PUBLICITY AND THE CANADIAN STATE

Critical Communications Perspectives

Publicity pervades our political and public culture, but little has been written that critically examines the basis of the modern Canadian "publicity state." This collection is the first to focus on the central themes in the state's relationship with publicity practices and the "permanent campaign," the constant search by politicians and their strategists for popular consent. Central to this political popularity contest are publicity tools borrowed from private enterprise, turning political parties into sound bites and party members into consumers.

Publicity and the Canadian State is the first sustained study of the contemporary practices of political communication, focusing holistically on the tools of the publicity state and their ideological underpinnings: advertising, public opinion research, marketing, branding, image consulting, and media and information management, as well as related topics such as election law and finance, privacy, think-tank lobbying, and non-election communication campaigns.

Bringing together contemporary Canadian analysis by scholars in a number of fields, this collection will be a welcome new resource for academics, public relations and policy professionals, and government communicators at all levels.

KIRSTEN KOZOLANKA is an associate professor in the School of Journalism and Communication at Carleton University. She has been an assistant press secretary to a political party leader on Parliament Hill, communications adviser to a cabinet minister at Queen's Park, and a communications manager in a federal government department.

Publicity and the Canadian State

Critical Communications Perspectives

EDITED BY
KIRSTEN KOZOLANKA

UNIVERSITY OF TORONTO PRESS
Toronto Buffalo London

© University of Toronto Press 2014
Toronto Buffalo London
www.utppublishing.com
Printed in Canada

ISBN 978-1-4426-4782-4 (cloth)
ISBN 978-1-4426-1590-8 (paper)

Library and Archives Canada Cataloguing in Publication

Publicity and the Canadian state : critical communications perspectives /
edited by Kirsten Kozolanka.

Includes bibliographical references and index.
ISBN 978-1-4426-4782-4 (bound). – ISBN 978-1-4426-1590-8 (pbk.)

1. Government publicity – Canada. 2. Communication in public
administration – Canada. 3. Communication in politics – Canada.
4. Public relations and politics – Canada. I. Kozolanka, Kirsten, author,
editor of compilation

JL86.P8P82 2014   352.7'480971   C2013-908148-8

University of Toronto Press acknowledges the financial assistance to its
publishing program of the Canada Council for the Arts and the
Ontario Arts Council.

Canada Council   Conseil des Arts
for the Arts   du Canada

University of Toronto Press acknowledges the financial support of the
Government of Canada through the Canada Book Fund for its
publishing activities.

Contents

Part Two
Publicity and the State

Part Three
Beyond the Publicity State

Tables

Acknowledgments

Government by poll. Non-stop advertising. Canada, the brand. Spin, but little information. The hard part about scholarship related to today's political communication is keeping abreast of the rapid shifts of fortune as new issues and vehicles emerge and others are overtaken or cast aside. Today, it is political marketing. Tomorrow ...? It is immediate and demanding but never boring. As the modern publicity state coalesces in Canada and in other late democracies, political communication has expanded its borders to include hitherto unimaginable areas of research, most of them involving new practices of publicity. Analysis of these new and emerging areas of political communication has been embraced by the intrepid authors here.

This edited collection would not have been possible without those first encouraging responses from scholars who saw the worth of such a project and agreed to be part of it, and I am in their debt. I have also had the pleasure of appreciating the scholarship of the other contributors who then joined the project, through both their contributions to this collection and also our many pleasant exchanges by phone and e-mail. I read every draft chapter with mounting excitement, and hope I communicated that to all of them. Now readers can do the same.

I also thank Patricia Mazepa and Herbert Pimlott for reading an early draft of the introductory essay, and Leslie Regan Shade, who mentors us all. Once again, Nicole Cohen did her editorial magic on the manuscript. University of Toronto Press editor Siobhan McMenemy also helped make this collection possible, moving it forward at key moments with her calm professionalism. Finally, I can have no better fellow travellers on this ride than my partner, Charles Brabazon, and our brilliantly shining daughters, Greer and Honor Brabazon.

PUBLICITY AND THE CANADIAN STATE

Critical Communications Perspectives

Introduction
Communicating for Hegemony: The Making of the Publicity State in Canada

KIRSTEN KOZOLANKA

Good government can be sold to a community just as any other commodity can be sold. I often wonder whether the politicians of the future, who are responsible for maintaining the prestige and effectiveness of their party, will not endeavour to train politicians who are at the same time propagandists.
– Edward Bernays (1928)

Taken at face value, propaganda godfather Bernays's utopian vision of a future rampant with politico-propagandists might seem to have taken concrete form in today's political persuaders. Many of those conversant with contemporary analyses of propaganda may dismiss Bernays's claim (or wishful thinking) outright, even as there has been a thoughtful revival of the term as it relates to political communication (O'Shaughnessy 2004; Corner 2007; Sussman 2010).[1] However, whether one rejects the label "propaganda" or encourages it as Bernays did, we all need to be concerned about the multiple persuasive trappings of the modern publicity state and the tendency for propaganda to come to mind when exploring publicity practices that are used in current political communication. In an increasingly commodified society, we need to probe the nature, context, and use of publicity as much as we need to explore the changing nature of the state itself.

To do so, we need to reveal the social and economic relations behind the commodity that political communication has become, beginning with the original triad of state, media, and public and its traditional social actors – political parties, journalists, and citizens – as well as a raft of newer players, including political consultants and other specialists. Taking a critical approach, the authors of the chapters in this volume examine the fostering of a promotional culture within the coalescing New Right[2] political project, specifically within the state and, more broadly, within capitalism. The analysis reveals how the public's relationship with the state continues to shift from citizen to consumer in today's market society in which the commercial and political worlds unite. The book focusses specifically on the publicity practices that have emerged to support ideological political projects, some generated by states and others by governments-in-waiting (opposition political parties), in what Golding (1992, 503) calls "communicating capitalism." Critical communication and political science analyses point to the widespread use of permanent campaigning in order to maintain the support and consent of citizens who, over time through the consumerization of society, have come to see politics as a marketplace in which they can purchase what appeals to them personally and individually, as they would any other consumer good. Late democracies such as Great Britain, the United States, and Canada undergoing this shift have been called "PR democracies," which entails "a pluralist society with a free media ... where much of the communication that comes out of the political system is designed to persuade the public" (Lilleker 2006, 168). Others have referred to this as a "public relations state" (Deacon and Golding 1994, 8) or simply "packaging politics" (Franklin 2004), while this volume uses the phrase "publicity state."

Together and separately, the chapters in this volume explore the specifics of how the interests of the state and capital are promoted through the articulation of material and discursive-strategic shifts by means of a growing and increasingly sophisticated tool bag of publicity strategies and practices. In the case of the turn in established democracies to what has been called, variously, neoliberalism, neoconservatism, or the New Right, these discursive practices of persuasion ultimately aid ideological and material state transformations.

In the current volume, I take seriously Jessop's (2003, 41) admonition to be wary of essentialism in analysis of the state's capabilities and strive instead for "more detailed accounts of the complex interplay of social struggles and institutions" in investigating state or hegemonic projects, as well as in statecraft – "the art of governing" – itself. Gramsci (1971, 195) also calls for the "extremely minute, molecular process of exhaustive analysis in every detail" in tracking how a shift in "collective will" takes place. The chapters here offer these detailed accounts and analysis of the evolution of political communication (media, state, and public) in part 1, particular publicity practices used by the state in Canada in part 2, and ways to move beyond the publicity state in part 3. All are grounded in actual examples and case studies that altogether illustrate an ongoing hegemonic shift towards a state that is dependent on publicity for its legitimation.

The Nature of the State

Jessop (2008, 6) offers a definition of the state that he acknowledges is heavily influenced by his analysis of Gramsci and Poulantzas: "One can define the state as an ensemble of socially embedded, socially regularized and strategically selective institutions, organizations, social forces and activities organized around (or at least actively involved in) making collectively binding decisions for an imagined political community." This characterization implies that the state is not static but partial, unstable, and contingent, depending on the balance of force and consent (Gramsci 1971, 80), both in the state apparatus and in society at any given historical conjuncture.

As we discuss the nature of the state and its practices in this volume, the critiques of the state by Jessop and others remind us that the state is more than simply "government" and instead refers to the entire apparatus of government (Held 1983). This is significant in recent and current times in which that apparatus is increasingly politicized, as well as its activities communicated in ways that are not neutral but are intended to serve the interests of power. Panitch (1977, 5–6) advises that we need to delimit our understanding of the institutional web that comprises the government apparatus in order to understand precisely how it operates: "The state is a complex of institutions, including the government, but also including the bureaucracy (embodied in the civil service as well as public corporations, central banks, regulatory commissions, etc.), the military, the judiciary, [and] representative assemblies." An understanding of the depth and extent of the apparatus of the state reveals not only the concrete linkages between the state and the dominant class but also the apparatus's key functions: that of accumulation (which is the base of its power) and legitimation. The latter, which Panitch (7–8) describes as "establishing and maintaining 'harmony,'" is a key element both in achieving power and in maintaining it. To be effective and maintain harmony, the legitimation function must permeate the governmental complex and, as we will see from concrete examples and analysis in the chapters in this volume, the state must make considerable efforts to legitimate its actions.

Furthermore, we cannot we lose sight of the fact that the use of publicity practices arises not only within a state complex but also within a state that is clearly capitalist. In fact, in marketized societies, it is impossible to analyse state publicity strategies and forms without situating capital at the centre of such analysis. As Schiller (1973, 44) wrote, "The dominant interests of the state-capitalist economy determine the character of, and controls on, the information flow" of all kinds. Typically found in what Jessop (2008, 15) terms "profit-oriented, market-mediated economies," those states with direct connections to capital – with capital being the "profit" gained by using such practices – can take many forms, including policy and electoral success. These forms can therefore be found in any state with capitalist features in which the quest for power dominates both the material and symbolic spheres of influence.

Thus, although the state acts on behalf of the dominant class, with its interests equated to those of commerce (Panitch 1977; Knight 1998), the state can and should be perceived further and more broadly as "an institution with various components which operate in a number of ways to facilitate, promote, and maintain capitalist relations of production" (Knuttia and Kubik 2000, 124) – the legitimation function noted by Panitch. As such, Schiller (1973, 11) points out that the state is not neutral but instead maintains "the myth of neutrality" in order to preserve the impression that its institutions are beyond reproach. The state is also embedded in social relations that are contingent and historically specific.

Moreover, as Jessop (2008, 16) theorizes, the state is itself a social relation with discursive dimensions that, similar to Gramsci's (1971, 263) conceptualization of the state as "political society + civil society," are increasingly articulated between political and civil society, as well as integrated into the structure-agency dynamic (113). As a social relation, the state has "discursive moments" (which we can understand occur through persuasive communication), but they are always connected to and grounded in "institutional materiality" (Jessop 2008, 7). The state does not apply these discursive moments haphazardly but as an essential and strategic element in articulating, shaping, and reshaping state projects. One such project, the turn to the New Right by conservatives and many liberals alike, is currently coalescing in late western

democracies. These discursive and material moments "mobilize support and deliver effective state policies" that in turn reorient the state in
what Jessop (2003, 7) has called "discursive-strategic shifts."

An interesting aspect of the discursive elaboration of state strategies
and state projects is that their articulation is "structurally selective"
(Jessop 2003, 36). In other words, their paths are neither inevitable nor
necessary but the result and product of ongoing interaction and negotiation that can take different directions. This emphasizes that political
and strategic choices can be made in how the state manages the content and articulation of its policies in order to embed them successfully
into social relations. By the same token, it bears remembering that,
however powerful the discourses and the political forces behind them,
there are no guarantees that state strategies and projects will meet with
success (40). As Gramsci (1971) tells us, state projects have alternatives,
and every project is born in struggle and needs to build a new "balance
of forces" (80) in the "formulation of a new collective will" (194).

In fact, Gramsci (1971) has much to tell us about how the legitimation aspects of hegemonic state projects such as the New Right are
formulated and embedded. As Jessop's (2003, 2008) recent work does,
Gramsci stressed a dialectic for social change that combined agency
and structure, and he synthesized interaction between material and
symbolic (or ideological) forces, with hegemony as the point of inter-
section. Further, he stressed that shifts in consciousness depend on conscious human action. By bringing human agency and symbolic fields
into his analysis, Gramsci's conceptualization of hegemony, which is
often referred to as "cultural hegemony," was a more open and inclusive understanding of the cultural and communicative forces at play in
establishing hegemony.

For Gramsci, hegemony has an active sense and is constituted by a
duality of coercion and consent. It is therefore more accurate to think
of hegemony as a relation, much the same way that Jessop speaks of
the state as a social relation. In addition, Simon (1982, 21) refers to hegemony as "consent by means of political and ideological leadership,"
so hegemony is not only a relation but also a process of gaining active
consent. Put succinctly, "hegemony is the political and ideological organization of consent" (Patten 1996, 99). As a relation and a process,
hegemony is understood as an active, ongoing process of continuous
creation. A process of constant negotiation exists between values and
dominant groups (e.g., ruling political parties and business leaders)

and their opposition (e.g., social movements). Within this negotiation, the legitimizing activities of the state, such as persuasive publicity practices aimed at achieving consent, have a darker side as "hegemony protected by the armour of coercion" (Gramsci 1971, 263).[3]

The consent-coercion duality is key to understanding how hegemony is constructed politically and ideologically and thus is germane to our understanding of the publicity state. The state exercises power over subordinate classes by a combination of consent and coercion; both are integral to how the state functions. Consent is not easily given. It is active and negotiated yet appears to be spontaneous. As Mosco (1996, 243) points out, not only is consent "very demanding," but also the very need for consent implies resistance and possibilities for change. When a hegemony is under development – that is, seeking consent – it is at its most vulnerable. The political, social, and economic upheaval in Ontario from 1995 to 1997 at the onset of the New Right government of Mike Harris serves as an example (Kozolanka 2007). Other homegrown examples of emerging New Right hegemonies across Canada include Ralph Klein's Alberta and British Columbia under Gordon Campbell. Hegemony "under development" can also characterize the several federal minority governments between 2004 and 2011 that followed a long period of first Conservative (1984–93) and then Liberal (1993–2004) majority governments.

Further, and critically for the present volume, when a hegemony is under threat, available state resources for legitimation can be pulled into play (Habermas 1975, 70). Thus the legitimating apparatus of publicity is available not only to those who seek political power but also to those who are already in power and strive to keep it. The spectrum of communications practices of legitimation used by the state to gain consent from the public is the subject of this collection.

The key understanding that underpins the present collection is that governments have shifted both structurally, from public service to commercial transactions, and symbolically, in the form of increased publicity that turns "messages … into marketable commodities" (Mosco 2009, 133) that have surplus value (profit) and reflect the interests of capital. Further, and importantly, as Mosco explains, "communication is taken to be a special and particularly powerful commodity because, in addition to its ability to produce surplus value (thereby behaving like all other commodities), it contains symbols and images whose meaning helps to shape consciousness" (134).

The Nature of Publicity

The legitimation function of the state bears further scrutiny to understand how, as Gramsci (1971, 263) uniquely describes it, the state is clothed in the "armour of coercion" as it seeks public consent. That armour includes a panoply of policies, strategies, and practices related to publicity, persuasion, and promotion. Despite a long history of state legitimation, there remain confusion and imprecision over naming the processes that have become so important in constructing all aspects of state activity.

Some of this is due to rejection of the term *propaganda*, which was a term commonly used to describe wartime promotion during the two World Wars of 1914–18 and 1939–45, although there are recent examples of deliberate and vigorous use of it (e.g., O'Shaughnessy 2004). Taking a critical cultural approach, Corner (2007, 671–4) examines the "nervous relationship between propaganda, political order, public opinion and the psychology of mass society" (671) through recent literature that variously describes propaganda as self-interested, practical and neutral, at times virtuous, needing to mean what users say, deceitful, mitigated by the contexts of motive and consequence, or organized lying. Choosing to use the term *promotional culture*, Corner concludes that propaganda is "still too crude a term to catch at the more stealthy, partial ways in which discourses of power are at work in culture" and is "an idea that media-political analysis should work beyond" (676). In contrast, Sussman (2010, xx), whose analysis is grounded in critical political economy, uses the term *propaganda* deliberatively – especially, but not exclusively, in international contexts – believing that, in an information economy that is "rooted in almost every aspect of daily life, the science of organized persuasion has extended propaganda to new boundaries, resulting in a promotional commercial, political, and popular culture."

Although *publicity* as a term to describe the communicative fields under discussion in this volume also has its doubters, including Corner (2007), it is nonetheless an open-ended term that carries with it the sense of publicness that situates it within a two-way state-public *relation* with connotations of the state's legitimizing function. It also acknowledges a *process* of becoming publicly visible; that is, it recognizes the state's obligation of accountability and transparency to the public in the public interest and what that might entail in terms of its publicity strategies and practices. Seeing publicity as a relation and a process reinforces Gramsci's understanding that hegemony is not fixed or absolute but can be mitigated or challenged by the counterpublicity of other social and political actors.

The concept of a "publicity state" has both Blumler and Golding as its antecedents. As early as 1990, Blumler (1990, 101, 113) suggested the existence of a "modern publicity process": "The modern publicity process involves a competitive struggle to influence and control popular perceptions of key political events and issues through the major mass media ... [It] could be likened to the irresistible force of a magnet, obliging those that enter its field to conform to its pull. This is then capable of altering the messages of opinion advocates, the issues and terms of political combat and public discourse, and finally perspectives and choices of citizens themselves."

Golding (1995, 35) studied the growth of what he referred to as the "public relations state" under British Conservative prime minister Margaret Thatcher in the 1990s and identified a build-up "on an unprecedented scale" within the government bureaucracy of persuasive communications. Aided by substantial increases in communications funding, the Thatcher government was then able to promote its controversial policies related to remaking – or unmaking – the state, basically engaging in "communicating capitalism" (Golding 1992, 503). Golding contrasted this with the concomitant urge of the government to secrecy, withholding the information needed for public life (see Rubin and Kozolanka's chapter for elaboration on government secrecy and access to information).

Although the term *publicity state* is relatively new, the idea of a state's embrace of persuasive communications was noted by Schiller in the American context by 1973. Schiller (1973, 44) charged that over time the US government behaved as a propagandist internationally and a "public relations agent" at home. Even earlier, Bernays played a major role in state-led propaganda efforts in the First World War. Other influential critiques of the materiality of the symbolic included Horkheimer and Adorno's ([1947] 2002) analysis of the impact of the culture industry on authentic culture and Habermas's (1989) examination of the threat of technical instrumental reason on the public sphere. More recently, Sussman (2010) has written about post–Cold War ideological clashes by the United States against emerging states through its controversial strategies of so-called democracy promotion.

The Cold War actually improved the status of public relations and persuasion, as PR agents who were credited with saving democracy turned after that war into a professionalized, managed, progressive force to save capitalism as it once had saved the states of the "Free World" (Miller 2005, 12–13). Williams, too, emphasized the link between publicity and the growth and dominance of capitalism. He suggested that the meanings of "consumption" altered as social relations and public life altered, beginning with a negative connotation of destruction and ultimately ending up as a positive way for people to refer to themselves in a modern "consumer" society (cited in Ewen 1992, 31). Streeck (2012) elaborates on capitalism's solution for its own stagnation as "sociation by consumption" (33), that is, acts of "self-identification and self-preservation" (35) that occur through the customization and diversification of consumption. In effect, consumption seemed to release citizens from the constraints of traditional social identities and obligations, although at a huge cost to democratic society.

Histories of the growth of various promotional practices in the United States demonstrate their emergence and use, first in the commercial sector and later in the political sector (Mayhew 1997, 4). This is also the case in Canada, which was influenced by and lagged behind its American counterpart. Mayhew (ibid., 189–90) demonstrates that the dominating principle behind the development of promotional industries was its rationalization. In the quest to construct a "new public" open to persuasion, marketers developed systematic research and systematically planned campaigns that were both effective and predictive. In this way, the techniques underlying advertising, market research, and public relations were developed. Once established in the commercial sector, the same practices were applied to the political sphere. Here, political consulting became the political equivalent of public relations, and other practices were developed, such as lobbying, endorsement by third-party experts, and policy certification through think tanks (ibid.; see also the chapter by Gutstein). Key to this ongoing process was the growing expertise in the commercial sector of techniques of persuasion.

In Canada, Robinson's (1999, 1–2) historical analysis contributes to our understanding of the development of persuasion by the state by situating the early growth of industries and practices of persuasion as steeped in the rhetoric of the public good as an antidote to rule by dictatorship. His analysis demonstrates that market research surveys began in the 1930s, followed by public opinion research a decade later, early in the Second World War (4). The Liberal government in power used polling in a limited way at that time and was the first governing party in Canada to use market research to target specific groups of potential voters (156). However, it was only in the 1960s that the techniques of market research fully made the crossover into the political realm (127). Although the early rhetoric of brave new vistas through market research has dimmed over time, market research in politics still promotes itself as serving the needs of the voters – for instance, by curtailing the influence of indiscriminate lobbyists and interest groups (5) – while it is clearly a rationalized technique for testing political messages that self-interestedly precludes the need for time-consuming personal contact and two-way dialogue with the (voting) public.

The implied neutrality of rationalization, measurement, and technique supported the extension of a new class of professional experts into the many spheres of the state and its apparatus, specifically within government. This shift could only have taken place if the post-war Keynesian consensus, a political project that fostered a larger government apparatus to administer its social programs, could be delegitimized in favour of a regime that curtailed or eliminated the social relationship with citizens and instead emphasized the economic "need" for less government. Thus the New Right political project emerged gradually with increasing confidence in western democracies in the latter part of the 20th century. It called for the technical management of a smaller and more efficient apparatus of government, specifically targeting the bureaucracy, that was premised on the persuasive message that large state deficits and cumulative debt would eventually destroy the state. Tupper (2003) describes the character of what has been called "New Public Management," one of many such private sector business exercises in delegitimizing the post-war administrative state by stripping it of credibility and expertise and replacing it with regimes that stressed rationalization through concrete measurement.[4] One impact was the loss of anything that could not be supported by calculable results; the broader impact was the loss of a sense of supporting the needs of citizenship, which can be less tangible, and therefore less expressible, and replaced by the more concrete customer service to the public as users and consumers. Overall, the new "politics of consumption" (Streeck 2012, 39) shifted away from the public-private balance of the post-war consensus and allowed for its replacement by a weaker and more business-oriented state. As Streeck points out, the old "political goods" of "social solidarity, distributive justice, and the general rights and duties that constitute citizenship" (41) did not fit into the new marketized standard of "product diversification" (41). Moreover, the new politics of consumption ensures inequality of those citizens unable to consume as society's collective provisions wither in the face of the New Right restructuring of the state (46–7).

More important for instituting the ethos of the New Right political project, smaller government allowed for private sector expertise to manage many aspects of government operations, not as public employees, but as contracted professionals. Many of these professionals provided strategic advice and services to communications divisions (Kozolanka 2006). Tellingly, communications was the only government division whose ranks rebounded quickly after state restructuring and retrenchment in the 1990s (ibid.). In this way, commercial expertise on publicity has entered into the political realm and has further extended into the workings of the state itself. The party in power can now count on the complicity of the communications apparatus of the bureaucracy, which includes private sector marketing professionals operating within a technically rationalized environment, to develop communications strategies that disseminate politicized messages. Thus not only is the publicity state grounded in capitalist relations, but it is also specifically "grounded in the ideology and practices" of the New Right (Sussman 2010, 7). As Wernick describes it, the promotion itself becomes the "communicative substance" of capitalism (in Aronczyk and Powers 2010, 4). Moreover, with politicized communication structured into the bureaucracy of government, the materiality of communication and its symbolic aspects converge as a powerful weapon in what O'Shaughnessy (2004, 172) terms "the symbolic state," where "the management of the state's communication may even rival in importance the management of the state itself." In this way, publicity shifts from being a mere tool of the state to "becoming its central organizing principle" (173) to enhance state legitimacy.

In fact, the new politics of communication fosters a tense relationship between the modern state's constructed need for publicity and its hypermanagement of information. As one-way, carefully crafted publicity dominates government communication, information needed for citizenship and accountability – a vital democratic countervalance – is often obstructed, even when requested formally under the *Access to Information Act* (see the chapter by Rubin and Kozolanka).

Publicity and the Canadian State

The idea of a "symbolic state," which characterizes forcefully the ideological direction being taken by governments in late democracies, allows us to understand the key role of communication itself in modern statecraft. Just as Shade and Shepherd elaborate on the impact of digitization in their chapter, Fuchs (2010, 22) points out that continuous technological development is a "condition for the existence and reproduction of capital," as knowledge workers – for the purposes of this volume, communications consultants and communications officers in government – labour to produce "immaterial" products, that is, knowledge. The increased embedding of the labour of communication into restructured and technocratic government ensures both the symbolic significance and material circulation of communication for public consumption, which is itself a form of labour (Sussman 2010, 6). As private sector interests embedded continuous consumption into the modern way of life as a social good, so now have governments reinforced and replicated the market and its relationship with customers, thus intertwining the capital-citizen relationship (Patten in Ewen 1992, 48).[5] Today's citizenship can be characterized more as "customership" (Streeck 2012, 41).

Further, we can understand that citizens, in their new role as consumers, labour as "promotional intermediaries" for free (Aronczyk and Powers 2010, 11). The "profit" from the citizen-consumer and government transaction emanates from the circulation and successful buy-in of a government's or a political party's publicity. Captured ideologically by publicity, citizens give tacit consent to be manipulated by engaging in the actions promoted by the state, from supplying personal information to governments and the private sector in many different ways to the ultimate complicity of voting for a particular party. Comor (2008, 43) further argues that consumption has a role in "normalizing *change itself*" (emphasis in original), so the voter-consumer, through the purchase and ownership of goods and services, is actually giving "a semblance of needed consent."

If we think of citizens as the audience for state publicity, we can hear echoes of Smythe's (1981a) visionary analysis that the (media) audience is a commodity in which the dominated agree to be dominated in "reciprocal relationships" with those who dominate (Mosco 2009, 137; Fuchs 2010, 32). There is no tangible product to purchase, just persuasive communications messages from the state that very often contradict the factual reality but make the audience complicit in its successful execution.

In addition, Mosco (2009) points specifically to the shift to the New Right as an example of how the state has transformed through commodification processes that have turned its "public service communication with social commitments to universal access and content that reflects the broad range of society into commercial communication that provides access to those who can afford it and content that delivers audiences to advertisers" (130–1). As for those who cannot afford to be. citizen-consumers, Streeck (2012) suggests that such exclusion by non-consumption in New Right societies depoliticizes and further contains and marginalizes them.

As the state has taken on the character of private enterprise, its relationship with the public has changed, as has its power balance with the media. The media are central to the modern political process and are key components in constructing hegemony. Media are what Herman and McChesney (1997, 3) call the "pre-eminent vehicles of communication through which the public participates in the democratic process." Media also are agents of legitimation for the purpose of constructing consent on behalf of their own hegemonic interests, as well as those of other elite institutions and social actors. Structural changes to the media wrought by concentration of media power foster institutions that are accountable to advertisers and shareholders for the reproduction of capital and only nominally reflect the broader public interest. At the everyday level of news production, the normative processes employed by the media are limited by economic and organizational constraints that narrow the possibilities for media products that reflect more than just a limited set of regular, reachable, and accredited sources for their perspectives. Thus, the media act as a "communications channel" for political elites who get to define the issues, have accredited access to the media (who are also elites), and exclude the members of the public, who remain "ill-informed spectators" (Davis 2007, 60).

The relationship of the media to the political sphere particularly has been described as an ongoing struggle in which politicians, supported by an expansive publicity apparatus, seek to frame the issues and set the political agenda. The task of both politicians and media is complicated by dwindling resources for newsrooms within media conglomerates, concurrent with growing perceptions by politicians of their increased need for publicity. There appears to be no easy conclusion to draw on which set of actors – the media or the politicians – has the upper hand, and the continual scrutiny of that relationship in recent years seems too narrow, as well as misplaced. Instead, the importance of the relationship lies in a different and more highly charged set of relations: the media still remain the general public's primary source in shaping the dominant discourse; the state-citizen relationship has shifted to a more consumer-oriented culture; and the constructed public's demands within this consumerized culture lead increasingly to a more market-oriented society and politics. Ultimately, the upper hand does not lie with either the media or politics per se, but instead more broadly with the underlying forces of capital that structure such a nation state.

Citizenship in the Publicity State

Am I in earth, in heaven, or in hell?
Sleeping or working? mad, or well-advised?

– William Shakespeare (2003)

Shakespeare's confused Antipholus of Syracuse could be said to sum up the dilemma of publicity used in politics or by governments: Is it the slippery slope to a weakened democracy, or is it a trouble-free pathway to electoral and policy success? Is it indeed madness or the best advice that money can buy?

The public does not naturally acquiesce to political publicity. As constructed consumers, members of the public apply the same logic to politics as they do to other consumer transactions and willingly give their consent, echoing the Marxian notion of false consciousness. Today's political decision making is less a deliberative process grounded in fully disclosed information as it is an orchestrated choice emanating from persuasive communications. In the latter, politics is just another "commercial service provider" (Lilleker 2006, 59). This was not always the case. Traditionally, voting and other aspects of political life were seen as ways for individuals to act on communitarian values, that is, acting on behalf of what was good for all citizens and not necessarily just in self-interest. The concept of a voter as a consumer emerged in recent years as private sector marketing techniques found their way into politics. This was partly due to the New Right's inculcation into the state apparatus of broader business ideologies based on rationalization and technique, such as New Public Management, as discussed earlier in this introductory essay. It was also due to the professionalization of communication departments within the public service through contracting with private-sector public relations experts. In addition, political engagement, as measured by voting, has been declining at the same time as political dealignment with traditional political parties has increased, creating strategic opportunities for new visions of politics (Lilleker 2008).

Over time, the "marriage of politics and marketing" saw the emergence of political practices that focused on techniques of persuasion used by private sector public relations firms under the aegis of *political marketing* (Lees-Marshment 2001, 692). In political marketing, market intelligence (such as public opinion research commissioned by governments or political parties) leads to product design (of a policy or a party's image), which is then tested (in focus groups) and adjusted before it is implemented as a political strategy. In effect, the party in power recrafts its messages, images, and even its policies to resonate with the voter and win elections. Recent research finds political marketing taking root in many late democracies, including Canada (see Paré and Berger 2008). This orientation shifts political parties away from the traditional ideological, moral, and ethical stances that characterize and differentiate a party and towards parties that base their beliefs and stances on in-depth segmented marketing. In Canada, this nascent market ideology was pioneered successfully in the 1990s in Alberta, British Columbia, and Ontario before eventually nurturing the federal Conservative Party (which dropped "Progressive" from its name) to a majority mandate in 2011.

Political marketing literature articulates the construction of an apolitical and nonaligned voter-consumer who votes with his or her own needs and wants in mind and is prone to populism and the bandwagon effect (Lilleker 2006, 155–7). Those making use of political marketing accept that such market research tends to move political parties to the homogenized centre of the political spectrum, ever able to shift to the left or right, depending on the results of the research and the persuasive communication efforts governments or political parties use based on that research. However, this voter behaviour does not reflect the absence of ideology, as has been claimed, but instead is a mystified form of ideology based in the New Right ideology of the market commodification of everyday life.

We need to understand how and why persuasive techniques based on the market intelligence of political marketing resonate with the politicians who perpetrate them and the public that acquiesces to them. In their analysis of contemporary democratic citizenship, Coleman and Blumler (2009, 3) problematize two divergent forms of what they call "democratic anxiety." Politicians are nostalgic for "the lost era of democracy, characterized by civic cohesion, dutiful citizens and clear political choices," while the public is "more concerned about the efficacy of citizens, whose experiences and expertise often seem to be diminished or marginalized" (3). Coleman and Blumler argue for "institutional innovation that could nurture critical citizenship and radical energy, while at the same time opening up representative governance to a new respect for public discourse and deliberation" (3). Their analysis not only reveals a cleavage between the needs of politicians and the public but also clarifies how the politician-public mutual frustration can make the promise of political marketing a viable option for politicians who still need to get elected and for members of the public who need to feel more in control. Unfortunately, it also fosters a modern state with market-oriented parties and voter-consumers in a permanent cycle of publicity.

Clearly, politicians, political parties, and governments use publicity because "the stakes are too high not to" (Lilleker 2006, 145). Is publicity then inescapable? Corner (2007, 672) suggests that political modernism and its changed administrative practices of government, in which public opinion matters more than it ever did before, might have a certain corrective in the higher visibility given to those who use more coercive actions. Given the power differential between state and citizen, however, it is difficult to see how coercive actions, such as those discussed in the chapter by Kozolanka, inspire citizens to anything more than further apathy and distance from their government.

If we look to the media, where societal expectations for correctives to mitigate political power lie, we find, as Fletcher notes in his chapter, that "audiences tend to accept the way in which the role of citizen is constructed in the news, as spectator, victim, or juror at best, passing judgment on political parties and leaders only at election time, with little reflection on other possibilities." Fletcher also notes that the mainstream media, "even with more innovative and diversified reporting, are too constrained to push civic engagement much beyond current levels or to offer alternatives to the dominant ideologies that frame their coverage and commentary." Moreover, the power of political persuasion emanating either from the state or the private sector "squelches inconvenient journalistic enterprise so that early warnings fail to resonate, and growing ills receive no mass attention" (Miller 2005, 26).

How can citizens, activists, movements, and the media renegotiate what Mayhew (1997, 190) calls the "instrumental persuasion" that is a hallmark of the publicity state? According to Mayhew, such use of persuasion leads to two distinct problems in a democracy: its strategies "are designed to avoid confrontations," and its influence is "based not on conversation but on token appeals ... which does not build commitment to a common cause" (190). Publicity entices us just as it seems to demand our response; however, it communicates with us not in our role as lifelong citizens but as one-time consumers.

Similarly, Barney argues in his chapter that "depoliticization arises not from failing to live up to the norms of publicity, but instead from their satisfaction." This echoes Schiller's (1973, 48) question about the "mind management" of the state and its institutions: "Is public awareness heightened or diminished by the information disseminated?" Therein lies the particularity of political publicity: it fosters acquiescence over action. Its work is successful when its carefully drafted and self-interested messages and images based on market segmentation cause only its targeted audiences to vote.[6] Little else is required of the commodified citizen. In effect, a disengaged, confused, and cynical public (Lilleker 2006, 145–6) is more easily susceptible to the velvet coercion by the state, as packaged in persuasive publicity.

As Mosco (2009, 134) writes, communication is "a special … and particularly powerful commodity." It is a commodity that lies at the heart of material-symbolic interaction and aids in the articulation of state political projects. It takes conscious and concerted actions and strategies to challenge the public relations democracy, where a permanent campaign requires permanent persuasion to maintain popular support, and a "single perception of reality" is perpetuated (Lilleker 2006, 169–70). Active audiences that transcend traditional roles to become producers and users of communication as well as receivers are a key element in reclaiming citizenship. While it is not possible or even necessary to fully reject persuasive practices in politics and government, Habermas suggests that "tight conditions" can be placed "both on the production of political discourse and on the terms of its reception" (in Corner 2007, 673), what Corner calls a "mean what you say" rule (673). In addition, Coleman and Blumler (2009, 7) are optimistic that new spaces for democratizing citizenship and policymaking exist in the "fluidity and indeterminacy of cyberspace," a contested position many of the chapters here also explore.

Purpose and Outline

The chapters in this volume articulate critical communications perspectives on the key issues confronting developments in persuasive political communication in Canada today. In doing so, they examine the nature, context, and use of publicity practices and, in so doing, demystify and reveal the commodified social, political, and economic relations underpinning state political projects, particularly those in late democracies such as Canada that devalue and diminish citizenship as they communicate for hegemony. More importantly for our understanding of the future of democracy, the chapters also explore what critical citizenship could look like, as well as how to foster it.

Moreover, the collection deliberately focuses on the communications aspects of political communication. Despite the clear connection of publicity to the state – and any history of public relations acknowledges that the birth of the PR industry was an offshoot of the state's wartime propaganda endeavours – academic analysis of the communicative and cultural aspects of state information and communication activity has been overdetermined by political science, the latter of which brings its own invaluable and specialized insights and analysis to the field. As practices of publicity become a more frequent subject within political communication, this volume also seeks to add to a relatively small body of critical communication analysis on this subject, particularly in Canada (see Lilleker and Scullion 2008, 3, 7). It also emphasizes the continuing role of persuasive communication by the state in Canada, a role that has intensified and accelerated through technological development, thus locating communication as a dominant force in state legitimation. Just as Bernays once said that propaganda can "help to bring order to chaos" (quoted in Olasky 1985, 17), this collection intentionally disrupts the deterministic and instrumental order of publicity practices in the modern state.

The chapter authors and this introductory essay use various critical conceptual entry points for their analysis. These complementary approaches reveal the theoretical underpinnings that ground a growing and diverse body of critical analysis in the field of political communication. Gramsci's (1971) cultural hegemony and other concepts, including the consent-coercion duality noted in this essay, add texture and understanding to how legitimation takes place. Smythe's (1981a, 1981b) concept of the audience as a commodity was a key break-through in critical communication scholarship, influencing scholars from Schiller (1973) to Mosco (2009), and is echoed in this essay and in various chapters. Bourdieu's (1990, 1993) field theory situates media power as acting within different institutional fields, some of them autonomous, while other fields are influenced by external factors and pressures. Thus field theory allows for a conception of the media that is not deterministic but open to opportunities for change while recognizing the external pressures under which the media work. Field theory is of considerable value to those who aspire to challenge persuasive practices of publicity. Building on Smythe, Mosco's (1996, 2009) immanent commodification sets out the process by which the audience commodity itself produces commodities. For this volume, this ongoing process of recommodification demonstrates the endless reach and capacity of practices of persuasion when applied to the audience as citizen-voter. Separately and together, these approaches demonstrate the ways in which the study of communication in politics has evolved to meet the need for analysis of the persuasive communications practices that inform, propel, and legitimate the modern publicity state. In addition, some chapters look to scholarly literature in such fields as varied as public administration (e.g., Savoie 2010) and journalism (e.g., McChesney 1999), as well as in contemporary scholarship particular to the subcategories of publicity that are the main theme in many of the chapters (see part 2 of the volume).

The current collection is divided into three parts, each with its own introduction that contains summaries of each chapter.

In part 1, the three traditional elements in political communication – media, state, and public – are reexamined in the context of the modern state. Over time, as the Canadian state grew, that traditional triad became more complex, adding new social actors and functions that complicated and shifted the balance of power relations among these three spheres. The chapters here challenge us to think critically about the democratic role the media play by keeping information flowing, the relationship between state communication and accountability, and the impact of excessive publicity on the public sphere.

The chapters in part 2 examine the specific practices of publicity that characterize the publicity state. The part begins with a chapter on the development of a "war on ideas," underpinned by persuasive communication, that enabled the growth of these practices. The chapters that follow illuminate and critically examine in whose interest public opinion can be quantified, the "uncharted and unchecked" field of state advertising, the importance and ramifications of finance in endless campaigning, and state branding as a constructed appeal to values that themselves are manipulated through marketing. This part concludes with two chapters that focus on information – specifically, on how governments manage and control information flow and the commodification of information through the invasion of citizen privacy.

While all authors of chapters in this volume explore the possibilities for challenging the modern publicity state and constructing a political environment in which alternative state projects can be fostered and renewed successfully, the chapters in part 3 speak specifically to what could lie beyond the modern publicity state. Chapters here examine the permanent nature of political campaigning in a networked online environment, the role that often-marginalized interest groups and social movements can play to influence the government and the public, and the need for economic resources to do so, the critical and unique role of alternative media in reframing and decommodifying information necessary for citizenship, and how media reform and activism can challenge the power of the publicity state.

NOTES

1   One expert, Stuart Ewen, who has written extensively on public relations and advertising, has said, "the term 'propaganda' at this point is very loaded and doesn't say much about anything." He suggests the use of "publicity" (Swift 1999, 17). For an extended discussion of the historical and contemporary use of the word "propaganda," see Corner (2007).

2   The New Right is a melding of economic libertarianism and moral conservatism and is the conservative response to the post-war Keynesian consensus. This market ideology became evident in the Thatcher (UK) and Reagan (US) governments, where it was referred to variously as "neoliberalism" and "neoconservatism," but the term "New Right" is inclusive of both these philosophical strands. See the chapter by Gutstein for a history of the shift from the post-war consensus to the New Right.

3   Some of the material here on Gramsci is adapted from the author's book, *Power of Persuasion* (2007).

4   It is now argued that New Public Management has become institutionalized as "New Political Governance" (see Bakvis and Jarvis 2012).

5   Consumption has also been used as an antidote to 'evil,' as when then President George W. Bush responded to the events of 11 September 2001 by asking Americans for their "continued participation and confidence in the American economy" (*Washington Post* 2001, 6).

6   Recent and ongoing political events in Canada have brought to the forefront the concept of "voter suppression" as a viable outcome of political communication. See particularly media stories on the automated "robocalls" used in the 2011 election, as well as chapter 2 in this volume. Using market research to target different groups of citizens, voter suppression is a tactic to reduce voter turnout amongst those likely to vote against one's political party.

PART ONE

Political Communication:
Media, State, Public

Introduction

This first part of the book examines the traditional political communication triad of media, state, and public as the basic ground on which we build our understanding of the publicity state. Starting in the latter years of the 20th century, as the Canadian state developed and became more complex, these three spheres also began to encompass ever more social actors – policymakers, social movements, lobbyists, independent media, pollsters, consultants – that shifted the power balance within the relationships amongst these social actors. Currently, in this changed public environment, citizens communicate on a more distanced scale with their government. Larger governments have more resources and more options for communicating with citizens, while the media – the intermediary between governments and citizens – must be more selective in the barrage of information they present to the public and, with an eye on decreasing editorial budgets, are likely to make use of the informational handouts that come their way from both government and well-resourced social actors.

In his chapter on media and journalism, Frederick J. Fletcher reminds us that whatever the relationships and contexts within which the media interact, "the flow of information is an essential element in a democratic public sphere." With that bedrock understanding, the emergence of mass media plays a dominant role in shaping the public agenda in active negotiation with policymaking and civic engagement. One positive aspect of traditional mass media lies in their unique capacity to foster a general (albeit incomplete) sense of common citizenship among citizens; today's mass use of social media could possibly provide an antidote to what otherwise could be growing citizen polarization and disengagement.

My own chapter echoes O'Shaughnessy's analysis that the material structure of the state has metamorphized to incorporate publicity as an integral element in regime success. I detail how the government apparatus in Canada has become politicized as a response to more aggressive attempts by politicians in power to take charge of their public image in a permanent campaign of publicity that, in response, requires permanent promotion to be successful. The chapter asks if the public interest is being served by recent governments, whose actions often breach existing accountability regimens without censure or redress. The longer this partisan use of government continues, the more likely that partisanship in government communications becomes the new "neutrality," as false as that is.

In his chapter on the public sphere, Darin Barney pulls back the lens to encompass a broader discussion of the public in liberal democracies. Despite the stated political nature of publicity – which is said to involve communication, information, and participation – an excess of publicity instead "has more to do with depoliticization than it does with moving people to act politically." When all is said and done, publicity doesn't lead to political action, according to Barney; instead, it is taken to be political action in itself. Publicity depoliticizes the public so that it does not act, and politicians have an alibi for not taking action. Why would politicians depoliticize the public? Because, as Barney writes, real politics is "exceptional, disruptive, antagonistic, burdensome, and dangerous." In other words, communication, information, and engagement create expectations that are difficult for politicians to manage. As for technology, the great hope for democratizing communication, it is reduced to clicking one's agreement or disagreement.

Overall, these three chapters demonstrate the shifts in our basic understandings of this original set of social actors and how their roles and fortunes have been challenged by developments in the state and society over the last generation. The roles and expectations of these social actors and their demarcation of territory is more fluid, as the state itself grows and contracts. Into this uncertain environment and over time, the private sector, in the form of business interests and communications consultants, begins to play a stronger role in the state. Questions also emerge about the quality of modern citizenship and the role of government in the modern state: Under what conditions can the media (both old and new) get access to the full information necessary to engage the public and foster citizenship? What demands can be made of self-serving governments to ensure the public can come to judgment knowledgeably on issues that concern them and the country? How can the public become reactivated and repoliticized?

1 Journalism, Corporate Media, and Democracy in the Digital Era

FREDERICK J. FLETCHER

There is a consensus among democratic theorists, whatever their vision of democracy, that a healthy public sphere is the foundation of good democratic practice. For media theorists, following Habermas, the modern news media, at each stage of their development, have altered the nature of the public sphere. From the coffee houses of the 18th century through the emergence of daily newspapers, news services, the electronic media, and the subsequent dominance of television, each has altered the nature of the public discourse so necessary to modern liberal democracies (Fletcher 2007).[1] The complex relationship among political communication, media systems, and the political-economic and cultural contexts in which they operate does not obscure the fact that the flow of information is an essential element in a democratic public sphere even though, as Barney argues in his chapter, surplus information can be problematic. Media systems, including social media, are an important influence on the political process and are in turn shaped by it. In Canada, the emergence of the Internet and social media in recent decades has added weight to a range of important challenges to critical elements of the public sphere. Driven by technological and political change, these changes include the fragmentation of audiences and declining revenue streams for traditional journalism, partially offset by Internet-enabled broadening of citizen involvement in public debate, a general shift to the Right in political and media commentary, and challenges to the national public sphere from the growing diversity of global and local communications networks. For the foreseeable future, the interplay between social media and traditional media will be a crucial element in the ecology of political communication and the evolution of the public sphere.

The hallmark of democratic political communication in the 20th century was the emergence of mass media as the dominant force shaping the public agenda. In the 21st century, this dominance has been challenged by the advent of a vast array of information and communication opportunities enabled by the Internet. Although the emergence of the Internet and social media has changed the public sphere in important ways, the traditional media, especially television news and major daily newspapers, are still the most visible arenas in which the struggle to set the public agenda takes place. However, as important as these traditional media are in the daily, if not hourly, flow of political information, they are no longer the gatekeepers in a top-down information flow. If we are to understand democratic political communication within the publicity state in Canada in the second decade of the 21st century, we must examine both the traditional media and the challenges posed to them by new social media.

The forces that shape the public agenda, including the established media and emerging online influences, are important elements in public policymaking and what is often called civic engagement, or the involvement of citizens in the political process. For example, "policymaking and the management of government now take place in a 24/7 media environment" (Thomas 2010, 81), which includes not only traditional media but also a vast array of online commentators and information services. Policymakers ask themselves how a government decision will play in the media – or at least the media they care about – and with their political base. In Ottawa and the provincial capitals, no policy is proposed without an accompanying communication strategy, often as carefully considered as the policy itself (Martin 2010, 58). As Thomas (2010, 117) has put it, "When political life resembles a permanent election contest, campaigning and governing become almost indistinguishable." What this means is that important aspects of public policy are shaped by the general orientation of the media, as well as the vastly increased capacity for scrutiny of political actors and instant commentary that began with the 24/7 news cycle; these aspects of public policy grew with communication mobility and the cell phone camera and culminated in the minute-by-minute commentary enabled by Twitter. To understand the modern publicity state, we must consider the full range of forces acting on the public sphere. These forces include an unprecedented increase in the capacity of governments, political parties, and well-funded interest groups to influence the public agenda. At the same time, the capacity of news organizations to resist the "spin" from the state is in decline. Do social media and citizen journalism provide effective alternatives? We will examine this question from a variety of perspectives.

The Canadian News System

The news media in Canada are an essential element of the public sphere because they are important sites where meaning is constructed. Even in the digital era, issues become part of the public agenda, regardless of where they originate, when they attract significant news media attention. Indeed, the major media – the large daily newspapers and television network newscasts – tend to set the agenda for other media. Politicians, advocacy groups, and even online bloggers measure their success largely on the basis of how successful they are in attracting news media attention and influencing the nature of coverage. Media-savvy political communicators have become highly skilled at influencing how an issue is framed in the major media. For example, in 2008, Conservative Party strategists and their supporters in the media framed the possibility of a coalition of the Liberals and the New Democratic Party (NDP; supported by the Bloc Québécois), which would have been an alternative to the minority Conservative government, as an illegitimate power grab by "socialists and separatists," effectively discrediting the idea. This framing drowned out the alternative view that if the Conservative government lost the confidence of the House of Commons, a coalition of opposition parties, which together received a majority of the popular vote in the previous election, would have been a perfectly normal option in a parliamentary system (Fletcher 2011, 37–8; Russell and Sossin 2009). Despite expert opinion, many Canadians were persuaded by the Conservative Party's message.

For a democracy to be healthy, the news media must fulfil some important social responsibilities. These include making available sufficient information about government and politics to permit citizens to participate effectively in the political process; maintaining ongoing scrutiny of those with power; investigating and reporting on important social, economic, and political issues; and presenting a wide range of viewpoints on public issues to facilitate debate. When asked which traditional journalistic roles they thought were most important, Canadians chose exposing abuses of power by government and other powerful institutions (90 per cent), reporting the story behind the headlines (89 per cent), and providing regular coverage of government actions

(86 per cent) (Fletcher et al. 2011, 5). Despite the increasing importance of nontraditional sources of news and information, most Canadians think these functions can be performed effectively only by traditional journalism (the chapter by Elmer, Langlois, and McKelvey discusses the role of blogging in disseminating this message).

In this respect, the media can be seen as an arena in which groups compete to gain public attention and support for their point of view. This formulation portrays the media as neutral, an objective referee perhaps, representing public debate in a fair and impartial manner. In fact, however, the news media approach their journalistic tasks with a series of structural biases, a result of standard journalistic practices and the commercial interests and ideological perspectives of owners and managers. As McChesney (2004, 17) writes, "The crucial tension lies between the role of the media as profit-maximizing commercial organizations and the need for the media to provide the basis for informed self-government. It is this tension that fuels much of the social concern about the media."

The Canadian news media, much like media in other industrial democracies, face important structural constraints in fulfilling their social responsibilities. Whether publicly or privately owned, news organizations are constrained in their reporting and commentary by public expectations, commercial pressures and related economic factors, and some aspects of government power. Since journalism depends on public attention for its economic survival as well as its influence, journalists must generally operate within the bounds of what the public considers legitimate political discourse. While it is possible to challenge the conventional wisdom, there are limits beyond which audiences turn away. Commercial pressures reinforce these social constraints and push news organizations towards the dramatic story and sometimes away from the important one as they try to build and maintain audiences. The pressure to maximize corporate profits may also threaten journalistic independence and effectiveness. Governments, which have found ways to limit access to information (see the chapter by Rubin and Kozolanka) and to select the timing and "spin" of public announcements, have a great deal of influence in framing both reporting and commentary. Statements by governments have a degree of authority that news organizations cannot ignore.

In the past decade, major news organizations have faced a series of challenges, threatening both their audience bases and their revenue streams. The proliferation of television channels and the increasing use of the Internet for both information and entertainment have resulted in a significant loss of audiences and income for major media corporations. As Hackett and Anderson (2010, 2) observe, "In the face of falling advertising revenues and large payments on debts incurred in escalating concentration of ownership in the past decade, Canada's big media corporations have made major cuts to the [budgets of] newspapers and local television. The Canadian Media Guild estimates that some 3,000 media workers were laid off between January and April of 2009 alone. At newspapers, layoffs and budget cuts led to ... narrowing specialized and local coverage." Most news organizations have faced reduced editorial budgets and have responded by withdrawing from or cancelling membership to news services such as the Canadian Press, as well as reducing staff (see also Winseck 2011a). Key institutions of political communication affected by the cuts include the Parliamentary Press Gallery in Ottawa, the home base for most of Canada's national political reporters, and the legislative press galleries in the provincial capitals. Many news outlets have opted out of the press galleries, relying instead on reports from journalists employed by newsgroups. The result, according to reporters, has been significantly reduced attention to stories of regional and local significance and regional angles to national stories. At the same time, the 24/7 news cycle, with reporters having to report continually not only for all news channels but also for online news Web sites, leaves reporters with little time to respond to requests for coverage from regional outlets, which is important in making coverage engaging for local audiences. These pressures have also reduced the time available for investigating more complex stories and, for many news organizations, the number of reporters specializing in covering specific beats, such as municipal politics or the courts (Canadian Association of Journalists 2010).

Because of the central role of journalists in the newsgathering process, reductions in the journalistic capacity of newspapers are of particular concern. Television continues to be the most important distributor of news for most Canadians, but newspapers initiate much of the original reporting in the system. As Shirky (2009, 1) has put it, "Print media does much of society's heavy journalistic lifting, from ... covering every angle of a huge story – to the daily grind of attending the City Council meeting, just in case. This coverage creates benefits even for people who aren't newspaper readers, because the work of print journalists is used by everyone from politicians ... to talk radio hosts and bloggers." In short, newspapers benefit society as a whole, despite the limitations imposed by their commercial business model. This business model – selling the attention of audiences attracted by journalistic content to advertisers in order to pay for the journalism – no longer works as it once did, challenged by growing competition for audience attention and advertiser dollars. It is unclear how journalism will be funded in the future. Although Canada has two distinct media systems, English and French, and a growing third-language sector, general developments in Quebec have been similar. For example, Quebecor, which dominates media ownership in the French system, owns major properties in the rest of Canada as well (Raboy and Shtern 2010, 73, 98). A good deal of ownership overlap also exists in the third-language sector. The power relations identified here, including commercial pressures and government control of information, operate in all these sectors, but the journalistic cultures and practices are notably different. While the third-language or ethnocultural media tend to focus on news from their homelands and local communities, the French media in Quebec are heavily invested in coverage of Quebec politics and Quebec interests in Ottawa (Nesbitt-Larking 2007, 247–9; Pritchard, Brewer, and Sauvageau 2005). Even the national public broadcaster, the CBC/Radio-Canada, is divided along language lines, with only moderate sharing of material in news and public affairs (Raboy and Shtern 2010, 113). These divisions in the Canadian media system are sources of concern to democratic theorists, who fear that a fragmented public sphere weakens the foundation needed for citizen engagement or serious political debate (Fletcher and Everett 2004, 429–31). Although the divisions remain important, all news organizations in Canada have had to adapt to rapidly changing technologies and audience patterns.

The Changing Media Environment

The traditional news media are, increasingly, one voice among many in a multimedia environment in which the competition for attention continues to grow with each new innovation. In this context, the role of the citizen is changing, with each of us having greater capacity to select the information we consume and to engage with and add to the information mix. Since the emergence of the Internet as a widely used way of engaging with the world, Canadians have spent increasing amounts of time not only seeking information online but also contributing their own thoughts and observations to public discourse. Several studies note that the Internet now rivals television as a source of information, although television is still dominant as a source of political news (e.g., see Decima Research 2011). Blogs and alternative news sites are increasingly important supplements to traditional media for many Canadians (Brown 2010, 178–9).

.Twitter is a good example of the emerging media ecology. Although less than 15 per cent of Canadian Internet users are on Twitter, mostly under 30 years of age (Zamaria and Fletcher 2012, table C3.325F), the vast array of content tweeted includes eyewitness reports and commentary on current events, which are increasingly used as news tips by journalists. The 140-character fragments of information can be pieced together to form a larger picture (Hermida 2010b, 3). A recent study by the Samara Foundation (Bastedo, Chu, and Hilderman 2012) examined 950,054 tweets related to political topics in fall 2011 and found that more than half of all tweets contained links to online content. Most of the links were to traditional media sites. For example, more than 70 per cent of links associated with the hashtag #cndpoli referred users to traditional media. With respect to #occupy and related hashtags, however, only 31 per cent referred to traditional media, a finding that supports the argument that social media platforms do, under the right circumstances, provide an alternative to traditional media sources. Nevertheless, as many commentators note, the traditional news media have specific strengths – reach, consistency, continuity, and professionalism – that are not easily matched. Even heavy users of the Internet rely on mainstream sources for verification, context, and interpretation (Fletcher et al. 2011, 5). Trends in mainstream media have a strong influence on online discourse; even the flow of influence is increasingly reciprocal.

Since the late 1980s, the culture of mainstream Canadian journalism has gradually shifted from a centre-Left consensus, generally supportive of the *status quo*, to a centre-Right position. Radical perspectives from either side of the political spectrum have traditionally been rejected or resisted, but in recent years, coverage and commentary have become more economically and (to a lesser extent) socially conservative. This is in part due to a concerted effort by business interests and conservative groups to influence the public agenda. As Martin (2010, 66), an Ottawa-based national columnist, commented on the media culture as of 2006,

The arrival of the *National Post* [in 1998] and the conservative CanWest chain, which owned most of the country's big newspapers, had given the Tories an edge. The tabloid *Sun* chain was conservative, as was *Maclean's* magazine, and AM radio was full of right-wing talk jocks. Neither CTV nor Global television was pro-Liberal. And while Conservatives railed against the CBC, it was no longer the Liberal bastion of old, at least not on the television side. Of its prominent pundits – Rex Murphy, Andrew Coyne, Allan Gregg, and Chantal Hébert – not one was on the political left.

Because a shift in journalistic culture is often subtle – expressed primarily in what is emphasized in news coverage – these observations are difficult to test. For newspapers, one measure is which national party was endorsed during the 2011 election campaign. Of the 62 largest circulation dailies in Canada (97.5 per cent of market share), 21 endorsed the Conservatives, 10 encouraged voting or supported more than one party, one endorsed the NDP (the *Toronto Star*), and 30 did not offer any party endorsement. Of the 13 daily newspapers in the Postmedia group, 10 endorsed the Conservatives. In the Sun Media group's 18 daily newspapers, six urged readers to vote Conservative. In both cases, the other outlets did not publish a specific endorsement (Winseck 2011b). Editorial endorsements do not necessarily affect news coverage, but they do indicate the general approach of the newspapers and their ownership groups.

Another indication of this cultural shift is the assessment offered by Kory Teneycke, an influential Conservative communication strategist and former director of communications for Stephen Harper. Teneycke is quoted by Martin (2010, 250) in providing a rationale for shifting the television operations of Sun Media into a version of Fox News for Canada: "We're doing well in print," Teneycke said, analysing conservative inroads in the media. "I think we're doing well in radio. I think we're doing all right online. But we're doing terribly on television." The Sun Media television experiment began in 2011 with a line-up of conservative commentators, much like the Right-wing tilt of its model, Fox News in the United States.

The shift to the conservative side of the political spectrum in the Canadian news media is, it appears, only indirectly related to American influences. The growth of Right-wing talk radio seems at times to reflect ideologies found on American radio, but in fact talk radio has a long history in Canada as well. Measuring American influence is not straightforward, but it is clear that Canadians have a strong preference for Canadian news sources. In a 2003 survey, for example, only

15 per cent of Canadians reported watching US television news on a regular basis (compared to 54 per cent who watched Canadian news daily), and 35 per cent said they never watched American news (Logan et al. 2004). A majority of the survey respondents reported disliking the sensationalism and confrontational style that is often featured on American television news. More recently, the best-known American example of Right-wing television news, Fox News (An et al. 2011), now available in Canada as a subscription-only specialty channel, has garnered a modest audience: less than 8 per cent of all its 887,000 cable subscribers, compared to 97 per cent for CBC News Network (11 million) and 72 per cent for the middle-of-the-road CNN (8.5 million) (see MediaStats 2010). In addition to Canadians' preference for Canadian news sources, Sun Media's modest ratings suggest style is also a factor.

In Canada, talk radio has a modest but committed audience. A recent count found 36 stations with an all-news talk format (Sampert 2012). A few, like CBC Radio One, are mainly news and interviews, but most privately owned all-news stations devote much of their time to audience phone-in shows. These stations are generally Right of centre in political ideology, and their hosts and commentators promote a form of "epistemological populism" that pits individual personal experience against science and expertise in general (Saurette and Gunster 2011, 195 and 214). The evidence lends support to Teneycke's view (mentioned previously) that radio leans towards the Conservative Party, with the exception of CBC Radio One and its French-language counterpart. Overall, radio news is quite popular, but a survey conducted before the 2011 election found that only 13 per cent of Anglophones and 7 per cent of Francophones expected to rely on talk radio for election news (Decima Research 2011). Thus, the direct influence of talk radio is limited. But, as Sampert (2012) argues, talk radio has considerable indirect influence on public debate because it is controversial and has the ear of mainstream journalists and, as one study suggests, the attention of conservative politicians concerned about the opinions of a key support group (Marland and Kerby 2010).

The struggle to influence the culture of public discourse takes place in all media. Government has important tools of influence in this regard but so too do political parties, think tanks, advocacy groups, and other institutions of civil society, as various chapters in this volume attest. However, the rules of the game still favour those who control the mainstream media, despite the increasing importance of social media.

Media Ownership and Control

The Canadian media system is dominated by a few large corporations that control most daily newspapers and many magazines and weekly newspapers, as well as most radio and television outlets, specialty channels, cable and satellite systems, and wireless Internet providers. The best-known news-oriented Web sites are operated by major news organizations. As of 2010, two large corporations owned more than half of Canada's daily newspapers, accounting for 54 per cent of total circulation. The *Globe and Mail*, one of two daily newspapers that circulate nationally, accounted for about 8 per cent of circulation, and the *Toronto Star*, Canada's largest circulation daily, whose parent company, Torstar Corporation, also owns three other daily newspapers, accounted for a little over 11 per cent (Canadian Newspaper Association 2010). There is also a great deal of cross-ownership, with major corporations in some cities (such as Vancouver) controlling the major newspapers and television stations.

It seems clear that ownership consolidation has reduced the capacity of the established news media to serve as an effective counterweight to the communicative power of the state. There is widespread concern among democratic theorists that concentration leads to undue influence on news by management and commercial interests and to a decline in the diversity of news coverage, especially reduced resources for the most costly forms of journalism, such as serious investigative work. The shrinking job market also means that journalists cannot easily walk away from existing positions, making them potentially more vulnerable to management pressure. Managers of large media corporations arguably spend more time worrying about the parent corporation's share value in the stock market and regulatory issues involving their broadcast interests than they do about journalistic quality.[2] The central concern for democracy is that declining journalistic competition reduces the range of perspectives needed to promote democratic debate and places limits on the kind of journalism that holds governments to account.

In responding to these concerns, media corporations argue that consolidation is necessary for their financial survival, given the fragmentation of audiences and advertising revenues in the past decade, and that in any case there is sufficient competition from other news providers to promote journalistic quality and diversity. Corporations also point out that the proliferation of television channels, including several national and international news services, and the growing access to the Internet, with its vast array of information services, provide Canadians with substantially more information opportunities than at any time in the past (Soderlund and Hildebrandt 2005, 91–6; Blake 2011). Although it is true that Canadians do consult more information sources than ever, the major outlets still set the public agenda. The availability of a wide range of nonlocal choices does not compensate for the absence of diversity at the local level, the most relevant political community for many Canadians. At this point, the Internet is a useful complement to traditional news sources, not a substitute. Even active citizens will pay only so much in information costs – whether in subscription fees and equipment costs or in personal time and effort – to be well informed.[3]

Changing Expectations

Although the Internet is gaining on traditional media, the latter are still the most important sources of news for Canadians. For national and international news, the major sources identified by Canadians are television at 40 per cent, Internet at 33 per cent, and newspapers at 15 per cent. For local news, printed newspapers are most important (38 per cent), followed by television (26 per cent) and radio (18 per cent). Among those who go online for news, the most visited sites are newspaper Web sites (66 per cent); portal Web sites, which derive their news from traditional news organizations (64 per cent); and television network Web sites (52 per cent) (Logan et al. 2010, tables 41–2, 86–7, 89). Social media networks are increasingly important as sources for news, especially for Canadians under 35 years of age, but these networks are used more to alert personal contacts about breaking news or for sharing reports and commentary from established sources than as a substitute for traditional news providers. Social media networks still do not set the agenda, although they influence it, because journalists themselves make substantial use of social media (Hermida 2010a; Hermida et al. 2011). In addition, as we have seen with Twitter, social media networks are effective in organizing dissent on topics that fall outside the boundaries of traditional media political discourse.

The continued importance of traditional media in setting the agenda is based largely on public trust. Nearly 9 out of 10 Canadians think that news and information in traditional news media is reliable and trustworthy. Trust in newer Internet sources, such as social media and personal blogs, is much lower. While younger Canadians are more likely than those 35 years and older to have confidence in nontraditional news providers, they also rely quite heavily on mainstream media for reliable information: "Many Canadians rely on social networks to alert them to news, even though they may often seek verification from traditional news outlets" (Fletcher et al. 2011, 2). In all age groups, Canadians trust information provided by newspapers (87 per cent) and television news (83 per cent) much more than information from governments (42 per cent) or private corporations (38 per cent) (ibid., 2–3).

Nevertheless, online news services have changed news consumption patterns in Canada quite dramatically over the past decade and, in the process, have changed expectations about how news should be delivered. Checking for news online is part of many Canadians' daily routine. For example, only 5 per cent of Canadian Internet users never check for news online and nearly 6 in 10 per cent do so at least daily (Logan et al. 2010, table 77). Online news consumers value the immediacy and search capacity of news delivered via the Internet, along with the ability to follow links to more detailed information or related reports, share content with friends and colleagues, and customize the news they receive (Fletcher 2010, 7–8). Canadians under 35 years of age are particularly attracted to those aspects of digital news delivery that have a social element. For example, the ability to share content was important to 83 per cent of Canadians under 35. The availability of online discussions is also important to a majority in that age group (Hermida et al. 2011, 1–2).

These findings underline a more general conclusion: that a growing number of Canadians see news not only as part of a broader information mix but also as an aspect of social life. This conclusion is supported by some of the reasons Canadians give for using social network sites (Logan, Fletcher, Hermida, and Korell, 2010, Table 105). The news-related motives for visiting these sites included the ability to "keep up with news and views from other places" (mentioned by 71 per cent), the capacity to get "firsthand information about important events" (63 per cent), and being "exposed to more news and information" through social networking contacts (59 per cent). According to Hermida et al. (2011, 1), "The survey shows how social networking sites are becoming a personalized news stream for Canadians of all ages, with news selected and filtered by family, friends and acquaintances." Clearly, news is seen as an element of ongoing conversations about what is going on in the world, and social networks have an increasingly important influence on how audiences direct their news consumption and, it seems likely, how news from traditional sources is interpreted.

For many younger Canadians, Internet news is valued because it offers convenient access to diverse points of view, including alternatives to mainstream media, and the opportunity to take part in discussions about the news. In a study of youth and the news conducted for the Canadian Media Research Consortium in 2006, many focus group participants reported visiting "sites conducive to discussions between users and created by interest groups or by individuals. Their objective is not necessarily to take part in discussions, but to obtain a wide range of views ... so they form their own opinions" (Boily 2006a). Alternative newspapers and Web sites "rarely constitute the main source of information" for the participants; they are regarded as complementary (see the chapter by Pimlott for an examination of alternative media). It was clear that information is a form of "social currency" for young adults and that they turn to their social networks as much as to news sources for validation (Boily 2006b, 50–5).

After a period of denying that traditional, top-down models of news delivery were losing support, news organizations have worked hard in recent years to meet these new expectations, though there are still strong top-down elements in the Web sites of most news organizations. In terms of promoting healthy democratic discourse, however, there is cause for optimism. These new expectations provide important opportunities for alternative media and for broadening public debate. The potential for support of independent public interest–oriented and community media may also be found in data on what Canadians want to see in the media environment in the next decade. Asked in 2008 what they would like to see in the next 10 years, Canadians mentioned less concentration of media ownership (42 per cent), more not-for-profit news organizations (44 per cent) and more community-oriented news organizations (33 per cent) (Fletcher 2010, 7–8). There is clearly support for a more diversified media system and the potential for more challenges to the domination of the public sphere by the state.

Journalism and a Healthy Public Sphere

The negative side of a more expansive public sphere is a more fragmented one. The combination of declining audiences for traditional media, which began with cable and satellite television, and the flood of information available online has raised concerns among democratic theorists about the future of the public sphere. The fragmentation of audiences and the competition for attention may be eroding the stock of common understandings necessary for healthy public debate. Beginning with the advent of television narrowcasting and enabled by the Internet and the emergence of a strong third-language media sector in Canada, targeted political messaging has grown dramatically. This has increased the likelihood of single-issue appeals, contradictory messages, and divisive ethnocultural messaging at the same time as it has broadened political dialogue.

To date, the most common response to audience fragmentation by news organizations has been to distribute their content through multiple channels, including print, broadcasting, news Web sites, and blogs. Although news and commentary are increasingly being delivered through numerous channels, many of which are Internet-based, much of the content still originates from established content providers, mainly major news organizations. It is this content that most Internet news consumers are using. In general, it appears that the best-known news organizations are maintaining their audiences, even though their online revenues do not come close to replacing those lost by the decline in offline readers and viewers (Logan et al. 2011, 1).

Theories of democratic citizenship tend to have high expectations of the news media. Even representative democracy, in which citizen roles are limited to passing judgment on elites who compete for power, places considerable responsibilities on the news media. Democracies that demand higher levels of engagement than periodic voting require even more of the media. The central requirement of a healthy representative democracy is an informed voter. The knowledge required to be an informed voter is not trivial. As Norris (2000, 29–30) puts it, "By this criterion, the news media succeed if they encourage learning about politics and public affairs, so citizens can cast informed ballots, if they stimulate grassroots interest and discussion, and if they encourage the public to participate through available channels of civic engagement, including voter turnout." In Canada, turnout is clearly related to voters' levels of information and interest (Blais, Gidengil, and Nevitte 2002, 197). While the election campaign system should provide parties and candidates with ample opportunity to make their arguments directly to the electorate through advertising, only the news media could provide the contextual information and critical scrutiny necessary for informed citizenship. Viewed in this way, the news has three major responsibilities during an election campaign: to report accurately and fairly the arguments that parties and candidates make; to provide a critical assessment of the factual claims and ideological assumptions underlying partisan communications, by investigating some matters themselves and by providing a forum for critical responses; and to provide a diversity of viewpoints in order to promote debate (Fletcher 2004).

As Norris (2000, 30) suggests, voters need "practical knowledge about the probable consequences of their political actions." For Norris, this means fewer stories about the game of politics and more reports on what electoral choices might mean for voters and their communities. In order to contextualize the electoral choices, voters need information about the strengths and weaknesses of party leaders and the general orientation of the parties. Drawing on citizen-oriented audience research, we can identify some useful principles for journalism. First, when news stimulates people to connect their personal experiences with political issues, people can begin to identify with others who have common experiences and think in terms of political actions that might make a difference (too often audiences cannot see the relevance that political reporting has to their lives). Second, news that points to alternatives for public action stimulates greater citizen interest and makes information easier for people to remember and recall (Fletcher 2004.) Many of the weaknesses in news coverage of politics can be traced to how journalism imagines the role of the citizen. According to Blumler and Gurevitch (1995, 106), "Of the three main elements in a political communication system – politicians, journalists, and audience members – it is the audience which, though most numerous, is least powerful, because it is least organized." It may well be that audiences tend to accept the way in which the role of citizen is constructed in the news, as spectator, victim, or juror at best, passing judgment on political parties and leaders only at election time, with little reflection on other possibilities. Mainstream media, even with more innovative and diversified reporting, are too constrained to push civic engagement much beyond current levels or to offer alternatives to the dominant ideologies that frame their coverage and commentary.

Recent Canadian election campaigns provide illuminating examples of the challenges and weaknesses of political journalism. For example, the high cost of providing ongoing television coverage of party leaders' tours – a key element of Canadian federal elections –led Canada's five major television networks to cut costs by sending one camera crew with each leader and sharing the visuals (Francoli, Greenberg, and Waddell 2011, 222). More importantly, recent studies conclude that in other respects campaign coverage has not changed much since the 1970s. Too much attention is paid to party leaders, which lets the parties set the agenda; too many issues are not covered effectively, especially issues that are complicated (such as climate change); too much attention is given to polling focused on voting intentions (the "horse race"); and there is not enough critical assessment of party policy proposals (Waddell 2009; Francoli, Greenberg, and Waddell 2011). The newspaper coverage had more policy content but was marked by less attention to reporting and more to opinion (Waddell 2009, 222–3). In short, although the traditional media still devote considerable resources to campaign coverage, voters' concerns rarely set the agenda and voters are not provided with the information that might stimulate citizen engagement.

In Canada, unlike the United States, the Internet and social media have not had a major impact on electoral communication. In the 2011 campaign, Facebook and YouTube were widely used by political parties and candidates but were employed mainly for fundraising and to extend the reach of more conventional forms of campaigning – posting press releases, videos of speeches, and television ads – and were viewed in small numbers and mostly by committed voters and partisans (see Francoli, Greenberg, and Waddell 2011, 231–3, 241–2; Small 2008). Even when the Conservative Party adopted the strategy of announcing a policy each campaign day, news coverage focused on the strategy rather than the policies themselves (Waddell 2009, 224). In short, it appears that social media sites have had only a modest influence on citizen engagement during past election campaigns (at least as recently as the 2011 federal election).

Social media sites have, however, had a greater impact on traditional journalism. Journalists are very attentive to political party Web sites and increasingly pay attention to citizen posts on social media sites. Based on their analysis of news coverage of the 2011 campaign, Francoli, Greenberg, and Waddell (2011, 244) conclude that, "for the mainstream media, social media offer another way of delivering news and information to audiences, but there is little evidence that news organizations, like the parties, are much interested in opening themselves up to the challenges and criticism that two-way social media debate can provide." While it is true that news organizations, accustomed to a top-down approach, have been slow to adapt the nonhierarchical values often attributed to social media, the most forward looking are slowly adopting a more conversational approach, with journalists increasingly engaging in dialogue with audiences on their blogs and on Twitter (Brown 2010).

There is little evidence that citizens are becoming more engaged or better informed because of these innovations. Indeed, citizens often hold alarming misconceptions about policy issues and processes. Nadeau and Giasson (2003, 26n46) offer two examples from the 1997 election survey. Results showed that an overwhelming majority of voters believed that violent crime is increasing and that the First Nations peoples are better off than other Canadians. Both beliefs are demonstrably false. Polls taken during the 1995 referendum in Quebec identified a number of misconceptions that were quite widespread, for example, that a sovereign Quebec could still send MPs to Ottawa. These misconceptions are challenging examples because in each case significant political actors had (and still have) a vested interest in perpetuating them. It requires a courageous and independent media to challenge misconceptions. Indeed, leading British theorist Keane (1991, 193) argues that a courageous and independent media is the best indication of a healthy democracy. A more recent example comes from a Dominion Institute survey that found that 51 per cent of Canadians believe the prime minister is directly elected by voters (Dominion Institute 2008), a misunderstanding that could be attributed to the leader-focused coverage of politics in the traditional media and the campaign strategies of the major political parties.

Although traditional media continue to dominate the public agenda, the Internet has provided new opportunities to broaden the scope of public debate and to modify mainstream journalism. In general, it is fair to say that the Internet has challenged the dominance of traditional media, has presented information in novel ways and raised questions about established definitions of news and the role of journalists, and above all, has created a new public sphere with the potential for greater public engagement. As with other new media, news on the Internet is taking on new forms, involving audiences in new ways (as both seekers and providers of news and commentary), and is altering news consumption patterns. It is essential to recognize the changed environment that the pervasive availability of online news – in all its variety – has created. The advent of bloggers and "citizen journalists" has led to unprecedented scrutiny of mainstream reporting and commentary, not only by identifying errors and presenting alternative perspectives but also by uncovering stories that have been overlooked or ignored. Audiences can with relative ease bypass traditional gatekeepers to access news from a wide range of sources and can seek out competing perspectives on a wide range of subjects,[4] even though only a minority may do so.

While most Canadians value the contribution of the Internet and wireless delivery of news and information, they also value the contribution of traditional journalism, which they still believe has an important role to play in a healthy democracy. Canadians rely on traditional media to expose abuses of power, report the story behind the headlines, provide analysis of important events, and provide regular coverage of governmental activity. In addition, Canadians are generally sceptical about the capacity of nontraditional forms of journalism to perform these critical tasks. For example, fewer than one in four Canadians believes that citizen-based media can fulfil these social responsibilities as well as professional journalism can (Fletcher 2011, 5–6). What these findings make clear is that efforts to promote a media system that would contribute more to a healthy democratic public sphere must include attention to traditional media. This conclusion is shared by spokespersons from a sample of progressive non-governmental organizations who told researchers in a recent study that the mainstream media, despite all their flaws, remain important (Hackett and Anderson 2010, 27). Of course, other more democratic alternatives may emerge as well.

Challenging the Traditional Media

In recent years, several instances of Internet-based activism have challenged the public agenda with considerable effect. During the 2008 federal election campaign, the broadcast consortium that manages the leadership debates excluded Elizabeth May, leader of the Green Party, from the televised debate, almost certainly out of concern that Prime Minister Harper would refuse to participate if May was included. Online petitions supporting May's inclusion generated many signatures and much mainstream media attention, which resulted in a change of policy (Waddell 2009, 227–8). In the face of two controversial adjournments of Parliament (prorogation) initiated by the prime minister to avoid possible defeat in the minority House of Commons, many Canadians, both partisan and non-partisan, went online to voice their objections. In late 2009, a Facebook petition opposing the prime minister's requests for a prorogation gathered more than 200,000 signatures and resulted in a dramatic change in public opinion (Canadian Press 2010a) and in media coverage.

At the beginning of the coalition controversy (both in 2008 and 2009), mainstream media treated the protests with disdain, apparently believing that Canadians did not care about such a complicated and technical issue. In fact, many journalists initially adopted the Conservative Party's message: "According to one dominant narrative [throughout 2009], which appeared to be the main Conservative talking point, the change of government [proposed by the Liberal and New Democratic Parties] was likened to an unprecedented *coup d'état*. There could be no change of government without a new election" (Schneiderman 2011, 20). To say the least, this is an unusual interpretation of parliamentary government. The Facebook protests, backed by rallies across the country, academic refutations of the Conservative argument, and eventually, polls that indicated public disapproval of the Conservative position, resulted in considerable backtracking by the mainstream media. As Dobbin (2010) put it, "It is rare that anything like a consensus develops on political issues in Canada, especially amongst the pundits, editorialists and academics routinely commenting on events. But the second prorogation by Harper set alarm bells ringing across the country." Commentators such as John Ibbitson and Andrew Coyne, usually regarded as conservative, as well as the editorial board of the *Globe and Mail*, expressed strong objections to the prorogation (ibid.). The public agenda was changed, at least for a time, and even though the Harper government was able to stay in power, the prorogation tactic was discredited. What the prorogation case demonstrates is that the public agenda set by the traditional media can at times be effectively challenged more quickly, more easily, and more comprehensively than in the past. The Facebook-generated protest resonated sufficiently with the public that it was voted the "best moment in Canadian democracy of 2010" by readers of the Samara Foundation's non-partisan Web site (Samara Foundation 2011).[5]

Media and the New Public Sphere

Web-based sources of news and information provide convenience, accessibility, ease of navigation, and a range of information and opinions, especially from other countries, not readily available in the established media. However, the vast majority of news and information accessed by online news consumers originates with mainstream news organizations, whether they are found using search engines, news compilers or aggregators, or the Web sites of newspapers and television networks. For example, while local newspapers dominate hard copy newspaper readership, most online readers check national or international newspapers. Although blogs and alternative news Web sites reach relatively small audiences, they provide both a check on and an alternative to the mainstream press, challenging the factual basis of reports, raising neglected issues, and offering other points of view.

Despite the fact that, with respect to news and information, the Internet is still used primarily as a supplement to traditional news services, it is nevertheless true that the Internet is changing the nature of the public sphere. As an American analysis put it, "Journalism is becoming a smaller part of people's information mix. The press is no longer the gatekeeper over what the public knows" (Project for Excellence in Journalism 2007). The Internet is indeed changing the nature of information seeking and news consumption, with younger citizens seeking more customized news and consulting multiple sources in an information environment that is more open and more global and includes a wider range of information and opinion. In the best-case scenario, the news media will become less purveyors of knowledge and more providers of context and meaning. Journalists will spend less time collecting information and more time "directing the social flow of information and public debate" (Boeder 2005, 8; see also Fletcher 2007).

The traditional news media, no longer the dominant gatekeepers of the public agenda, are struggling to define themselves in new ways in order to retain a significant role in the digital age. As citizens, we have unprecedented opportunities to customize the information we consume and, indeed, to add our own voices to the information mix. Yet, most Canadians continue to rely on traditional journalism for verification, context, and interpretation of the news. Nevertheless, indications are that the new online media, as long as they remain open to dissenting counter publics, will help limit the influence of powerful media organizations, challenging their version of events and publicizing alternative perspectives. These developments offer hope that the proliferation of information and commentary online will contribute to the reinvigoration of the public sphere or, more likely, to the rise of an overlapping series of public spheres.

The new public sphere, then, involves new opportunities for participation and the formation of counterpublics to challenge dominant ideologies. For media democracy theorists, this is a positive development. At the same time, however, the emergence of more narrowly focused public spheres threatens the common public sphere upon which democratic discourse depends. If the sense of common citizenship is diminished, social cohesion is threatened. If increasing numbers of citizens do not share in a common public agenda and a widely shared vocabulary of precedents, deliberative democracy is harder to achieve. In this respect, the convergence of social media and the evolving news media is a reason for optimism. It is essential, however, to remember that the online community is by no means open to all and, indeed, may never be equally open to all. The digital divides – whether by age, income, education, or geographic location – still constitute an important inequality in the new public sphere, one that requires public access policies (for further discussion, see Fletcher 2007). In addition, the growth of a more opinionated and confrontational style of discourse, whether in traditional media (talk radio, Sun Media) or online, may reduce the likelihood of dialogue and civility in political debate.

Any movement towards a more democratic media system, one that can effectively promote deeper civic engagement, will necessarily involve a range of reforms (for more on media reform, see the chapter by Cross, Hackett, and Anderson). Finding a balance between an opening up of the political communication system to promote diversity and the need for common understandings for effective debate will not be easy. At the same time, increasing numbers of citizens are consulting a wider range of online sources in Canada and around the world and many seek out a broader range of perspectives. There is concern that citizens may be increasingly customizing their news so that they rarely encounter perspectives that challenge their own. Whether that leads to greater polarization and more disengagement or to a higher quality of debate remains to be seen.

On the one hand, then, it is important to recognize the importance of traditional media and to try to encourage journalists to take a sceptical approach to the social distribution of power. Many journalists do – and some excellent journalism is published in Canada – but they are constrained by the structures within which they must work. As a public broadcaster, the CBC aspires to serve the public interest, but its journalists are also constrained by government scrutiny and, ultimately, by the dependence of their institution on government funding. The role of the CBC is important not only because, with its multiple platforms (including a popular Internet service), it has a major impact on the Canadian public sphere but also because it has long served as an exemplar of journalistic quality. Citizens can try to hold traditional news organizations to higher standards, for example, by advocating for reduced market concentration, public or community ownership, and more critical journalism education, to name a few possible reforms (Hackett and Anderson 2010, 27ff). Alternatively, citizens may look to innovative forms of online journalism, including outlets such as TheTyee.ca and experiments that feature collaboration between citizens and professional journalists, such as "Go Public" on CBC television news or more radical alternatives in other countries. (For a discussion of these experiments, see Singer et al., 2011.) Or, citizens may look to public interest research groups to take up the kinds of investigative journalism that traditional news organizations cannot or will not undertake. Others may content themselves with the increased opportunities for dialogue offered by the traditional media, through online town halls, comments sections, and so on. The Internet does not yet provide a public sphere for democratic discourse for most citizens, but it has the potential to serve that purpose. Nor does it consistently challenge the persuasive communication strategies of governments and political parties that successfully frame much of Canada's public debate within the publicity state. Yet online media developments and innovative forms of journalism have the potential to improve dramatically the capacity of citizens to resist hegemonic discourse. Technology is an enabler. The political will of citizens and journalists will determine whether Canada pushes the boundaries of democratic political discourse or simply replicates past patterns.

NOTES

1 For a summary of this argument, see Boeder (2005).
2 For discussions of this issue, see Skinner, Compton, and Gasher (2005, 8, 53–4, 62–3) and Soderlund and Hildebrandt (2005, 91–6, 162–3n2).
3 This argument is set out in Fletcher (2005).
4 For more on this argument, see Fletcher (2007).
5 For useful accounts of the 2008 and 2009 prorogations and the public response, see Paulsen (2010) and Dobbin (2010).

2 In Whose Interest? Government Communication and Public Accountability

KIRSTEN KOZOLANKA

In recent years, burgeoning publicity practiced by governments in Canada has been in the media spotlight, raising questions about the appropriateness of how governments communicate with the public. The scandal over a federal government promotional program involving sponsorships was dissected widely and publicly mostly between 2004 and 2006. That, and the use of public funds over several years for an ongoing advertising campaign to sell the subsequent government's 2008 stimulus plan, speaks to the lure and potency of publicity for political parties in power. While successful publicity is intended to do its persuasive work invisibly, according to Schiller (1973) and others, or at least without drawing negative attention, the fallout from these examples and other cases indicate that publicity practices that benefit the party in power, and use public service administration and funds to do so, remain a vital component of successful policymaking in Canada.

This chapter examines how successive governments have entrenched publicity practices within the apparatus of government. It discusses the main organizational mode of centralization to enable efficient publicity, the politicization of the public service in carrying out publicity tasks that benefit the political party in power, and the professionalization of the public service and advisors to the government that is built on technical advances in publicity. It does so within the context of troubling ethical issues, relating to accountability and transparency to the public being served, and reveals the chill under which public employees now operate. In so doing, the chapter draws attention to the nature of political communication within the permanent campaigning endemic and in a publicity-oriented state that also affects both the media and the public, as the chapters in this part by Barney and Fletcher elucidate.

Further, the chapter demonstrates how these instrumental practices of communication actually serve to contain transparency and accountability to citizens.

Conceptualizing State Bureaucracy

In 1995, Golding commented on an interesting development in government communications in the United Kingdom under Margaret Thatcher, prime minister from 1979 to 1990. While noting that all states generally want to promote their policies, Golding said the Thatcher government was subjecting the media to "unprecedented pressure to reflect and disseminate government views" at the same time that it also "engaged in a build up of its own publicity and press relations activities on an unprecedented scale" (35), becoming a "major public relations enterprise" (36). As the introduction to this volume outlines in more detail, this is the core and initial understanding of how modern states could conduct their policymaking by using the labour and other assets of the bureaucracy or public service.

Over the years, the build-up of the capacity to undertake publicity within governments both in the United Kingdom and in Canada, which required compliance and support at the highest level of the public service, did not reflect the traditional concept of the role of a state bureaucracy. As Weber (1969, 196) theorized, the traditional concept of bureaucracy within what he identified in an earlier era as the modern state had "bureaucratic authority" through fixed, official, and regular duties, rules, and rights. To support the bureaucracy, he envisaged a "stable system of taxation" as the precondition for retaining the bureaucracy as a permanent structure (208). The state, he said, was "absolutely dependent upon a bureaucratic basis" (211).

To Weber (1969, 215), the concept and structure of bureaucracy grew alongside capitalism, which demanded some form of administration, and provided a countervalence to the interested nature of politics and capitalism by virtue of bureaucracy's new traits of objectivity and rationality. Modern bureaucrats or "political officials" were expected to be loyal to their office in an impersonal and functional way and were not to be exploited by an "exchange of services" or to act "under the personal command of their master," as they had done in labour relationships prior to the modern state (199). Once fully established, the expert bureaucracy was a "power instrument" that was "among those power structures that were among the hardest to destroy" (228). Wielding its own power, the relationship of the bureaucracy to the interests of state power depended absolutely on the rational, objective advice of bureaucrats.

At the same time, Weber (1969) did not glorify the concept of a neutral bureaucracy, even though he saw the emergence of bureaucracy as stemming the power of authoritarian or absolute leadership. Like Marx, with whom he is often contrasted, Weber understood that those who labour in public institutions, as well as in large capitalist enterprises, can also be separated from the means of production (221, 224). In addition, although bureaucracies are intended to lessen social and economic differences and do not seek power for their own use (231), they do not in themselves become democratic, and in fact, once established, they are subject to direction from above that is nonetheless in the interests of capitalism and domination (230–1). The development of constitutional government, considered an advance in democracy, also has the result of concentrating the power of a bureaucracy under a prime minister and against other parliamentary parties (234).[1]

Weber's approach to bureaucracy can be critiqued for its idealist foundation and administrative essentialism (Mosco 2009), as its underlying belief in neutrality both in theory and practice cannot and should not be ignored. What Weber fails to take into account we can find in Marx, who centred his analysis on domination and inequality. Moreover, Schiller (1973) points out something very interesting about neutrality: citizens themselves must believe in the neutrality of their institutions, from the government to the media, in order to have faith in their government itself. This "myth of neutrality" insulates citizens from doubting both the integrity and the non-partisanship of government (11). The myth of neutrality may be a factor in how citizens in their role as voters react to blatant partisanship in the publicity practices within the bureaucratic arm of government.

For the purposes of the current chapter, however, Weber lays some early and influential sociological groundwork for understanding how the concept of a bureaucracy developed in the modern state that cannot be ignored. Further, his historical insights have surprisingly accurate relevance to how bureaucracies act today. Weber (1969) perceived how a ruler would develop a need to dominate and capture the power of an expert bureaucracy by setting up permanent advisory bodies (such as privy councils[2]) rather than rely on ad hoc advice. He also understood how fear of losing power could turn to hatred and distrust of the bureaucracy (236). Startlingly, given the discussion in this volume on how governments use the apparatus of the state, Weber even addresses how the influence of administrative bodies wanes when technology hastens communications; thus faster, more streamlined, and unified decision making from advisory bodies becomes more important than being thorough in preparing expert bureaucratic advice: "This is the case as soon as parliamentary institutions develop and – usually at the same time – as criticism from the outside and publicity increase" (238).

This mention of publicity by Weber reminds us that governments have been concerned about their public profiles for a great many years prior to the developments in Canada discussed in this chapter. They have also sought to enhance their reputations with citizens, particularly those citizens who vote and can hold them accountable.

The Long Slide into Centralized Government Communication

Just as Weber's first mention of communication within bureaucracy was primarily focussed on transportation, the first report in Canada of the Special Committee on Communications in 1830 was on roads, not information to the public (Lower Canada 1830). Although it developed slowly, politicians recognized the importance of personal communication with citizens beyond election campaign posters, slogans, and speeches. To feed this need, the Parliamentary Press Gallery was established in 1867 at the time of confederation. And what, after all, is the iconic 1885 photo of "The Last Spike" that joined the West with the East by rail, if not the product of public relations? Or the many advertising campaigns from 1891 to 1914 by Minister of the Interior Clifford Sifton that portrayed a positive image of Canada to lure potential immigrants to the country (Rose 2000)?

Propaganda bureaus established inside government during the First and Second World War were the precursors of today's communications branches, moving from temporary entities with a specific purpose to peacetime press offices that fed information to the media. Much of the organization of government, however, remained relatively constant until the early 1960s. In 1963, a royal commission on the organization of government recommended a decentralized approach to management, along with a central agency of government (the Treasury Board) to coordinate operations (Canada 1962–3). Perhaps in response, the then prime minister, Lester Pearson, expanded and standardized both the all-party standing committees and the cabinet committees. Since then, prime ministers have personalized the organization of this part of the executive part of government to their own style and priorities.

This was particularly evident in the mandates of two long-term prime ministers who followed Pearson and sheds some light on how the communication apparatus developed in government. Pierre Trudeau's (1968–79, 1980–4) style of governance was based on what we can call a Weberian technocratic rationality, or government by logic, systems, and reason (Doern 1977, 190). His was a collegial style of decision making (Schacter 1999, 8), built on information sharing and open discussion. To support this, he expanded his cabinet over time, gave more authority to fewer standing committees and had a large number (13) of cabinet committees (I. Clark 1985, 189). Diverging from past practice, he also brought "openly partisan political advisors" into the Prime Minister's Office (PMO) (Schacter 1999, 6). In contrast, Brian Mulroney (1984–93) preferred a more informal decision-making style that gave him more political control over policymaking unfettered by elaborate bureaucratic systems and long debate and brought rapid results (Schacter 1999, 7–8). Despite this, Mulroney had the largest cabinet ever (until Harper in 2011) and 10 cabinet committees, which included a restarting of the on-again–off-again communications committee (Doern 1977, 191). During Mulroney's time in office, both the PMO and the Privy Council Office (PCO) became more politicized, with "an unprecedented degree of intervention by the PCO in detailed policy and operational matters across government," as well as the "expansion of non-civil service political staff for ministers and the Prime Minister" (Schacter 1999, 7–8).

Absent from discussions of the differing styles of these two prime ministers, who had such influence on the character of both the political and bureaucratic sides of government, is any sustained discussion on the role of communication. Yet there are signs that politics began to change dramatically during this period and that communication had a hand in it. This is evident in examining the table of contents of *Apex of Power: The Prime Minister and Political Leadership in Canada* (Hockin 1977). The first edition (published in 1971) and the second edition (published in 1977) are similar in content, and both include a chapter on the images of party leaders in the 1968 election. Trudeau and the Liberals won that election after an extended period of what was called "Trudeaumania," which carefully constructed a modern, exciting image for the new prime minister. However, the second edition adds several more chapters related to prime ministerial government, the powers and privileges of prime ministers, and more importantly, "the prime minister as public persuader" (Fletcher 1977). On his part, Mulroney was so concerned about his image that he was known to pore over his media coverage; one of his favourite questions to ask his press secretary became the title of a book about him by that press secretary: "So, what are the boys [sic] saying?" (Gratton 1987).

Beyond the use of the ubiquitous press release, the importance and growth of actual communication capacity specifically within the PMO and PCO and in the public service of government were slower to be acknowledged. This is partly due to the untravelled ground upon which initial publicity efforts trod; the infiltration of political actors into the PMO and PCO noted previously who would focus more proactively on obtaining good media coverage likely went unnoticed. But the absence of a history that tells us precisely how communication came to play a key role at the political level and within the supposedly neutral public service, including its "head office," the PCO, also reveals how ordinary and natural this process was considered at the time. A communications desk has existed in the PCO since before 1971, and by 1981, it included an assistant secretary for communication (Canada 1981a), as well as a communications branch. Within the public service, 14 of 29 government departments had some measure of a structured communication or information function by 1980 (Canada 1980). In addition, a self-standing cabinet committee on communications has existed intermittently since before 1984, although, as we will see, the sponsorship scandal put an end to the most recent one in 1999.

In terms of bureaucratic support for publicity efforts, communication became more prominent as a government function in the late 1980s and the 1990s, as the number of information officers on staff grew at a faster rate than other occupational groups during times of severe cost-cutting in the public service (Kozolanka 2006, 350). The PCO published the first principles for communication in 1981 (Canada 1981a), which laid out "who does what" and was followed by a more complete guide later that year (Canada 1981b). In 1988, the first communication policy for government was published, and over time it has been revised to include many more functions, most of them related to publicity practices and many of those functions and practices requiring technical expertise that the eventually downsized bureaucracy did not have. New functions included advertising, marketing, sponsorships, fairs and exhibits, and risk and crisis communications (Canada 2002).

In addition, both the PMO and the PCO, the highest political and bureaucratic authorities, respectively, of the state, have transformed over time in ways that have centralized power and, in the case of the traditionally neutral PCO, have become politicized by serving the political needs of the PMO. This was first evident in the structural changes within both offices, which added many more functions, staff, and budgets. The Pearson PMO in the early 1960s had 30 staff members and a budget of $182,000, while Trudeau's PMO in the late 1960s had a staff of 85 and a budget of $901,000 (Lalonde 1971a, appendix ii). The rationale at the time for the increase was the new prime minister's openly stated desire to include "individuals who would serve him in various political capacities" (22)[3] and possibly because he was an outsider to federal politics, but the changes had actually become visible under Pearson with the slow "formalization of roles that had been informally developed in previous years" (Doern 1977, 193). In comparison, in 2007, Harper's PMO had 106 staff, seemingly not much more than Trudeau 36 years earlier, but a key departure is that in Harper's PMO, almost 35 per cent of staff were engaged in communication and publicity-related activities (Canada 2009a). A second departure is the increased use of professional political advisors from the private sector to staff the PMO, a practice that accelerated in the 1980s under Mulroney, who was suspicious of the "liberal" bureaucracy and routinely bypassed the PCO.

In contrast, the Harper government's strategy has been to co-opt the PCO by having that office operationalize its publicity strategies. Over time, the PCO has also been growing, adding to its staff and budget. From 10 officers in 1945, the PCO grew to 68, excluding support staff, in 1971 (Robertson 1971, 493). By 2008, it had 128 staff and a budget of $10.4 million but a whopping 902 employees if all its business lines are included. Since then, its total number of employees has hovered between 902 and 1,066.[4] For example, between 2009 and 2011, the PCO added 20 new staff and received an extra $7.2 million specifically to manage an extensive and questionable advertising campaign (on the Economic Action Plan, the government's stimulus response to the economic recession, which is discussed later in this chapter) (Canada 2010e, 14, 22). This has raised questions about the propriety of that office in undertaking clearly political work. As Savoie (2010, 93) suggests, current and recent politicians understand the importance not only of communications to winning elections "but also of the political and policy processes within governments," specifically for controlling the media.

Historically, as laid out in government documents and in scholarly analysis, the PCO is responsible for managing the public service and administering government programs. Through the late 1950s, the PCO and PMO worked closely together and even shared accounting, personnel, and administration units (Canada 1958, 53). In its relationship with the political office of the PMO, the PCO plays an advisory role by supporting the prime minister on "prerogatives of government organization, ministerial mandates and senior personnel; secretariat support for Cabinet operations; [and] briefing of committee chairmen [*sic*] on relationship of new proposals to priorities and to other activities" (I. Clark 1985, 196). This seems clear; however, it also leaves considerable room for interpretation, as there is an unspoken "honour system," in which all participants know the roles they are expected to play, roles that both separate them and bind them together. Gordon Robertson, a former clerk of the PCO, famously described the relationship between the two offices in this way: "The Prime Minister's Office is partisan, politically oriented, yet operationally sensitive. The Privy Council Office is non-partisan, operationally oriented yet politically sensitive"(Robertson 1971, 506). This, too, is helpful, especially when Robertson adds that the two offices "share the same fact base but keep out of each other's affairs" (ibid.). One further key aspect of the PCO's role, however, may get to the core of its mandate. It is what has been described as "the challenge function," by which the PCO challenges government departments to ask one vital question when putting forth positions and initiatives for prime ministerial and Cabinet approval: "*Is this in the public interest?*" (Schacter 1999, 19; emphasis added).

As recent history shows, however, the operational and advice-giving role of the PCO has been challenged by prime ministers, such as Jean Chrétien, who desire a more accommodating approach from the PCO[5] or, as most recently in the case of the Harper PMO, by taking on the role of the PCO itself. This is when the public interest risks not being served, as discussion of the sponsorship scandal under Chrétien and the many ethical issues facing Harper will demonstrate.

Chrétien and Harper: Politicizing the Public Interest

Harper is not the first prime minister to want more control over the state bureaucracy, specifically over its communications capacity, but only recent prime ministers have pushed to harness the PCO and the public service into political activity. This breaches the traditional "bargain" that existed between politics and administration of government that each has a distinct space from the other in which it operates (Savoie 2003, 6). It also reflects the perceived need by prime ministers and their parties to take charge of their image in a modern state in which the media cycle is ever faster, media content is more superficial and based on entertainment, and citizens are more cynical about government, are less personally involved in politics, and need motivation to vote. These conditions of play lead to politics that is always in campaign mode, thus perpetuating a continuing need for persuasive politics. The administrative side of government has little choice but to respond and be led by political demands that edge ever closer to, if not beyond, the boundary between mere implementation of policy and unacceptable politicized promotion of policy. In doing so, questions of ethics and transparency come into play.

A further condition involves the preference of recent prime ministers to look for expert advice outside the government bureaucracy. In the 1980s, Mulroney, the outsider with trust issues, bypassed the public service – stopping long enough to downsize it and introduce technocratic business management practices – and instead relied on outside political advisors. But it was under Chrétien in the 1990s that the massive retrenchment of the state took place, with the entire public service contracting sharply in size. In sharp contrast, communications began to increase rapidly in order to help sell the government's policies, and massive attention was paid to constructing the positive "brand" of Canada, as Nimijean discusses in his chapter. To ensure consistent and constant image making across government, Chrétien restarted the Cabinet Committee on Communications and eventually reorganized publicity efforts into a self-standing government department, Communication Canada. Here, the bureaucratic apparatuses for publicity practices such as advertising, public opinion research, fairs and exhibits, the national householder program,[6] and nation branding were handled, along with the then little-known sponsorship program. For several years (1999–2003), the government even conducted its own national polling survey, which included asking respondents their priorities on public policy issues and how well the government was performing on them, as well as their voting preference.[7] Budgets for advertising and polling increased sharply during the last years of the Chrétien government (Kozolanka 2006, 350). Although the communication branches in government were still growing, much of the work involved specialized expertise, so the government contracted with private sector suppliers, which included polling firms and advertising companies to do much of the work, and advisors to provide strategic advice and direction.

This unprecedented build-up of government publicity practices did not go unnoticed by the media, and it was media stories that alerted the political opposition and the public to the excesses in one particular area: the sponsorship program. It seemed an inoffensive goal to promote the positive brand of Canada by placing the wordmark (the stylized word "Canada" with the small red maple leaf over the final letter) in such places as hockey arenas where Canadians gather to enjoy being Canadian. But two auditor general's reports and one inquiry later, it appeared that most of the money was spent in Quebec, a key electoral battleground for Chrétien's Liberal Party. Further, $145 million of public money went to inflated commissions to ad companies in Quebec, and $100 million in donations and kickbacks ended up in the party's Quebec wing (Canada 2005).

A worrisome aspect of the sponsorship scandal that eventually played a role in toppling the Liberals from power in 2006 was how long it and other dubious publicity efforts were allowed to continue and grow. In the case of the sponsorship program, which sought to bring a positive profile to the Canada brand, and in doing so foster national unity, the seeds were sown years earlier in the 1980s in debates over Quebec separation (Rose 2000). Altogether, this raises questions of bureaucratic oversight, political ethics, and the role of the PCO: Were the checks and balances, normally a part of decision making in the public service, downsized out of existence? Should parties in power be able to co-opt and use the public service for political purposes? While this was happening, did the PCO ask the important question, "Is this in the public interest?"

Harper and the Conservative Party came to power in 2006 with an election platform promise to be accountable and transparent after the ethical failures of the Liberals. Instead, it seems that the new government merely found different, but no less controversial, ways to ensure a positive public response to its policies through massive expenditures on publicity. This self-promotion relied on an even tighter grip on the bureaucracy with the complicity of the PCO. While the Chrétien government was more blatant with its intentions and actions, with the confidence that comes from being in power for many years, the Harper government chose an "incremental" approach (Flanagan 2009, 283) or what I have referred to elsewhere by the oxymoronic phrase "communication by stealth" (Kozolanka 2009, 223). One of the new government's first and positive steps was to pass the *Federal Accountability Act*, which implicitly called for neutrality and transparency in government. The act provides oversight to many agencies of government, as well as to new, independent commissioners for ethics and integrity. It also oversees already existing commissioners for languages, privacy and information access, the auditor general, and the Public Service Commission.[8]

In contrast to these positive steps, another initial step was to bypass the Parliamentary Press Gallery or control the access of its members to the prime minister, thus preventing the media from their democratic function of getting information and opinion to the public quickly and professionally. Instead, the new government preferred to use more direct ways of getting its message to the public through regional and online media. Through the PCO, the government has also enlisted the bureaucracy in managing media requests, which were formerly dealt with by individual departments and by having appropriate subject-expert public employees give out information and answer routine questions. Now, expert employees are not allowed to speak directly to the media. All media requests undergo a centralized process in which requests make their way through departments to the PCO and then to the PMO. Once vetted, they make the slow return journey, often by which time the media have missed deadlines or no longer need the information (Kozolanka 2012). Opposition parties also often found that they could not get information from departments or from government members of parliamentary committees, where much of Parliament's work is conducted. In 2007, it was discovered that the government had prepared a manual for its own MPs to advise them on how to deal with hostile questions from opposition MPs in committee meetings. As Hansard records, Conservative MPs were directed to "obstruct" and "disrupt" committee meetings when things got hot (Canada 2007a, 27–30). More recently, as a majority government, Parliamentary committees go *in camera* routinely, which means the public and the media are not privy to the discussion.

Also troubling in the battle for control over image and for positive publicity is the fate of other measures put in place by the Harper government to make good on the election promise of a more transparent and ethical government. Along with the promised *Accountability Act* in 2006, the position of parliamentary budget officer was established to "provide independent analysis to Parliament on the state of the nation's finances" and "estimate the financial cost of any proposal for matters over which Parliament had jurisdiction" (Canada 2007b, 1). Unfortunately, unlike the independent ethics and integrity commissioners, the budget officer operates inside government jurisdiction. In early 2011, the Speaker ruled that the government was in contempt of Parliament when it did not properly report the costs of its plans on a series of expensive policy announcements widely believed (correctly, as it turned out) to be a lead-up to a spring election. Embarrassingly for the prime minister, the parliamentary budget officer whom he appointed to ensure transparency publicly rejected the government's cost estimates – only one of many times when he openly criticized government spending (Fitzpatrick 2011). In 2012, the budget officer fought the government to get details on the $5.2 billion in cuts announced in the annual federal budget, charging that there was no public transparency without this information (Bruno 2012b, 1).

In 2007, in another move to demonstrate commitment to transparency, the government enacted the *Public Servant Disclosure Act*, part of the implementation of the *Accountability Act*. The new act set up an independent agency under an integrity commissioner to investigate disclosures of wrongdoing ("whistle-blowing") in the public service. As it turned out, the first integrity commissioner resigned after an auditor general's report found that the commissioner had "failed to properly perform her mandated functions" over several years (Canada 2010b, 1). She was later ordered to appear before an all-party parliamentary committee to explain her lack of action. A further piece of legislation to promote accountability in government was the *Lobbying Act* in 2008. The mandate of the commissioner of lobbying is to ensure transparent and ethical lobbying by having lobbyists disclose their meetings with ministers, senior public employees, and their respective staffs. The commission has garnered less interest than many of the government's other efforts at accountability, since its main activity of merely listing "who met with whom" cannot in itself be clearly quantified into influence. But other than revealing a structured lack of access to the powerful by those who do not agree with government, as the chapter by Gutstein in this volume reveals, few or less meetings could just as easily mean that ministers or deputy ministers are not consulting as much as they should (Vongdouangchanh 2010, A1).

The government has hit other roadblocks that reveal it to be obstinate if not duplicitous in its repetition of its communications messages to the public on its exemplary ethical goals and behaviour and its transparency, despite growing evidence that its actions do not match its rhetoric:

• Early in the Conservatives' mandate, there were media reports
  on questionable, under-the-radar advertising practices from
  their winning 2006 campaign. Elections Canada eventually filed
  documents in the Federal Court that said the Conservative Party
  moved more than $1.2 million to 67 local ridings and back to the

national party campaign. Elections Canada alleged that the money was actually spent on the national campaign, which put the party over the legislated finance limits. The Conservative Party challenged Elections Canada, and it wasn't until March 2011 that two Conservative senators were charged for illegally transferring the money, prompting a debate in the House of Commons (see the chapter by MacDermid).

- At times, transparency seems to lie in the hands of the prime minister to decide. In 2010, Harper fired Cabinet minister Helena Guergis for reasons that he refused to make public, while in early 2011, he refused to fire Cabinet minister Bev Oda even though all the details were known publicly on how she misled a Cabinet committee when it became clear that she had overturned a funding decision previously approved by federal bureaucrats. In the Guergis case, there was no transparency and no way for the public to judge if the decision was in the public interest, while the Oda case was transparent but accountability to the public was missing (a year later, Oda suddenly resigned from politics).

- Parliamentarians and the public were misled about who made the decisions related to $80 million set aside for 2011's G8 summit, which took place outside Toronto in the riding of industry minister Tony Clement. Not only did $50 million end up in 32 infrastructure projects in Clement's riding to show a good image to the international guests, but information obtained through access to information requests also showed that public employees, along with Clement's constituency staff, undertook the political task of deciding which projects were to be funded. Yet, this seemed to contradict the account that Clement provided to Parliament. In addition, when requesting information on how the G8 projects were funded, the auditor general had been told by Industry Canada that no documents were available, clearly in an attempt to avoid scrutiny (Minsky and Thompson 2011, A4).

- In 2012, reports emerged that the government had started to analyse results of some of the polling it commissioned from its external contractors rather than have the companies supply their own impartial analysis, as is standard practice (D. Butler 2012, A3). This was seen as an attempt to frame the issues in the surveys in ways positive to the government. It also avoided measures under the *Accountability Act* that legally require commissioned reports, including their analysis, be deposited with Library and Archives Canada.

- Reports of election irregularities surfaced in 2012 that involved mysterious phone calls to voters on the day of the 2011 election (Ryckewaert 2012, 1). These automated "robocalls" targeted eight ridings where Liberal candidates were leading Conservatives by a small margin in the polls. The calls, allegedly from Elections Canada, misrepresented to potential Liberal voters where they were to vote. By coming late on election day, the calls may have denied some voters their right to vote. Election Canada was investigating what could not only be a violation of the *Canada Elections Act* but also a breach of public trust in the government. Revelations on the robocall scandal continued throughout 2013.
- In late spring 2012, the Conservatives introduced a massive omnibus bill that was more than 420 pages long with 700 clauses affecting more than 60 pieces of legislation. The bill was intended to implement measures from the federal budget that needed legislative revisions, but its length and breadth beyond a normal annual budget were staggering. Moreover, the government voted against pleas from the political opposition – who called the bill "unethical," "undemocratic," and "an abuse of power" (Fekete 2012, A3) – to break the bill into separate parts to allow more time for democratic debate. Communication and information on the bill from both the PMO and the clerk of the PCO were so deficient that the parliamentary budget officer commissioned an opinion from a constitutional expert who concluded that "senior bureaucrats had breached the law and should turn the information over" (May 2012, A3). In effect, the budget and the implementation bill were being used as a cover for significant structural changes to the state – far beyond a budget's purview – with the government's extensive ability to communicate with Canadians in this case all but absent.

Altogether over several years, these breaches of public expectations and the public interest reveal a disturbing tendency to preserve the image over the reality of ethical behaviour and transparency in government in a post–sponsorship scandal environment. Some might argue that we may not be satisfied with the low level of accountability and transparency exposed in the aforementioned examples but that it could be considered an improvement that the public is aware of the transgressions due to accountability measures put in place by the Conservatives; however, most of the previously listed examples emerged from media investigative reports. Nonetheless, these serious issues were overshadowed by a communications-related government publicity campaign lasting several years that has gone far beyond providing simple information to citizens and that reveals the extent of the self-serving behaviour of the government to market itself.

As a response to the world recession of 2008–9, the Harper government undertook a massive advertising campaign to promote its Economic Action Plan to lead the nation to economic recovery. The saturation campaign involved six ads each for radio and television, as well as Internet and print ads, all in both English and French. Since the funds had already been allocated and since rumours of an impending election were rampant, the ad campaign was seen as priming voters for what turned out to be the 2008 election while using public funds. In other ways, the ad campaign revealed itself to be promoting the Conservative Party. The plan's Web site was awash in Tory blue, media releases used the phrase "Harper government" instead of the mandated "Government of Canada," and a few government MPs used giant novelty cheques with the Conservative Party logo in photo ops when promoting funds received in their ridings – which, as investigative media reports found, was allocated in higher amounts to ridings with government MPs (McGregor 2009, A1). The ethics commissioner, another of the new transparency officers set up by the Harper government, said the cheques "had the potential to diminish public confidence in the integrity of elected public officials and the governing institutions they represent" (Canada 2010a, 2).

In fall 2010 and in spring 2011, new ads promoting the same economic plan played seemingly endlessly. Both of these periods were rife with election fever, and once again, ads were criticized for being overtly promotional rather than informational, as well as priming the electorate. Altogether, the government spent a record $136.3 million on advertising in the 2009–10 fiscal year, a 42 per cent increase over the previous year and three times higher than the amount spent in the first year after Harper came to power (Canada 2011b, 2).[9] In the first quarter of 2011, the government spent $26 million on the ads, which still used the Economic Action Plan logo and linked to the plan's Web site.[10] One media report quoted a marketing specialist who said a major commercial advertiser would not spend that much on such a campaign over a year (Cheadle 2011a). In the same period (2010–11), PCO's budget hit a high of almost $160 million (Bruno 2012a, 1). After the 2011 federal election in which the Conservatives gained a majority mandate, the Conservatives capitalized on public recognition from the long Economic Action Plan campaign and resurrected the logo and name to promote their annual budget and other ongoing activities.[11]

Once again, as with the sponsorship scandal under Chrétien, the neutrality of the bureaucracy, a key aspect of the *Federal Accountability Act*, took a direct hit. Although communications branches in government continued to grow, just as with other areas of government, the strategic function and expert guidance of public employees are less in demand (Canada 2009a). Therefore, the impact of the act's strict conditions under which public employees can speak to the public and the media should also be considered. This became clear in the fifth annual report of the prime minister's Advisory Committee on the Public Service. The committee is charged with providing oversight on the government's accountability mechanisms. In March 2011, its report concluded that "the costs of operating this complex regime may be disproportionate to the benefits" (Canada 2010a, 4) and overall that the regime "is doing more harm than good" (Butler 2011, A1). The report said the accountability system is now "less clear rather than more effective" and "hampers" public employees from serving the public (Canada 2010a, 4).

In addition to transparency issues and their impact on public communication, the status and role of the PCO should cause concern. Disturbingly, the recent increases in budget and staff were to allow the PCO to manage the government's overtly politicized campaign on the Economic Action Plan. Yet, as Robertson (1971, 506) emphasized, the PCO should be "deliberately kept small" and its officers "work hard *not* to be encumbered by program responsibility. To expand beyond a certain critical size would be to deny the other principles that help control [it]" (emphasis in original). This action by the government also confirms Savoie's (2003) charge of the broken bargain that differentiates the traditional political role and the administrative side of government. This has also been referred to as a shift from the ethos of the New Public Management of the public service since the 1990s (Tupper 2003), which focused on streamlined management and led to a lack of balance in how the bureaucracy and the political office interacted, to what Aucoin (2012) calls the "new political governance" (NPG), in which permanent political campaigning by governments puts continuous pressure on the public service to be partisan on its behalf rather than on behalf of the public interest. Moreover, NPG also "constitutes a corrupt form of politicization to the extent that governments seek to use and misuse, even abuse, the public service in the administration of public resources and the conduct of public business to better secure their partisan advantage over their competitors" (178).

Permanent campaigning requires permanent promotion. Despite its media lines to the effect that it has made government transparent and accountable, the Conservative government instead has enrolled that bureaucracy in its tactical implementation of its own political strategies, while controlling that implementation from within the PMO.

Conclusion

As Weber (1969, 231) has said, bureaucracies are subject to direction from above in the interests of domination. He also distinguished the "rational" from the "democratic" (217), saying that one does not automatically result in the other. Government decisions and actions can be rationally devised but can still be lacking in ethics or morality. In contrast, the new normal in government is that the PCO has become a de facto adjunct of its political counterpart, the PMO, in ways that were never imagined when it was constituted in 1867 or when Weber was writing about how a bureaucracy's role is to level power, not enhance it by using the bureaucracy's status as expert as its weapon.

In the modern state – not Weber's anymore, but today's radically different and more complex version – governments have found their own experts outside of the public service. This is partly due to the long and only sometimes successful drive over many years, starting with Mulroney, to reduce the size of the public service. Although this has always been communicated to the public as efforts to reduce state debt, it should also be seen as political efforts to reduce the influence and expertise of the public service. Over time, prime ministers have also bypassed the PCO and built their own advisory capacity within their own domain, the PMO. Power is no longer situated within the neutral and rational bureaucracy, to use Weber's language, but in the PMO's professional political advisors. The new experts are "contract professionals" (Savoie 2010, 97–8), part of what has been called a "new politico-bureaucratic class of spin doctors shouldering aside public servants" (Hood and Lodge 2006, cited in Savoie 2010, 95). Simultaneously, whatever power is left in the public service is managed and controlled centrally by the PCO but increasingly more often by the publicity-sensitive PMO itself – unless the PCO can be of service, as we saw in the tactics used for the Economic Action Plan. The PMO has armed itself with the expertise to control its image within its own boundaries and thus can fight the permanent campaign in the snap of a finger. It seems there is no need for the self-standing government department Communication Canada, Chrétien's blatant image-management empire, when the PMO can do the job itself (Kozolanka 2012). As O'Shaughnessy (2004, 173) has said, "the management of the state's communication may even rival in importance the management of the state itself," but, he also adds, "at least according to its leaders." Yet, as we also saw in the case of the budget implementation bill, sometimes that means not communicating with citizens when it is *not* in their own self-interest.

The future for genuine communication by governments to citizens and media may seem unrealistic if not impossible in an environment in which any political slip or error can find its way to a front page or the top story in a television line-up, let alone be dissected instantaneously and endlessly in social media. Yet accountability and transparency depend on the clear division between the political and the administrative sides of government, not only the implied division, but also one that is entrenched in policy and practice. Franks (2004) has called for reasserting the accountability and responsibility of deputy ministers, an important step in wrestling control back from the PMO and rehabilitating neutrality in the public service. A system for vetting potential clerks of the Privy Council, currently the prerogative of prime ministers, could be devised, perhaps by way of an all-party parliamentary committee – one that cannot resort to in-camera sessions. A protocol for the role of the PCO itself could be developed that specifically reaffirms its traditional and historical relationship with the PMO. Establishing a commissioner of public appointments to head and staff such key offices as budget, ethics, integrity, access to information, privacy, and accountability – such as exists in the United Kingdom – would help ensure non-partisan appointments. This could minimize appointments such as that of the integrity commissioner mentioned earlier. The parliamentary budget officer, currently reporting to the prime minister, should be independent and report directly to Parliament. In the important, high-volume area of communication, a new policy for contracting (for both services and strategic advice) and a more transparent system to identify contracts awarded to external contractors could add considerable oversight. The public interest group Democracy Watch recommends that the laws governing who has the power to order and control investigations into government actions be changed to allow a majority of any parties, not just the ruling party, to initiate inquiries concerning government activities (Conacher 2011). All party leaders – not just the prime minister – would need to agree on who would be named as the inquiry commissioner. Currently, only the party in power, which is likely to be the subject of the investigation, can order such an inquiry.

One only has to review the changes that Judge Gomery recommended in his 2006 report on the inquiry into the sponsorship scandal to understand how accountability in government could be improved (Canada 2006c). Gomery concluded that the large size of the PCO made decision making overly complex. Importantly, he expressed concern about the politicization of the PCO's clerk and the blurring between the administrative role of the PCO and the political role of the PMO. Both the clerk's role and the office itself should be reiterated so that they emphasize the neutral administrative role of public service to the prime minister and his or her cabinet. In the reverse direction, the role of the clerk in presenting the prime minister to the public service should be eliminated, thus clearly identifying the clerk's role as separate and representative of the public, not political, interest. Gomery also recommended that the Library of Parliament, as purveyor of neutral research to politicians, and all-party parliamentary committees, which rely on testimony from expert witnesses from across the country, should have more resources to be able to work effectively in the public interest. Further, he recommended that deputy ministers, the head administrators in government departments, should not be appointed by prime ministers on the advice of the clerk of the PCO, but instead recruited in an open process directed independently by an executive group search. Gomery also called for stronger access to information legislation that put the onus on government to prove that documents were not in the public interest. To date, none of these recommendations has been acted on. Moreover, instead of improving transparency, severe budget cuts across government in 2012 saw reductions in the information and privacy commissioners' watchdog operations and Elections Canada (Karstens-Smith 2012, A4).

Long ago, Trudeau spoke about the importance of government's place in a modern society in which technology accelerated the pace of decision making. His inclusive, dialogue-driven, Weberian rational approach was intended to avoid a scattergun approach to problems and crises, which, the former prime minister said, "ignor[ed] the underlying conditions which caused each crisis. It would be prescribing for the symptoms rather than the disease" (Doern 1977, 193). Although decision making in Trudeau's administration was also lengthy and somewhat unwieldy, as recent and current prime ministers lurch from one ethical scandal to the next, public trust in government wanes and voter turnout in federal elections hovers around 60 per cent. The longer this state of affairs continues, the more likely that partisanship in government communication will become the new neutrality. Governments are treating the disease with ever more sophisticated promotional medicine, but they are ignoring the underlying symptom: a growing malaise in our democracy, for which recent governments must be held accountable.

NOTES

1 Here, Weber is clearly referring to an early form of constitutional government and bureaucracy, but his point of centralization of political power within a bureaucracy is increasingly relevant in today's context.
2 Again, here Weber is not speaking specifically of what we understand as a privy council today, but his point that an administrative body should exist within the bureaucracy between those who rule and the neutral, expertise-providing bureaucracy remains valid.
3 These figures were first noted in a speech by Marc Lalonde, a Trudeau Cabinet minister. Interestingly, when Lalonde's speech was published later that year in *Canadian Public Administration*, this rationale about growth in PMO staff was softened to take the emphasis off the political nature of the added staff members (Lalonde 1971b, 520).
4 Estimates vary widely on the size of the PCO, depending on whether one includes all of its business lines, which can include the Office of the Prime Minister, ongoing commissions of inquiry and task forces, the Cabinet Secretariat, the Federal-Provincial Relations Secretariat, corporate services, and support staff (Privy Council Office 2004).
5 Interestingly, it was during Chrétien's time in office that the clerk of the PCO became responsible to the prime minister instead of the public service (Savoie 1999, 113).
6 Householders were centralized mass mailings to many ridings at once on issues of importance to the government (such as the economy). These mailings were little more than advertising for the political party in power. They were axed after the sponsorship scandal when Communication Canada ceased to exist. However, quite separately, Parliament allowed Members of Parliament to send "ten percenters" to 10 per cent of their ridings at one time. Unfortunately, these morphed into very aggressive and negative advertisements. Once the huge cost to Parliament (and to Canadians) of these partisan flyers was exposed, their frequency, tone, and influence were diminished substantially.

7 The latter question was later deemed inappropriate by the Paillé report into government public opinion research practices (Canada 2007c).
8 In 2013, the government's credibility on the issue of accountability took a beating when it emerged that the expense claims of several Conservative senators were being probed for excessive spending.
9 Since the 2009–2010 report was inexplicably delayed almost a year until April 2011, more timely scrutiny of polling costs was avoided.
10 According to the PCO, the ads drive people to the plan's Web site; however, the cost of the Web site itself is not included in advertising costs (Cheadle 2011a, 2).
11 Polling in 2013 found that Canadians considered the ongoing ads "political advertising, a waste of taxpayers' money, or 'junk'" (McGregor 2013, A3).

3 Publics without Politics: Surplus Publicity as Depoliticization

DARIN BARNEY

As the last straw breaks the laden camel's back, this piece of underground information crushed the sinking spirits of Mr. Dombey.
– Charles Dickens, *Dombey and Son* (1848, 15)

Perhaps the most interesting thing to emerge from the 2010 episode during which WikiLeaks dramatically published reams of secret diplomatic cables and state documents was the candour with which the organization's leader expressed its intentions. In an interview with *Time* magazine, Julian Assange said, "It is not our goal to achieve a more *transparent* society; it's our goal to achieve a more *just* society" (Stengel 2010). It came as no surprise when the architects of mainstream discourse moved swiftly and successfully to slot Assange into the various categories now routinely used for anyone who is seriously impolite to wielders of power: terrorist, criminal, conspiracy theorist, narcissist, sociopath. The same was true for the apparent source of many of these documents, US Private Bradley (now known as Chelsea) Manning. Despite clear indications that he had been motivated by disillusionment with American foreign policy (he had reached a tipping point after witnessing US-backed Iraqi police forces detain several people who had distributed a critique of Nouri al-Maliki, Iraq's prime minister) and his statement that he hoped his actions might "actually change something," mainstream media accounts of Manning followed a script typically reserved for serial killers and child molesters. Thus, we learned that Manning was a frustrated homosexual; the child of a broken marriage; a victim of schoolyard bullying; a high-school dropout; an itinerant, heartbroken, vain, suicidal, and "troubled young man" who had experienced "trouble fitting in at school" (Verma 2010). What a relief.

"Troubled" though he may have been in his youth, at least Manning was not tortured. It is not clear the same can be said of his experience after he was arrested. Prior to his court martial, Manning was held for 11 months in solitary confinement at a marine base in Quantico, Virginia, where he was also subjected to prolonged, forced nudity. According to UN special rapporteur on torture Juan Mendez, this "constitutes at a minimum cruel, inhuman and degrading treatment in violation of article 16 of the convention against torture. If the effects in regards to pain and suffering inflicted on Manning were more severe, they could constitute torture" (Pilkington 2012). What would prompt an ostensibly democratic government to treat one of its own citizens, one of its own *soldiers*, with such brutality? Was the content of the information Manning allegedly disclosed so dangerous to national security? (At the time of this writing, the American state is still intact.) Or was the true danger that he had obeyed his conscience rather than his superiors? Was it the scandal of publicity or the horror of political action?

Even more telling than the ease with which the protagonists in this drama were pathologized (as I will suggest later in this chapter, there is, after all, some truth to this: political action is pathological by definition) was the consistency with which the mainstream imagination of what happened in the WikiLeaks case steered clear of the express motives of its perpetrators. Despite their explicit assertions that, in this case, publication was merely instrumental to more substantial, albeit vaguely defined, political goals of "justice" and "change," the issues raised by WikiLeaks were framed as concerning the incendiary value of information under technological conditions that have allegedly *changed everything*. Isn't information supposed to be public in a liberal democracy? Aren't some secrets necessary to protect and promote democratic freedom? Where do you draw the lines between transparency, privacy, and security? Who gets to decide? Has emerging media technology made it impossible to enforce these limits? Is this a good thing or a bad thing for democracy?

These are all interesting questions. They are not, however, intrinsically unsettling ones, or even questions that a liberal democratic political culture is incapable of handling. A conversation about transparency is one that a liberal democratic society is well prepared to have, just as we are well prepared to live with the contradiction between the ideological promotion of "openness" and its ongoing material denial. And it is a conversation we are content to have stand in for the more demanding and disruptive sorts of actions that might be required to open the possibility of justice. Conveniently, the conversation about transparency directed attention away from what was arguably most re-markable about the case of WikiLeaks: not the fact that so much secret information was publicized, but that two people, collaborating with a network of others, took serious political action in the face of extreme personal risk and aimed at massively disrupting the operation of state power. This small but exceptional fact points to the heart of the matter. For, if the issue is the political significance of WikiLeaks and every-thing it purportedly represents, then the central question must be this: Once information is made public and people know what is going on, *what will they do?* In light of events in the Middle East shortly after the WikiLeaks cable dump, it is tempting to answer that once they are in-formed, people will be moved to act politically, and even dramatically, in favour of justice. After all, US Embassy diplomatic cables document-ing the corruption of the Ben Ali regime in Tunisia and first leaked by WikiLeaks and then translated and circulated by a range of social me-dia networks, as well as by the Al Jazeera broadcasting service, have been widely credited in 2011 with sending Tunisians into the streets in numbers that the regime could not deny, an action which proved conta-gious in other parts of the Arab world (Sanina 2011).

Presumptions of this sort conform to certain widely accepted ideas about the relationship between democratic politics, publicity, and me-dia technologies. By "publicity," I mean to indicate not just the sort of organized promotional activity typically associated with public rela-tions both inside and outside what can be called the publicity state but also the broader condition of *publicness* – public goods, public spaces, public citizens, public exposure, public information, public discussion – that is thought to distinguish political activity from a range of "merely" private experiences, practices, and interests. Feminist theory and ac-tivism have provided us with good reasons to reject the claim that the private, domestic, and personal realms – saturated as they are by authoritative permissions and prohibitions and unequal distributions of power and status – are somehow devoid of politics, and emerging technologies have rendered the distinction between public and private more difficult to discern. Nevertheless, in the liberal democratic imagi-nation, political life remains largely equated with public life. Politics is carried out by citizens who appear before, with, and against each other in public encounters. These encounters, in which political judg-ments are made and political actions are taken, unfold in a variety of communicative spaces, sites, and practices that together comprise the *public sphere* (Habermas 1991). Our experience of the public sphere is one of being simultaneously separated from, and connected to, a multiplicity of others, which is to say that all public experience is *mediated* experience: whether it is in a city square or a community hall, or over the radio spectrum or an Internet connection, to experience publicity is to be joined to others by media that stand between us, separating and connecting us across both time and space (see Fletcher's chapter for the role of the media in political communication). Liberal democratic publicity also entails a set of practices that are thought to be characteristically political: *communicating* with others in a variety of modes; producing, consuming and circulating *information* in various forms; and *participating* with others in discussion, debate, and decision concerning common affairs. These characteristically public activities invoke a set of normative expectations according to which we can evaluate the democratic quality of the various media that make public life possible. Media that provide expanded means of public communication, improved access to publically relevant information, and enhanced opportunities for public participation are understood to support the possibility of democratic politics. It is in this light that emerging media technologies – digital networks and the various devices and applications connected by them – are widely thought to optimize publicity in a manner that supports the possibility of democratic politics, an equation that the case of WikiLeaks and the Tunisian revolts would seem to confirm as universal.

Those who are interested in the political implications of digital information and communication technologies surely have much to learn from the events that took place across the Arab world in winter 2011 and later, and it will require careful study to take full measure of the role emerging media played in those events. With that said, two early lessons stand out. The first concerns the ease with which sensible (and nervous) liberal elites rushed to fetishize "information" as the motive force behind these uprisings. As in the Dickensian epigraph at the start of this chapter, a focus upon "the last straw" tends to obscure long-standing structural and material conditions of inequality and brutalism, borne over time by the camel, such that its back is made ready for breaking – conditions that, when it comes to the illiberal regimes of the Arab world, western governments and their citizens have been complicit in perpetuating for a very long time. It also entails more than a hint of condescension. As Eltahawy (2011) put it, "By buying into the idea that leaked US embassy cables about corruption 'fuelled' the revolution, commentators smear Tunisians with ignorance of the facts and perpetuate the myth that Arabs are incapable of rising up against dictators." As if Tunisians (or Egyptians, or Bahrainis, or Libyans) had not actually *lived* for decades under corrupt and authoritarian regimes, or at least did not *know* they did, until it was revealed to them by a leaked diplomatic cable from the US Embassy. That the alleged last straw in this case happened to be "a piece of underground information" also served to confirm liberal prejudices about the relative "openness" of western democracies, as well as liberal fantasies about the simultaneously solvent and galvanizing power of information itself (see Morozov 2011).

The second early lesson of these events is that the character of the relationship between publicity, its technologies, and political action depends heavily on the context in which the relationship is situated. This means that the supposed universality of publicity as a normative category needs to be approached critically. In what follows, I will suggest that the relationship between publicity and political action has become marginal in liberal, capitalist democracies where emerging media technologies continue to proliferate and that, under these conditions, publicity has more to do with depoliticization than it does with moving people to act politically. However, it would be doctrinaire to suggest the same is automatically true of illiberal and undemocratic contexts in which emerging media technologies might bear on the possibility of politics quite differently. In situations where access to mass media is tightly controlled by state authorities, the ability of citizens, noncitizens, and activists to communicate via such technologies can be crucial to their political prospects. Recognizing this is not to fetishize the WikiLeaks cables or to condone the branding of every popular uprising with the commercial trademark of whatever social networking application happens to have been favoured by those carrying it out. The point is that the meaning of these technologies in relation to the possibility of politics is not universal but depends heavily on the particular conditions in which their use is situated.

This appeal to context in assessing the relationship between publicity and politics should be distinguished from the sort of phony and patronizing multiculturalism that for so long has vouchsafed western "tolerance" of authoritarian regimes in the Arab world (from whose capacity to enforce order the west has profited so handsomely) on account of alleged "cultural differences" that left their people naively unprepared for democracy and vulnerable to fundamentalist theocracy. In an interview on Al Jazeera English television during the 2011 Egyptian revolt, Žižek (2011) put paid to this sort of particularism:

Where we are fighting a tyrant, we are all universalists: we are immediately in solidarity with each other ... It is the struggle for freedom. Here we have direct proof, a) that freedom is universal and b) against that cynical idea that somehow Muslim crowds prefer some kind of religiously-fundamentalist dictatorships ... No! What happened in Tunisia, what happens now in Egypt, is precisely this *universal* revolution for dignity, human rights, economic justice. This is universalism at work ... They gave us the lesson against this falsely respectful but basically racist prejudice that says, "Oh, you know, Arabs have their specific culture, they cannot really get it." They got it. They understand democracy better by doing what they are doing than we do in the West.

The meaning of the appetite for dignity, equality, and freedom, and of political struggles to contest their systematic denial, does not vary significantly from one context to another. The role that something such as publicity and its mediating technologies might play in relation to those universal appetites, and to the struggles to satisfy them, does. In a context where denial of access to publicity and its technologies is indexed to the denial of dignity, equality, and freedom, a sudden proliferation of emerging technologies that afford opportunities for enhanced public communication will have one set of implications for the possibility of politics (Mohammed 2011). However, in a context where people already enjoy a surplus of publicity and ready access to its technologies, and where this corresponds to an experience of relative material security and liberty, the implications of emerging media for the possibility of politics might be altogether different. We fortunate western liberal democrats have lived with extensive publicity, including the sort intensified by digital networks, for quite some time now, long enough at least to suspect that this most recent explosion of access to information might provide what publicity has always provided for political action in liberal democratic contexts: an alibi for not taking such action.

This is what is at stake in Assange's assertion that his actions were aimed at justice rather than transparency for its own sake. Justice, he wagered, might have a chance if constant exposure means that state authorities can no longer function in the manner to which they have grown accustomed. What would happen, he asks, if under the threat of total disclosure, American political parties "gave up their mobile phones, fax and e-mail correspondence – let alone the computer systems which manage their subscribers, donors, budgets, polling, call centres and direct mail campaigns?" (Assange 2006, 5). Under these conditions, some new, more just way of organizing power and authority might possibly emerge. As Assange put it in his 2006 manifesto on conspiracy, the aim is "to radically shift *regime* behaviour" (1); save for a couple of asides about "resistance" that are clearly meant to indicate a radicalized minority (of one?), the text makes no reference at all to information motivating or "empowering" citizens to become democratically "engaged" or hold their representatives "accountable." Indeed, the words "democracy" and "citizen" do not appear in the tract at all. Assange seems well aware that information, or knowing what is going on, has never been enough to move good, liberal citizens to act politically against organized injustice. Neither his manifesto nor his subsequent actions were primarily about technology *enabling* liberal democratic citizens; rather, they were precisely about technology *disabling* liberal democratic government. His was an insurrectionary political act that had nothing whatsoever to do with the terms in which the relationship between emerging technology, publicity, and democracy is presently discussed in respectable circles. This suggests the lesson of the WikiLeaks incident is not so much about the increased political potential of publicity in the emerging media environment as it is about its limits.

Politics, Pathology, and Publicity

Wherever it arises, politics can be recognized by its pathological character. Politics is what happens when we are confronted with a wrong (definitively, the wrong of inequality) that calls for judgment under conditions of undecidability, in which the outcome of that judgment cannot be given in advance, and it inheres in the action that arises from such judgment – disruptive, exceptional action that typically unfolds at the borders of inclusion and exclusion, and which opens onto a terrain of radical uncertainty and unpredictability. As such, politics entails judgment and action that alter the parameters of the possible and the impossible in any given situation. It is in this sense that politics that can be distinguished from what Rancière (1999, 28–30) calls "police," referring to those agencies, practices, and institutions – including the institutions of liberal democratic government – whose function it is to contain the disruptive possibility of politics, even as they give the impression that politics is taking place.

Under such conditions, being carried away by political judgment and action is not normal. Instead, politics is a pathological event that a person would normally avoid if given the choice. Politics is exceptional, disruptive, antagonistic, burdensome, and dangerous. It is like a sore that erupts on the smooth skin of democracy. According to Rancière (ibid., 30), politics arises only in response to a fundamental wrong, a wrong that takes the form of a structuring exclusion or silencing, a basic miscount that produces an antagonism between the whole and the "part that has no part." This wrong is materialized in the structure of publicity itself, at the border between those who are counted as part of the public and those who are not. We tend to associate publicness with inclusivity, but the truth is that every public is as much defined by those who are not part of it as it is by those who are. We might say that politics arises to refuse or contest the social, conventional, and material inequalities and exclusions that are institutionalized over and against the incontestable equality that is otherwise basic to our humanity and that publicity is one of the names for this inequality and exclusion. It is for this reason that politics is always threatening and why its relationship to publicity is more contradictory than what is typically attributed to it in the liberal democratic imaginary.

Politics happens when and where people can no longer afford the luxury of its absence. In situations where the experience of inequality and exclusion are acute, and where this coincides with a deficit of publicity – whereby actionable information is scarce, communication is tightly controlled, and participation denied or meaningless – the expectations attached to information, communication, and participation take on the character of political demands, and the practices of communicating, informing, and participating can achieve the status of political action. Politics presents itself as a material imperative at the threshold between affluence and deprivation, both within comparatively prosperous societies where violence and misery persist but are safely consigned to the margins of mainstream public experience and between these societies and the global poor. At this threshold and on these margins, the camel's burden is always already heavy, and there is no telling when an additional straw, even something as light as a piece of "underground information," might break its back and raise the imperative of politics, an imperative with which the situation is already pregnant. Under conditions where people are hungry and brutalized, and their opportunities to communicate, inform themselves and others, and participate in altering their situation are minimal, expansions of the horizon of publicity can open political possibilities where before there seemed to be none. Conversely, in situations where inequality and exclusion are experienced in tolerable moderation (where injustice seems to be not so great, or not experienced directly by so many), and where this experience is compounded by a surplus of publicity – abundant information, free communication, and a surfeit of opportunities to participate – the politicizing function of publicity is reversed and tends in the direction of depoliticization.

This is the great insight of Dean, who argues that the norms of liberal publicity – information, communication, and participation – have come to stand in for the political ends that they might otherwise be presumed to serve, ends such as material and political equality and social and economic justice. This substitution is abetted by the apparent materi-alization of the promise of publicity in emerging media technologies. As Dean (2005, 63) writes, in established liberal democracies, "the complexities of politics – of organization, struggle, duration, decisiveness, division, representation, etc. – are condensed into one thing, one problem to be solved and one technological solution. So the problem of democracy is that people aren't informed; they don't have the information they need to participate effectively." This is a problem that emerging media technologies solve in advance, although it is not clear that lack of information is really what prevents most people from engaging in political judgment and action. Indeed, as Dean (2006, 9) has shown convincingly in her rendering of Žižek's political thought, the ideological hold of liberal democratic capitalism and its militarist and imperialist state forms operates not under the sign of ignorance or false consciousness but rather under the sign of knowledge and awareness. The definitive gesture of contemporary ideology is the fetishistic disavowal – "Je sais bien, mais quand même ..." (I know very well, but all the same ...) – which, together with the thumbs-up and thumbs-down signalling of likes and dislikes online, suggests the essence of publicity in the emerging media environment. I know very well that the prime minister is lying when he says he supports freedom of expression, but all the same I congratulate him for condemning foreign governments who censor the Internet (👍 for freedom of expression!). I know very well that Petro-Canada paid the Libyan government (i.e., the Gadhafi family) a $1 billion "signing bonus" in 2008 to secure the right to drill for undersea oil (Saunders 2011), but all the same I need to gas up the car and get the kids to hockey practice (👍 for WikiLeaks! 👎 for Arab dictators!). I know very well that the Quebec firm SNC-Lavalin is building a $275 million prison in Libya for the Gadhafi regime (Waldie 2011), but all the same I got a tweet linking to an article that says the prison will be "built according to international human rights standards" (👎 for torture! 👍 for

Twitter!). *I know very well, but all the same ...* Not all people are as well informed as they could be, but information alone has never been sufficient to motivate political judgment or action, and a lack of information is not what prevents most of us from taking the risk of disruptive judgments and action. The distribution of possibility and impossibility is a material question more than it is a question of information.

The same can be said of communication. The traditions of western political thought, and the traditions of western political culture, give us many reasons to believe that political judgment and action are somehow identical with communication. And to the extent that emerging media technologies appear to liberate the potential of intersubjective communication, it is hard to resist the conclusion that they contribute to the possibility of politics. Once again, emerging media technologies would seem to deliver precisely what the normative framework of publicity has habituated us to expect from politics. However, one could also say that the proliferation of communication sponsored by emerging media acts as a vaccine against other, more burdensome and disruptive expressions of political judgment and action. In the contemporary climate, whenever there is a threat that genuine dissent, discord, or disagreement might break out, a threat that something political might actually happen, the liberal democratic response to these disruptions is always the same: more, better communication. In the age of social media, blogging, and user-generated content, emerging media stand ready to absorb potentially pathological political energies into the relatively innocuous world of dialogue and circulating contributions. However, as Dean (2009, 32) points out, it is not so much the technology that guarantees this form of depoliticization as it is the normative framework of publicity that enables the "reduction of politics to communicative acts, to speaking and saying and exposing and explaining, a reduction key to a democracy conceived in terms of discussion and deliberation."

The question is not whether communication is *necessary* for politics but rather whether communication is *adequate* to politics. According to Dean (ibid.), "When communication serves as the key category for Left politics, whether communication configured as discussion, spectacle or publicity, this politics ensures its political failure in advance: doing is reduced to talking, to contributing to the media environment, instead of being conceived in terms of, say, occupying military bases, taking over the government, or abandoning the Democratic Party and doing the steady, persistent organizational work of revitalizing the Greens or Socialists." Dean refers here to "Left politics," but her observations would seem to apply to any sort of politics that actually seeks to do something rather than just say something. The trouble is that saying something has always been much easier than doing something, and emerging media technologies have made it easier than ever to say something without doing anything. Most of us embrace the ease with which we can use *saying* something as an alibi for *doing* nothing not because emerging technologies force us to, but rather because the norms of publicity have conditioned us to accept, and even to expect, the reduction of politics to communication. The problem of depoliticization arises from convenience, not apathy. As Dean (2005, 61) observes, "The circulation of communication is depoliticizing, not because people don't care or don't want to be involved, but because we do."

This line of argument is similar to one advanced in 1948 by Lazarsfeld and Merton (1971, 565) in their account of the "narcotizing dysfunction" of the mass media:

> The interested and informed citizen can congratulate himself [*sic*] on his lofty state of interest and information and neglect to see that he has abstained from decision and action. In short, he takes his secondary contact with the world of political reality, his reading and listening and thinking, as a vicarious performance. He comes to mistake knowing about problems of the day for doing something about them. His social conscience remains spotlessly clean. He *is* concerned. He *is* informed. And he has all sorts of ideas as to what should be done. But after he has gotten through his dinner and after he has listened to his favorite radio program, and after he has read his second newspaper of the day, it is really time for bed.

Politics is pathological in that it invariably aims at the fundamental disruption of the milieu in which it emerges, a redrawing of the horizons of the possible and the impossible. As with any pathogen, the viability of the organism in which it arises relies upon its containment. Depoliticization is the name given to the various strategies and techniques whereby the pathological threat of politics can be managed without recourse to the sort of outright repression that is more likely to motivate resistance than to contain it. We are accustomed to the long-standing accounts given by critics of mass culture that locate depoliticization in the operation of ideology – manipulation of the subjective consciousness of individuals in a manner that immobilizes them, either through the cultivation of false but system-reinforcing needs or through deception and distraction (Marcuse 1964; Horkheimer and Adorno [1947] 2002).

In these accounts, it is a failure to really meet the expectations of publicity that is held responsible for depoliticization. The emerging media environment brings us to consider an alternative possibility, namely, that depoliticization arises not from failing to live up to the norms of publicity, but instead from their satisfaction.

The role that emerging media technologies, combined with contemporary normative expectations surrounding publicity, play in regard to the problem of depoliticization is not captured by the figure of "narcotization" – the induction of stupor (stupidity) or slumber (in Lazarsfeld's and Merton's account, the newspaper reader literally *goes to bed*) – but rather are better characterized in terms of inoculation. Inoculation is a technique that came to the west in 1700 when small quantities of smallpox virus were introduced into bodies "in order to induce a mild and local attack of the disease, and render the subject immune from future contagion" (Oxford English Dictionary 2010, s.v. "inoculation"). After 1799, inoculation began to be carried out by means of vaccination, whereby the pathogen introduced was attenuated or weakened so as not to be dangerous. We might note that one of the secondary meanings of inoculation associates it with information: to inoculate is to "imbue a person or community with a feeling, opinion or habit" (ibid.). As we know very well from recent experience with a potential influenza pandemic, the best way to contain the outbreak and spread of an unwanted pathogen is to inject a little bit of the pathogen into the system we are seeking to protect – an attenuated bit with the dangerous part neutralized. When we are seeking to contain the spread of a pathogen or disease, we do not *narcotize* people, we *inoculate* them: we introduce a weakened strain of the pathological agent, provoking a benign form of disease that generates immunity to more dangerous strains.

Ironically, inoculation against the pathology of politics has arguably always been a primary function of "normal" politics. To think of politics in this way is to concede that most of what goes for politics in liberal democratic contexts comprises a routinized habit aimed at containing the possibility of politics itself. As Rancière (1995, 19) observes, "Politics is the art of suppressing the political ... Depoliticization is the oldest task of politics, the one which achieves its fulfillment at the brink of its end, its perfection on the brink of the abyss." In his book *Political Machines*, Barry (2001, 207) locates depoliticization firmly within the normal context of what goes by the name of politics in contemporary liberal democracies: "One of the key functions of established political institutions," he writes, "is to place limits on the possibilities for dissensus and restriction on the sites in which political contestation can occur. What we generally term politics thus always has something of an anti-political impulse." My suggestion is that the depoliticizing impulse of conventional political participation operates not in the manner of narcotization but rather in the manner of inoculation. The pathogen of politics is contained not by the logic of repression, manipulation, and exclusion but rather the logic of per-mission, participation, and inclusion – the logic of publicity, a logic whose effectiveness is dramatically enhanced in the emerging media environment. As Barry (ibid., 129) puts it, describing the proliferation of network-enabled forms of "interactivity" in governmental contexts, "In an interactive model, subjects are not disciplined, they are *allowed*" (emphasis in original).

Information and communication have long been understood to play a privileged role in managing pathological forms of politics. This is true not only of Lazarsfeld and Merton but also of other foundational figures in communication studies such as Lasswell (1971) and cyber-neticists such as Wiener (1948). Communication and the circulation of information contribute to equilibrium, not disequilibrium; feedback (arguably the paradigmatic mode of communication in the emerging media context) performs a system-stabilizing function, even without resort to repressive forms of propaganda and covert surveillance. The habits of information, communication, and participation sponsored by emerging media are particularly well suited to perform this function. In capitalist, liberal democratic, technological societies such as ours, emerging media provide subjects with ready access to copious volumes of high-quality, factual, and interpretive information in which the truth about power is exposed, explained, confirmed, and contested. These same media also provide for a proliferation of opportunities to choose, vote, rank, comment, discuss, create, debate, collaborate, engage, con-tribute, interact, access, share, deliberate, and communicate. Every day, millions upon millions of people take advantage of these opportunities to participate. In some cases, the information and communication me-diated by these technologies mobilize events that are potentially dis-ruptive. But in many more cases, for most people most of the time, the innocuous habit of participating in the emerging media environment comes in lieu of more burdensome, inconvenient, and disruptive forms of political judgment and action. For most of us, clicking ☙ simply leaves us sitting with our thumbs up our asses, and we are comfortable with that because the discomfort of politics is too much to bear.

To experience a political situation is to be uncertain as to what might happen next. In contemporary liberal democracies, there is perhaps nothing that is more regular, in terms of both its occurrence and outcome, than the absorption of periodic popular grievance into the circuits of social media. In Canada in late 2009, the Conservative government of Prime Minister Stephen Harper prorogued Parliament, a move widely attributed to the government's desire to avoid scrutiny of its role in placing enemy Afghan detainees at risk of human rights abuse and torture by transferring them to the custody of Afghan state security agencies. It is interesting to note that Canadian complicity in the torture of Afghan detainees had been revealed in the mainstream national press as early as 2007, information that, at that time, failed to prompt significant political protest by Canadian citizens (Koring 2007). Nevertheless, something about the democratic affront represented by the prorogation of Parliament (and not, it must be stressed, the fact that the Canadian state had been revealed as having facilitated the illegal torture of enemy combatants[1]) prompted what by 2010 had become an utterly predictable occurrence: somebody started a Facebook group. Quickly, Canadians Against Proroguing Parliament (CAPP) gathered over 200,000 friends, some of whom were organized to participate in anti-prorogation rallies held across Canada on 23 January 2010 as part of a national day of action. Pundits were quick to inaugurate a new era in Canadian publicity: "Never before has Facebook filled Canada's streets. It did today" (Capstick 2010). This was Canadian politics' Facebook moment.

Like many aspects of this particular episode, "filling the streets" was somewhat of an exaggeration. Sympathetic estimates put the total number of participants in the day's rallies at 25,000, the majority of those concentrated in Toronto, Ottawa, and Vancouver (ibid.). According to organizer Shilo Davis (2010), "That makes it not only the biggest Facebook group in Canada, but also the quickest large-scale grass-roots political mobilization in Canadian history." The modifier "quickest" is, one supposes, key to this distinction. Otherwise, the number 25,000 would probably call to mind the number of workers who took to the streets of Winnipeg on Bloody Saturday during the General Strike of 1919 (Bumsted 1994). And for sheer size in multiple cities, one might think back to the Days of Action against the neoliberal economic policies of the Ontario government under Mike Harris's Conservatives in the late 1990s, in which the numbers of demonstrators in London (20,000), Hamilton (120,000), and Toronto (250,000) were perhaps all the more impressive precisely because they were mobilized without the aid of social media platforms such as Facebook and Twitter (Turk 1997). Notwithstanding the relative modesty of the CAPP mobilization, organizers were quick to inflate its impact. Much was made of a drop in public support suffered by the government, attributed to the Facebook campaign. According to S. Davis (2010), "The growing buzz around the CAPP Facebook group helped turn the prorogation issue from a political non-event on Dec. 30 to a major headache that cost Mr. Harper approximately ten points at the polls two weeks later." A few days before the rallies were to take place, the Facebook group's founder, Christopher White (2010), declared his constituents to be "the new power brokers in Ottawa." To put this claim into perspective, if every one of the 25,000 Canadians who joined the anti-prorogation protests on 23 January 2010 had moved to Calgary Southwest and voted in the 2008 election for Harper's nearest rival, they still would not have been able to prevent the prime minister from winning his own seat in Parliament.[2]

The truth is, the Conservative government was never in jeopardy over this issue, which (along with the issue of the Afghan detainees) quickly receded from public view. Roughly a year later, the government remained standing and its percentage of public support was again polling the high thirties, roughly 10 percentage points ahead of its nearest competitors (who had valiantly taken up the Facebook nation's cause in opposing prorogation). Indeed, the Facebook nation itself had largely stood down. Organizers had boldly declared that "a 200,000-strong Facebook group and nationwide anti-prorogation rallies show the government that, regardless of what else divides us, Canadians will not stand for the suspension of Parliament for partisan advantage" (S. Davis 2010). Except, of course, that they did stand for it, and they will. In a flourish of insurrectionary rhetoric, White (2010) had decried Parliament as "an institution that has turned its back on its people" and called upon the disenfranchised multitude to "work together and take it apart brick by brick and build it anew," which made the campaign's defence of Parliament as a democratic institution, and its ultimate goal of convincing MPs to "return to the Hill," all the more incoherent. As one supporter put it, somewhat more modestly, "Canada needs its House of Commons up and running" (Capstick 2010). This is exactly what Canada got – an outcome that was never in doubt – a few short months later. Perhaps this is what explains the message on the CAPP (renamed, but conveniently with the same acronym) Facebook page a year later: "Canadians Advocating Political Participation does not have any upcoming events."

Conclusion

In this chapter, I have tried to show that despite the tendency to equate communication and access to information with democracy itself, publicity is not the same thing as politics. Under conditions where access to information and communication is tightly controlled and restricted in ways that bolster existing inequalities, demanding these resources can certainly have a political character, and emerging technologies that loosen such control and restrictions definitely have political implications. However, under conditions where access to information and communication are relatively widespread already, demands for more of the same might not be so politically challenging, especially when emerging technologies stand ready to extend and intensify access to these resources. Under these conditions, the identification of democracy with publicity can serve to absorb political energies that might otherwise be devoted to contesting other forms of persistent inequality, marginalization, and disadvantage. If this is true, then the emerging media environment should prompt us to reevaluate, rather than uncritically celebrate, our commitment to publicity as the primary and defining norm of democratic society. This is not to say that transparency or enhanced capacities for interactive communication are unworthy of our investment or concern. Rather, it is to remember, with Manning and Assange, that these are merely means to a much more substantive and challenging end.

Emerging media hold out the promise of realizing publicity's dream of universal inclusion, but the possibility of politics is more likely to arise in response to the experience of publicity's structuring exclusions. As soon as one is included in the public sphere – or even merely *feels* included or as if one could *choose* to be if one so desired – the wrong of structural exclusion is absorbed back into the promise of liberal publicity and deprived of its motive potential. We might recall here the Habermasian prescription that, in an adequately democratic public sphere, it is not necessary that citizens actually *are* equal but rather only that they interact *as if they were* (Habermas 1991). Inclusive publicity, even if only apparent, provides liberal capitalism with an alibi for structural inequality. To the extent emerging media technologies make it possible for most everyone to be included in the public sphere *as if* they were equals, they mitigate against pathological outbreaks of the sort of political judgment and action that might arise when people are confronted with the fact that they are actually not equal after all. Faced with publicity's exclusions, the struggle of and for politics is not simply the demand to be included (a demand that technology promises to meet) but rather rejection and reconfiguration of the very terms of inclusion and exclusion altogether.

Most of us do not really have the stomach for this; politics is inherently risky, incalculable, unpredictable, and disruptive, and so we are more than prepared to accept information, communication, and participation as ends in themselves, ends that become identified with politics as such. Emerging media technologies stand ready as means to deliver us to these ends. But the true end of politics is justice, not information, communication, or participation, and getting to it is hard, not easy. Whatever debates we might have over degree and quality, one thing that emerging media technologies appear to have accomplished is a massive expansion of access to information, communication, and participation. They provide precisely that form of shallow encounter with the possibilities of judgment and action that contemporary liberal democratic subjects have been habituated to expect from politics. And it is in this respect that emerging media contribute to depoliticization – to the closure of spaces and options for political judgment and action – even as they apparently satisfy the prevailing normative framework of publicity. As Dean (2002, 165) writes, "The public is an ideal whose materialization undermines its very aspirations." Emerging media, like the media that have gone before them, sustain depoliticization not because they fail to meet the normative expectations of contemporary publicity but because they succeed.

Acknowledgements

Thanks to Joseph Sannicandro for research assistance and Kirsten Kozolanka for editorial advice.

NOTES

1 A survey of members of the group revealed that while 33 per cent of respondents identified the Afghan detainee issue as their primary reason for joining, 53 per cent joined because "prorogation is undemocratic" (Killeen 2010, 4).

2 Stephen Harper polled 38,545 votes in the riding. Marlene Lamontagne, the Liberal candidate, polled 4,918 votes (Chief Electoral Officer of Canada 2008).

PART TWO

Publicity and the State

Introduction

The second part of this collection examines the various practices of persuasive communication that characterize the modern publicity state. The focus here is on the shifting social relations as these practices evolve and come to dominate the political sphere, concurrently as they contribute to and reflect the material and symbolic restructuring of broader society into a consumer marketplace of ideas. A central theme in this part is how the different forms and practices that commodify the public sphere are shifting the non-commercial citizen-state relationship away from the broader public interest and into a more individualized and marketable consumer relationship in which the state has something to sell and to which citizens "choose" or otherwise consent, with choices ranging from a service to a vote.

However, the section begins with a contextual historical chapter by Donald Gutstein that delves deeply into the pathology of ideological institutions, such as global think tanks, and their manifestations in Canada. He traces how global elites acted to establish a "new common sense understanding" of how the post–Second World War world would work that relied on its own "carefully managed" research and persuasive communications. The resulting well-funded "war of ideas" elevated conservative views on key economic and social issues, which market research showed would resonate with the public and would be amplified by the media. Simple messages and carefully contrived, authoritative-sounding statistics disseminated the positions and values of what became known as the New Right. Over time, this political project, fanned by the communication efforts of think tanks and other conservative organizations, was eventually translated into political power in Canada.

One of the earliest publicity practices, public opinion research, has evolved considerably over time but retains and exacerbates problems related to how and in whose interest "the public" can be quantified. When used in the political sphere, public opinion research is a favoured tool of the powerful because it allows politicians first to frame "reality" in ways that legitimate their own beliefs and ideologies, and then define issues, prime the electorate, and set the political agenda. As Paul Nesbitt-Larking notes in his chapter, "Those who can afford the high costs [of public opinion research] are also those who have the greatest investment in the outcomes and the most powerful input into promoting those dominant ideas and ideals in the political society that disproportionately shape opinions in the first place." Nesbitt-Larking also points out that even technology does not resolve the problem of those publics that are still marginal and apart from political life and whose voices are not heard in public opinion research.

Governments have used advertising to promote policies and programs almost as long as private business has. Although advertising is universally understood as a persuasive form of communication, the very knowledge of that breeds complacency and lack of analysis. As Jonathan Rose explains in his chapter, state advertising is uncharted and unchecked – until it transcends boundaries that remain undefined. Controversy breaks out only when governments "use the power of the state to sway public opinion on matters where there are significant differences of opinion between the governing party and society." An unresolved issue is how governments make use of advertising for partisan purposes. This is a nebulous area of growing importance as governments pass less legislation and instead rely on state-paid advertising to prime the public prior to election campaigns. In effect, they are persuading the public rather than using the deliberative, democratic multiparty processes of Parliament (an institution increasingly marginalized). While the media focus on the huge expenditures involved in state advertising, the content of the ads themselves and their symbolic messages draw less scrutiny but have a vital impact on the quality of democracy.

"There can be little political communication without money." The stark first line of Robert MacDermid's chapter tells us immediately that today's political parties are commodities to be bought and sold, with their changing fortunes virtually preconditioned on the ability to purchase the services and products of publicity. Financial regulation enacted by parties in power can make or break a party or an election.

Recent changes to financial reform have shifted the power and ability of parties to fundraise, thereby creating winners and losers before the writs for an election are even dropped, as some parties stay indebted for years between elections. According to MacDermid, the bottom line for political communication is that "the need to raise money, and the existence of groups that are willing to provide it, shapes the messages that are communicated."

Richard Nimijean demonstrates in his chapter how consumer branding has worked its way into politics, with governing political parties using image management techniques to brand the state itself. A successful state brand must appeal to a citizen's sense of national identity and values, so political parties in power seek to redefine a country's brand for partisan advantage. In effect, "the rhetoric of nationalism and the promotion of national solidarity are state strategies that provide security to citizens," as well as an "emotional connector" to ground them in a global world. The emphasis in national branding on values also allows governments to "camouflage rhetoric-reality gaps between stated values and public policy," thus avoiding contentious public debate. The brand message, rather than policy itself, becomes the effective response to citizen demands and anticipates those demands by winning buy-in from the public even prior to launching initiatives that might otherwise prove controversial.

The next two chapters elaborate on a key dichotomy that has emerged in the publicity state and that was noted in the introductory essay: the tension between government publicity and government secrecy. The one-way torrent of publicity that the state engages in is strikingly at odds with its attempts to close down information access needed by citizens for accountability, judgment, and engagement. The first of the two chapters, by Ken Rubin and Kirsten Kozolanka, reminds us that information itself is a "high-stakes commodity and its management by government is key to political success." Although successive governments in Canada have paid lip service to access to information, over time it has become clear through actual practices that the state does not like to disclose information and seeks ways to get out of doing so. Governments centralize and control access to the information environment within political offices rather than having it administered by the public service. Rubin and Kozolanka point out that within the Harper government, "practices of hyper-control of information that might impede its policies and public image" have resulted in often-considerable delays in providing information becoming the norm. In addition, perceived needs for security and safety in the post–11 September 2001 environment threaten public accountability by greatly widening what records can be classified in the category of security. Altogether in the publicity state, information is a political battleground.

In the second of the two chapters on the dichotomy between publicity and secrecy, Leslie Regan Shade and Tamara Shepherd examine the politics and history of privacy, reinforcing the commodification of information. They situate private sector marketing techniques and technologies as the source of online practices that track, profile, and target the "consumer" audience in an unequal relationship in which the commodified user retains the perception of control over his or her environment. In fact, they point out that "privacy is contextually dependent, where the context is always inscribed within capitalist business practices." Echoing Barney's contention in chapter 3 that information, communication, and participation in the hands of the modern state actually quash political action, Shade and Shepherd note that the perception of individual control over privacy is elitist and disenfranchising, as citizens need a high degree of informational literacy to keep up with the constant changes to privacy controls and features.

All the chapters in this section scrutinize the intensifying publicity practices used by governments that bombard the public on a daily basis. From its gentle beginnings as simple political ads in discrete election campaigns to the all-encompassing war on ideas within a consumerized political marketplace, publicity on behalf of the state has increasingly dominated our understanding and consciousness of how politics works and how the public understands its political role in a democracy. A refrain throughout these chapters is the concern expressed for the quality of our democracy, leading to key questions: How can the publicity state be challenged? What resources and strategies can be mustered to renew and foster communicative democracy?

4 The War on Ideas: From Hayek to Harper

DONALD GUTSTEIN

The Fraser Institute (FI) released its *Economic Freedom of the World Annual Report* in September 2010. This index, which the institute has published annually since 1996, purports to measure the degree to which government policies and institutions support what the FI calls economic freedom. "The cornerstones of economic freedom," the document declares, "are personal choice, voluntary exchange, freedom to compete, and security of privately owned property" (Gwartney, Hall, and Lawson 2010, v). Canada rated seventh, just behind the United States and ahead of Australia. This was higher than Canada's ranking the first year the index was published, when, under Liberal Prime Minister Jean Chrétien, Canada ranked 14th. Canada's problem that year, the index claimed, was excessive government spending levels, which were "looking more like those of the European welfare states and less like the United States" (Gwartney and Lawson 1997, 71). The following year the Paul Martin budget slashed spending on social programs and improved Canada's ranking on the economic freedom index (the campaign to cut government debt and deficits is described later in this chapter). The 2010 ranking was good news for the government of Stephen Harper, which was negotiating a series of bilateral free trade agreements, using economic freedom as one supporting argument.

The FI released its 2010 report at a policy briefing at Ottawa's Rideau Club with guest speaker Peter Van Loan, Harper's minister of international trade. Van Loan applauded his government's "commitment to free trade, open investment rules and lower taxes" (Canada 2010d). Free trade was key to economic recovery, he declared: "In Canada, prosperity and quality of life are dependent on trade with the world." He also declared that "we need to continue building a broad base of support for the importance of a competitive, globally engaged Canadian economy of the future" (ibid.). He ended with an invitation: "So let's work together to continue convincing Canadians ... of the importance of economic freedom" (ibid.).

Convincing Canadians – and the world – of the importance of economic freedom has been one mission of the neoliberal[1] project since it was formally constituted in 1947. That year, Austrian economist Friedrich Hayek invited leading European and American intellectuals of various free-market persuasions to consider the post-war creation of a welfare state and the rise of demands for social and economic rights. These developments, Hayek argued, would lead to a nightmare world of collectivism and socialism, to slavery, not freedom (Hayek 1944). Hayek and his colleagues formed the Mont Pelerin Society to engage in a war of ideas to promote an individualistic, non-egalitarian society governed by market transactions. Working together with government to achieve economic freedom, as Van Loan invited his FI audience to do, would have been unthinkable then.

This chapter traces the trajectory that began with the meeting of 39 classical liberal intellectuals – united by their belief in individual liberty – and how it was transformed, over 60 years of intense activity, into a global network of scholars, journalists, business executives, politicians, and think tanks spreading the message of economic freedom and establishing a new common-sense understanding (or hegemony) of how the world works. The chapter examines these developments in Canada, from the formation of the FI in 1974 to the invitation from the Harper government to work with the institute 35 years later to promote economic freedom.

In doing so, this chapter will demonstrate how the war of ideas solidified neoliberal ideology into a coherent political project. The chapter will also explain how it achieved this goal by building its own body of carefully managed research and then communicating it through media- and public-friendly ways. Thus, the war of ideas can be seen as a forerunner and a model of publicity campaigns to shift public opinion over time that have become so ubiquitous in the modern publicity state.

Creating the Neoliberal Project

It wasn't always so. During the 1930s and 1940s, classical liberals were a beleaguered minority outgunned by Keynesians, social democrats, and Marxists. This section describes, briefly, how neoliberals rose to prominence after the election of Margaret Thatcher in the United Kingdom in 1979.

The market society that the Mont Pelerin Society founders desired would become reality, they understood, only if they could capture and reorganize political power. This activist ambition differentiates Mont Pelerin Society liberals from those who came before and justifies the label "neoliberal." In the early years, they did call themselves neoliberals – conservative American economist Milton Friedman used the word in the title of a 1951 survey of his comrades (Friedman 1951) – but they stopped using the term in the late 1950s. They didn't want to dwell on the fact that the ideas they espoused differed radically from the laissez-faire ideas that stretched from Adam Smith (1723–90) to their time, because they demanded dramatic government action to create and enforce markets (Mirowski 2009, 427; Van Horn and Mirowski 2009, 161). According to Harvey (2005, 2), "The role of the state is to create and preserve an institutional framework appropriate to such practices," using force, if necessary, to guarantee "the proper functioning of markets. Furthermore, if markets do not exist (in areas such as land, water, education, health care, social security, or environmental pollution) then they must be created, by state action if necessary."

In post-war Europe and North America, the Mont Pelerin scholars realized they could not capture and reorganize political power by entering politics directly because of the hostile climate of ideas. Instead, "to capture political power, they would first have to alter the intellectual climate" (Mitchell 2009, 387). To alter the intellectual climate, Hayek (1949, 417) argued, they would have to influence what he termed "professional secondhand dealers in ideas." These were journalists, teachers, commentators, ministers, lecturers, publicists, radio commentators, fiction writers, cartoonists, and artists. They "decide what views and opinions are to reach us, which facts are important enough to be told to us and in what form and from what angle they are to be presented" (419). To accomplish this further task, Hayek and his colleagues designed their own network of dealerships, or think tanks. According to Mitchell (2009, 387), "Backed with funds from corporations and their owners, usually channelled through private foundations, think tanks repackaged neo-liberal doctrines in forms that 'second-hand dealers' could retail among the general public. Doctrine was supported with evidence presented as 'research.'" This research was packaged within books, reports, studies, teaching materials, and news stories and distributed to news organizations and other secondhand dealers. Later, think tanks developed a variety of simplistic indexes because these were more likely to receive favourable distribution to target audiences. Annual indexes are effective in persuading people to change their minds because they prey on most people's discomfort with statistics, and they are repeated year after year. The FI has made effective use of this device. As of 2010, its ongoing indexes are tax freedom day (34 years), hospital waiting list (19 years), and British Columbia's secondary school report card (11 years). The economic freedom of the world index (13 years) fits comfortably within this mould.

Half a century after Hayek (who was feeling despondent at the prospect of a welfare state) invited his fellow neoliberals to Mont Pelerin, Anderson (2000, 13) observed that "whatever limitations persist to its practice, neo-liberalism as a set of principles rules undivided across the globe: the most successful ideology in world history." The project would have floundered had it not been for financial and organizational support from a group of conservative businessmen (Phillips-Fein 2009), who could see the value in financing seemingly arm's-length organizations that would benefit mainly themselves. A key figure in expanding the reach of the Mont Pelerin neoliberals was Antony Fisher, a British businessman who made a fortune by introducing factory-farmed chicken in Britain after the Second World War. Hayek encouraged Fisher to fight the war of ideas by setting up a think tank "to supply intellectuals in universities, schools, journalism and broadcasting" – the secondhand dealers – "with authoritative studies of the economic theory of markets and its application to practical affairs" (Frost 2002, 49). Fisher established the Institute of Economic Affairs in London in 1955, which, along with other neoliberal think tanks and over 20 years of effort, was instrumental in altering the British climate of ideas to such an extent that Conservative Margaret Thatcher could be elected prime minister. The model the neoliberals devised was ready for export.

The War of Ideas Invades Canada

Over the next 30 years, as this part describes, the neoliberal project established think tank outposts in most Canadian provinces and, in 2008, in the nation's capital. This section also explains the crucial importance think tanks play in masking the corporate interests that finance them by appearing to be independent and arm's-length from business.

The project made little headway during the 1950s and 1960s – the heyday of the Keynesian compromise. The 1973 oil shock, other economic and financial challenges to the welfare state, and business concern about an "excess of democracy" (Crozier, Huntington, and Watunaki 1975, 113) created the conditions for a vast expansion in business support for neoliberalism. To exert more influence on government decision making, business set up umbrella organizations comprising a nation's major corporations, such as the Business Roundtable in the United States and the Business Council of Australia. In Canada, the imposition of wage and price controls in 1975 by the Trudeau government was a powerful signal that the decades-long truce with the welfare state was over (McBride and Shields 1997, 46–50; Langille 1987). Business needed an organization to take charge of a newly constituted pro-business agenda. The Business Council on National Issues (BCNI) was established within a year, comprising the CEOs of the 150 largest corporations. The BCNI produces favourable research on public policy issues that affect business and uses its economic clout to sell its ideas to government (McBride and Shields 1997, 47–50). With its deep pockets, the BCNI quickly became Canada's chief business organization (Dobbin 1998, 166). But because its self-interest is transparent, business requires the support of seemingly arm's-length, but business-backed think tanks that provide a scholarly, or at least independent, patina to the promotional efforts. The think tank model developed by Antony Fisher in the United Kingdom 20 years earlier was perfect for this project.

With the continued activism of the early Trudeau government in Ottawa and the election of the New Democratic government of Dave Barrett in British Columbia in 1972, business executives became alarmed. Noranda chairperson Alf Powis, who helped organize the BCNI several years later, felt "what was needed was a think tank that would re-establish the dominance of free enterprise ideas, the values of the market, and property rights" (Jeffrey 1999, 420). Antony Fisher was invited to Vancouver by economist Michael Walker (who, through his friendship with Milton Friedman, knew of Fisher) and forestry executive Patrick Boyle. They asked Fisher to establish a think tank that would replicate the success of Fisher's Institute of Economic Affairs. The FI was set up in the same mould; it employed a core group of researchers and engaged like-minded academics to conduct specific studies that would package neoliberal doctrine in research, which would then be published in book and report formats and distributed widely and promoted heavily in the media (Fraser Institute 1999, 1–4).

While the FI was gearing up to become the first Canadian neoliberal think tank, business established additional organizations to address other concerns. Wealthy corporate executives established the National Citizens Coalition in 1967 to defend their political and economic freedom. In Calgary, some of Canada's wealthiest tycoons founded the Canada West Foundation (in 1972) to promote western business and financial interests. In the same year, Bay Street financiers and CEOs did the same for central Canada by funding the C.D. Howe Institute, which focused on federal government monetary, economic, and social policy.

Fisher also founded two more think tanks: the Manhattan Institute for Policy Research in New York and the Pacific Research Institute in San Francisco, selecting geographical names to blur their ideological purpose. He received requests from business people around the world to help them set up similar organizations in their own countries to promote the free market. In 1981, he established the Atlas Economic Research Foundation to automate the process of setting up and running such think tanks, having perfected a formula for funding, projects, experts, and promotion. Eighty Atlas-related think tanks participate in the "economic freedom of the world" project, ranging from the Afghanistan Economic and Legal Studies Organization to the Zambia Institute for Public Policy Analysis.

With organizational support from Atlas and start-up funding from the Donner Canadian Foundation, conservative business executives founded regional think tanks during the 1990s: the Atlantic Institute for Market Studies in Halifax (1994), the Montreal Economic Institute (1999), and the Frontier Centre for Public Policy in Winnipeg (1999). The FI set up a branch office in Calgary to tap into neoliberal scholars at the University of Calgary, started a Toronto satellite office to support the work of the Mike Harris government, and in 2007, opened a branch office in Montreal. The regionalization of corporate-sponsored think tanks followed the American model, where such organizations were created in most states to provide a business-oriented perspective on policy issues at state and municipal levels (Soley 1998). Montreal Economic Institute executive director Michel Kelly-Gagnon explained to the *National Post* that "we are trying to change the climate of opinion in Quebec." The FI and C.D. Howe Institute "do good work but they fail to penetrate Quebec. The message needs to come from within the tribe" (Kelly-Gagnon, quoted in Cosgrove 1999). Finally, in 2008, the Macdonald-Laurier Institute was established in Ottawa with Donner funding and Atlas support to assist in pushing federal government policies further to the Right. The formation of this new think tank demonstrates how close corporate-sponsored organizations and the Harper government had become. In June 2009, Finance Minister Jim Flaherty hosted a private dinner at Toronto's Albany Club to raise support for the institute and wrote a letter inviting corporate executives to the event. In the letter, he said he was "giving [the institute] my personal backing ... and I hope that you will consider doing the same ... My office will follow up with you" (Best 2009; McQuaig 2009). Was the finance minister using his office to raise funds for the new think tank?

The project to influence secondhand dealers in ideas requires prodigious amounts of cash to set up think tanks, support conservative scholars, publish their works, and disseminate the results widely in the media. Currently, about $25 million a year is invested in neoliberal think tanks in Canada. During the 1990s, the Donner Canadian Foundation was the lifeblood of this activity. Buoyed by its success in participating in funding the Reagan revolution in the United States, the Donner family decided to move the Donner Canadian Foundation to the right (Rau 1996). After consulting with leading conservative journalists and academics, the foundation launched a new grant-making program, pouring $2 to $3 million a year into conservative efforts, helping establish the regional think tanks and single-issue advocacy groups such as the Dominion Institute, the Canadian Constitution Foundation, the Society for the Advancement of Excellence in Education, and many others (Gutstein 2009, 161–2). This foundation, "with real money to spend, has accelerated the growth of a conservative intellectual network," Harper and Flanagan (1996, 37) acknowledge.

In 2006, a new foundation began funding the neoliberal infrastructure at a high level. Peter Munk, who made a fortune in mining as head of Barrick Gold, created the Aurea Foundation (*aurea* means "golden," in Latin). The foundation grabbed public attention as sponsor of the Munk Debates, which pits high-profile liberals against conservatives to debate controversial topics such as "I would rather get sick in the United States than Canada" (Munk Debates 2010), "Climate change is mankind's defining crisis and demands a commensurate response" (Munk Debates 2009a), and "Foreign aid does more harm than good" (Munk Debates 2009b). The debates serve two purposes. They elevate conservative positions to parity with long-standing liberal viewpoints, crowding out progressive ones. They also mask the foundation's more financially significant activities: quietly doling out over $1 million a year to Canadian neoliberal organizations (Canada Revenue Agency 2009). In 2010, the FI, which received over $800,000 from Aurea and a second Munk foundation, the Peter and Melanie Munk Charitable

Foundation, awarded Munk the T.P. Boyle Founder's Award at a gala dinner in Toronto "in recognition of his unwavering commitment to free and open markets around the globe and his support for enhancing and encouraging democratic values and the importance of responsible citizenship" (Fraser Institute 2010), cleverly equating free and open markets with democratic values.

Money is also supplied directly by corporate Canada, but little is known about this funding. Few Canadian think tanks reveal their sources of corporate backing, which is not required by the *Income Tax Act* (Gutstein 2009, 163–7). If they do provide any information about their corporate supporters, as the Atlantic Institute for Market Studies does, they do not reveal the amount of the contributions, which pay for studies by academics whose work is compatible with the think tank's goals. Think tanks must also build staffs of reliable researchers and analysts who do much of the day-to-day research, writing, and promotion of the institute's products. With a budget of $12.8 million in 2009, the FI supports a staff of 64, plus 25 senior fellows, making it by far the largest think tank in Canada (Fraser Institute 2009).

The studies produced by a neoliberal think tank seem to head in the same direction. The mission of the Frontier Centre for Public Policy, for instance, is to apply market principles to the economic and social life of Manitoba and Saskatchewan. It covers issues such as agriculture (privatize the wheat board), poverty (reduce by cutting taxes and regulations), housing (reduce zoning bylaws), environment (protect by entrenching property rights), health care (promote health-care industry), education (increase school options such as vouchers), and Aboriginal governance (move from band to individual ownership).

By the turn of the century, Canada and the globe were blanketed with neoliberal think tanks, a result of financial backing from conservative business executives, organizational support from the Atlas Foundation, and the efforts of supportive academics and conservative policy entrepreneurs. Almost all of these Canadian think tanks are ideologically conservative. The net effect was to elevate neoliberal ideology to supremacy in the war of ideas, challenging and ultimately removing social democracy from hegemonic dominance.

Think Tanks Target the Media

With a mission to influence secondhand dealers in ideas – particularly the news media – and through them, target audiences, think tanks are, not surprisingly, preoccupied with their media impact. This section outlines think tank strategies for ensuring their messages are well received by news media. It also describes the process by which corporate news media were shaped by their conservative owners into organizations more accommodating to neoliberal messages. In 2010, Canadian neoliberal think tanks outgunned their progressive rivals, with the leading neoliberal think tanks mentioned 4.0 times more frequently in the commercial media than their progressive rivals.[2]

As the nation's largest neoliberal think tank, the FI has the greatest media presence. According to the institute, "Reaching decision makers, policy makers, and the public through the mainstream media remains one of our primary tactics" (Fraser Institute 2007, 8). About 30 news items mentioning the institute appear in print, broadcast, and online every day of the year, with about half appearing on various Web sites (Fraser Institute 2009, 33–5).

By providing news releases, op-eds, and tailored news stories, think tanks subsidize news. Their corporate and foundation backers pay them to undertake studies and package them for free distribution to the media. The FI's school rankings are a case in point. For more than a decade, the institute has produced report cards for schools in British Columbia, Alberta, Ontario, and Quebec. The institute arranged exclusive distribution rights with leading media outlets in each province, resulting in over 300 pages of free copy a year for these papers, which are owned mainly by CanWest (now Postmedia News) and Quebecor (Cowley 2007). Along with dozens of pages given over to detailed school rankings, the think tank supplies ready-made stories that newspaper education reporters can easily rewrite under their own bylines. The Weston Awards for schools that receive the highest rankings allow the communication department to "customize and personalize our message for specific communities" (Fraser Institute 2007, 38). The effort has assisted in the destabilization of the public education system, as families with the means flee low-ranking public schools and a private system becomes more appealing (Gutstein 2010a). This is an outcome desired by Mont Pelerin Society members such as Milton Friedman, who recommended that vouchers be given to the families of all school-age children "as a means to make a transition from a government to a market system" (Friedman 1995, C7).

The FI understands the critical importance of the media in shaping public opinion. The institute's leaked 1997 draft five-year plan, "Towards the New Millennium," revealed an ambitious media relations program. This document provides a rare glimpse of think tank thinking. In it, executive director Michael Walker bragged that the FI had "outpaced not only each and every one of our competitors, but the sum total of their efforts in [the creation of a media presence]" (Fraser Institute 1997).

Walker vowed that the focus during the next five years would be "the expansion of our penetration of the national media." He proposed to double the institute's $2.5 million budget – a target he easily met – with a sizable portion going to media outreach and influence. He described ambitious plans to develop a database of journalists who respond to the institute's material and catalogue the extent to which particular journalists cover its news releases. Each new project area the institute undertook "will have a component focusing on the approach to the media and to other second hand dealers in ideas," a characterization that harkens back to Hayek's 1949 paper. It suggests that devising strategies for media dissemination is a key input in determining which projects to adopt (Fraser Institute 1997).

Projects that "provided a tangible empirical focus for the policy concern" were key in the media penetration efforts, as the five-year plan predicted. These are endeavours such as tax freedom day, the hospital waiting list survey, the economic freedom of the world index, and the school report card (Fraser Institute 2002, 25). They are misleading (Gutstein 2009, 172–5) but attract media attention because they can grab headlines and are easy to report. They are also effective because most people tend to accept statistics as being authoritative.

Canadians would hear little about economic freedom if it were not mentioned in the press. Almost everyone reads newspapers, listens to radio talk shows, or watches news on television, at least some of the time. Even those who obtain their news primarily from online sources will hear about economic freedom, since much of online news is derivative of traditional media (Coleman and McCombs 2007). Neoliberal ideas would have little impact without the participation of the news media, which are perceived by their audiences to be generally free of bias and not beholden to corporate or other special interests (Winter 1997, 71). But behind the general perception is the reality that media owners are members in good standing of Canada's corporate elite. Many are active members of the Canadian Council of Chief Executives (formerly the BCNI).[3] As McQuaig (1995, 12) observes, "We must always remember that virtually all media outlets are owned by rich, powerful members of the elite. To assume that this fact has no influence on the ideas they present would be the equivalent to assuming that, should the entire media be owned by, say, labour unions, women's groups or social workers, this would have no impact on the editorial content." Given that big business finances the production and distribution of news, it would be naive to expect media owners to question seriously the structure of society or to entertain far-reaching proposals for change. For 100 years, the press has been a profit-making enterprise operating in a capitalist system and has thoroughly assimilated the values of business. The owners' ideological convictions and interests in influencing the political agenda, and their reliance on advertising dollars for their revenues, create an ideal context for disseminating neoliberal messages. As for the journalists they employ, Sparks (2007) suggests that senior journalists are likely to identify with media owners and political and corporate elites. Other journalists in the organization, in contrast, are "subordinates in a hierarchical division of labour and their activities are directed by their superiors" (79). Their ability to select relevant sources and provide comprehensible accounts depends on their power in the newsroom, which depends on being represented by a trade union (82).

For many, knowledge of the world beyond immediate experience comes largely from the news media. How the press treats events and issues has an impact on what people know and believe. Cohen (1963, 13) observes that the press "may not be successful much of the time in telling people *what to think*, but it is stunningly successful in telling its readers *what to think about*" (emphasis added). McCombs (2004, 2) says that "for all the news media" – newspapers, television, radio, and even the Internet – "the repetition of a topic day after day is the most powerful message of all about its importance." If, on the other hand, a topic is rarely or never discussed in the media, it has almost no chance of being deemed important by the public: "In a world where media set the public agenda and drive the dialogue, those things media ignore may as well not exist" (Pitts 2001).

More than 400 studies confirm that the media agenda (i.e., the items receiving the most frequent and most prominent coverage) sets the public agenda (i.e., the issues members of the public think are worthwhile to hold opinions about) (McCombs 2004, 5). If think tanks can influence the issues on which the media report and comment, they will influence the issues people consider important. And if they can influence the public agenda, they can push governments in desired directions. As FI annual indexes pile up and receive positive or even controversial coverage, the public comes to believe these are important issues that need to be addressed by policymakers.

While think tanks developed sophisticated strategies to influence what Canadians read, hear, and see about issues important to the neoliberal project, media owners and executives were making their organizations more conservative and neoliberal friendly. The political tenor of Canadian newspapers shifted dramatically when Conrad Black took over the Southam newspaper chain in the mid-1990s. He remade the *Ottawa Citizen* and *Montreal Gazette* into more conservative papers; started a dedicated conservative daily, the *National Post*; and moved the entire Southam chain Rightwards by hiring a half-dozen conservative commentators from outside the organization (Gutstein 2009, 211–13). Black fostered a close relationship with the FI. His company, Hollinger Inc., donated $100,000 to the institute's building fund, and his two long-time business partners and his journalist wife joined the institute's board of trustees. Black also brought FI staffers into the editorial rooms of the *Vancouver Sun, Calgary Herald,* and *Ottawa Citizen.* The Asper family maintained the conservative complexion of the chain when it bought out Black in 2001. Son David Asper joined the boards of the FI and Frontier Centre before he became publisher of the *National Post.* In addition, the company that took over the papers in 2010 – Postmedia Network – is likely to continue the chain's Rightward slant, given that CEO Paul Godfrey had been the *National Post*'s publisher and had started the *Toronto Sun* as a conservative daily in the 1970s. In 2005, billionaire tycoon Ted Rogers made his flagship magazine, *Maclean's,* into a more conservative organ by hiring as his new editor Ken Whyte, former editor at the *National Post* and a director of the Donner Canadian Foundation. Whyte populated his newsroom with former *National Post* staffers. Corus Radio, owned by the billionaire Shaw family, presents a line-up of mostly conservative talk-show hosts. The *Globe and Mail* gave a twice-monthly column to retired oil industry executive and FI vice chair Gwyn Morgan, who donated $1 million to the FI Foundation, which funds the FI, in 2007 (*Fraser Forum* 2007), and a twice-weekly column to long-time newspaper editor and former Libertarian Party of Canada president Neil Reynolds. In addition, in 2011, media tycoon Pierre Karl Péladeau, who bought the conservative *Sun* newspaper chain from Paul Godfrey and his backers, launched a conservative television news channel, dubbed Fox News North.

If the media are gatekeepers to the public mind, the gates were opened wide to the flow of neoliberal – and social conservative – messages. Hayek's dictum that the war of ideas is waged and won through the secondhand dealers was being demonstrated in the Canadian media.

Influencing Public Policy

The prodigious and expensive efforts of the neoliberal message machine would be for naught if, as was the hope of the Mont Pelerin Society founders, they could not eventually be translated into political power. This section provides a case study of neoliberal success with a Liberal government that had previously espoused social spending and job creation but was swept up in the rhetoric of debt and deficit reduction. During the 1980s and 1990s, the FI and other business-backed organizations had a significant impact on government policies. Provincially, FI recommendations were embraced by provinces such as British Columbia (1983), Saskatchewan (1988), Alberta (1992), and Ontario (1995) (Gutstein 2009, chap. 4; Kozolanka 2007). At the federal level, FI policy prescriptions were influential, if not embraced, during the Mulroney and Chrétien years. In addition, FI-allied academics at the University of Calgary were instrumental in establishing the policy orientation of the Reform Party, combining neoliberal economics with Preston Manning's social conservatism to create Canada's first federal New Right party (Laycock 2001; McDonald 2004, 43).

The multifaceted attack on government deficits and debt culminating in Liberal finance minister Paul Martin's 1995 budget was a milestone in limiting the federal government's ability to provide social programs (Klein 1996; Dobbin 2003, 51–4). After business won the free trade fight in 1988, it turned its attention to Canada's public debt, mounting a long campaign to convince Canadians that the debt situation was not just a problem but also a crisis demanding dramatic action. That Canada would soon "hit the debt wall" unless spending on social programs was sharply curtailed became a central theme. Key players outside government were the BCNI, the C.D. Howe Institute, and the FI. The BCNI spoke directly to the Chrétien government, ensuring it was "in the camp of correct economic thinking" (Ferguson 1994a), a phrase BCNI president Tom d'Aquino applied to Paul Martin after Martin announced his intention in October 1994 to dump the Liberals' long-standing goals of creating jobs and promoting growth and instead focus solely on cutting the deficit and debt: "The answer is spending cuts. Larger cuts. More immediate cuts," d'Aquino explained (Ferguson 1994b).

The C.D. Howe Institute, which is funded by the same corporations, banks, investment dealers, and insurance companies that make up the BCNI, reports that its mission is to "promote the application

of independent research and analysis to major social and economic issues affecting the quality of life of Canadians" (C.D. Howe Institute
2008, 5). This characterization gives the organization more credibility
with the public, at least with the attentive public. Howe claimed to be
arm's-length from business; nonetheless, it supplied rationales congru-
ent with BCNI policies (Gutstein 2009, 32–4). This is not to argue that
corporate funders can tell researchers what to write, but that researchers are selected whose views are known to be aligned with corporate
interests. During 1994, Howe released a blizzard of studies with such
titles as *Digging Holes and Hitting Walls* (Robson 1994), urging the Liberals to cut the deficit, not by raising taxes, but by cutting government
spending. By the end of the year, Howe president Tom Kierans reported
that "this has been a time of high visibility for the [institute]. In recent
months, our studies have reverberated in newspaper editorials across
the country, on television news, and in parliamentary debates" (C.D.
Howe Institute 1995, 2–3).

Like the C.D. Howe Institute, the FI is funded by BCNI companies
and conservative business executives. Its role seems to be to push public discussion further to the Right by supplying positions that are more
radical and unlikely to be immediately adopted. A 1994 FI study of government finances – a precursor to the economic freedom of the world
project – concluded that Canada was in reality a Third World country
because of its severe indebtedness, ranked ahead of Morocco but behind Burundi, Ethiopia, Ghana, and even war-ravaged Rwanda. Such
a dismal situation arose because of excessive spending, the Donner Canadian Foundation–financed study reported. The solution to the crisis was, among other recommendations, balanced-budget legislation,
which meant governments would have to balance their budgets every
year, regardless of the business cycle (Beauchesne 1994; McKenna 1994).
Some editorials rejected the allegation that Canada was a Third World
country but applauded the think tank's call for drastic cuts in spending
(*Calgary Herald* 1994). The FI's second contribution to the campaign to
scare Canadians into supporting deep spending cuts was a two-day
conference later in the year with the attention-grabbing title "Hitting
the Wall: Is Canada Bankrupt?" The institute repeated its claims that
Canada was one of the most indebted nations in the world, garnering
another round of media attention. The tone of the conference was set
by the recently retired chief economist of the Royal Bank, who warned
darkly, "Everything hinges on the next federal budget. We don't have
much time" (*Vancouver Sun* 1994).

The slash-spending lobby could not have succeeded without largely uncritical access to corporate news media. The CTV's Eric Malling was among the most effective voices supporting the business position, with his fallacious claim that the New Zealand government killed a baby hippopotamus because the government had no money left to build an enclosure at the zoo (McQuaig 1995, 1–5). Most corporate news media called for deep and dramatic spending cuts as the only responsible means of bringing deficits under control (Klein 1996, 79). Every new study by the FI and C.D. Howe Institute received sympathetic, often front-page, attention, while alternative perspectives presented by the Canadian Centre for Policy Alternatives (CCPA) and other progressive groups – which often called for higher taxes, especially on the wealthy – were ignored or dismissed. During 1994, the C.D. Howe Institute was mentioned in 28 stories about the deficit and debt in the *Globe and Mail*, the FI was mentioned in 24, and the CCPA in only five. But two of these were critical of the CCPA. C.D. Howe coverage, in contrast, was mostly laudatory. The day after the institute released one study calling for deep spending cuts, the *Globe* gave it a 1,200-word front-page story, a 700-word excerpt, and two glowing columns in the business section. The institute's name was mentioned in the paper 14 times that day (Little 1994; *Globe and Mail* 1994; Cook 1994; Corcoran 1994).

By the turn of the century, neoliberal ideas had come to dominate public discourse. Summarizing the success of neoliberal efforts, Flanagan and Harper (1998, 191) wrote, "The purpose of the conservative movement is to change public opinion and public policy, not solely to elect to office a party with a particular name. Much has already been achieved and can be advanced further by working on public opinion and pressuring the governing Liberal Party."

The New Right Captures Power

Less than a decade later, the conservative movement had worked on public opinion sufficiently to allow for the election of a minority Conservative government, one that openly espoused the New Right program of neoliberalism and social conservatism. The Liberal government it replaced had paved the way for the turn to the New Right through its implementation of neoliberal policies, as explained in the previous section. Of course, other factors were involved, such as the festering aftermath of the Liberal sponsorship scandal, as Kozolanka mentions in her chapter in this volume.

This final section describes the close connections between Stephen Harper and the neoliberal infrastructure. It presents Harper's formula for success – uniting neoliberals and social conservatives into an authentic New Right party that was able to gain and hold power. Highlighting the changed circumstances from a decade earlier, former Harper mentor Flanagan (2009, 274) observed, "Winning elections and controlling the government as often as possible is the most effective way of shifting the public philosophy ... If you control the government, you choose judges, appoint the senior civil service, fund or de-fund advocacy groups, and do many other things that gradually influence the climate of opinion."

Harper was familiar with neoliberal ideas, having been introduced to Hayek's ideas as a student at the University of Calgary after he arrived there in 1981 to study economics. Hayek's work became the foundation of Harper's master's thesis (Gray 2009; Johnson 2009, 25; McDonald 2004, 44), and it continued to influence his thinking as he rose from graduate student to Reform Party policy advisor, to MP, to president of the National Citizens Coalition, to leader of the Canadian Alliance Party and later to leader of the Conservative Party, and in 2006, to prime minister.

Harper courted the neoliberal infrastructure throughout his journey. As leader of the Canadian Alliance, he spoke at the Montreal Economic Institute in 2003, where he declared, "The Québecois sovereigntist movement as we've known it is dead. And Pierre Trudeau's vision of Canadian sovereignty is already dead" (Gordon 2003). (After becoming prime minister in 2006, Harper appointed Montreal Economic Institute executive vice president Maxime Bernier as his first minister of industry.) The following year, as leader of the Conservative Party, Harper conveyed his remarks by videotape to the FI's 30th anniversary bash in Calgary. Harper showed off his $45 FI silk Adam Smith tie and confirmed he was a big fan of the institute (Olsen 2004). He did attend the 10th anniversary of the Atlantic Institute for Market Studies the same year and called the organization "dollar for dollar the best think tank in the country" (Atlantic Institute for Market Studies 2011, 1). He also spoke that year at the Frontier Centre for Public Policy on tax policy and in 2009 gave his special greetings at the centre's 10th anniversary. "Frontier's ongoing contribution to serious, informed public policy debate in Canada has been outstanding," Harper said (Frontier Centre 2010, 2). In 2010, Harper appointed Nigel Wright as his chief of staff. Not only was Wright an executive at

Onex Corporation, but he was also a trustee of Peter Munk's Aurea Foundation, which was doing so much to fund the neoliberal think tanks and advocacy groups.

Harper also maintained close connections with the Civitas Society, the secretive association of 250 economic and social conservatives that set up shop as a discussion group after they failed to create a unified New Right party at the "Winds of Change" conference in Calgary in 1996 (Gutstein 2009, 186). In his speech to the 2003 conference, Harper (2003, 75) claimed that the ideas of the economic conservatives had already been adopted by government. As a result of the Reagan and Thatcher revolutions, Harper argued, "socialists and liberals began to stand for balanced budgeting, the superiority of markets, welfare reversal, free trade, and some privatization." Of course, much more needs to be done, he reassured them, specifically "deeper and broader tax cuts, further reductions in debt, further deregulation and privatization, and especially the elimination of corporate subsidies." But the arguments for this program "have already been won," he declared (76). The task was now to bring social conservatives of various stripes into the Conservative tent. There aren't enough economic conservatives to win a majority government, so alliances must be formed with ethnic and immigrant communities, who historically voted Liberal but espouse traditional family values. We need to change gears from "neocon" to "theocon," Harper told his audience. Movement towards the goal must be "incremental," he insisted, so that the public won't be spooked. "Any other approach will certainly fail" (78).[4]

In 2006, after 30 years of effort, a New Right government was finally installed in office and made many such incremental changes during its years in power. Most were on the social conservative side of the ledger, as Harper foretold in his Civitas speech:

- Appointing socially conservative lawyers to the bench
- Eliminating the court challenges program, which provided funding for those who could not pay for lawyers to fight for their constitutional rights
- Cutting funding for the Status of Women for advocacy, lobbying, and research
- Providing unconditional support for the state of Israel
- Reversing the trend of recent Governor General appointments, which were inclusive of Canada's diversity, and appointing instead a conservative, business-oriented establishment figure

- Undertaking a review of federal affirmative action policies based on the principle the public service should hire based on merit, not race or gender
- Rewriting the Canadian citizenship guide and creating a new picture of Canada for future newcomers, one in which feminists, unions, Aboriginal people, poverty, Medicare, and housing were deleted and replaced by war, the prime ministers and "great moments" in history (Gutstein 2010b)
- Launching a comprehensive tough-on-crime agenda

In addition, the new government's elimination of Statistics Canada's mandatory long-form census and its replacement with a voluntary survey was a far-reaching neoliberal stratagem. The decision was widely condemned by many governmental and non-governmental organizations (Canadian Press 2010b). But the Harper government ignored all calls – even from some business-backed organizations – to reinstate the census. Ideology trumped business interest. The FI supported the government's action. While such support may seem puzzling emanating from an organization whose motto is "if it matters, measure it," the puzzle is solved by realizing that different things matter to the FI and the neoliberal project than to advocates for social welfare. As this chapter has demonstrated, the former create their own statistics to prove the superiority of markets. The latter, in contrast, use Statistics Canada information to discover inequalities in society and then "lobby the government … to reduce inequalities through social programs" (Saurette 2010). Programs that redistribute income challenge neoliberal hegemony and must be repelled. In the market society envisioned by neoliberals, inequality is an essential ingredient. As the FI observes, "Taking more money from successful Canadians and redistributing it to lower income Canadians will only decrease the incentives for lower income Canadians to become successful" (Karabegovic and Veldhuis 2009).

The elimination of the long-form census was a Mont Pelerin moment: a pre-emptive strike for the market society. Even if the Conservatives lose an election, much has been accomplished and will not be easily reversed. The neoliberal information infrastructure will continue to influence secondhand dealers in ideas, regardless of the political stripe of the party in power. The project will continue because of its emphasis on training and supporting the next generation of scholars and activists.

Neoliberal hegemony is the result of a 60-year-long project to reverse the gains of the welfare state. A key element has been business-sponsored think tanks that waged the war of ideas and helped gain hegemonic control. Eventually, the climate of opinion shifted enough to provide for the election of a federal New Right government, which accelerated the shift to a market society. As a result, the publicity state was given more muscle because government and think tank infrastructure could leverage their efforts, as they set out to accomplish in the campaign to promote economic freedom. It should be clear that a market-dominated, non-egalitarian society is not inherent in nature (George 1997). It should be just as clear that waging a war of ideas for a different kind of society is just as possible.

NOTES

1 This chapter uses the term "neoliberal" rather than the more common "New Right" because it focuses primarily on the economic policies promoted by a select group of think tanks rather than on the array of social and economic issues included under the New Right label, which includes neoliberalism, as well as neoconservatism. It will be applied in this chapter to the program of the Reform and Canadian Alliance Parties and the government of Stephen Harper. See also note 2 in the introductory essay.
2 Mentions in the Canadian Newsstand database for neoliberal think tanks total 1,724 (FI, 1,179; Frontier Centre, 329; AIMS, 93; Montreal Economic Institute, 63; and the Macdonald Laurier Institute 60) and for progressive think tanks total 432 (Canadian Centre for Policy Alternatives, 398, and the Parkland Institute, 34).
3 In 2010, CCCE media members included representatives from Astral Media (radio stations), BCE (CTV television network [pending], Corus Entertainment (radio stations), Power Corp. (*La Presse* and six other papers), Rogers Communications (radio stations, CityTV, *Maclean's*), and Woodbridge Co./ Thomson family (*The Globe and Mail*).
4 Harper was ruling out a second method of policy change, the "blitzkrieg," or lightning strike. This strategy also involves "a policy goal radically different from the existing configuration" but is "attained in a short period following a surprise announcement and a very rapid implementation" (Easton 1994, 215). Such an approach had been applied in New Zealand in the 1980s (ibid.) and in the Canadian provinces of British Columbia in 1983 (Magnusson 1984) and Ontario in 1995 (Kozolanka 2007).

5 The Politics of Public Opinion

· PAUL NESBITT-LARKING

Political party leaders, social movement activists, spokespersons for interest groups, journalists, government officials, and other political actors make periodic references to public opinion. Understood as the collective political will of a sovereign and deliberative people, public opinion is invoked and interpreted to support a range of political claims, preferences, and decisions among a range of political agents. Political choices are legitimated and strategic decisions are justified on the basis of public opinion data. Consistent with the principal themes of the volume, this chapter explores in detail an increasingly important commodity in the publicity state: public opinion. Through a critical elaboration of the meaning of both "opinion" and "public," the chapter explains how political values may be used in the service of those in the struggle for control over persuasion and influence and how the strategic communication of public opinion may serve to legitimate governments and regimes.

The chapter consists of a critical enquiry into the composition, interpretation, and uses of public opinion by today's publicity state and the broader public in three interrelated sections. The first concerns the ontology of public opinion or what we can say about those objects and practices that are referred to as "public opinion"; the second section explores how public opinion is measured, or its methodologies; and the final section is concerned with the ideological uses made of public opinion.

In the first section, the core existence and nature of both "public" and "opinion" are under scrutiny. Using contemporary approaches to rhetorical and discursive psychology, attitudes and opinions are taken to be conditioned by both the sociopolitical setting and the tactics of argumentation and are shaped by privileged discourses and narratives available to agents in the process of political formation. Thus, opinions are always already conditioned and shaped by both distal discourses and more proximate social circumstances. As such, the taken-for-granted abstracted individualism of opinion formation is called into question. If studies of opinion are overindividualized, analyses of the public are oversocialized. Among the assumptions of those who employ public opinion analyses is that democratic citizens are engaged in public spaces in sustained and meaningful acts of deliberation and interchange. While not denying the existence of the agora, the section questions the extent of democratic deliberation and formation of will in contemporary Canada. Moreover, the rhetorical assumptions of a singular public are called into question as the section explores the plurality and multiplicity of distinct publics, quasi-publics, and non-publics.

The second section, on methodology, investigates how polling and opinion research scans, identifies, isolates, assigns, collects, measures, and assesses aggregates of individual opinion. Public opinion is ontologically complex, and there are associated methodological challenges associated with operationalization, sampling, validity, and reliability. Serious challenges have arisen regarding the capacity of polling organizations to reach members of the public and to deliver fully representative and random samples. The very lack of meaningful public dialogue combined with the capacity of dominant discourses and narratives to inform attitudes impoverishes attempts to meaningfully capture individual opinions in formation. Practices of public opinion assessment become increasingly circular, even tautological, as the act of interviewing is increasingly a matter of seeking confirmation. The innovative adoption of new information and communication technologies, such as the use of social networking sites for attracting respondents, resolves certain problems of access and response but only serves to perpetuate the challenges of public opinion assessment. Given the growing technical challenges, effective and persuasive public opinion polling is increasingly expensive. Those who can afford the high costs are also those who have the greatest investment in the outcomes and the most powerful input into promoting those dominant ideas and ideals in the political society that disproportionately shape opinions in the first place. Going beyond quantitative approaches to research methodology, the section explores both qualitative approaches and the ideas of those for whom the act of empirical research itself only reveals the vacuousness of the category "public opinion."

The commissioning of polls facilitates the selective use of those results that further entrench dominant ideas and ideals. This is the focus
of the final section on ideology, which profiles the capacity of those with
political capital to privilege and prefer their interpretations of what exists, what is good, and what is possible. Partial and preferred values
and orientations, having been adopted by the majority whose access to
information and deliberation is limited, are now measured, tabulated,
and presented back to those agents as the "facts" of public opinion that
then further amplify the dominant discourses and justify the actions
grounded in them, based upon the appearance of widespread consent.
Thus, ideologies are privileged and informed by the selective invocation of ideas and ideals.

While no simple reflection of prior public dialogue, the data on public opinion are nonetheless valuable in a strategic and tactical sense
to political operatives, in the publicity state, whose routine tasks are
driven increasingly by market research and persuasive communication. Data can be invoked not only to legitimate certain courses of action but also as resources to gain advantage in political encounters and
struggles. More importantly, the chapter argues that the agora is not
entirely meaningless and that individuals, communities, and groups
are capable of advanced and relatively autonomous processes of deliberation. Evidence of this is in the propensity of publics to generate patterns of opinion that do not meet the expectations or demands of those
able to commission polls. Under such circumstances, unwelcome data
can of course be concealed or leaked strategically by those who have
commissioned the survey, even if the raw political will that underpins
such opinion cannot be so readily suppressed.

Which Public? What Opinion?: The Ontology of Public Opinion

Regimes that claim legitimacy will characteristically ground their authority in the consent of the citizenry. A republic is etymologically a *res
publica*, a Latin expression meaning briefly "the people's thing" or, in
an elaborated form, "an affair or issue of the political people." The idea
that political authority is in some way grounded in the collective will
of a sovereign people – that government is their "thing" – is a universal
standard of legitimacy in all but the few remaining theocracies in the
contemporary world. The question of what exactly constitutes the public as the sovereign people is in need of scrutiny. Who exactly is being
hailed when political leaders refer to the public? As I shall argue later

in the chapter, in a global world there are complexes of partial, hybrid, and overlapping publics, quasi-publics, and non-publics.

If the political sociology of the singular public is in need of deeper scrutiny, so too is the political psychology of opinion. What constitutes an opinion? The complexities of this question have been explored in depth by the social psychologists Ajzen and Fishbein in their book *Understanding Attitudes and Predicting Social Behaviour* (1980). Attitudes are the ways in which we respond internally to certain stimuli in the world around us. They are both cognitive (based on what we know) and affective (influenced by how we feel). Opinions are the overt expression of such attitudes. The relationship between attitudes and opinions is often taken for granted. In the idealized "rational choice" model (or in its political science variant, the "public choice" model), a rational, informed, and free individual forms an attitude with regard to a political object and then acts according to that attitude. A basic political action is the voicing of an opinion in the public sphere. In reality, the expression of opinions is not so clean and simple. Among the many challenges emerging from social psychology to this model is the research of Scott (1957), who demonstrated that through reinforcement people tend to adopt as their own attitudes that which they have been asked to espouse publicly. In other words, expressed opinions can give shape to the very internal attitudes that were said to underpin them. Applying the insights of Bachrach and Baratz (1963), we can also appreciate how it is possible for attitudes to have no corresponding action, if action is meant as an empirically observable event in the world. According to Bachrach and Baratz, a nondecision can exert as much impact as a decision. In other words, not voicing an opinion can be as powerful as expressing one's attitudes and beliefs. To appreciate the power of opinion, it is necessary to take into account not only its manifest occurrence but also the consequences of opinion not being voiced or being voiced in such a manner that the opinion is not registered. I shall return to the latter theme later in this chapter.

Among the earliest precursors to the work of Ajzen and Fishbein is that of LaPiere (1934). In a famous sequence of experiments on racial discrimination, LaPiere visited about a hundred hotels and restaurants with a Chinese couple as he travelled across the United States with them in the early 1930s. In almost each instance, he and his guests were welcomed. Following each visit, LaPiere sent a letter to each establishment asking the owners whether they would accept Asians in their establishment. The overwhelming response was negative.

LaPiere discovered that there are often large distinctions between attitudes and actions, and he used his research to caution overreliance
on questionnaire-based research as a surrogate for investigating how
people act. In a conclusion that has stood the test of time, LaPiere alerts
us to the contextual variability of human agency and in particular to the
need to explore deeply the origins and development of opinion rather
than taking it for granted as an independent variable: "The question-
naire is cheap, easy and mechanical. The study of human behaviour
is time consuming, intellectually fatiguing and depends for its success
upon the ability of the investigator ... Yet it would seem far more worthwhile to make a shrewd guess regarding that which is essential than
to accurately measure that which is likely to prove quite irrelevant"
(LaPiere 1934, 237).

Behind every action, including the expression of an opinion, there is
a complex of factors that pertain to the social and psychological constructs that eventuate in that action. Ajzen and Fishbein (1980) identify
many of these factors and their interrelationships. Behind every action
are one or more "behavioural intentions" that serve the actor as reflexive scripts of what the actor intends to do. To identify behavioural intention is to recognize that human agency is both self-monitored and
distanced from the self as behavioural object. One can see oneself performing in a certain way in the future, including stating an opinion,
and plan for it in various ways. Knowing this also means that actors can
change their minds. Thus, between the behavioural intention and the
action there can be breaches of various kinds.

The voicing of some opinions may serve the actor as trial balloons.
Depending upon the context, an expressed view might be regarded as
unpopular or even unacceptable. As Billig (2001) has demonstrated,
deeply racist and offensive comments made among friends are readily
laundered through the use of innuendo and modes of symbolic racism
in the broader context of polite society. Where the actor is unaware of
the norms of those copresent, he or she might employ a formulation
such as "Look, some of my best friends are ..." or "I'm not prejudiced,
but ..." in order to hold the opinion utterance at some distance from
the self, at least temporarily until social assurances have been given
by those copresent. If those social assurances are not forthcoming, of
course, the actor can then disavow the already distantiated opinion
through some mechanism designed to heal the social breach. While
ordinary actors move in an atmosphere of doubt and uncertainty and
have to test the waters, both for themselves and for others in their orbit,

a strong opinion stated forthrightly by an opinion leader can have an impact by contributing to the stock of subjective norms available to all relevant actors. In fact, skilled "entrepreneurs of identity"[1] are already aware of the discursive potential of what has so far remained unspoken. Invoking tropes of nation, race, religion, gender, class, or some other category, such leaders know that they have touched a nerve when they hear the refrain "It's about time somebody spoke up for the likes of us" or "Never mind all this political correctness, I agree with ..." In describing the construction of social identities, Reicher (2004, 936) argues that "the issue of what is an appropriate comparison group is a matter of argument – something that involves a rhetorical dimension and is used strategically." The capacity to define the situation or object, or at least to have a claim to offer an alternative take on reality, is a powerful source of political influence. This is the politics of agenda setting, framing, and priming. Bennett (1983, 187) writes, "To a remarkable extent, the actor who controls the selection and symbolization of critical information in a political conflict may possess a decisive measure of control over key political considerations ... defining the issues."

Attitudes are rhetorical positions adopted in the context of a social world of doubt, dispute, and conflict. Moreover, attitudes are adopted contingently, reflexively, and strategically. Their utterance as opinion depends very much on the perceived circumstances of their reception (Billig 1995). The contingency and variability of attitudes receive advanced statistical analysis in Zaller's *The Nature and Origins of Mass Opinion* (1992). Zaller's work has been highly influential in public opinion research. Zaller is aware that question wording and question order can profoundly influence responses. He cites research in which subjects are prepared to express an opinion on non-existent legislation. More importantly, he references the research of those cognitive social psychologists who employ "top of mind," "drunkard's search,"[2] and other models of mental processing that place the emphasis on the ready availability of mental schema at a given point in time as responses to the cues of those conducting surveys. For Zaller, an attitude is "a 'temporary construction' which depends on peculiarities of the process by which a person has constructed it" (35). While he explores the potential for highly partisan and highly aware individuals to resist political persuasion, Zaller's model lacks a thoroughgoing social theory of the origins of attitudes.

The key to Zaller's overindividualized and voluntaristic model of public opinion is his explanation of ideology: "Ideology ... is a mechanism by which ordinary citizens make contact with specialists who are knowledgeable on controversial issues and who share the citizens' predispositions" (327). Thus Zaller conceives ideology as a tool of those individuals who wish to locate and lock into others who share their views. It is "an agglomeration of views of different specialists sharing a common predispositional bent" (327–8). Zaller's definition of ideology begs the question as to why such common predispositional bents would arise in the first place. He offers little explanation. If there is a political theory behind his model, it is a version of elite theory. As the title of his book implies, there are masses and therefore the elites that the masses tend to follow: "When elites divide, members of the public tend to follow the elites sharing their general ideological or partisan predisposition" (9). Such a conception of ideology is lacking in an account of its most important element, the matter of interests and behind them the social structures and relations that have given rise to those interests. Of course, there is evidence of elites deliberately distorting and twisting the truth in order to control the benighted masses (Bennett, Lawrence, and Livingston 2007). However, such strategies are of limited use in the long run. Such are the insights of Gramsci (1971) and Althusser (1971), both of whom argue that ideology is matter of deep and long-term cultivation towards ways of seeing, grounded in lived social relations, rather than a matter of the arbitrary and voluntary choice of beliefs from a menu of available preferences. Gramsci and Althusser do not appear in Zaller's reference list, even though their works are foundational to contemporary understandings of ideology.

To summarize, the origins and character of opinions have been over-individualized and understood according to principles of abstracted individualism. We have seen that opinions are far from the voluntary and open-ended consequences of independent processes of cognitive reasoning and arbitrary choice. If opinions have been overpsychologized, then the notion of public has been oversocialized in that it has been taken for granted that the public is an undifferentiated mass or agglomeration of the political people. To conceptualize the public in this way is to limit our appreciation of the struggle for control of knowledge, symbolic manipulation, and the strategic use of information. To speak of an undifferentiated public is to adopt one of two models of liberal democratic society, each of which is limited in analytical capacity. The first is elite theory, in which the public is conceived as "the masses" that serve little purpose in history other than an inert mass to be manipulated by the much-smaller elites who vie for their attention and support. The second is liberal pluralist theory, which regards the emergence of groups in society as a matter of the aggregation of a series of open and free individual choices, each of which is grounded in little but pure volition. While both elite and pluralist theories have their merits, in order to begin to unearth the workings of that object which is called the public, we require elements of a critical theory of political society. Such a critical theoretical orientation is grounded in a political economy and an analysis of cultures and discourses that seek to understand both how objective social structures arise and how the social forces and relations that arise from such structures cause patterns of contradiction and conflict. Thus, to understand "the public," we need to undertake a historical exploration of the politics of class, gender, sexual orientation, race and ethnicity, religion, and region, among other criteria of social differentiation, in order to develop an understanding of those forces that condition significant group and community growth. There is no one singular public, and at best we might say that there are a series of publics. Public policy analysis makes use of concepts such as "issue publics" and "attentive publics." Depending upon how they are conceptualized, they serve a stronger analytical purpose than reference to a generic and otherwise underinvestigated public. As we shall see later, the very invocation of a singular and unified public is an ideological act.

To the extent that we have problematized the concept of a singular and unified public, we open up the possibility not only for there to be multiple publics but also for there to be both quasi-publics and nonpublics. Quasi-publics arise whenever there are movements of historical collective significance in which many people, groups, and communities come together for the attainment of a common purpose (see the chapter by Smith in this volume on social movements and interest communities). The nurturing and growth of a quasi-public is often ideological, but a quasi-public can also achieve near universality, as in the popular eruptions of opposition to communist regimes across Eastern Europe in 1989. If there are multiple publics, then we also require a concept of nonpublic. Going beyond the bland statement that everyone is a citizen and that all belong to the public, the existence of distinct publics opens up the necessary logical corollary that there are those who remain outside specified publics, who are in some way marginal to and apart from organized and recognized political life. These categorizations are of great importance. Putting together denizens, guest workers, migrant labourers, and those for whom the existing system is of little relevance or use creates a large collectivity of those who are not "political people" or at least those whose politics are obliged to find other modes of expression. As Noelle-Neumann (1995, 46) writes, "Public opinion consists of opinions that *may* be expressed in public without risk of isolation, or opinions that *must* be expressed if one wishes to avoid isolation."

Measuring Public Opinion: The Methodologies of Public Opinion Research

Notwithstanding the challenges of identifying the very object of public opinion, it is nonetheless important to identify those techniques that can be employed to best assess the stated viewpoints of those we seek to understand. To argue that notions of both public and opinion are frequently misconstrued and oversimplified does not exonerate us from the need to develop the best methods of empirical enquiry. While all public opinion research is empirical, meaning that it involves some kind of engagement with those who can inform us of their values, interests, and views, it is not necessarily quantitative. What is conventionally understood as public opinion research is quantitative and consists of the accumulation of large numbers of machine-readable responses to questions on widely administered questionnaires. As we shall see, however, opinion research can also use qualitative research methodologies or, more dramatically, may reject the use of empirical methods altogether.

The pitfalls of large-scale survey research are well known and therefore require only a brief listing here. In attempting to register the views of the public, researchers rarely have access to each individual. Therefore, they rely upon select samples of an entire population and in doing so need to follow the science of sampling to avoid misrepresentations grounded in unrepresentative samples. Among the key criteria for the selection of adequate samples is the notion of randomness: a sample must be composed on the basis that each potential member of the population from which the sample is drawn has the same opportunity to be included as each other member. Social scientists have known since the 1930s that both researcher-selected and self-selected samples generate unrepresentative data. For this reason, the July 2010 decision by the federal Conservative government to convert the 20 per cent sample, long-form, five-year census from a scientifically selected sample of Canadians to a document that Canadians could complete on a voluntary basis was declared to be unscientific by the Canadian social scientific community and those relying upon dependable and valid research from Statistics Canada (Chase and Grant 2010, A1).

Even if surveys are distributed according to the principles of adequate scientific sampling, the design of the survey itself establishes a potential set of decisions that will introduce biases. Given the decisions that must be made regarding question order and question wording, a certain degree of bias is inevitable. The key consideration is how the more glaring and obvious degrees of bias in survey design can be managed. Among the most important considerations in the administration and interpretation of opinion polls are the following seven criteria.

First, questions must be phrased so as to avoid leading the respondent. Words carry a great deal of ideological and cultural weight, and the connotations of a word or phrase can make all the difference to responses given to questionnaires. The use of certain heavily loaded words such as "Islamist," "feminist," or "terrorist" is likely to induce certain response patterns.

Second, question order must be organized to avoid leading the respondent. The order in which questions are asked can stimulate particular patterns of response. If one wishes to encourage a high degree of opposition towards multiculturalism, first asking a battery of questions concerning terrorism, illegal immigration, transnational crime, cultural isolation, and the oppression of women would frame the consideration of multiculturalism and prime respondents towards negative responses.

Third, decisions must be made in advance about how to treat undecided respondents, "don't knows," refusals, and spoilt responses. Such data must be reported. There are at least four categories of those who produce a "non response." We can call them the vacillators, the ignorant, the angry brigade, and the jokers. We need to think in advance about how we want to categorize them in our analysis. Large numbers of people may simply not have a formed opinion about a topic but might nonetheless feel obliged through social desirability to express a point of view (Schuman and Presser 1980).

Fourth, related to this, the proportion of nonrespondents in standard random-digit-dialling telephone surveys of public opinion (notably those using landlines) has been steadily increasing in recent years (Groves 2006). While not always damaging to the reliability of a survey, the systematic omission of certain strata of respondents introduces survey bias. Inadequate attempts to compensate for such biases will generate unreliable survey results. Such unreliability may then be further amplified through the distortions of selectivity and framing associated with the presentation of data for partisan or ideological purposes.

Fifth, any sponsors of polls must be clearly identified. It matters a great deal who sponsored the report. Sponsors will have had input on the survey design and control over the generation and reporting of results. Such control can make a great deal of difference to interpretation. If the multinational agribusiness biotechnology corporation Monsanto commissions a poll on public opinion of genetically modified foods, such information is vital to an adequate interpretation of the results. The results do not speak for themselves.

Sixth, in reporting data, the confidence interval (CI) or margin of error (i.e., the range of variation around each reported percentage, maybe plus or minus 3 per cent or 4 per cent) must be reported. The CI or margin of error – calculated on the basis of the total sample size and the acceptable confidence level (see below) – tells us how confident we can be that the percentage given is the right one. If we read that 40 per cent of Canadians support a reintroduction of the death penalty and that the result is accurate to within 3 percentage points, this means it is possible that as many as 43 per cent of Canadians (40 plus 3) or as few as 37 per cent (40 minus 3) support a reintroduction of the death penalty (Ekos Research 2010).

Seventh, in reporting data, the confidence level must be stated; that is, on the basis of the sample size and the CI, the chances that the sample is truly representative must be stated. Is it 19 out of 20, or is it 99 out of 100? Once we know how many people are in the sample and how broad the CI, then the universal properties of probability theory can be used to tell readers what risk there is that the sample does not reflect the larger population from which it was drawn. There is always a chance that in picking 1,000 Canadians at random, we will select 999 seniors, 999 New Democrats or 999 curlers. Employing proper rules of sampling, we can calculate the probability that our sample is an unrepresentative or rogue sample. The normal acceptable minimum is known as the .05 level of probability. This means we are prepared to accept the probability that, on one occasion out of every 20, the sample will not be representative. In order to achieve this level, we can do two things. Assuming that it is properly selected, we can increase our sample size (clearly the larger the sample size, other things being equal, the better it represents a population), or we can increase the breadth of our margin of error or CI. Thus, if we move our margin from plus or minus

3 per cent to plus or minus 4 per cent, we can be more confident that the sample range includes the true population figure.

Given the importance of methodological rigour in the administration and reporting of questionnaire-based opinion research, the Canadian federal elections law was amended in 2000 to require all public media henceforth to list the key methodological criteria, including the CI and the Confidence Level, of any polls they reported. As Ferguson and de Clercy (2005) report, however, the compliance of the media has been weak and enforcement has been non-existent.

Although the democratic potential of public opinion polling has been widely praised as a clear source through which the wishes of the people can be registered and then acted upon by the leaders, not all researchers have been as convinced by the use of quantitative methodology. The methods of quantitative polls tend to isolate individuals in their homes, and many are conducted by random-digit dialling techniques that employ land telephone lines. As noted earlier, these have a very low and potentially biased response rate, and matters have not been assisted by the use of the Internet or social media. What are the consequences of isolating a series of individuals in their homes and asking them to comment on public policy options? Can we in some way register informed views in such a manner? More valid opinions are attainable only through the frank, sustained, and difficult dialogue of people in their community. In the absence of this, according to Habermas (1984) and other critics, what is measured is little more than highly conventional reflections of the dominant values in a society. For the development and assessment of deeper opinion, we require a new public domain for deliberative democracy, for sustained dialogue, argument, and reason. This must occur in an environment of equality, freedom, mutual respect, and plentiful resources for teaching and learning from one another. Such an approach necessitates deeper and more intensive qualitative methodologies such as the in-depth interview, focus groups, and narrative and discourse analysis. Deliberative polling brings together the measurement of opinion with techniques of deliberative democracy. While it is an intensive and expensive method of garnering opinion, it results in the generation of better-informed perspectives grounded in deep dialogue and fuller consideration of the issues at hand. Having said this, there are just as many potential pitfalls and limitations inherent in qualitative research as there are in quantitative. Any empirical research methodology needs to be systematic.

Among those who have attempted to theorize and operationalize a more deliberative approach to public opinion research is Fishkin. Fishkin (2006) begins from the perspective that the act of responding to an unanticipated phone call for an opinion on an issue that may not have been considered and being distracted momentarily from the domestic daily routine is likely to produce superficial, invalid, and unreliable responses. Such responses are better described as pseudo-opinions. However, *"when effectively motivated*, the public is awesomely competent" (158). Fishkin's model of deliberative polling gathers citizens together for a weekend of instruction and dialogue on the issue or issues under consideration and assesses their opinions before and after participation. Participants are given balanced information and are asked to treat one another with civility and respect, to make arguments on their merits, and to ensure that all points of view shared by significant portions of the population receive attention (Fishkin and Luskin 2005, 285). In contrast to the findings of those who have relied on impersonally administered one-shot questionnaires, Fishkin reveals that his participants are a better informed and more ideologically consistent group, who are able to attach policies to political parties and exhibit a greater willingness to venture an opinion than those contacted impersonally.

In the end, the most appropriate methods for discerning and reading public opinion are those that incorporate what anthropologist Geertz (1973), following Gilbert Ryle, refers to as "thick description." In contrast with the superficial tallying of precoded responses garnered from subjects voicing opinions in isolation of any immediate social context for their utterances, a thick descriptive approach is always deeply contextualized in the social psychological circumstances of the encounter, integrates multiple sources of judgment and insight, and generates layered and nuanced expressions of opinion. Only thick methodologies are able to capture non-opinions and breaches between attitudes and opinions and between opinions and actions. If we wish to read the meaning of what has come to be called public opinion, we need to pay attention to what sociolinguists refer to as pragmatics, the social and psychological context of the utterance, and deixis, an understanding of what is being referenced in context. Thick methodologies necessitate an immersion into deeper social structures, historical movements, and local particularisms. Such an approach is necessarily also critical in that the transformative character of the social research act is recognized, along with a range of associated ethical questions and scientific challenges.

Certain theorists reject the entire enterprise of empirical enquiry into public opinion. According to Baudrillard (1996), opinion polls purport to display the values and beliefs of the public but in fact do no such thing. The methodological and statistical laws of opinion polling construct a hyperreal simulation of the social order that is based on nothing more than a convoluted set of procedures. Opinion polls cannot reflect social values because the social as such does not exist. There is no "real" society of discourse, dialogue, and collective decision that can be reflected back on itself. Thus, opinion polls foist upon us an arbitrary construction of our social selves, a fantasy, and an illusion. They can hardly be said to misrepresent our wills or distort our true values, because "they do not act in the time-space of will and of representation where judgement is formed" (61). Baudrillard describes opinion polls as, quite literally, "obscene" (62). He employs the word according to its Latin roots: *ob* meaning "removed from" or "lost to" and *scene*, the place of human activity and life. Polls are an alienation of human activity, a removal from the scene through their arbitrary construction of who we are supposed to be. Although Baudrillard rejects the notion that polls reflect who we are in a meaningful way, he does allow that they can make us anxious because of their power to define ourselves back to ourselves. He refers to this as a kind of "hypochondriacal madness" (62) through which we chronically search for our essence through the distorted fragments (re)presented to us as our volition or desire. For Baudrillard, there is no such thing as a subjective agency beyond the play of discourses. His subjects are passive, indolent, naive, and reactive.

As we have seen, there is abundant evidence to reject Baudrillard's view of human agency. People are agentive and capable of more than hypochondriacal madness in their responses to polls. Nevertheless, Baudrillard's take on opinion polls sensitizes us to some important considerations. First, in order to resist the persuasive power of polls and not be overwhelmed by them, we should pay attention to the artificiality of their scientific and substantive assumptions. Second, polls do not reflect public opinion because they are usually conducted in private, especially now that telephone polling has become dominant. The views of aggregates of isolated individuals do not make a public. For this reason, too, polls can hardly reflect any meaningful opinion. However, simply because opinions are often assessed technocratically and ideologically on the basis of limited methodologies does not necessitate the abandonment of opinion research through thicker methodologies.

Making Meaning: Ideology and Public Opinion

Ideologies do a job: they work. The Swedish thinker Therborn (1982, 18) argues that any ideology has three things to say about social reality: "what exists," "what is good," and "what is possible." Ideologies appeal to us as imagined communities, and when ideologies work, they construct us as viable, if artificial, communities. They create publics with ready-made opinions. An ideology describes the world in a certain way. It states what is wrong, what needs to change, and most importantly, what is possible in this world and therefore, by implication, what is impossible. This point deserves some elaboration. One of the greatest powers of ideology is its ability to prevent or limit certain questions from being asked and to render certain visions or hopes unimaginable or unspeakable. A corollary to this is that certain voices, ideals, and persons are labelled eccentric or egregious. Ideology conceived in this way crafts a hermetic form of reality. As Giddens (1983, 20) writes, "The most subtle forms of ideology are buried in the modes in which concrete, day-to-day practices are organized." Among the more powerful characteristics of an ideology, then, is the capacity to frame and privilege a way of seeing that excludes and marginalizes those whose perspectives lie beyond the frame.

Ideologies are those interested and invested partial appropriations of culture that serve to systematize knowledge and understanding in a manner that justifies and underpins the interests of particular groups such as classes, genders, and races. Attempts may be made, more or less successfully, to universalize a particular reading of "the real" and to mobilize people on the basis of such an ideological project. In a capitalist political economy, under the leadership of a socially and economically conservative government, the privileging and promotion of pro-corporate, anti-collectivist, and socially conservative ideologies is to be anticipated.

For an opinion or a set of opinions to exert an impact in the public domain, they have to be registered, heard, or attended to. Whose voices are heard? Lewis (2001) offers an elite theoretical response to this question. Among his more important research findings is that even when the methodologies of opinion research demonstrate that clear majorities favour a certain course of political action or a policy option, it is by no means certain that such views will be taken into account if they are contrary to the views of those who are in advantaged positions of political influence. In the political context of recent ideologically driven governments of the Right in both the United States and Canada, elected into office by minorities and special-interest coalitions and driven by wedge issues, Lewis's contentions regarding the uses of incumbency are of critical importance. Lewis states, "Public opinion is ... molded – as a form of representation – in ways that render it compatible with the views of the powerful" (ibid., xi). Lewis argues that state and media elites frame and prime the public to respond to the elite agenda and, in doing so, ignore a great deal of what people actually believe. He correctly points out that the media gloss over distinctions of gender, race, and class in their construction of a single and unified public opinion (ibid., 65–6). He also demonstrates that clever research design techniques can elicit very different assessments of public opinion from the same population.

Lewis (2001, 5) argues, "To interpret poll responses ... requires an understanding of the constrained, ideological conditions in which they are produced." While he is correct to point to the importance of the ideological circumstances of poll production, his statement that they are always constrained gives too little credit to the autonomous will formation of social agency. As active agents in their own socialization, people are indeed conditioned by the ideological discourses that surround them, but they are not thereby determined once and for all, and the capacity to redefine, resist, and refuse is of critical importance at key junctures in history. Ideologies themselves are in process, in question, and in contestation. The media and the elites do not always agree, nor do they have a coherent and singular perspective. Their interests may differ. Ideologies also operate in an open field of hegemonies and counter-hegemonies. In such an environment, today's dominant ideology can be tomorrow's laughing stock. Lewis's analysis is too strongly elite-driven and does not permit sufficient capacity for resistance, refusal, and rejection on the part of the non-elites. Lewis states that a great deal of actual public opinion is to the Left of the spectrum in the United States. Quoting Knight and Erikson, Lewis (ibid., 94) claims that American public opinion is "philosophically conservative but it is operationally liberal." But how does he know this? If public opinion can be so easily constructed as he theorizes, then surely his Left reading is itself every bit as constructed as any Right or moderate reading?

Despite these criticisms, there is clearly something in Lewis's claims. His paradox of an independent-minded American public that nonetheless allows itself to be misrepresented, misguided, and even duped by its elites in government and the media would benefit from a series of thicker descriptive explorations. For instance, we might explore the matter of what we construct as political knowledge. Since Pateman's (1980) and MacIntyre's (1972) critiques of Almond and Verba, we have known that the very delineation of what is political (or "the political") is itself an ideological matter. Given that "civics" matter very little to most people, what do those who have not conventionally been included as core members of the public care about? Instead of arguing that they have no opinions or little ideological constraint, it seems more useful to understand what politics has actually been to them. In this regard, most questionnaires would do well to have a greater proportion of regime "output" items (such as laws, regulations, surveillance, and policing) than government "input" items (such as voting, joining parties, and contacting MPs). We require thicker techniques to begin to understand those occasions where our polling simply gets it wrong and does not see the emerging realities. Writing of the velvet revolutions and specifically of the fall of the Berlin Wall, Beck's (1999, 100) words compel us to think about how such movements might be expressed – if at all – as structures of opinion: "There, the citizens' groups – contrary to all the evidence of social science – started from zero with no organization, in a system of surveilled conformity, and yet, lacking even photocopiers or telephones, were able to force the ruling group to retreat and collapse just by assembling on the streets ... In a society without consensus, devoid of a legitimating care, it is evident a single gust of wind, caused by the cry for freedom, can bring down the whole house of cards of power."

Polls have a legitimating effect, and they are taken to be the bedrock of authoritative public policymaking when invoked by leaders. The manipulation and construction of a certain range of poll results and the omission of inconvenient others are ideologically constructed acts. How questions are framed, who does the administration, how results are analysed, and how the results are reported and then represented make large differences to what the results can be made to support. In the latter part of his book, Lewis (2001, 118–66) generates numerous instances of these ideological practices. He correctly writes, "Polls are used to *sell* policy positions rather than *construct* them" (37).

To conclude this chapter, the ideological manoeuvrings of the Canadian federal Conservative government of Prime Minister Harper illustrate many of the points under consideration. The decision of the government to convert the long-form census from a mandatory duty to a voluntary opportunity, as discussed earlier, was met with universal opposition from those academics, planners, leaders in other orders of government, and members of various communities who depend upon Statistics Canada for vital information. It was a move that generated widespread incredulity. How could the government of an advanced state in the context of a global order increasingly dependent upon reliable information knowingly subvert its own central agency designed to generate valid and reliable data? Stuart Soroka, director of the Canadian Opinion Research Archive at Queen's University, explained how both the decision to make the long-form census optional and the dramatic cuts made by the Conservative government to departmental public opinion polling "occurred without much serious discussion" (Soroka 2010). While the decision did not make sense in terms of the needs of Canada as an information economy and for the achievement of informed social planning, it did make sense ideologically. Put simply, the decision, along with a series of others made regarding limiting funding for pure research and cutting a range of moderately progressive programs, fit into the trend towards anti-intellectual populism that characterizes the government's agenda. While the Conservative government cut back on public polls and public information, its own private spending on polling and other private research continued to be extensive and went far beyond that of previous governments in office. Clearly, the Conservative government wanted valid and reliable data on public opinion, but it also needed to exert control over its generation, distribution, and uses (Valpy 2008; Galloway 2010). As Kozolanka (2009, 222–3) writes, "The Conservative government has a deep strategy of strictly managed, hidden and incremental change" in which the political marketing of targeted constituencies is at the centre of operations in the Prime Minister's Office. Recent revelations regarding the unethical and potentially illegal uses of "robocalls" and push polls have generated evidence of the extent and the depth of the Harper government's investment in the technology of opinion management (Elections Canada 2012).

The techniques employed by the Conservative government represented a significant departure in the ideological uses of information. What Butler (2007, 116–17) refers to in the American context is relevant to the Canadian Conservative Party in office: "Leaders are more likely to rely on carefully crafted communications to win support from the electorate for their policy objectives ... Polls are mainly used as tools to monitor the acceptance or rejection of policy options put forward by government and to show the number of those who are amenable to changing their views." While both federal parties have used polls in this way in recent years, the Conservative administration has done so with greater frequency and consistency, thereby devoting substantial public expenditures to the private advantage of promoting the party line.

Conclusion

The basis for a critical examination of the politics of public opinion is an understanding of its core characteristics. The chapter began with an exploration of the complexity of both terms *public* and *opinion*. The principal contention was that social scientific research has tended to overpsychologize the concept of opinion and to oversocialize the concept of public. The complexities and contingencies of opinion formation were revealed, notably those related to their argumentative or rhetorical variability across social settings. In contrast with common-sense assumptions that there is a singular and unified public, the chapter explored the political sociology of group formation and the plurality of groups and communities whose social relations constitute the fabric of political society. The concepts of quasi-publics and non-publics were introduced to broaden the conceptualization of the public.

With respect to the methodologies of public opinion research, the chapter reversed the positivist tendency to profile large-scale questionnaire-based research as the standard and to relegate qualitative research techniques as minor afterthoughts. While affirming the value of properly conducted questionnaires, the chapter promoted the thick-descriptive methodologies of qualitative opinion research, including deliberative polling.

A critical understanding of the nature of public opinion and how we might empirically assess the opinions of groups, communities, and citizens alerts us to the ideological uses and abuses of opinion research, some of which can be encountered in governments that rely on such research to underpin their communication strategies and campaigns of persuasion. While avoiding instrumentalism or reductionism, an analysis of ideology constitutes the core of the politics of public opinion in that it (with apologies to Harold Lasswell[3]) addresses the matter of who gets to define what reality, through what media, with what resources, at the expense of whom, and to what effect.

NOTES

1 The phrase is developed by Reicher and Hopkins (2001).
2 The drunkard's search is a metaphor used to describe the cognitive process of locating the information that is most readily available to introspection. In the original joke, a drunkard, who has dropped his car keys, searches for them in the light of a street lamp. It is the availability of the convenient source of light that guides his search rather than any comprehensive assessment of where the keys might have in fact fallen.
3 Lasswell (1953, 178) wrote, "Who says what in which channel to whom with what effect?"

6 Taming the Untameable? Constraints and Limits on Government Advertising

JONATHAN ROSE

Government advertising is one of the last uncharted areas of state communication. It is only when governments transcend the boundaries of appropriate advertising that we have a sense of its scope and its unchecked nature. But determining where the line of non-partisan advertising ends is not an easy task.

In March 2011, two incidents in particular made this clear. Cheadle (2011b) wrote of the shift from the "Government of Canada" to the "Harper Government" on Web sites and other department communications. Days later, Curry (2011, A1) divulged that the government would spend $4 million to sell its Economic Action Plan, a central plank in the Conservative Party's 2011 election platform. While there was much debate about the propriety of this behaviour, both of these stories highlighted a real problem. There are few, if any, regulations outside of the Federal Identity Program and Cabinet committee guidelines that can limit the behaviour of the government to spend taxpayers' money for partisan purposes. This chapter reviews some recent attempts to regulate government advertising both in Canada and elsewhere to demonstrate that the primary preoccupation of governments is around expenditure rather than content. This may be due to the public's concern for value for money and its reluctance to impose limits on free speech.

The relatively little attention paid to the regulation of government advertising may have something to do with the lack of clarity around the definition of advertising. Advertising is traditionally understood as paid placement in a medium such as newspaper, television, magazines, or radio. This is relatively uncontroversial, but governments also advertise on the Web through banners. If a government sponsors a local theatre production and is recognized as such in the theatre program, should that be understood as advertising? If a government underwrites a municipal infrastructure project and places a road sign to indicate its financial support, should that be considered advertising? While the media in which advertisements occur are evolving, they all share one attribute: they constitute a message placed in a medium paid for by the government. By this definition, signs by the side of the road touting "Canada's Economic Action Plan" ought to be considered advertising, as should theatre programs, Web banners, and ads that appear before the start of a film in cinemas. The government of New Zealand recognizes the importance of payment in its definition. Its Cabinet manual states, "Government advertising is any process for which payment is made from public funds for the purposes of publicizing any product, policy or activity provided at public expense by the government" (Cabinet Office 2008, appendix B). Like New Zealand, the Canadian federal government's definition puts an emphasis not only on payment but also on the medium: "Government advertising is defined as any message conveyed in Canada or abroad and paid for by the government for placement in media such as newspapers, television, radio, Web, cinema and out-of-home" (Canada 2009b, 1). Thus, government advertising must be paid for by the government (as opposed to the governing party) and be in a mass medium, that is, not addressed to a particular individual but undifferentiated within a target audience.

In addition to the fact that governments have paid for a message to be placed in a communications medium, advertising is characterized by a certain kind of content. While we might agree on the importance of payment as a criterion, there is wide variation on considerations of content. Most governments are silent on this, while others suggest very broad parameters for legitimate content. The Canadian Code of Advertising Standards, the professional body that regulates commercial advertising, defines advertising as "any message (the content of which is controlled directly or indirectly by the advertiser) ... communicated in any medium ... to Canadians with the intent to influence their choice, opinion or behaviour" (Advertising Standards Canada 2011, 1). This definition is similar to Qualter's (1985, 124) definition of propaganda as "the deliberate attempt by the few to influence the attitudes and behaviour of the many by the manipulation of symbolic communication." If there is something common to all definitions, it is that advertising is a vehicle of persuasion because ads are consciously trying to sell you something. In the case of commercial advertising, the product is easy enough to identify (most of the time). In the case of government advertising, the "product" is often more elusive. Government ads try to motivate viewers, readers, or listeners to *do* or to *feel* something. That something can be as direct and specific such as changing our thoughts on the use of seat belts or life jackets. Or it can be as complex as changing our attitudes towards well-engrained habits such as eating, drinking, or voting. At its core, however, advertising is directed at using the tools of persuasion to elicit behavioural or attitudinal change.

While all advertising does this, government advertising also exists to provide information. This is often the primary rationale for governments to spend taxpayers' money but also has its roots in liberal democratic theory. Governments see advertising as a way of raising awareness of its programs, supporting government priorities, informing Canadians about their rights and responsibilities, or encouraging or discouraging behaviour in the public interest (Canada 2009b, chap. 1; *Government Advertising Act 2004*, s. 6.1). Liberal democratic thought views an informed citizenry as a foundation for enlightened decisions. Communication by government, including advertising, is one way to ensure that citizens have the informational resources to make good judgments about policy choices of elected representatives.

Advertising that provides information on non-controversial issues is rarely questioned by the public. The vast majority of what government advertises is non-controversial and performs legitimate functions of responding to citizens' needs and informing citizens about rights, responsibilities, policies, or programs (Canada 2003a, 9). These types of ads can make bold claims often without evidence to support them because there is general agreement on the goals of the policy. For example, a famous ParticipACTION ad campaign that extolled Canadians to become fit used the tag line "The average thirty-year-old Canadian is as fit as the average sixty-year-old Swede." This provocative statement had no basis in reality and, though it was completely fabricated, was not controversial (Christie 1990, A1). Like positive, "feel good" ads of political parties, there are more falsehoods in non-controversial advertising than there are for issues around which there is little agreement. The reason for this has to do with expectations that the state should not intervene in a public debate or change public opinion around issues for which there is no consensus. Not only are controversial ads held to higher scrutiny, but there is also a higher burden of proof placed on them. Or as American Democrat consultant Bob Squier says simply, "Most lies in politics are told in positive ads" (cited in Geer 2006, 4).

The Elements of Ads

Advertising is composed not just of words or verbal claims but also, and perhaps most crucially, of images. Print, television, and Internet advertising are visual forms of communication. The point that an ad is attempting to make can be made through words explicitly. In 2011, the Ontario government ran a series of ads that said, "You could get money back. File your taxes and find out." This is a clear pitch that is made entirely through words. But government ads also make arguments through images. In 2000, a federal government ad called "Health Pieces" used an image of a young girl working on a puzzle of Canada to make the argument that health-care funding was dependent on all partners working together "to put the pieces together." This associative logic invites the reader to make inferences between the explicit images shown and the implicit claims being made. In the case of "Health Pieces," the image of the girl putting together a puzzle made the case that the problems associated with health-care funding were not intractable but rather dependent on a proper fit. Though it may seem otherwise, such a presentation is political.

Justice Potter Stewart said about pornography, "I know it when I see it."[1] Notwithstanding that many would say the same of government advertising, it can be understood as having several identifiable qualities. First, it is communication paid for by government in a mass medium. Second, it is a form of communication designed to persuade. To this we might add that, with few exceptions, it is generally unregulated by the state.

With the exception of radio, another characteristic of all advertising is a reliance on the juxtaposition of images and language to frame its message. The visuals in ads constitute the frame that is used to portray an issue. Like a picture frame, these are the borders that direct your eyes and give structure to what you see. As Iyengar (1991, 11) has written, frames are about "subtle alterations in the statement or presentation of judgment and choice problems." So the selection, construction, and choice of images in an ad very much shape the way in which the policy is understood, a political leader is summarized, and how responsibility is attributed. In the case of government ads, the frame of visual metaphors can help reduce the complexity of policy. Advertisers use them as shortcuts to understanding a policy, and according to a body of research, these visual images are often more memorable than the verbal elements (cf. Grabe and Bucy 2009). When we have to make the connection between the image presented and the argument being made, we are actively involved in our own persuasion. This is the most powerful form of persuasion, called an enthymeme, which forces the viewer to fill in the connection between the visual and verbal. In "Health Pieces," the argument that health-care problems are like a puzzle is never made. The viewer constructs this enthymeme through the logic of the image and the choice of language.

If advertising is a visual form of persuasive communication, it is also one that relies on different kinds of rhetorical appeals. Aristotle described these as logos, or reason; ethos, or the quality of persuader's character; and pathos, or emotion. Appeals that are made according to reason (e.g., buckle your seat belt if you want to reduce potential injury) are often found in ads that are deemed "informational" or that make their arguments through verbal claims. Most ads, government and otherwise, do not rely on fully formed arguments that have a claim, evidence, and a conclusion. Rather, they use the other two forms of rhetorical appeals to make their case. Anyone who has seen a celebrity pitch for a product recognizes that the person making the appeal can be part of the appeal itself. Government ads trade on the stature of the persuader. It is reinforced through the ever-present wordmark or logo and a tag line: "Paid for by the Government of Canada." As Easton (1965, 125) argues, the state is the "authoritative allocation of values," and viewers may be persuaded of the claims in the ad by virtue of the fact that the message originates with the state. Another kind of persuasive appeal found in advertising generally is an appeal to emotions. Good political advertising can make us feel patriotic, angry, motivated, or fearful, among other things. Brader's (2006, 129–31) work on emotions in ads suggests that positive, feel-good ads are more likely to reinforce the status quo, whereas ads that play on fear are more likely to alter the bases of political judgment.

Government advertising that relies on emotion is most likely to employ patriotic images, much as Nimijean describes in his chapter. In Canada, emotional appeals have a storied and lengthy history. This is most apparent in government advertising for immigrants in the early 20th century. Clifford Sifton, who was Wilfrid Laurier's minister of the interior, romanticized Canada's climate, geography, and employment opportunities in advertising to target "desirable" immigrants (Rose 2000, 49). One campaign used the tag line of "Free Land Clubs." Another euphemistically described winter in Winnipeg as "bracing" and "invigorating." Later, in both World Wars, governments would use patriotic images to both reinforce domestic popular opinion for the war and shape animus towards the enemy.

Emotional appeals were also used in early government advertising campaigns in Australia. Ads in 1899 said, "The climate is healthy ... The soil is rich and productive" and emphasized an education that was "free to all classes" (Young 2007, 182). Nationalist appeals during the war emphasized what Young calls "mateship and masculinity," with slogans such as "Be a man! Enlist today" (182). Notwithstanding cultural differences, a survey of comparative immigration ads reveals a similarity of appeal in both substance and rhetorical style.

The kind of emotional appeals found in immigration ads laid the groundwork for subsequent wartime ads. Here, the state was engaged in the manipulation of images of one's own country to make claims against adversaries. In most countries, the adversary was an external threat. This was true not only during wartime but also after the Second World War. The most recent example of this is in the US government's efforts after the terrorist attacks of September 2001. The Department of Homeland Security was created in part to ensure that terrorism remained a salient issue domestically and to use advertising and pre-packaged media stories as the means to achieve this. But we find a similar pattern elsewhere. In Australia, the "Let's Look out for Australia" anti-terrorism campaign was an $18.5 million high-profile campaign that told citizens to "be alert, but not alarmed" (Sinclair and Younane 2007, 212). The UK government's Home Office spent £8 million on its "Preparing for Emergencies" campaign (United Kingdom 2007), but additional advertising was created by both London Transport and the city of London that told transit riders, "If you suspect it, report it" (Metropolitan Police 2008).

In contrast to these examples, emotional appeals in advertising by the Canadian state have been used to shape domestic opinion against internal threats. This has been most notably to respond to Quebec nationalism and threats to succession. The federal government had a significant presence in both the 1980 and 1995 Quebec referendums. It created the Canadian Unity Information Office, an unofficial propaganda office, to disseminate advertising. Nominally about federal programs, the ads were often an emotional appeal about the strengths of federalism or provided reasons for Quebec to remain in Canada. One of the most (in)famous government ads, "Flight," broadcast in 1980, showed a flock of geese flying with the national anthem as a soundtrack and a narrator stating the importance of "working together to make our hopes

and dreams come true for all Canadians." Another ad by the federal
government prior to the 1980 referendum was an antismoking ad that
proclaimed, in capital letters, "SAY NO!" While this was an obvious
reference to the federal position in the referendum, it was defended as
an important part of Health Canada's anti-smoking campaign. The slogan of Tourism Canada at the time, "So much to stay for," was equally
transparent in its intention (see Rose 1993).

In 1992, the federal government was in negotiations with the provinces around a series of constitutional provisions that would later
be called the Charlottetown Accord. Prior to its proposals being defeated in a referendum, the federal government primed public opinion through a $25 to $30 million advertising effort (Ryan 1995, 268).
The campaign was not about the specifics of the Charlottetown Accord
but used the 125th anniversary of Canada's confederation as a pretext.
Canada125 extolled the virtues of Canada's ranking by the United Nations as a good country in which to live. The campaign also lauded such
important nationalist symbols as the Royal Canadian Mounted Police,
Terry Fox, Rick Hansen, and Canada's first female astronaut, Roberta
Bondar. These transparently feel-good ads relied heavily on emotional
images to subtly shift public opinion around federalism and the virtues
of the federal government.

In many of these campaigns, opposition parties decried the scope
of advertising by government, but until recently, little changed. This
may be a result of several factors. First, political parties historically
have been beholden to advertising agencies during election campaigns.
These agencies have donated their labour and talents to help get parties
elected and, according to Whitaker (1977), were quick to establish close
relationships with the government of the day because of the lucrative
advertising contracts that would inevitably follow. This suggests that,
for agencies, the free labour given at the time of the campaign is seen
as an investment that will yield dividends through future government
contracts. The second reason advertising has gone largely unchallenged
has to do with self-interest. As long as the major parties alternated time
in office, there was little reason to change a practice that benefited the
governing party. While in opposition, the parties are fierce critics of
advertising. This changes when in office (see Ryan 1995, 269), when the
incentives are structured such that this form of self-promotion is too
irresistible for any party. The third reason for the pervasiveness of advertising has to with the complexity of federalism in Canada. Our constitution gives significant spending capacity to the provinces but places
the burden of taxation on the federal government. At the federal level,

advertising has been seen by all federal parties as a legitimate way to provide information about programs, such as health care, that may be delivered by the provinces but are paid for by the federal government.

A fourth reason has to do with institutional imperatives of government. In this volume and elsewhere, Kozolanka (2006) argues that communication has become embedded within the structure of government. This has its roots in wartime bureaus of information but has been hastened with reorganization of government departments. In 1998, there began a coordinated approach to government advertising (Canada 2003b, 4.11). Kozolanka (2006, 353) identifies the creation of Communication Canada in 2001 as a pivotal moment in this centralization tendency. This also coincides with the Privy Council Office (PCO) beginning a brand rationalization process to coordinate the visual presence of the government of Canada. It was also at this time that a government advertising committee in the PCO oversaw the planning and development of government-wide advertising plans.

The growth of government advertising and the lack of oversight cannot be separated from other organizational changes in government. The most significant of these are the centralization of power in the Prime Minister's Office and the creation of a Cabinet committee on communications formed under Pierre Trudeau. The series of three minority governments from 2004 to 2011 put the government in perpetual election mode. This contributed pressure both to have a clear message and to use advertising to disseminate that message. When combined with a prime minister such as Stephen Harper, who is known to favour centralized communications, the result is both a culture and structure of central control. This centralized structure reached a nadir in 2010 when it was revealed that Harper employed message event proposals (MEPs) for events large and small. These documents provide the script for the details of announcements and events, stage-managing them so that the government message is not lost. The MEP template includes such things as a desired headline, a desired sound bite, an ideal backdrop for spokespersons and speakers, tone, media lines, and even attire (Blanchfield and Bronskill 2010, A1).

The Sponsorship Scandal and Its Impact on Government Advertising

If changes in behaviour are motivated by crises, the most significant change in the behaviour of the government of Canada's advertising activities was precipitated by an event in November 2003.

It is practice for the auditor general of Canada periodically to examine specific policy areas of the federal government to assess the value of money and audit program management and issues of accountability. The 2003 auditor general's annual report was noteworthy for its focus on three such policy areas: advertising, public opinion polling, and the government sponsorship of cultural events. The federal auditor at the time, Sheila Fraser, found egregious violations of rules relating to contracting agencies. The sponsorship program devoured $250 million of taxpayers' money, which was directed to sponsoring activities that were often of marginal value. More alarming was that over $100 million of this money went to communications agencies as fees and commissions (Canada 2003b, 1).

Other chapters in this volume also note the widespread impact of the sponsorship scandal on various aspects of the publicity state. In terms of advertising, however, the auditor general found that the choice of advertising agencies rarely, if ever, met the requirements of the government's contracting policy. Fraser's report found that there were often irregularities for work that was invoiced but that was never done. The conclusion one could only reach from her findings was that government advertising was unregulated, unenforced, organizationally chaotic, and did not follow any semblance of normal business practices. In short, it showed reckless disregard for taxpayers' money and, as the auditor general's report bluntly put it, "little regard for Parliament, the *Financial Administration Act* ... transparency, and value for money" (ibid.).

Following the auditor general's November 2003 report being tabled in February 2004, the then prime minister, Paul Martin, immediately established a Commission of Inquiry chaired by Justice John Gomery to investigate the sponsorship program and other advertising activities of the government. The immediate changes were significant: a temporary moratorium on government advertising was announced, as well as 15 per cent reduction in overall expenditures over three years (Sadinsky and Gussman 2006, 308). As important as these changes were, they were only a precursor to what would come later.

The Gomery inquiry facilitated a significant reevaluation in the financial management of advertising but was silent on the content of advertising. The changes to the financial regulation and efforts towards transparency were significant. Among them were increasing the number of suppliers for advertising, eliminating commission-based payment for agencies, and decreasing Canadian ownership of advertising firms doing business with the government from 100 per cent to 80 per cent. The agency of record – the central buyer on behalf of government for media time and space for advertising – would be selected through a competitive process that was much more transparent than previous practices. In terms of transparency, Gomery held consultation meetings in several cities across Canada to solicit feedback on changes in accountability, transparency of the bidding process, and protection for whistle-blowers (those who would "tell" on wasteful or illegal practices). Finally, Public Works and Government Service Canada, the department responsible for government advertising, was to produce an annual report that would indicate total advertising expenditure and list the advertising agencies that received contracts and the amount of those contracts.

The shock that followed the auditor general's report and the Gomery inquiry resulted in the federal government in Canada undergoing a sea change in financial practices associated with government advertising. Once secretive and opaque, the government is now a leader in the amount and quality of data and information it makes available about its advertising activities.

This evaluation of government advertising in Canada mirrors similar practices elsewhere in the world. A survey of these practices demonstrate that there are common themes that emerge, all of which have to do with financial issues, such as whether the state is applying market efficiencies or is respecting the principle of value for money. In Northern Ireland, a 2006 review of advertising made 28 recommendations, all of which had to do with making advertising contracts more competitive, consolidating the purchasing of classified advertising, and decreasing costs associated with advertising (Office of the First Minister and Deputy Minister 2006). In Australia, the Australian National Audit Office has produced two studies on government advertising. The first, conducted in 1995, was an efficiency audit designed to "encourage better practice in managing difficult and complex campaigns" (Grant 2004, 3). The second review by that office in 1998 was begun at the request of the political opposition, which was concerned about the government's advertising on the goods and service tax (GST). Like the GST advertising campaign in Canada, the report noted that there are no protocols distinguishing between government and party advertisements and that controls over expenditure prior to an election were needed. At the provincial level in Canada, there are very few, if any, regulations around the content and scope of government advertising.

Reviews of government advertising based on sound public administration principles and adherence to rules of transparency are important
elements to oversight. However, as important as they are, they miss
an important aspect of advertising by the state: an evaluation of the
content of the ads. Until recently, much of the review of government advertising was around financial improprieties. In Canada, the Gomery
inquiry put this issue on the front burner, and as a result, the process
related to government advertising expenditures is much more transparent. These kinds of reviews apply standards to advertising used in
other aspects of government procurement, but what standards should
be used to assess its content? On this matter, the challenges are great
and the criteria are as slippery as a wet bar of soap.

The content of advertising by government comes under scrutiny
if its message is ill timed, controversial, or implausible. On the first
criterion, the Canadian government used taxpayers' money to fund
a GST advertising campaign in 1989–90 before legislation had passed
Parliament. This angered both the opposition parties and the Speaker,
who saw it as a blatant attempt to change public opinion and an affront to the powers of Parliament. Opponents were also not persuaded
that the ads responded to informational needs of citizens, arguing that
arguments made were selective and partial (Roberts and Rose 1995).
Similar to this, in 2005 the Howard government of Australia spent
$120 million on WorkChoices, an industrial relations policy that had
not even been introduced in Parliament (Tiffen 2011). These ads were
egregious not only because a High Court judge pronounced that they
were "propagandizing in advance of the [the legislation's] enactment"
(quoted in Young 2007, 200) but also because they were a direct response to ads broadcast by unions. Closer to home, in 2012 the government of Alberta spent $1.3 million on government ads touting the
benefits of the proposed budget (Henton 2012). The timing was particularly egregious, since the message of the ads – that there would
be no new taxes – mirrored a key plank of the governing party in the
imminent provincial election. The ads were rightly seen as supporting
the partisan message of the governing Progressive Conservatives at
taxpayers' expense. Other provincial governments in Canada have enforced advertising bans prior to their elections. For example, Manitoba
prohibits government advertising 60 days prior to an election while
Saskatchewan bans advertising 30 days prior. This is only possible if
there are fixed election dates and is virtually impossible to enforce in a
minority Parliament.

Government ads are seen as controversial when they use the power of the state to sway public opinion on matters where there are significant differences of opinion between the governing party and broad sections of the public. Again, Australia provides a good example. In 1995, the Labor government spent over $9 million on its "Working Nation" campaign designed to change perception about unemployment when it was being criticized for its inaction on high unemployment rates. Nominally designed to persuade employers to give the unemployed a chance, the campaign featured actors who would later turn up in Labor party ads and highlighted the unregulated nature of advertising content. This was a Gomery moment for Australia, as it was "the first time that there was a major debate in Australia over a federal government advertising campaign" (Young 2007, 195). It also made advertising an election issue, with the opposition party leader promising a ban on partisan advertising and that all advertising be approved by the auditor general. While this was never done, it did form the basis of the law in Ontario that does this very thing.

The government of Ontario provides many examples of controversial advertising. Between 1996 and 2003, the then Ontario premier, Mike Harris, used advertising to support his government's "Common Sense Revolution." Central to his task of government downsizing was Bill 160, the *Education Quality Improvement Act*, which dramatically changed the working environment and collective bargaining of teachers, as well as classroom sizes and curriculum for students. The act was a radical reshaping of education in Ontario. In an effort to shore up public opinion, a hard-hitting campaign was created that attacked teachers and their "union bosses." "Let's put our children first" was the slogan of the campaign (Kozolanka 2007, 197), with one ad framing the issue as simply "asking teachers to spend a little more time with their students." The controversy associated with this campaign has as much to do with the aggressive ad hominem nature of the persuasion as it did with the propriety of using taxpayers' money for arguably partisan purposes. This campaign was supported by a Conservative Party–funded campaign that was directed at Liberal leader Dalton McGuinty. The combination of government ads that implicitly attacked the opposition's position and party ads that explicitly attacked the opposition made it difficult to make a distinction between the claims of the two.

The Harris "Common Sense Revolution" campaign has much in common with the Australian government's GST campaign in 1998. According to Young (2007a, 196–7), the campaign, which cost over

$100 million and was centred on Joe Cocker's "Unchain My Heart," was controversial because of the volume of advertising. In addition, the campaign was short on reasoned arguments and "laden with emotional references" that provided little or no information. Like the Harris government ads, the campaign was timed to appear prior to an election and thus seemed to be a proxy for political advertising by the government. The ad made the claim both visually, through people being shackled in chains, and verbally, through Cocker's lyrics that the proposed GST would set consumers free. This argument was as implausible as the claim that teachers were not interested in the quality of education.

These controversial ads are united not only by the scope of their campaign but also because they are on policies, the goals of which are not universally shared. This is a marked change from past government practices where, for the most part, advertising responded to a policy that had significant popular support. Formerly, advertising followed a longer-term strategy that saw the government run years-long campaigns (such as ParticipACTION to encourage physical fitness or antismoking campaigns). Modern controversial campaigns are responses either to legislative opposition or to ad campaigns by interest groups that target government initiatives. They are short-term campaigns on salient election issues. Because they often run before an election, they raise the possibility of government advertising being party advertising in disguise.

Government Advertising and the Timing of Elections

The federal government in Canada is prohibited from advertising once an election is called. Its communication policy (Canada 2006a, sec. 23) states that all government

> Institutions must suspend their advertising during general elections ... Advertising is only permitted when: an institution is required by statute or regulation to issue a public notice for legal purposes; an institution must inform the public of a danger to health, safety or the environment; or an institution must post an employment or staffing notice. Otherwise, advertising plans and activities must be held in abeyance effective the day that the Governor in Council issues a writ for a general federal election, and must not resume until the day the newly elected government is sworn into office.

Table 6.1. Canadian government advertising spending and federal elections

Fiscal year (April 1–March 31)	Nominal amount (in millions)	Amount in 2011 dollars (in millions)	Election date
2002–3	111.0	134.0	—
2003–4	69.8	80.8	—
2004–5	49.5	56.8	28 June 2004
2005–6	41.3	46.3	23 January 2006
2006–7	86.9*	95.5	—
2007–8	84.1	90.3	—
2008–9	79.5	84.3	14 October 2008
2009–10	136.3**	140.7	—

Sources: Annual Report of the Government of Canada's Advertising, 2002–10; the Bank of Canada's Inflation Calculator was used to produce real dollar amounts.
Shading indicates federal election years.
* includes $11.1 million for the 2006 census.
** represents data from Perlman (2011).

While these caveats might seem broad enough for an unscrupulous government, advertising by the government during the 2006 federal election still amounted to 1 per cent ($440,000) of its yearly total. At the time of writing in 2012, data were not available for the 2008 or 2011 elections.

The absence of spending by government on advertising during an election is, of course, not enough assurance that the governing party is not using taxpayers' money to prime its partisan message. To determine whether the governing party is using taxpayers' money, we would need to examine whether government advertising increased immediately before an election. Table 6.1 provides some data but is skewed because of the timing of elections within the government's fiscal year. For example, the 28 June 2004 federal election appeared earlier in the 2004–5 fiscal year than the 23 January 2006 election that came close to the end of the 2005–6 fiscal year. One pattern is clear from these three elections: advertising expenditure is lower in an election year than the previous year. This may have to do with the moratorium placed on advertising during the formal election periods, which would depress overall expenditure. It might also tell us something about the timing of communication priorities of governments in their mandate. In other

Table 6.2. Rank of Canadian federal government among top advertisers in Canada, 2002–10

Year	2002	2003	2004	2005	2006	2007	2008	2009	2010
Rank	2	3	8	4	4	4	4	2	3

Source: Nielsen Media.
Rank represents total media dollars per calendar year.

words, governments may choose to advertise their program immediately *after* being elected. A second pattern that emerges from these data is the significant jump from the 2006 election when Harper's Conservatives were elected. Advertising doubles in real dollars after the 2006 election and did not vary significantly until 2009.

In Australia, several studies have noted the increase in advertising prior to an election. Young and Tham (2006, 74) note that in two months in 2004, the government spent twice as much on advertising as any party could during the official campaign. A report by Australia's parliamentary library notes that governments of all political stripes engorge on advertising months before an election. The pre-election spikes are on issues that the governing party covers in its campaigns, suggesting a strong indication of priming (Grant 2004, 3). As indicated previously, this pattern of pre-election priming has occurred in Canada as well, most recently in the Alberta election of 2012.

But is it too much? The amount of money that the federal government spent on advertising needs to be put in context. If we look at the rank of government as advertiser, prior to the 2003 auditor general's report, Canada was either the top or almost the top advertiser in the country (Rose 2010). Since 2005, the federal government has ranked among the top five advertisers in the country (see Table 6.2). If it is examined as spending per capita, federal government advertising ranks among the top five international spenders (Young and Tham 2006, 80).

The pattern of increased government expenditure on advertising may tell another story that is not immediately evident from the data. There is some evidence to support the claim that governments in Canada use advertising as a form of policy exhortation to offset the decline of policymaking. The amount of legislation that governments pass has been steadily declining since Lester Pearson was prime minister in the 1960s. The success rates of government bills have declined from 96 per cent in the King–St. Laurent period to 8 per cent in the first Harper government of 2006–8 (Franks 2009, 4). In an environment where governments either are unable or choose not to pass their legislative agendas, advertising might be a proxy for policymaking. This decline also coincides with a significant drop in the amount of sitting days in Parliament from 163 days in 1969–73 to 105 days from 2004 to 2008 (5).

The decrease in Parliament meeting may speak to its increasing irrelevance as the place where our national conversations occur. Governments, in turn, rely on advertising to bypass Parliament and take their message directly to citizens. This was the case with the Canadian government's campaign around the GST in 1990 and more recently with the government's Economic Action Plan (EAP), which is also discussed in the chapter in this volume by Kozolanka.

Prior to the March 2011 budget, Harper's government spent an estimated $53 million on advertising its economic stimulus program. To provide context for the EAP spending, in that year $23.5 million was spent on H1N1, a health pandemic. Advertising the EAP used up more than a third of the government's entire advertising budget. Included in this was $5 million spent on an intensive media buy during *Hockey Night in Canada*, the Oscars, and other prime-time spots (Cheadle 2011c).

The EAP campaign received significant criticism in the media and from the opposition for several reasons. The scope of the EAP campaign was massive. It combined television, radio, print, Internet, billboards, and road signs to present a virtual omnipresence that an opposition member said was tantamount to "carpet-bombing the country with self-serving messages at the taxpayers' expense" (ibid.). The reforms of 2004 established a "set-aside" amount of $65.4 million each year from which most government information campaigns were to be funded (Canada 2011a). That the EAP used up over 80 per cent of this pre-established amount speaks to the importance of the EAP to the government and to the extraordinary nature of the campaign. Indeed, many government departments, such as the Canada Revenue Agency, the Department of Finance, and the former Human Resources and Social Development, ran concurrent campaigns on the same issue.

The campaign was also questioned because of its timing. The pre-election advertising spike of $26 million began just weeks before an expected election. Because it was a minority Parliament, the timing was beyond the government's control, but there were clear signs that the government would fall on a vote of no confidence, and it did. The argument that these ads were an adjunct to partisan advertising was reinforced with the political ads ran by the Conservative party within days of launching EAP ads. According to the testimony of an assistant deputy minister, a Conservative ad and a government ad appeared within 10 minutes of one another during the Oscars that year (Perlman 2011).

The effect was to help prime the electorate on the governing party's key messages: competence of leadership (extolled in the party ads) and the importance of economic management (in the content of the government ads).

Advertising can be justified if it provides information to citizens. The content of EAP ads was not new and therefore cannot be justified on these grounds. Rather, they focused on the $60 billion of stimulus spending that had already been spent in prior years (McKenna 2011). The EAP ads highlight very clearly how unregulated government advertising is in Canada.

The Next Wave: Constraining Government Advertising?

Constraints on policymaking can be internal through instruments such as legislation, written guidelines, and procedures. They can also be cultural, such as working in an environment that provides the boundaries in which legitimate behaviour is understood. International experience shows that governments of all political stripes in different political environments use advertising for partisan purposes. There are examples of governments providing some context for advertising but few examples where it is explicitly limited or controlled.

The most notable example of legislation limiting government advertising is in the province of Ontario with its *Government Advertising Act, 2004* (GAA). Brought in by the Liberals as a response to what was perceived to be dubious advertising by the previous Conservative government, the GAA is intended to ban partisan government advertising. The legislation is noteworthy not only for the standards it sets but also because Ontario is the only province in Canada to create legislative constraints around government ads. All government ads by the provincial government must adhere to specific standards, such as stating that they are "paid for by the government of Ontario"; ads cannot feature a minister or the premier (unless they are part of a tourism campaign internationally), and more importantly, the ads "must not be partisan" (*Government Advertising Act*, s. 6.1.4). This is a crucial part of the act, but how does one determine what is partisan? The act mandates that the provincial Office of the Auditor General of Ontario (OAG) review every government ad before it is broadcast or published. The OAG relies on an Advertising Review Panel composed of a lawyer whose practice includes advertising law, a political scientist whose research is on government advertising (*viz.*, the author of this chapter), a journalist, and a former manager in the auditor's office. The advice that the panel provides is given to the OAG, which then deems whether the proposed ad is compatible with or in contravention of the law. The scope of the law is broad, as evident that the GAA gives the OAG power to examine "additional standards" (ibid., s. 6.4) such as the timing of the ad in the electoral cycle and whether the ad delivers self-congratulatory or party-aggrandizing messages.

The GAA is a significant milestone because it gives final authority to the OAG (there is no appeal) and provides criteria that all ads must fulfil. A similar bill was introduced in the Manitoba legislature in 2008 but failed to receive majority support. Because this type of legislation is unique in the world, there have been some gaps in its coverage. It is, for example, silent on Web-based advertising, although the OAG and the government have come to an agreement that the content of government Web sites mentioned in ads would be seen as a continuation of the ad based on the "first click" after the landing page. This is the fastest growing area of government advertising, almost doubling from 6 per cent in 2006 to 13 per cent in 2008 at the federal level (Canada 2009b, chap. 23), so it is a significant omission. The pattern of online growth exists at the provincial level as well. In 2010, for example, the government of New Brunswick pulled tourist ads from television, opting for Web-based ads that were cheaper and that have greater impact.

In addition to the lack of Web advertising guidelines, another gap in the Ontario legislation pertains to outdoor billboards. In 2010, Infrastructure Ontario billboards that appeared on government-funded projects were initially outside the scope of the GAA. The government argued they were "signs" and not "ads." After some negotiations between the OAG and the government, these billboards were deemed to be within the context of the GAA (OAG 2010, 403–4) and are now reviewable items. How governments use billboards and new modes of communication, including social media and Web-based marketing, has been underexplored by academics or policymakers.

Legislation is only one method of constraining advertising by government. In New Zealand, the Office of the Auditor General created and administers guidelines for government advertising campaigns. There are also guidelines for government advertising in its Cabinet manual, but like Ontario's GAA, the guidelines are broad. For example, ads have to be accurate, factual, and truthful; fair, honest, and impartial; and lawful and proper (Cabinet Office 2008, chap. 5). How these guidelines are defined and enforced is not stipulated.

In Canada, there are no federal legislative constraints, although the government is guided by its corporate communications policy and the federal identity program, both of which provide some parameters. Opposition parties have attempted to use other levers of the state, such as the ethics commissioner, but have had little success. In 2009, Liberal MP Martha Hall Findlay asked the commissioner to investigate her claim that the prime minister and various Cabinet ministers were in violation of the *Conflict of Interest Act*, which prohibited use of one's elected position for personal gain. She argued that the Conservatives' use of government advertising benefited their "private interests" as members of that party. The ethics commissioner dodged the question by rejecting the complaint on a technicality, arguing that the Conservative Party was not covered by the act because it was not a legal "person" and therefore could not have "private interests" (Canada 2010c, 4).

The massive spending by the federal government on advertising in 2010 and prior to the 2011 election suggests that there is a need for some oversight. This chapter has discussed some of the options used throughout Canada and around the world but argues that virtually all the constraints on government advertising are around expenditure rather than content. While cost is an issue for those concerned about public finance and transparent administration, the "work" of an ad is done through its content. A study of American political ads suggests that citizens do learn from advertising (Freedman, Franz, and Goldstein 2004). Ads can provide information; they can help create engagement by the use of emotion, which may motivate people to become more involved in politics; and they are good shorthand cues for those who have the least information. All of these functions can be applied to government advertising.

In short, advertisements by the state do matter. They do have a role to play in creating values of citizenship, are symbolic markers about the preoccupation of governments, and are an important element in government communication efforts. While governments are quick to point out the noble functions of advertising, past practice suggests that parties of all political stripes use advertising for more immediate partisan gain. The next wave of reform needs to impose some control over content, which, up to now, has been untameable.

NOTE

1 *Jacobellis v. Ohio*, 378 U.S. 184 (1964).

7 Political Funding Regimes and Political Communication

ROBERT MACDERMID

There can be little political communication without money. Money is the power to spend on the communication skills and resources to fashion influential political communication. We live in a media-saturated society, where almost all political communication is forced through the conduit of the news industry, shaped by the communication potential of the Internet or compressed into phone calls and messages. Money can demand the time of people who know how to produce words and images that cause insecurity and phrases that can placate it, people who can formulate implicit arguments in the shape of images or slogans, and people who know or half know through polls and focus groups the half-understood and largely constructed apprehensions that people have about political ideas and persons.

Without money to purchase the skills and time of experts who shape messages, manipulate images, and produce symbols or to purchase broadcast airtime or newspaper ads and generate Internet traffic or social media activity, political communication in the publicity state is limited, and the ability to continuously communicate a message in various forms and ways is tightly constrained. The hundreds of millions of dollars spewed out to communicate political arguments that public spending is wasteful, that tar sands oil is environmentally benign, that taxes are too high, or that public health care is unsustainable speak to the power of those who can marshal resources to convey their messages over long periods and in a multitude of ways. In this sense, money seems always to be a precondition for political communication in democratic societies that, of course, look a lot more plutocratic when we think of it in this way.

The general point, that the wealthy can communicate their arguments much more effectively than others, also carries over to communication between political parties and citizens, the subject of this chapter. The financial regulation of Canadian federal political parties, the regime of rules that determines how much, from whom, and how money can be raised and spent, determines the ability of parties to communicate with and engage the electorate in democratic politics. Indeed, fundraising itself is a form of political communication. When disclosed, information regarding who gives how much money to what party or candidate communicates something to citizens about what interests that party or candidate represents. The fact that corporations, unions, banks, or the real estate development industry support one or two parties or candidates over all others is a revelation that those backers believe those parties or candidates are most likely to advance their interests. In addition, that moment of fundraising, "the ask," where the telephone fundraiser, the party's "bagman," or the fundraising letter communicates "the pitch" and asks for support, is an opportunity for communication to flow both to supporters and back to parties. Of course, the intimacy and the seriousness with which that feedback is considered varies from the fundraising bagman asking an individual for thousands or even hundreds of thousands of dollars to the letter in the mail that can never shed its impersonality and provides no more than standardized ways of responding, and nothing more empowering than ticking a box. In yet another way, political party fundraising and how it is conditioned by the set of rules created not by all parties, but by those parties in power, also determines a strategy of communication that begins to align with a strategy of fundraising. In other words, the need to raise money, and the existence of groups that are willing to provide it, shapes the messages that are communicated.

To understand how the regime of campaign finance rules can affect the form and content of political communication by parties – much of it is intended to persuade citizens to support policy positions that may not be in their best interests – we need to look closely at those rules and briefly at the messages parties have tried to convey, most visibly through election campaign advertising and in the growing volume of advertising and other methods of persuasion between election campaigns that play a key role in the permanent campaign in the modern state. This chapter also endeavours to redress the limited amount of scholarship on campaign finance, which has a considerable, if not overriding, impact on political success.

Recent Campaign Finance Changes in Canada

Campaign and party finance rules are often the ground upon which broader political appeals are fought in the most practical sense. The fact that Canadian finance rules have changed frequently in the past 35 years, that each province has a unique set of rules, and that municipal campaign finance regimes vary from province to province and sometimes even within provinces suggests that every set of rules is the result of a compromise or, more likely, the imposition of a set of rules favourable to the party in office and the interests that support it. Every arrangement has a unique history that reflects the power of different groups to mobilize votes and resources in support of a preferred set of rules. Campaign and party finance regimes that predominately represent business interests tend to have largely unregulated and secretive systems that hide the extent of reliance on large donors. For much of Canadian history, this was the pattern at the federal level, and until party deficits began to pile up as a result of repeated elections and minority governments in the 1960s, the regime remained closed and secretive (Paltiel 1970; Stanbury 1991). Alberta provincial politics was captured decades ago by energy, mining, forestry, and related interests and continues to have a party financing system that is open to influence through large contributions and, until very recently, was somewhat opaque. The UK political finance system was, until 2000, similarly reliant on large donors and intensely secretive.

Reforms to campaign and party finance rules have three main causes. Often they are a response to the surfacing of corruption, evidence that political influence is being bought. When reforms have occurred in Canada, they have often been in response to scandals such as the 1873 Canadian Pacific Railway scandal, the Beauharnois scandal of 1930, or more recently, the sponsorship scandal. Changes can also occur when the largest parties are in debt and cannot raise enough money to conduct electoral politics in an advantageous manner. This is often the result of increasingly expensive campaign technologies such as polling, television advertising, or image-making leaders' tours that quickly exhaust the financial resources of parties. At other times, reform is the result of a number of elections in a short amount of time that plunge the major parties into debt that inadequate fundraising cannot repay. In these instances, reforms are intended to give the parties access to new funding sources, most often state subsidies. On other occasions, reforms, or rather changes, are made by governing parties to create or cement a fundraising advantage over opponents. This might include raising or removing contribution limits or admitting more funding from corporations by parties that are favoured by wealthy interests, or it could include the reverse: banning corporate money and setting very low contribution limits to stem the influence of the wealthy.

On limiting funding from organized groups, three provincial examples come to mind. First and foremost, in Ontario in 1999, the Mike Harris Conservative administration changed Ontario's campaign finance laws to take advantage of corporate wealth that supported his neoliberal policy directions (MacDermid 2000). Harris raised the total limits from $14,000 to $25,000, allowed parties to spend more on central campaigns, and even redefined election expenses to exclude polling and research costs and leaders' tour expenses. Even though a limit was placed on how much one could contribute in an election period (set at $4,000), the limit applied to each and every general election and by-election campaign, so those with the money to do so could spend up to the limit multiple times (MacDermid 1999, 11).

In 2001, the Manitoba New Democratic Party (NDP) government did the opposite and banned corporate and union contributions, established a contribution limit of $3,000, and limited expenditures on campaign advertising (Thurlow 2008, 8). Quebec has banned corporate contributions to political parties since the first election of the Parti Québécois and limited contributions to $1,000 in any year (3). In 2010, the newly elected Nova Scotia NDP government legislated a ban on corporate and union contributions and imposed a $5,000 contribution limit.

In the discussion that follows about recent reforms, we should keep all of these reasons for change mentioned above in play as ways of understanding the reforms and the forces that lay behind them.

Before the federal reforms of 2004–6, federal parties were often in debt, sometimes for several years following an election, whether they won or not. The debt was usually the result of large loans from banks to fund the central election campaign and often took several years to retire, leaving little time to build up a reserve for the next campaign. Any contemplated expensive broadcast advertising between elections was often out of the question, given the limited financial resources. Parties borrow substantial sums of money to fund election campaigns. Once campaigns begin, supporters contribute to the central party and candidate campaigns. However, to pay for the immediate costs of the campaign, and particularly the advertising costs that escalate as soon as the campaign begins, parties have historically turned to the banks for loans to start the campaign. For example, in 2008, the Conservatives borrowed $15 million to start their campaign (Elections Canada 2008), and the Liberals borrowed the same amount in 2011. These borrowings are always made in anticipation of funds raised during the campaign and in the years following. This can be an uncertain basis for borrowing. Parties and candidates habitually and perhaps necessarily overestimate future election success and rarely consider how failure will limit future fundraising. Before 2004 and the inception of the party allowance (discussed later in this chapter), parties often spent several years paying off campaign debts, crippling their ability to advertise and communicate with voters and party members between elections. Typically, party offices, staff, and expenditures shrank between elections, as all fundraising went to pay off the past election debt. New leaders often inherit parties divided by leadership battles or defeated by the electorate and must spend years fundraising to pay off party debts. The merger of the Alliance and Progressive Conservative Parties weighed down the new Conservative Party with debt from its predecessors, debt mostly incurred in 2000 that was not paid off until 2008. While the sums parties now borrow to underwrite campaigns have grown, paying off those debts is much easier, given the Liberal and Conservative reforms of 2004 and 2006.

Before those reforms, a good portion of fundraising by the Liberal and Progressive Conservative Parties was accomplished by a party bagman (almost without exception a male), a party insider who almost always came from the business community, preferably Bay Street, or had very good connections to the business elite. The bagman's job was to collect very large contributions from the very small set of corporations and wealthy individuals who had the wherewithal and interest to support and influence government policy. This meant most large corporations and particularly the banks that were ever sensitive to the regulatory hand of the federal government. The bagman could raise a very large amount of money in a very short time and at almost no cost since all it required was the bagman's donated time.

The bagman was also a communications conduit to the party leadership. The bagman not only brought the message of the party but also relayed the feelings or, more specifically, the policy inclinations and wishes of the contributors back to the party leadership. The amounts the bagman collected were a gauge of the business community's approval of the party's actions. Recent Canadian party leaders Brian Mulroney, Paul Martin, and Jean Chrétien have all been bona fide members of the corporate elite, while one of Stephen Harper's jobs before entering formal politics was as president of the conservative lobby organization the National Citizens Coalition, which at one time battled the government on election finance reform (National Citizens Coalition 2013). These leaders communicated with corporate elites on a regular basis, both formally and socially, and were actively involved in fundraising. Communication in this kind of fundraising is very personal, close, two-way, and receptive. Raising large amounts of money from a few donors is quite different from the one-way, standardized party-to-supporter communication techniques for raising small sums from party supporters.

The political finance regime at the federal level in Canada has been extensively rewritten in a very short span between 2003 and 2006 with changes from three successive administrations, the Chrétien and Martin Liberal governments and the Harper Conservative administration. The reforms were not the result of a long-term policy process that welcomed extensive public input on central democratic questions about how parties and candidates should be funded but were the initiatives of particular administrations, apparently in response to political crises and partisan opportunities. A few of the reforms or variants of them had been suggested in the 1991 Royal Commission on Electoral Reform and Party Financing and in its supporting academic research, but other reforms had not been publicly debated prior to their inclusion in legislation (Canada 1991).[1]

In 2004, Bill C-24 (*An Act to amend the Canada Elections Act and the Income Tax Act*), a Chrétien Liberal initiative, radically reformed the federal campaign system (see Table 7.1). The bill introduced limits on contributions where there had been none and where annual contributions of over $100,000 from corporations, individuals, and unions were not infrequent. From 2004 onward, individual contributors were limited to giving an annual total of $5,000 to a central party and its candidates, constituency associations, and nomination races. Even more surprising, given the Liberals' past reliance on corporate money, Bill C-24 limited corporations and unions to a total of $1,000 per year. This radically changed the campaign and party fundraising terrain, for both the Liberal and Progressive Conservative Parties had depended on corporations for at least half of their finance. In contrast, the Reform Party, later reshaped into the Alliance party, had cultivated a broad base of individual supporters, and by the time it merged with the Progressive

Table 7.1. Key changes to federal election finance, 2004–12

2004 (Liberals)

- A contribution limit (where there had previously been none) of a total of $5,000 per year from individuals to any one party, constituency association, nomination contestant, or candidate in any year.

- A contribution limit (where there had previously been none) of a total of $1,000 per year from corporations and unions to any one party, constituency association, nomination contestant, or candidate in any year.

- The creation of a central party allowance of $1.75 per year for every vote won at the preceding election.

- Contribution and expenditure limits and the party allowance were allowed to rise with inflation.

- An increase in the subsidization of central party election campaign expenditures from 22.5 per cent to 50 per cent and candidate expenditures from 50 per cent to 60 per cent.

- An expenditure limit for candidate nomination races of 20 per cent of the candidate election expenditure limit.

- The requirement for the disclosure of contributions and expenditures for party leadership and candidate nomination races.

- The political contribution tax credit, the portion of a contribution returned to the contributor, was substantially increased to 30 per cent.

- The election campaign spending limit for central parties was raised by 12 per cent.

2006 (Conservatives)

- A complete ban on contributions from corporations and unions to political parties, candidates, nomination races, and leadership contests.

- A contribution limit of $1,000 per year from individuals to any one political party.

- A contribution limit of $1,000 per year from individuals to local constituency parties, candidates, and nomination contestants of any one political party.

- All contribution limits indexed to inflation.

- A requirement that political parties file quarterly financial reports where previously they had filed only annual and election campaign reports.

2012 (Conservatives)

- The central party allowance to be phased out by the end of 2014.

Sources: Act to Amend the Canada Elections Act and Income Tax Act, 2004; Accountability Act, 2006.

Conservative Party in 2003, corporate support was just under 25 per cent of its funding.

Bill C-24 also introduced a party allowance to replace the now very much reduced corporate money. The party allowance, almost entirely for parties with elected representatives (the one exception was the Green Party, which in 2006 and 2008 won enough votes to secure a public subsidy), was to come from general state revenues and was initially set at $1.75 per vote won by the party at the prior general election and continuing for each year or part thereof until the next election. The allowance was to be paid quarterly to the central party and most or all of the allowance stayed at the party centre with very little, if any, distributed to constituency parties (see Coletto and Eagles 2011; Coletto, Jansen, and Young 2011). The allowance gave the parties stable, predictable quarterly and annual incomes. Parties could now devise budgets for the inter-election years that did not depend wholly on the inevitable ups and downs of fundraising, party popularity, passing scandals, or things such as leadership races that tended to siphon away inter-election finances.

Bill C-24 also very significantly increased subsidies for election campaign expenses. Candidates who attracted at least 10 per cent of the votes now got 60 per cent of their campaign expenses back, and central parties would get a subsidy of 50 per cent for their expenditures as well. The change more than doubled the previous 22.5 per cent subsidy for central party expenses.

The 2004 reforms also boosted the tax credit for contributions by about 30 per cent, raising the maximum credit from $500 to $650, a benefit to the very small group of largest contributors, those who give more than $800 to a party every year.[2] The tax credit, where contributors receive a portion of their contributions back when they file their taxes, is a way of funnelling state subsidies (in the form of tax expenditures) to parties through what are effectively loans made by citizens to the parties. It has helped parties raise money in small amounts from citizens by giving a large part of the contribution back to the contributors at tax filing time. The tax credit should encourage parties and candidates to create a broad base of financial supporters, not to mention the claim that it increased citizen involvement in politics, albeit at a fairly passive level. However, as Tables 7.2 and 7.3 show, building on its Reform Party base, the Conservatives have done this far more successfully than any other party and boast a list of financial supporters that is almost three times the length of the Liberal list in 2009.

Bill C-24 also raised campaign spending limits, required more frequent reporting of party finances, and brought into the campaign regulatory framework the finances of constituency associations and nomination and party leadership races that had, up until then, been unregulated and largely hidden. This increased disclosure could be seen as the quid pro quo for the massive increase of public funds now pouring into parties.

While parties continued to raise funds from individuals, corporations, and unions until funds from corporations and unions were banned in 2006, they now had a steady basic income achieved without incurring the costs of raising funds. Party fundraising tends to be a very expensive exercise partly because the tradition has been to hold large and expensive dinners where a significant part of the ticket price goes to pay the cost of the event itself. It is not unusual for parties or candidates to spend $1 to raise $2 or less, a ratio that Revenue Canada would consider unacceptable if it were reported by a registered charity.

The reasons for the Liberal reforms of 2004 still need to be examined closely. One interpretation is that the Liberals were responding to allegations of kickbacks in what became known as the sponsorship scandal, a scheme that illegally returned money from government advertising contracts in Quebec to the Liberal Party (see the chapter by Kozolanka and the chapter by Rubin and Kozolanka for related discussions on this scandal). The Liberal Party president of the day, Stephen LeDrew, called the changes as "dumb as a bag of hammers" and led the corporate interests within the Liberal Party in a prolonged but unsuccessful campaign against them (*The Economist* 2003a, 1). It may have been that Chrétien and his advisors – and it is not clear who led on this file, as Chrétien (2007) says nothing about it in his memoirs – believed that the unified Conservative Party would become the party favoured by the business community and gain an increasingly large share of money from corporations. Some elements of the business community may have withheld contributions from the two parties on the Right in the 2001–3 period and tried to starve them into an eventual marriage. The pattern of contributions from major contributors such as the banks certainly supports this suggestion. For the Liberals, reducing those renewed corporate contributions to a unified Right-wing party and instituting a party allowance perhaps seemed one way of negating a potential Conservative advantage.

Attempts to explain the Liberal reforms through the lens of the dominant parties working together as a cartel, a now conventional explanation of parties' actions, have had limited success (Katz 2011; Young and Jansen 2011). A clearer understanding of the motives behind the Liberal-inspired reforms is a future project for interested researchers that will require interviews with the key actors who have so far remained silent.

The Harper Conservative reforms of 2006, part of the *Accountability Act*, banned all contributions from unions and corporations and reduced the maximum annual contributions from individuals to $1,000 to each central party and another $1,000 in total to the riding associations, nomination contestants, and candidates of each registered party (see Table 7.1).[3] While an annual limit of $2,000 spread across a party is far beyond the average contribution size and much more than 99.9 per cent of citizens would ever consider or be able to give to a party, this makes federal contribution law one of the most restrictive in the country, far below provincial limits (with the exception of Quebec) and even less than some municipal campaign contribution limits.[4]

The reforms of 2004 and 2006 changed the way parties raised money, who they raised it from and how they communicated with those contributors, and arguably how parties related to the part of the electorate that is likely to fund them.

Those who make a contribution to a political party or candidate are a very small subset of the electorate. While in recent years, the Conservatives have drawn an ever-increasing number of contributions, many of these are from the same donor and the number of contributors is very small. For example, in 2009, about 20,300 individuals made a contribution to the party that was greater than $200; that is less than half of 1 per cent of all of those who had voted for the party in 2008.

While the party allowance provided a constant base of funding between elections, there was still competition to raise money above the allowance and create or close a gap between the parties that was greater or lesser than the now-funded voter total difference – a difference that during a minority government might not be that great.

Table 7.2 gives a snapshot how the parties adapted to the reforms. The Conservatives, drawing on the broad base of individual supporters established by the Reform and Alliance predecessors, have in several years raised twice as much money as the Liberals and left the other parties far behind. The Liberals have yet to successfully establish a system for raising small amounts from a large number of people. Battles over the party leadership have left the party divided – never a good thing for fundraising – and the party administration has not successfully built a broad base of consistent contributors. This may have to do with the party's "big tent" appeals in which all who are loosely small-L liberal are welcome, as opposed to the Conservatives' strategy of building a coalition of issue voters who feel strongly enough about a single issue – for example, the abolition of the gun registry – and who can be

Table 7.2. Contributions to Canadian federal central parties, 2004–12

Year	Conservative	Liberal	NDP	Green	BQ
2012	$17,251,793	$7,833,015	$7,922,394	$1,640,083	$506,119
2011	$22,727,706	$9,890,405	$7,382,364	$1,726,640	$1,016,285
2010	$17,408,565	$7,363,082	$4,361,513	$1,296,206	$834,548
2009	$17,702,401	$9,087,756	$4,006,641	$1,863,155	$858,226
2008	$21,177,952	$6,318,031	$5,415,236	$1,292,385	$923,265
2007	$16,983,000	$5,397,297	$3,912,029	$972,022	$593,036
2006	$18,631,685	$11,261,293	$3,954,501	$962,927	$689,682
2005	$17,915,780	$9,121,716	$5,073,310	$409,357	$965,089
2004	$12,907,357	$6,085,121	$5,187,142	$351,031	$1,051,851

Sources: The figures in the table are taken from the audited financial statements of the respective political parties and do not include government transfers, membership fees, or other sales revenue (Elections Canada 2013).

squeezed repeatedly for funds. I link this idea to the Conservatives' campaign advertising below.

Table 7.2 also highlights the failure of Bloc Québécois fundraising efforts. In 2009, the Green Party, without representation in the House of Commons, raised more than twice as much money as the Bloc. The Bloc had the lowest 2009 average contribution, just above $100, and relied very heavily on state subsidies, as Table 7.3 shows. It is hard to disentangle whether this is an indication of inept fundraising techniques or a Quebec fundraising culture that has relied heavily at the provincial level on state finance, small donations, and relatively low levels of campaign spending. Between 2006 and 2010, while leading minority governments, Harper often complained that the party allowance gave the Bloc the ability to recharge its finances and constantly threaten a future election. The Bloc's stunningly poor showing in the 2011 election coupled with the phasing out of the party allowance will mean that the Bloc will have to significantly broaden its base of individual funders if it is to run a competitive campaign in the future.

One result of the 2004–6 reforms was that the Liberal and Conservative Parties shifted in two years from a heavy reliance on large corporate contributions to an even heavier reliance on public funds. This was most obviously the case with the creation of party allowances and less

Table 7.3. Canadian federal central party funding sources, 2009

2009	Conservative	Liberal	NDP	Green	Bloc Québécois
Total contributions	$17,702,201	$9,060,916	$4,008,521	$1,123,095	$621,126
Total contributors	101,385	37,876	23,704	9,115	6,052
Total contributions greater than $200	$9,794,225	$6,926,592	$2,456,462	$631,355	$271,711
Total contributors greater than $200	20,314	10,920	5,876	1,457	646
Tax credit value on contributions greater than $200[1]	$6,526,198	$4,243,995	$1,691,670	$434,378	$193,848
Total contributions less than or equal to $200	$7,907,976	$2,134,324	$1,551,709	$491,014	$349,416
Total contributors less than or equal to $200	81,071	25,504	17,604	7,589	5,401
Estimated value of tax credits on contributions less than or equal to $200[1]	$5,930,982	$1,600,743	$1,163,782	$368,261	$262,062
Annual party allowance	$10,351,071	$7,215,857	$4,998,191	$1,863,155	$2,742,215
Total public funding	$22,808,251	$13,060,595	$7,853,643	$2,665,794	$3,198,125
Total party revenue[2]	$29,168,153	$19,990,407	$10,085,163	$3,055,128	$3,604,866
% public funding 2009	78.2	65.3	77.9	87.3	88.7
% public funding 2008	79.5	89.2	89.0	84.6	95.2

Source: Elections Canada (2009).
Public funding sources are shown in italics.
This table does not include money raised by the parties' constituency associations.

[1] These totals are calculated by applying the tax credit to the actual disclosed contributions and assumes that all individuals claimed the refundable tax credit.

[2] These totals include contributions, the party allowance, membership fees, and other income.

obviously as a result of the enhanced tax credit. By 2009, as Table 7.3 shows, all the parties relied on public money for more than three-quarters of their funding with the one exception of the Liberal Party, where it approached two-thirds of all funding.

As the second to last row of Table 7.3 shows for 2009, a not atypical year in the post-2004 period, all the parties, including the Conservative Party, have come to rely very heavily on the different sources of public funding. Jansen and Young (2010) conducted a similar analysis in the election year of 2008 and found that with election subsidies included, in some cases percentages were even higher, as the last row of Table 7.3 indicates. The Bloc tops the charts with almost $9 out of $10 coming from state subsidies in 2009, but the Conservative Party is not far behind, at almost $8 out of $10. While the Harper government has specifically attacked the party allowance, as I discuss later, the party took in more money in 2009 as a result of the tax credit subsidy than it did from the party allowance.

The Aftermath of the Reforms

The rule changes in Bill C-24 and the *Accountability Act* have continued to be the grounds for partisan struggle. Following re-election in 2008, the Conservative minority government's "Economic and Fiscal Statement" in November, mostly a response to the crisis in the financial system, took the opportunity to propose the cutting of the party allowance as an austerity measure in the face of collapsing public finances and an escalating deficit. The finance minister sanctimoniously intoned,

> Canadians pay their own bills, and for some Canadians that is getting harder to do. Political parties should pay their own bills too, and not with excessive tax dollars. Even during the best of economic times, parties should count primarily on the financial support of their own members and their own donors. Today, our Government is eliminating the $1.95-per-vote taxpayer subsidy for politicians and their parties, effective April 1, 2009. There will be no free ride for political parties. There never was. The freight was being paid by the taxpayer. This is the last stop on the route.[5] (Canada 2008, 5–6)

The savings would have been minuscule in comparison to the burgeoning deficit, and the intent was transparently partisan. The Conservatives saw the financial crisis as the excuse to hobble the opposition and greatly improve their own chances to massively outspend the opposition before and during the next election. The opposition parties were furious with the government's attempt to change the rules without consultation. The Liberals, who had put in place the party allowance, were incensed by the move. The Bloc Québécois depended on the per-vote party allowance in nonelection years for as much as 75 per cent of its revenue and faced the prospect of layoffs of party workers and near organizational collapse. As much as anything, the threat to cut the allowance joined the opposition in a common cause to defeat the government, based on what they considered to be undemocratic reforms that constrained the work of political parties, especially smaller ones. Only a contentious proroguing of Parliament in December 2008 saved Harper's minority administration from defeat. When the Conservatives returned to Parliament with a Throne Speech, the plan to cut the per-vote party allowance had disappeared.

But the Conservatives had not given up. Their 2011 election platform promised to abolish the party allowance: "We have always opposed direct subsidies; and a Stephen Harper-led majority Government will phase out the direct subsidy of political parties over the next three years" (Conservative Party of Canada 2011, 63). During the campaign, Harper said, It is partly in my view this per-vote subsidy – this enormous cheque that keeps piling into political parties every month, whether they raise any money or not – that means we're constantly having campaigns ... The war chests are always full for another campaign. You lose one; immediately in come the cheques and you are ready for another one even if you didn't raise a dime" (Chase, Galloway, and Perreaux 2011, A8).

The idea that the per-vote party allowances rather than government policy and actions had led to the fall of two minority governments was overstating the case. The Conservatives still had a huge fundraising lead over the Liberals, with or without the party subsidy. The real target was the Bloc Québécois, and raising the issue again had as much to do with Harper reminding his supporters that the Quebec separatist party was being funded with everyone's tax dollars. It must have been vexing to the Conservatives that a party dedicated to separatism could, with so little money, help thwart their majority ambitions.

Conservative opposition to the per-vote party allowance – or "subsidy," as they like to refer to it – is no doubt ideologically and politically motivated. But it is also hypocritical. The Conservatives have never suggested removing campaign expenditure subsidies that in 2008 brought

$9.7 million to the party or the massive subsidy to parties provided by the political contribution tax credit (Elections Canada 2008). Following their 2011 election win, one of the first actions of the majority Conservative administration was to change the *Canada Elections Act* to begin phasing out the per-vote party allowance, reducing it to zero by 2015.

Some, like Thurlow, have suggested that the now defunct party allowance encouraged parties to campaign more broadly and against the incentives of the first past the post electoral system that encourages parties to focus their campaign efforts in ridings that they can win (Flanagan 2010). Perhaps the allowance and the anticipation of a per-vote subsidy did encourage parties to seek votes everywhere rather than just in seats in winnable ridings. But falling national turnout figures suggest otherwise, and a closer examination of this thesis would require a look at riding vote totals, local candidate expenditures, and financial transfers between the central and local parties and candidate campaigns.

According to Boatright (2009, 37–8), another unexpected result of changes to elections acts that limit or eliminate contributions from corporations and unions is that some groups, such as organized labour and advocacy organizations, have tended to increase their work at the grass-roots level or use the media more often to communicate their political and electoral goals. This certainly seems a likely response by unions in particular, although union membership has never translated into votes for the NDP. Corporations and business-sponsored organizations such as the Fraser Institute have always invested heavily to frame the political agenda (Gutstein 2009; see also the chapter by Gutstein in this volume). However, there has been no large upsurge in regulated third-party election period spending since 2004. We do not know where the millions of dollars of corporate money that once flowed into the Liberal and Progressive Conservative Parties have gone, although lobbying activities and other forms of influence seem a reasonable guess.

The "In-and-out" Court Case

While the Conservatives have raised far more money than the Liberals since 2004, as Table 7.2 shows, during election campaigns they were and are limited to spending the same amount, a situation that must have irked them. The per-voter spending limit for the central party's campaigns makes it difficult to translate a fundraising edge into as clear a campaign period spending advantage.[6] Even if the Liberals did not raise as much as the Conservatives, they could still borrow money during the campaign, pay it off afterwards with the help of the per-vote party allowance, and come very close to Conservative Party spending totals. This may, in the 2006 election, have led the Conservatives to devise a scheme to circumvent the central party expenditure limit and allow them to spend more on television advertising. In 2011, Elections Canada finally charged the party and four leading party figures with spending more than the central party limit in 2006. Prior to going to court, the Conservative Party and the individuals involved pled guilty to the violation of the expenditure limits and the filing of false financial statements. More than five years later, the party was fined $52,000 and the individuals involved, including two Conservative senators, had all charges dropped (Payton 2011).

The Conservative scheme took advantage of the ability to transfer money back and forth between the central party and constituency parties. Parties often transfer contributions received at one level of the party to another level. The central party will often levy a charge on constituency parties to pay for some part or specific element of the central party campaign. Or, the central party may transfer funds to constituency parties to assist in the running of a local campaign, especially if there is a high-profile candidate and the riding association has not been able to raise sufficient funds to run a competitive campaign. These types of transfers are permitted by campaign and party finance legislation and are important to maintaining central and local party structures and visible campaigns in a region where a party may not be popular. However, the Conservatives transferred funds to a number of ridings they knew would not approach constituency spending limits and then had the local ridings transfer the money back to the centre as an expenditure for local advertising. The "Agreed Statement of Facts"[7] confirmed that the money did not go to locally made and local candidate-centred advertising but back to the central party for its national advertising campaign, thus allowing them to, in effect, exceed the limit on central campaign expenditures.

Fundraising as Political Communication: Conservative Campaign Ads

Several times above, I have referred to a connection between political fundraising and political communication. This relationship is increasingly important in the modern publicity state where permanent campaigning is deemed by political parties to be necessary to maintain public approval and consent. Not only does a party fundraise in order to communicate during a campaign and to pay for the repetitive 30-second spot ads, but a party can also communicate in order to raise funds. In other words, campaign ads can contain messages that are targeted at very specific segments of a party's supporters, particularly those groups that are most likely to respond by contributing to the party. (For an in-depth history and analysis of political advertising, see Rose's chapter in this volume.)

The 2008 Conservative election campaign advertising budget was one of the largest ever. The party spent almost $10.6 million on advertising, about 55 per cent of its total budget, outspending the Liberals and NDP by about $2 million. At least 14 different English television ads appeared, and there may have been regional variants as well. Some of these ads were translated into other languages and ran on channels with Hindi or Mandarin programming. The 11 ads in French were thematically very different, a practice that has become commonplace since the Bloc Québécois created a unique, competitive situation in Quebec.

The number of ads aired by parties during election campaigns has been growing over the past 25 to 30 years as the cost of production has declined and the speed of production has accelerated. In the 1980s and 1990s, parties usually made no more than 10 ads, and often fewer and those tended to be fairly broad appeals to a wide audience. Technological advances have made the almost immediate production of ads possible, and rather than being prepared in advance of the campaign, ads are now created during the campaign to respond to specific situations, such as negative ads launched by competitors. In addition, many of the simple ads used today can be produced at a very low cost.

Ads and ad buys, the quantity and placement of specific ads in a growing multichannel television universe, have allowed parties to target specific audiences according to channel demographics. In the 2004 campaign, all the parties, including the Bloc, took advantage of specialty channels, running ads on some of the following channels: APTN (Aboriginal Peoples Television Network), Discovery, Vision, the Women's Channel, and the various sports channels (MacDermid 2006). It is very likely that political party election campaign advertising has grown on these channels and in programming that offers advertisers very specialized, albeit usually small, audiences, as television channel fragmentation of the viewing audience allows parties to narrowcast specific messages to specific groups of people without the need to explain these messages to other nonviewers.

The Conservative Party's adaption to the new campaign finance rules and its bias towards raising small amounts of money from a large number of individuals followed a logical pursuit of groups that were strongly committed to a particular issue and had a proven track record of financing organization and communication around that issue. The gun lobby, the pro-Israel lobby, and sections of new immigrant communities had all demonstrated abilities to organize and financially support the communication of their issues. It made sense then that the Conservatives should speak directly to those groups, appeal to their issues, and reassure them that the Conservative Party would unequivocally speak for them. One of the vehicles the party used to do this was a series of campaign ads that has been dubbed "the sweater vest series" after the attire worn by Harper.

Each of the seven ads opens with the same waving Canadian flag filling the screen and the same solo piano tune that sounds like a hundred other soundtracks – easy, nostalgic music that swells to strings at the end. Each ad is staged as what might be a conversation with the prime minister, who appears causally attired in an open-necked blue shirt and sweater vest, seated in a wingback chair in a palatial room, apparently responding to one or more interviewers or perhaps people – that part is not clear. The attire and situation suggest a leader at ease. The fact that he is seated when important messages are always delivered standing, the casual attire, the demonstrative use of the hands, the apparently shy averting of the eyes, and the smile that never escapes feeling just a bit manufactured are all intended to convey authenticity. This translation of a politician from the formal attire and surroundings of the House of Commons or a formal speech, where we are most likely to see him nightly, to what we are encouraged to think of as how he appears as outside, reflects what many would see as that realm of phony duplicitous politicians. Of course, it is in just these fleeting 30 seconds, with viewers' disbeliefs suspended, that ads do their convincing.

The target groups for the messages in these ads are some of the organized groups that the Conservatives drew on or have tried to convert to constant funders of the party. We can only guess which groups are targeted, but some come readily to mind. One of the ads, "family is everything," is an obvious appeal to social conservatives, whereas the crime and punishment ad appeals to the law and order faction. Others are possibly more distant in their connection to fractions of the electorate being courted by the Conservatives. For instance, for a number of years, they had struggled mightily to win the Toronto and Montreal Jewish vote away from the Liberals but without a great deal of success until they dropped Canada's long-standing policy of balance in the Middle East and adopted a pro-Israel stance. The ad "Canada must take a stand in the world" may have been a way of communicating that issue to an important group of voters and funders.

Lessig (2011, 98–9) describes how American parties and candidates have taken more extreme policy positions after realizing that those who hold those positions are often the best source of campaign finance: "The more campaign funds an issue inspires, the more extremely it gets framed ... So long as there is a demand for endless campaign cash, one simple way to supply it is to sing the message that inspires the money – even if that message is far from the views of most." Similarly, and again in the US context, Johnson (2010, 890, 906) notes that "an incumbent's ideological extremism improves his or her chances of raising a greater proportion of funds from individual donors in general and small individual contributors in particular. Extremism is not the only way to raise money [... but] to some legislators, extremism is an advantage."

While there is still much research to be done on the effects of campaign and party financing reforms of the last few years, tying together the changing sources of funding, party messaging, and the rising importance of single-issue groups may tell us a lot about how the reforms have changed our politics in a state obsessed with publicity.

Conclusion

Following the Conservatives' election win in 2011, one of the first acts of the newly formed Conservative majority government was to phase out the per-vote party allowance over four years. The broad base of Conservative supporters and the relative wealth of those supporters will ensure that the party is not outspent at future elections, at least until the other parties can adapt to the new fundraising regime. But can they? The Liberals' centrist, brokerage party heritage has left them without a strong funding base rooted in issue groups willing to finance the party. The social conservative base that is regularly harvested by Harper's statements and policies provides support for Conservative advertising between and in future elections. One should not forget that much of the television advertising that drove negative appraisals of Liberal leaders Dion and Ignatieff occurred between election campaigns, when spending is unregulated. Ironically, at the time of its greatest success with the election of their leader, the Green Party will lose the funding that was significant in bringing it to prominence. It seems likely that future Green Party campaigns will be more modest and the party may have reached its zenith. The Bloc Québécois's future seems more likely to be influenced by the decline of separatist support than by the loss of the per-vote party allowance – but the two go hand in hand. The NDP, while the official opposition for the first time in 2011, has not been able to build a broad base of individual supporters in the union movement or among workers. In fact, the party is running away from that base, as it seemingly aspires to replace the Liberals as the brokerage party of the centre-Left. From a party funding perspective, that may condemn the NDP to a very unequal contest with the Conservatives.

Political finance regimes to some extent determine the breadth of democratic discourse within party politics. The more open and supportive finance regimes are of minority voices and new parties, the richer and more diverse the dialogue and the more likely citizens are to get involved. The 2004 and 2006 reforms supported these goals, but the more recent end to the party allowance has moved the regime in the opposite direction. The in-and-out scandal and the emerging robocall scandal[8] suggest that parties continue to seek partisan advantage through the manipulation of the campaign finance and election rules and with the help of generally lax enforcement provisions. While the per-vote party allowance will disappear before the next election, it may well reappear following it if the Conservatives are defeated. It is even conceivable that corporate funding will find its way back into the system in the future. The history of party and campaign finance reform suggests that the search for partisan advantage is unceasing, regardless of the effect on participatory democratic politics.

NOTES

1 Jenson (1991) discussed the importance of state funding in building responsive parties in the research studies that accompanied the Royal Commission. The commission's research remains virtually unique in its history and depth on electoral finance in Canada, having devoted four of its 23 volumes to it.
2 In 2009, the average contribution to the central organizations of the four parliamentary parties was about $185.

3 By 2011, these inflation-indexed amounts had risen to $1,100 and $2,200 in total.
4 For example, the limit for contributions to campaigns for the mayor of Toronto is $2,500.
5 The inflation-indexed per-vote party allowance had risen to $1.95 and reached $2 by 2011.
6 In 2011, central party spending was limited to $0.70 multiplied by an indexation factor of about 1.3, or about $0.91 per elector where the party nominated a candidate.
7 The "Agreed Statement of Facts" can be found in the *Sentencing Digest for the 2006 Election,* on the Elections Canada Web site at http://www.elections.ca.
8 At the time of writing, reports had surfaced that "robocalls" (automated phone calls) to voters in some federal ridings during the 2011 election had misdirected some identified Liberal voters to incorrect or non-existent voting stations. Such irregularities were alleged to have taken place in eight ridings in Ontario in which Liberals and Conservatives were in a tight race. Elections Canada is still investigating and one Conservative Party campaign worker has been charged with violations of the Canada Elections Act.

8 Domestic Brand Politics and the Modern Publicity State

RICHARD NIMIJEAN

As other chapters in this collection demonstrate, the nature of political communication has changed in the era of the modern publicity state. Rather than simply providing information, the modern publicity state focuses on the promotion of its activities. Through issue definition, the modern publicity state attempts to persuade citizens of the merits of its actions in order to get society to agree on how to approach issues of the day. This has important democratic implications, as elected *governments* consisting of representatives of political parties use *state* resources obtained from the citizenry to advance narrow partisan goals. Thus, public funds can be used to advance private agendas.[1]

The emergence of the modern publicity state has coincided with the appearance of a new form of political communication: domestic brand politics. Inspired by an emerging literature on nation branding, this approach shows how governments use lessons from branding nations globally to change how citizens perceive their governments (Nimijean 2006b). In the era of domestic brand politics, politicians use issues central to the national political culture to create an emotional attachment between government policies and public opinion. Elements of national identity – such as symbols and "national values" – connect policy and citizens. While this may be seen as a normal dimension of political communication, it affects the quality of democratic practice, for the government in power is able to use state resources, notably state-sponsored public opinion research, to identify and track public opinion and then reshape public policy in ways that resonate with the electorate.

There is a strong connection between analyses of the modern publicity state and domestic brand politics. They both demonstrate that contemporary emphases on communication, branding, and image management have reached new heights: institutional restructuring of the state allows governing parties to use communication and marketing techniques, which are increasingly integrated into the daily operations of government, to gain and cement their hold on power.[2] The communication of a national brand (or an element thereof) to a national audience can be politically motivated, reflecting the concerns of critics of the modern publicity state. Indeed, domestic political branding accentuates their concerns.

Nation Branding and Domestic Brand Politics

Nation branding is a recent state technique allowing countries to stand out in a crowded international marketplace. Its emergence in the 1990s coincided with the end of the Cold War and the rise of globalization and neoliberalism. In this environment, people and capital became more mobile, and shifting political considerations affected the potential power and influence of countries. Governments realized that national image was increasingly a key determinant in their ability to attract skilled labour and foreign direct investment and increase their influence in international relations (van Ham 2001b; 2008).

There is an important domestic and historical dimension to nation branding exercises. For example, nation-branding exercises can increase national pride, as seen in the hosting of mega-events such as the Olympic Games or World's Fairs, even though the benefits are less tangible than anticipated (Whitson 2004; 2005; Whitson and Horne 2006). The nation branding literature largely treats domestic politics and policy implications as secondary considerations, addressing domestic concerns when they affect the truthfulness of a country's external message (among others, see Anholt 2004, 216–17; a notable exception is Tatevossian 2008). Governments must avoid the temptation of propaganda, instead building their image on a foundation of domestic accomplishments: "A [country's] reputation can never be constructed through communications, slogans and logos; it needs to be *earned*" (Anholt 2009; emphasis in original).

Might the new governmental emphasis on articulating its national image abroad also be aimed at domestic audiences? van Ham (2001b, 3–4) argues that state branding represents a shift in political paradigms to a "postmodern world of images and influence" that is "gradually supplanting nationalism." This affects not only how the state projects its image internationally but also how the state conducts its relations with citizens, who are influenced increasingly by consumerism and branding. A new state-citizen relationship has emerged, along busi-ness to customer lines, using techniques such as focus groups, re-sulting in the redefinition of citizens "as consumers of public policy" (van Ham 2001a). Governments use nationalist symbols for domes-tic purposes, though van Ham (ibid.) suggests that it is a response to citizen-consumer demands. The function of national identity therefore changes in the era of the brand state as "brand states exploit their heri-tage and history as logos and folk-motifs" (van Ham 2002, 263). Van Ham concludes that "location branding ... plays an increasingly impor-tant internal function of identity-formation" (ibid., 254); the national brand makes "citizens feel better and more confident about themselves by giving them a sense of belonging and a clear self-concept" (van Ham 2008, 131).

Alternatively, branding national identity may have become a substi-tute for public policy. For example, Rose, who has written a chapter on advertising for this volume, argues that van Ham's "sanguine view of marketing" requires examination, for it allows governments to focus on changing *perceptions* of policies rather than the policies themselves. He contends that state branding is a "deeply conservative development, one that sees propaganda replace policy" (Rose 2003, 12).

Rose's critique provides a useful starting point for examining the do-mestic brand state and its connections to the modern publicity state. It draws our attention to the link between public policy and government communications, emphasizing the articulation of values and national image. When articulated policies and programs are framed in terms of values, stated values can point to shortcomings in policy. This was the case in Canada during the 1990s, when neoliberal policies that resulted in growing socioeconomic inequality were presented as reflecting pro-gressive values of "caring and sharing" and a new value of "fiscal sover-eignty." This allowed governments to ignore demands from the citizenry for more extensive support for social policy (Nimijean 2005b, 46).

When the state links the externally projected national image to sup-posed values shared by its citizens, the paradoxical nature of national identity is reinforced: governments promote the celebration of ideals rather than the accomplishments that shaped the national identity, ignoring the current state of public policy. This creates rhetoric-reality gaps that undermine branding efforts (ibid.). Thus, while van Ham (2001b, 2) defines the brand state as "the outside world's ideas about a particular country," the concept must be expanded, for it also applies domestically, representing a citizen's idealized view of a country, complete with emotional resonance. For example, the idea of Canada as a country of peacekeeping, a core element of Canada's international image, resonates strongly with Canadians, even though in the past two decades Canada's participation in international peacekeeping has declined steadily, to the point that it now hardly performs peacekeeping and that the nature of Canadian peacekeeping has changed (Anker 2005; Simpson 2002).

The connection between international branding campaigns and the domestic political culture – the international-domestic nexus of nation branding (Nimijean 2006b) – is inherently political. There is a form of domestic governance that regulates political life (Howell 2005), and values and symbols linked to the international image can be used to shape policy choices. For example, the Harper government's promotion of Arctic sovereignty and Canadian patriotism is connected to the government's policy agenda of promoting the Canadian military. Thus, the planned $9 billion purchase of F-35 stealth fighter jets has been defended in terms of protecting Canadian sovereignty (Clark and Chase 2010). Most recently, the Harper government used a key Canadian symbol (the national flag) and a key day (National Flag Day) to honour two "Red Friday Ladies," who encouraged Canadians to wear the colours of the national flag (red and white) in order to show support for Canadian military members (Harper 2011a).

In the Canadian case, using the principles of nation branding to achieve policy goals not only transformed the state but also transformed domestic politics. The federal government promoted the celebration of Canadian ideals and identity at home, reflecting a growing sense of Canadian pride. In recent years, politicians have used the ideals and institutions promoted abroad to sell domestic policies.

Like governments of other countries, the Canadian federal government began a concerted branding campaign in the mid-1990s. The Liberal government of Jean Chrétien (1993–2003) tried to rebrand Canada's international image. Focus groups in the United States revealed that Canada was seen as a country of hockey, snow, and ice and not one of high technology and advanced capitalism, thus hurting its ability to attract foreign direct investment. The economic imperative was reinforced by the Liberal government's 1995 foreign policy statement, *Canada in the World*, which emphasized public diplomacy and the "export" of Canadian values. The federal government also emphasized diversity and official multiculturalism and the associated values of caring, sharing, tolerance, and hospitality. The goal was to communicate a new image emphasizing Canada as a place of economic dynamism and as a country in which all people of the world would feel at home and able to prosper economically (Nimijean 2006b). The Liberals portrayed Canada as a "middle power" that used "soft power" and peacekeeping, reflecting its values as a country of redistribution and social justice to both foreign and domestic audiences. This was captured in the speech "The Canadian Way in the 21st Century" (Chrétien 2000), presented by Chrétien to the Progressive Governance for the 21st-century conference of "Left-leaning" countries in 2000 hosted by the German Social Democratic government. Chrétien claimed that Canada was at the global forefront of countries seeking to marry progressive social and foreign policies with "responsible" fiscal policies, claiming that Canada had "invented" the "Third Way" politics that dominated policy circles at the time, and indeed that this had always been "the Canadian way." By skilfully weaving a selective overview of Canadian history with Liberal accomplishments over the years, this vision of identity effectively suggested that Canada's national identity was linked to the Liberal Party (see Nimijean 2005b, 37–9).[3] More importantly, given that most Canadians have a "mixed bag" of values, this mirrors the self-image many Canadians have held of themselves over the past two decades as socially progressive and fiscally conservative (Nevitte and Cochrane 2007).

It is fair to ask if the Chrétien government's exercise in adding a partisan twist to a redefined national narrative was a one-off. The answer is no. Since assuming power, the Harper government has sought to redefine the Canadian identity with a Conservative twist, linking pride in the nation and a celebration of Canada with the military, sports, and the Canadian North, to produce a Canada that is not a soft "middle power" – an outlook associated with the Liberal Party – but a world leader and, in the words of the prime minister, a "very special place in the world" that is the envy of others (Slater and Ibbitson 2010).

The external projection of Canada is one of a military power with a glorious military past, embodying what the historian Ian Mackay has called "Warrior Nation" (McKay and Swift 2012). This can be seen in the ongoing celebration of the armed forces, including:

- Canada's participation in the 2011 Libya intervention by NATO, which was portrayed as a victory not only for democracy but also for the Canadian Forces. It culminated in an $850,000 victory celebration on Parliament Hill – including a military fly past – that was planned months before the end of the actual conflict (Pugliese 2012). As the prime minister noted, taking a swipe at Canada's diplomatic and peacekeeping traditions that may be associated with the Liberals, "the fact that there is now 'new hope' in Libya gives some proof to the old saying, 'a handful of soldiers is better than a mouthful of arguments'" (Harper 2011b).

- This muscular rhetoric began early in Harper's tenure in power, where he attempted to get Canada to be seen as a world leader on the world stage via militarism, thus framing the Afghanistan conflict in terms of Canadian values. Speaking in New York City in 2006, the prime minister stated that Canada was taking "real casualties" (CBC News 2006a). Losses, he suggested, were "the price of leadership" (CBC News 2006b). In response to critics who said Canada should withdraw, he declared that "there will be some who want to cut and run, but cutting and running is not my way and it's not the Canadian way. We don't make a commitment and then run away at the first sign of trouble. We don't and we will not, as long as I'm leading this country" (CBC News 2006c).
- A celebration of Canada's military tradition, including a $5 million celebration of the War of 1812, about which the Heritage Minister James Moore said, "Canada would not exist had the American invasion not been repelled during the War of 1812, and for that reason, the war is a defining chapter in our country's history" (Boswell 2012).
- Looking at putting military bases in the Canadian North (Woods 2011) and linking a controversial $9 billion purchase of F-35 fighter jets to the protection of Canadian sovereignty in the North (Pugliese 2010).
- A celebration of the Canadian military and a military flyover at the 2011 Grey Cup.
- Featuring Canada's national Vimy Memorial on a new $20 bill (replacing an Aboriginal sculpture, Bill Reid's *The Spirit of Haida Gwaii*).
- The Department of National Defence restructured its annual departmental performance report, devoting more space to the military's connection to the Canadian identity and arguing that military values shape the Canadian identity, using public opinion results showing that 87 per cent of Canadians see the military as a source of pride (Meyer 2011).

This approach has been complemented by an emphasis on Canada's historic links to the monarchy, which included several 2011 initiatives (Boesveld 2011):

- Organizing a high-profile 2011 visit of Prince William and Catherine, the Duchess of Cambridge
- Restoring "Royal" to the titles of the Air Force and Navy
- Ordering Canadian embassies abroad to hang pictures of the Canadian monarch Queen Elizabeth II (This followed a controversial replacement of modern Quebec art in the Department of Foreign Affairs and International Trade by a portrait of the Queen.)

Prime Minister Harper and his government have also wrapped themselves in country and flag, which has replicated the elevated and ceremonial stature of the presidential brand prevalent in the United States. This includes

- Travelling with a lectern called "Canada" wherever he goes
- Considering changing the colours of the prime minister's official airplane from military grey to one on which "Canada" and "True North Strong and Free" may be painted on it (Raj 2011)
- Supporting Bill C-288, the *National Flag of Canada Act*, a bill protecting the right of citizens to fly the Canadian flag wherever they wish
- Indeed, 35 per cent of photos of the prime minister issued by the Prime Minister's Office in 2010 included Canadian flags (Delacourt 2012)

Finally, the Harper government adopted what it called "principled leadership" on foreign policy – notably a strong pro-Israel stance at the United Nations, in contrast to Canada's more balanced and nuanced historic position (Clark 2011), which may be associated with the Liberal Party. Indeed, it appears that the Conservative government instructed foreign policy officers to stop using foreign policy terms and language associated with the Liberals (Davis 2009a, 2009b). The stark contrast between the two parties was made clear by the prime minister in 2011, when he stated, "We campaigned on this new Canadian reality. Not on a dream or a fantasy or a slogan, but upon the reality of this great country rising – a country founded on great principles – a courageous warrior, a compassionate neighbour, a confident partner – and under a strong, stable, national, majority, Conservative government – the best country in the world" (Harper 2011c).

That these positions and views are often complex and controversial do not detract from the political strategy being employed. The goal is to consistently create the impression in citizen's minds that Canadian values and institutions – which inform the Canadian identity – are linked to and defended by the Conservative Party.

The Chrétien and Harper cases show how promoting foreign images of Canada and recasting the national identity along partisan ideological lines domestically occurs; in turn, this image can be used to nurture domestic political support. As we will now see, this has been enabled by the rise of the domestic brand state.

The Domestic Brand State

The international-domestic nexus is the foundation of the domestic brand state. In a Westminster political system such as Canada's, the party forming the government can use national images to advance its partisan interests by taking advantage of institutional changes that accompany the shift to the postmodern world of images. These include the promotion of national symbols by the government; control over major policy development and linking the communication of policy to national identity; framing policy initiatives in terms of national values and, by extension, framing opposition perspectives as outside the national consensus; and extensive use of public opinion research, increasingly sponsored by the state.

Governments can exploit these issues in three dimensions of the domestic brand state. First, the domestic brand state is preoccupied with values politics and national identity, using it as the basis for its political strategy. Second, the domestic brand state relies heavily on public opinion research and political marketing – in essence, tracking consumer preferences – to sell and reshape its "product." Third, the domestic brand state is very centralized, allowing it to execute the strategy.

Values Politics and National Identity

The essence of branding is the creation of an emotional connection between a consumer and a service or good. Brands are not actual products or services; branding refers to how products and services are represented and perceived. The use of qualities and emotions to represent products and services creates an emotional connection between them and the consumer. This connection sees consumers willing to pay a premium in exchange for a high-quality product, for it becomes a mode of expression of the consumer (among others, see Clifton, Simmons, and Ahmad 2004; Holt 2004; Kelly and Silverstein 2005; Klein 2000).

The emotional connection is also important in brand politics, though it operates in a slightly different manner. A country brand, as promoted by the state, embodies values and emotional qualities, and citizens connect to their sense of citizenship through national identity. The centrality of a national image is the key distinguishing feature of the domestic brand state. It is the emotional connector between government and citizen in an era of globalization and the brand state. While many believed that globalization would reduce the appeal of a national identity, globalization at its outset was an elite phenomenon, and local and national connections remained important for citizens (Guibernau 2004, 138); consequently, citizens have turned to their nations in order to feel more grounded during such a turbulent period. Indeed, in the mid-1990s, the Canadian government acknowledged that there was a role for social policy to address such feelings of insecurity in order to avoid social upheaval potentially caused by the downscaling of the welfare state (J. Brodie 2002, 389; Nimijean 2005b, 32–3).

Citizens articulate national exceptionalism through displays of national pride. Often displayed in response to mega-events such as the Olympic Games, in Canada national pride is also expressed through anti-Americanism and a belief that the "Canadian way" and, in particular, programs such as health care are much better in Canada. Political parties and governments appeal to citizens' sense of national identity and their values and stoke pride in order to form the connection necessary to develop a successful brand.[4] Parties also try to redefine the nature of national identity in order to gain a partisan advantage. Thus, the consumer brand relationship is transferred to the political sphere.

This is accomplished through the political appropriation of national values and symbols: "The bonding power of national symbols is sometimes invoked with instrumental ends in mind" (Cerulo 1995; 19). Symbols have a strong resonance with the citizenry, so invoking them involves efforts to exert control over citizens by merging their personas with the symbols. This strategy is reinforced by rhetorical articulations of national identity in efforts to rally the citizenry: these are "politically consequential" and influence a country's laws, policies, and sense of imagined community (Bruner 2002, 1). Canadian politicians regularly invoke images of Canada to link their parties to supposed Canadian values. For example, in the past decade, Canada has been both a "northern tiger" (the Liberals' John Manley seeking to promote an entrepreneurial Canada; *The Economist* 2003b, 34) and a "wolverine" (Prime Minister Harper saying that Canada was like the small but fierce creature that defended itself against stronger adversaries; Boswell 2007, A15) to communicate images of Canada to foreign and domestic audiences.

This builds upon a long-standing tradition of prime ministers using national visions to promote their political agendas: we can think of John A. Macdonald's "National Policy," John Diefenbaker's "Northern Vision," or Pierre Trudeau's "Just Society." However, the role of a national identity changes in the era of the brand state, due to the homogenizing policy effects of globalization and the widespread adoption of neoliberalism. Symbolic differences, as opposed to ideological or policy-based differences, assume greater importance in the political competition between parties on the Left and the Right: "We are beginning to see product parity in the political arena just as in the consumer goods arena; policy is converging and the key differences between the major political parties in much of the western world are attitudinal, rather than substantial" (Anonymous 2001).[5]

In Canada, this has centred on the belief in balanced budgets, low taxes, universal health care, and a fair degree of public services (Centre for Research and Information on Canada 2004, 3–5). As Nevitte and Cochrane (2007) argue, while values have become more important in Canadian politics and while different groups of voters have different "bundles" of values, the overall direction of value change is "Leftward," a factor that parties of the Right must acknowledge. This explains the incrementalist approach of Prime Minister Harper in advancing a non-Liberal, "centre-Right" agenda. He has been reluctant to tackle controversial issues in the areas of social values (abortion, same-sex marriage), social policy (two-tier health care), and economic policy (despite a record deficit, he has stated that there will not be "radical" spending cuts). His government has been careful to link more controversial issues, such as its "law and order" campaign and increased military spending, to Canadian values and patriotism.

Consequently, political competition is increasingly based on a party's ability to frame its platform in terms of national values, as well as its ability to frame opposition policies as beyond the national consensus. Indeed, this is one of the key features of domestic brand of politics: the ongoing attempt of governing parties to present themselves "in the flag." For example, the 2004 and 2006 Canadian federal elections were highlighted by Liberal leader Paul Martin's attempts to frame

Conservative leader Stephen Harper as Americanizing and to remind Canadians that only his party truly embodied their values (see Nimijean 2006a, 88–90). Since winning the 2006 election, Harper has adopted a strategy of trying to convince Canadians that his party, and not the Liberals, reflects the Canadian consensus. This is part of his effort to achieve his main goal of challenging the hegemony of the Liberal Party (Martin 2010, 6; Wells 2006, 5). On the first anniversary of his government, Harper stated, "East and West, French and English, immigrant and native born, we are all proud champions of these founding values, all champions of the Canadian way. Conservative values and Canadian values, I think we've demonstrated in the past year that these are one and the same" (quoted in Mayeda 2007, A4). This quote is telling, for it implies that values that are not Conservative are also not Canadian. Ironically, Harper criticized the Liberals for questioning his patriotism in the 2006 federal election, asking if it was possible to be a Canadian without being a Liberal (see Nimijean 2006a, 90).

When values are consistently used to support governmental actions, critics and political opponents will challenge the government narrative. Values associated with a national identity are therefore rearticulated by governments to reconcile rhetoric-reality gaps (Nimijean 2005b) in a manner similar to Stuckey's notion of "celebratory othering." Stuckey (2004, 6) argues that the state can use the language of inclusion even if the state is maintaining stratification, for inclusion is defined by the dominant culture, seeking to recognize minority groups but first and foremost seeking to include minorities in the polity; this recognition often precedes policy initiatives or legal recognition.

In this vein, the *rhetoric* of nationalism and the promotion of national solidarity are state strategies providing security to citizens at a time of great disruption. This allows the state to implement public policy that is at odds with this rhetoric. For example, we can understand the Chrétien response to the challenges of globalization, neoliberalism, and national unity through the articulation of a redefined Canadian identity. Chrétien's economic policy response to globalization was a series of neoliberal measures reducing the size of the Canadian welfare state. As Armstrong (1996, 251) so aptly described the era in a chapter title, Canada, once "caring and sharing," became "greedy and mean." However, a simultaneous rhetorical strategy articulated the "Canadian way": a set of inclusive values that defined Canadian exceptionalism in terms of an ongoing concern for the less well-off in society. Thus, while inequality and stratification grew in the Chrétien era (Yalnizyan

2005), Chrétien politically contributed to a growing sense of pride and national solidarity. In other words, while the rhetoric of the Canadian way harkens to a socially progressive Canada, increasing its appeal, the Liberals essentially redefined citizenship to reflect the neoliberal times (J. Brodie 2002). Consequently, Canadians and their governments became more vocal and proud of their socially progressive identity just as the policy-based nature of such identity was disappearing and as a growing consensus on neoliberal economic and social policies emerged (Nimijean 2005a).

The Chrétien government also employed nationalist symbols and appeals to pan-Canadianism as part of its national unity strategy after the 1995 Quebec referendum. This followed advice the government received from prominent public opinion analysts who highlighted the need to create an emotional connection between Canada and the Québécois in order to diminish the popularity of the sovereigntist option in Quebec (see Greenspon and Wilson-Smith 1996, 356–60). The federal sponsorship program – promoting the visibility of the federal government in Quebec and the creation of a National Flag Day in 1996 – was a conscious effort to stoke patriotism and attachment to the country. Chrétien articulated a shared emotional sense of national identity while also stressing that Canadian values were threatened by fiscal doom and the prospect of separation. Canadian values – linked explicitly to the Liberal Party – could save the day (and the country). For example, in the 2000 election campaign, the Liberals prepared an ad that explicitly stated that Liberal values were Canadian values: "Canada is a Great Nation. Built on Liberal values. Freedom … justice … sharing … tolerance. Today, Canada can be a leader in the New World. What is important for me, Jean Chrétien, is that each and every Canadian can take their place in this New World … without ever losing sight of our fundamental values. We have a bright future. It is up to us to achieve it" (cited in Kinsella 2001, 72).

Harper's appeal to patriotism in order to slowly move Canada to the political Right also shows why rhetoric and the use of a national identity are central to brand politics. Harper's attempt to expand the base of the party beyond social conservatives reflects Nevitte and Cochrane's (2007, 268) argument that parties of the Right may need to move to the centre on moral and economic grounds or else possibly suffer electorally. Harper has tried to appeal to urban and suburban voters who would be attracted to policies based on market economics and patriotism (Wells 2006, 11–12) and to link these values to the Conservative

Party, as seen for example in the "Stand Up for Canada" theme of its 2006 election campaign (Martin 2010, 52).

Thus, promoting national symbols and linking them to the government in power is central to brand politics. Governments recognize that there is a symbolic dimension to nationalism that has considerable currency: "Politics – especially the emotionally laden politics of nationalism – seems to be more about wielding prominent symbols in popular culture than it does about choosing substantive policy alternatives" (Rose 2000, 1). Such promotion not only connects the nation to the state but also allows the state to define the nation (Geisler 2005, xv–xvi). For example, the Chrétien government advanced pan-Canadianism by highlighting national identity – through the articulation of Canadian values and the promotion of symbols of Canada, such as Flag Day, the federal sponsorship program, the Canada wordmark, and the Federal Identity Program, all prominently displayed in Liberal red.

This was not simply a tactic of the Liberal Party. Prime Minister Harper and his Conservative Party have employed similar tactics. Among other tactics, the Conservative government has changed the colours of government Web sites from Liberal red to Conservative blue and adopted the slogan "Canada's New Government" for official government communications rather than the traditional "Government of Canada" (Nimijean 2007), and in early 2011, controversy arose over the sudden proliferation of references to the "Harper Government" on official government communications (Cheadle 2011d). The Conservative Party has rewritten the *Canadian Citizenship Guide* to be more reflective of Conservative values of patriotism and celebration of the military (Ivison 2009). Early in his tenure, the banner of the prime minister's Web site (http://pm.gc.ca/eng) proclaimed the "True North Strong and Free," a key line from the national anthem, reminding Canadians of the need to promote sovereignty and resist "foreign" claims to the North while also connecting the Canadian brand to the Conservative Party. Lawrence Martin (2010, 51) argues that Harper was proud of Canada's war record and did not like the rise of "soft power." Thus, supporting the war effort and the armed forces "were part of an effort to shape a Tory patriotism, one predicated on symbols and traditions. This was central to his goal of taking the flag away from the Liberal Party" (L. Martin 2010, 51).

Therefore, far from the state responding to more consumerist citizens, as van Ham claims, the domestic brand state has a considerable instrumentalist interest in national identity. The key is to pitch it properly, as

Chrétien reminded Canadians shortly after the 1995 Quebec referendum: "The Parti Québécois did not win, Canada won. We have such a good product that, put it under the proper light, and the people will buy it" (Ha 1995, A4). The Canadian case shows how leaders appropriate national images and values in order to advance their agendas.

Public Opinion, Advertising, and Marketing Brand Politics

The second dimension of the domestic brand state is the increasingly important role of state-funded public opinion research in support of a more politicized governmental communications strategy. While this is not a new issue in political communications (for an overview, see Page 2006), the increase in public opinion research contributes to the "development in government communications that has politicized public employees and public policymaking as an extension of partisan interests ... Government communications has become state communications by equating its work with the perspectives of the governing political party" (Kozolanka 2006, 344). This phenomenon assumes greater importance for developing and communicating the identity narratives central to domestic brand politics. Thus, while Nesbitt-Larking's chapter in this volume examines the ontology and methodologies of public opinion research and how they structure and influence research findings, this section focuses on the brand politics of public opinion research, specifically its messaging.

Scammell (2007, 188) argues that polling and market research are reflective of an older style of political marketing, namely "the permanent campaign." They are central to what Lees-Marshment (2004) calls the political marketing revolution. Voters are now political consumers: they are no longer deferential and are instead demanding changes to public policy and political institutions. Consequently, market-oriented parties seek to win elections by reflecting voter demands and responding to them. Even after winning an election, parties and governments endure the "pressure to deliver," requiring that they demonstrate to the public that they are meeting their needs. This extends to various state organizations as well, as Lees-Marshment documents in the British case: "A market-oriented party in government needs to deliver, and therefore put pressure upon health and education services to use marketing" (236).

This means that parties must continue to campaign in noncampaign periods. Scammell (2007, 188) notes, "The permanent campaign focuses on the instruments of media politics; the brand concept uncovers the underlying strategic concerns of efforts to maintain voter loyalty through communication designed to provide reassurance, uniqueness (clear differentiation from rivals), consistency of values, and emotional connection with voters' values and visions of the good life." Thus, the identification of the opinions and demands of citizens is critical, as increased emphasis is placed on linking government programs and services to citizen values.

While some argue that polling provides government with valuable information that can improve the development and delivery of public services (Butler 2007, 118; Soroka 2010), the lens of domestic brand politics provides a different perspective of polling and the permanent campaign. "Values politics" allow governments to camouflage rhetoric-reality gaps between stated values and public policy; the brand message, rather than policy itself, becomes the effective response to the "pressure to deliver" noted by Lees-Marshment. Domestic political branding effectively builds on this foundation, with politicians emphasizing values and national identity in order to connect with voters. Thus, in looking at the operations of government and political parties in the context of the modern publicity state, it is necessary to go beyond the narrow focus of political marketing. It is important to situate political action within the broader contextual environment in which political actors operate. It is not possible to understand the changes noted in the political marketing approach without understanding the consequences of the changing understandings of national identity.

There is a fine line between public opinion research that surveys Canadian attitudes for the development and improvement of public policy and government services and the government use of such data that allows the government to craft its message in a way that resonates with citizens. Page (2006, 5) notes that governments may argue that their policies have legitimacy when they are doing what the public wants; these results help shape policies, determine what options are politically acceptable, and help determine priorities (Savoie 2003, 109–10). Polling can greatly influence agenda setting and the broad direction of government policy, as outlined in Throne Speeches (Page 2006, 58–9). In effect, governments can determine if they have public "buy-in" before they implement initiatives, especially controversial matters, thus reinforcing the "permanent campaign" (Butler 2007, 132). Indeed, in his comprehensive study of the federal government's use of public opinion research, Page (2006) notes that this research can help frame communications strategies in order to increase acceptance of policies. He noted that 20 of his interviewees (more than one-fifth) used the word "sell" to describe this phenomenon. He concludes, "The selling of policy is the foremost purpose of government communications" (68). This makes it easier for governments to frame opposing views as outside the national consensus, thus making the balance of political competition more unfair.

Public opinion research funded by the state does not simply allow governments to develop an understanding of public attitudes. It also allows the government to shape the narrative that it uses to communicate with citizens, introducing a decidedly partisan dimension to state advertising. As Angus Reid states, politicians do not use polling simply to determine the public will; "it is equally the case that politicians want to change the public will" (cited in Page 2006, 194). This explains why governments are "addicted" to polls and focus groups, according to an anonymous public servant (cited in Savoie 2003, 109).

Domestic brand politics takes political advertising to the next level, as nationalistic political communication appears to involve the promotion of symbols rather than the debate of complex policy issues (Rose 2000, 1–2). Using national narratives to sell policy and political agendas replicates this phenomenon. Indeed, Rose (2003, 8) argues that "it's easier to change perceptions than the material conditions of citizens." Thus, we can understand how the Liberals in the 1990s emphasized Canada and Canadians as caring and sharing; polls showed that this is how they saw themselves and that they wanted policies reflecting these values. Michael Marzolini, Chrétien's pollster at the time, argued that Canadians had to be convinced of the need for drastic budget cutting in 1995. Selling patriotism could increase social cohesion. Selling neoliberal policies within a progressive rhetoric allowed the Liberals to frame the New Democratic Party and parties of the Right as outside the Canadian consensus on progressive social policy and conservative fiscal policy (see Marzolini 2002).

Marzolini noted that such an approach would minimize the political risk for the government, thus pointing to the connection between political interests and policy communication. This continued under Harper's Conservative government. Several government polls conducted in 2006–7 asked citizens for their opinion of the performance of the current (Conservative) government. A review of federal government public opinion polling practices noted that a number of opinion polls went beyond measuring satisfaction with the Government of

Canada and entered into the realm of political partisanship, an area expressly forbidden by federal regulations (see Canada 2007c, 15–18). The government polls conducted during this time included one that asked Canadians if they supported the five major Conservative priorities as outlined in the 2006 election (Woods 2006, A3). The Prime Minister's Office (PMO) also undertook public opinion research on Canadian ethnic communities – a key target of the Conservative electoral strategy – and their attitudes regarding the Conservative government's five priorities in a report called *Exploring the Views of Canada's Multicultural Communities* (Ditchburn 2007, A7). Clearly, such public opinion research allows governments to change the tone and content of their message for political purposes. Thus, while the Conservatives have been targeting new Canadians in order to increase their support, the Conservatives stress that their values reflect Conservative values: traditional, family-oriented, entrepreneurial, and tough on crime (Wells 2010). Such strategy reflects Page's (2006, 73) observation that public opinion research is often used not to provide clarity of government initiatives, but to "make a message more persuasive."

The link between domestic brand politics and the modern publicity state can be seen in how the Conservative government manages communications with respect to policies that may undermine Canadian sovereignty, seem "American," or align Canada too closely with the United States, as these are areas in which the Conservatives are weak politically. State-funded public opinion research has combined with communications strategies to attempt to both dampen the effects of unpopular policies in the sensitive area of Canadian identity and support the government's political brand. This is significant, given that the Liberal Party under Paul Martin warned that a Harper government would "Americanize" Canada (see Nimijean 2006a, 89).

For example, the Harper government used focus groups to test citizen reactions to its first budget speech in 2006: respondents stated that the speech should sound "less American" when discussing international affairs (Aubry 2006, 21). Similar results emerged from focus groups who were asked to share their views on Canada's participation in the war in Afghanistan. Citizens suggested that government communications should avoid words such as "freedom, democracy, and liberty," which sound "too American" and reminded people of the US government's message on Iraq and to drop tough language such as Canadians don't "cut and run" – used in defence of the Afghanistan mission – and instead employ a rhetoric of human rights and diplomacy involving iconic language such as "peacekeeping" (Freeman 2007; Woods 2007a, 2007b). In effect, this was using state funding for political purposes. Given the sensitivity of Canadians to their national identity and their overwhelming desire to be seen as distinct from Americans, using public funds to reframe messages that initially are not seen as embodying the Canadian identity transcends the democratic spirit. Thus, given this record, one must question why, in one of his first major pronouncements on foreign policy as prime minister, Harper suddenly emphasized that Canada was quite distinct from the United States (Foot 2007).

This points to the ongoing use of public opinion research for partisan ends. While public opinion research can potentially increase two-way communication between citizens and government, it can also be used to reshape public opinion in favour of a government's preferred policy options. In essence, the state has developed regulations that benefit the party in power, for public opinion research is far more important for governmental communications strategies than it is for determining the content of public policy (Page 2006, 187).

The Centralization of Power

The third dimension of the domestic brand state is the growing centralization of power in central agencies, notably the PMO and the Privy Council Office (PCO), the PMO's counterpart in the public service. This has coincided with a growing power of party leaders in Canadian political parties, which allow leaders and their close advisors and strategists to focus on messaging party policies and tactics ("talking points"), with little role for parliamentarians or party (Whitaker 2001). This is where the worlds of political communications and domestic brand politics intersect. The growth of the communications apparatus, controlled by the centre, allows politicians to use state resources not only to advance partisan agendas but also to link party to state and national image.

The power of central agencies has become more pronounced in recent years, amplified by the diminishing policy capacity of the federal public service due to budget cuts. Decision making in Canadian foreign policy, and in government in general, has shifted away from line departments to centralized agencies such as the PCO and PMO and to economic ministries such as the Finance and Treasury Board (Copeland 2005, 746).

Consequently, the PMO has grown in part to control the bureaucracy through the use of communications, including the PCO's development of a senior position to control all public service communications and the 1998 formation of a Cabinet Committee on Communications (Kozolanka 2006, 347, 353). The centralization of power allows for a very tight bond between the political (PMO) and the policy (PCO) worlds, allowing for increased political direction over government communication. Kozolanka, for example, demonstrates how strategic government communications have become standard practice in the public service. Communication, rather than substance, becomes the priority, thus explaining how the communications corps of the public service could grow by 7 per cent in the 1990s, at the peak of government cutbacks (it grew 30 per cent between 1987 and 1999) (350). The case of the federal sponsorship program, Kozolanka argues, shows how this tendency has challenged democratic practice by allowing the government in power to benefit from its control of state resources.

This practice continues under Harper, whereby the communications section is the largest division of the PMO (Hall 2009), resulting in a 30 per cent increase in the cost of running the PMO. Minister John Baird argued that these were necessary costs for communications and travel by the prime minister to promote the Economic Action Plan (Kennedy 2010, A4). In 2009, the PMO increased spending by an additional $1.7 million on video distribution of the prime minister as well as events preparation, leading journalism professor Christopher Waddell to suggest that the government is funding public relations, not communications based on the journalistic principles of access (Cheadle 2009b).

It can be argued that this seeks to promote the visibility of government members to the point of affecting the public service. For example, in 2008, a senior bureaucrat stated in a briefing note that promoting smaller projects of a federal infrastructure program provides "excellent visibility for regional ministers and local MPs" (De Souza 2010, A3). Priorities can be misplaced. In 2009, the Conservative government spent five times more tax dollars promoting its economic action plan than it did on raising awareness about the H1N1 flu virus (Cheadle 2009a); in addition, the Economic Action Plan Web site directed citizens to a Web site with Conservative Party colours that featured 40 photos of the prime minister and referred to "the Harper government," against government regulations that federal advertising should not promote a political party or entity. Photographs of the prime minister quickly disappeared, even though a spokesperson said they were not removed (despite evidence of cached images showing they were there; Cheadle 2009c). Despite these regulations, official government documents – funded by taxpayers – continue to refer to the "Harper Government."[6] Thus, the *Ottawa Citizen*

(2010, A14) editorialized that "centralizing communications in the PMO does not necessarily mean *more* communicating; it might just mean that the information that is communicated is more controlled and spun than ever." When it comes to communications, Canadians are getting less for more money. As political communications expert Jonathan Rose noted, "It's using taxpayer's money to do what the [Conservative] Party should be doing" (cited in MacLeod 2009, 1).

It appears that the PMO is driving the management of government communications and is politicizing communications using state resources (for a detailed overview of the process, see Cheadle 2011e). Most routine government communications are now cleared by the PMO through a system known as "Message Event Proposals," which seeks to anticipate media reaction to events, desired headlines, and desired sound bites. This has slowed down the communications process and reduced the amount of information shared with the public (Blanchfield and Bronskill 2010, A1; J. Davis 2010; Martin 2010).

This reflects trends elsewhere. In Britain, the Blair government showed how government marketing became more important in communicating with citizens and in the delivery of government services. Citing Scammell's analysis of the Blair government, Garbacz Rawson (2007, 215) states that "the marketing focus must be at the centre of decision making rather than something that is considered after the decision is made." This reflects van Ham's conception of state branding. However, this concern with the centralization of the marketing strategies in locations of power also underlines what is called "political marketing," "which uses marketing strategies to better execute government election campaigns on local, federal or national levels" and which focuses on "the comprehensive strategy of the party, rather than the specific promotional techniques" (ibid.).

Conclusion

I have argued in this chapter that domestic brand politics are integral and necessary to the modern publicity state, which is underpinned by obsessive image management. Recent governments in Canada – and here I have focused on the emergence of brand politics under Chrétien (1993–2004) and its further development under Harper (since 2006) – have increasingly striven to define themselves and project their positive image both at home and abroad. This chapter argues that three interconnected factors mark the era of domestic brand politics in Canada.

First, politicians engage in domestic brand politics by embedding values politics, which emphasize shaping an emotional connection with citizens, and national identity, the state's distinguishing feature, into their core political strategy. This has become more significant as economic ideological differences between the major political parties diminish. Instead, reflecting the nature of branding, values are emphasized to form a bond between party and voter, highlighting the personal dimension of political outlooks (this leader or party best reflects my values) as opposed to traditional political relationships in which party platforms and policies were presented to voters. Consequently, rather than conceiving of one set of "Canadian values" that all parties seek to embody, we may be entering a period of competing sets of Canadian values linked to parties. Efforts to define and redefine national symbols and historical memories become crucial, as these influence the brand. Thus, the Harper government's message on the 200th anniversary of the War of 1812, which has been framed as no less than an epic feat of survival against an American juggernaut and the foundation of the Canadian nation and identity, can be associated with a party and leader that is fiercely patriotic and militaristic. Indeed, the prime minister proclaimed in July 2012 that the War of 1812 was "the Fight for Canada" that produced "a common identity that would eventually make our Confederation possible" (cited in Wherrey 2012).

Second, in order to amplify the brand, political parties must rely on the persuasive publicity practices that have become endemic in the modern state, particularly the expensive tools of public opinion research and, more recently, political marketing. The chapter notes the increasing blurring of lines between government and state, as public opinion research can be used to help governments reframe messages that blur rhetoric-reality gaps and address partisan shortcomings. This was seen, for example, in the case of the Harper government using findings from focus groups to reshape messages, making the government sound less American, and seeking public opinion that supports government priorities.

Finally, the brand state requires the centralization of power within the government in order to effectively direct the cohesive implementation of the brand in all government "products." The growing role of central agencies in managing communications allows the domestic brand state to flourish, as the centralization of power requires and cements a close relationship between the political (PMO) and the policy (PCO) spheres of the state, thus allowing for more direct influence and direction on the national brand. This trend began long before Harper assumed power, but it continues.

Thus, I conclude that domestic brand politics are here to stay. The Harper Conservatives, elected on a platform of accountability, "value for money," and governing differently than the Liberal Party, have continued and sometimes surpassed some of the practices they condemned when in opposition. The challenge of domestic brand politics is that it emphasizes the symbolic in its efforts to link party with state. So far, the Conservative Party has been able to keep the party base satisfied with its law and order agenda, its muscular foreign policy, its defence, and a revival of the monarchy.

However, murmurings of discontent from prominent fiscal conservatives such as journalists and commentators including Andrew Coyne and Gerry Nicholls suggest the Conservatives may continue to face challenges. It is perhaps understandable that a minority government could not implement far-reaching fiscal changes. This is reflective of the desire to constantly present the government in favourable terms according to its own narrative to increase support – as part of the permanent campaign – rather than acting according to convictions. This tendency increases the impact of high-profile cases of governments acting inappropriately, ranging from incompetence and self-interest, in opposition to their stated goals, to egregious violations of Canadian values and interests. It also has the potential to quickly undermine support, despite the best efforts to micromanage the political scene. Now that the government has obtained a secure majority (in 2011), that barrier has been removed. In 2012, in its first budget since the election, the government made huge, more Conservative-like cuts to programs and services. It remains to be seen if the carefully framed Harper brand is sufficiently established to withstand this shift.

Two scholars recently asked if democracy was good for a nation's brand (Kemming and Humborg 2010). However, it is also important to ask if nation branding is good for a country's democracy. The case of Canada suggests that the articulation and manipulation of a national image and identity for foreign audiences, when transferred to the domestic political scene, detracts from a country's democratic spirit. As Fan (2010, 101) notes, "Nation branding, in essence, is to align the nation's image to the reality." However, as we have seen, both Liberal and Conservative governments have attempted to reshape the national image to their partisan reality.

This is a troubling development in political discourse and practice, one that is antithetical to the guiding principles of democracy, which are based on civic engagement and respect for the rule of law. Not only do many of the practices of domestic brand politics seek to shape the public will by using state resources for partisan ends, but they also flout the democratic spirit. For example, the Paillé investigation into Liberal polling practices, appointed by the Conservatives in an effort to make the Liberals look bad, cost taxpayers $610,000 (Martin 2010, 119). In the controversy over how the Conservative government promoted its Economic Action Plan, it was recently revealed that the PCO – which should serve the prime minister bureaucratically but not politically – sought exemptions from the "Common Look and Feel" regulations (designed to ensure that state communications are non-partisan) for the EAP Web site. Ultimately, Vic Toews, president of the Treasury Board, overruled bureaucrats who stated that the exemptions were not merited (Cheadle 2011f). This incident suggests that critics of the modern publicity state should be concerned about not only the use of public funds for partisan purposes but also the phenomenon of domestic brand politics, which affects the quality of democratic life.

NOTES

1 Thanks to Kirsten Kozolanka for her insights on the nature of the modern publicity state.
2 Many thanks to Jeff Ruhl for offering this insight and for comments on an earlier version of this chapter.
3 The irony is that Canada was not invited to this conference. Canada's last-minute invitation was the result of American President Bill Clinton's lobbying. I have explored this incident and the politics of the Canadian Way elsewhere (see Nimijean 2005b, 37–9).
4 In this environment, corporations adopt a similar strategy. Tim Hortons, Roots, and Molson Coors have all successfully appealed to a strong sense of patriotism to connect their products to the Canadian identity (see Carstairs 2006; Cormack 2008; Millard, Riegel, and Wright 2002; Seiler 2002).
5 This comment was posted to an online discussion about the link between politics and branding on the BrandChannnel.com message board, which is sponsored by Interbrand, a major branding company.
6 Delacourt (2009) drew attention to this phenomenon in June 2009 by asking her readers to search "Harper Government" in the Canada News Centre (http://www.news.gc.ca). As of July 2012, searches reveal that some departments continued to use "Harper Government" in their press releases.

9 Managing Information: Too Much Publicity, Not Enough Public Disclosure

KEN RUBIN[1] AND KIRSTEN KOZOLANKA

The politics of access to information in Canada exposes a critical dichotomy in contemporary Canadian society: the right to information from our government and the power of the government to withhold, distort, or provide that information. Two fault lines characterize the government information field. The first, in which information is juxtaposed against privacy, will for the most part be discussed by Shade and Shepherd in their chapter in this volume. This chapter focuses on the second fault line, the publicity-information line, and the nature of the contradiction between too much publicity versus not enough information from government. Issues involving information such as the wide cleavage between transparency and secrecy cut across all issues related to a government's public image and have an impact on how it governs.

In today's politics, in today's publicity state, information is a high-stakes commodity and its management by government is key to political success. In Canada, information has become both centralized and politicized. Savoie (2008) has noted the concentration of power for communications in the Office of the Prime Minister, as well as the general tendency for governments to centralize power and control, particularly in relation to communications. More broadly, governments are adopting a permanent campaign mode, in which governing itself has become synonymous with campaigning, thus also requiring ongoing campaign-style information management (Bowman 2000).

In addition, government communications departments are actively involved in information management and messaging, including playing a role in handling access to information requests. These communication departments have been given increased resources (many times more than those communication officers engaged in providing access to information) and are more ready to play an active and important role to publicize government achievements (Kozolanka 2006). Yet the public is being increasingly told to obtain information not from government communications services but by filing access to information requests, despite the cumbersome and nonresponsive process of filing access requests.

Putting information queries into an access-to-information channel invariably leads to a government's perceived need to control that information channel; therefore, the government chooses to either withhold or not release fully any information that might reflect badly on the government. In this way, the ground rules and practices adopted for information access can help further erode public trust rather than enhance public participation and confidence. In an "information society" where nowadays a government is primarily in the information business, the power a government has in holding and using that information is not likely to be fully shared with its own citizens.

Establishing the Right to Information Access and Codifying Secrecy

To give the impression that they want their citizens to have some information, governments have developed and codified ways to control the way they handle public information requests. In Canada, the *Access to Information Act* was passed in 1982 under the Trudeau government. The motivation for the legislation was less to give out information but more to plug escalating leaks and to ensure that information could be protected as secret.

There were those in Canada, however, who wanted a law for greater disclosure. The issue of trust in government and better access to its records led in 1972 to a public interest coalition called ACCESS that included public relations consultants, civil libertarians, journalists, and individual backbench parliamentarians. ACCESS's decade-long lobbying for more open government gained momentum after the infamous Watergate scandal in Washington politics led to changes in the American *Freedom of Information Act* in 1974.

As co-author of this chapter Ken Rubin (1975, 1–2) saw it, the government of Canada was "the centre for evasion and secrecy" and was "married to the *Official Secrets Act*," which requires that "civil servants take an oath to be secretive, not to serve effectively the public," and "hide their mania for confidentiality behind the word security."

Some of the information access problems identified by parliamentary committees reviewing limited government transparency included no public access to central information systems, no independent access appeal processes, conflicting and vague policies, and poor responses to queries on policies and procedures. A further study in 1977 for ACCESS showed cases where even members of Parliament had been denied information (Rubin 1977).

The 1982 *Access to Information Act* gave Canadians limited rights to information within the purview of many, but not all, government institutions. The process was deceptively simple: individual citizens would apply to get access to information and would receive that information for a small fee within the limits set out in the act. However, exemptions were also set for access to information concerning individual privacy and confidential information on commercial entities, national security, policy advice, and other areas, as well as Cabinet confidence exclusions. Fairly unique at the time, a complaints mechanism was also put in place and was administered by an information commissioner to try to broker a solution satisfactory to both the requester and the department in question. But the commissioner could not compel the government to release the information. Ultimately, the requester had the right to appeal the decision to the Federal Court.

Even at the time, although heralded justifiably as a milestone for merely existing, the law was considered flawed in key ways, both administratively and politically. Administratively, the access process was complicated, had high fees, and had the potential for expensive time extensions, thus creating its own barriers to access (Rubin 1983, 9). Politically, the act exempted swathes of information reputedly in the public interest, including much policy advice to ministers, much commercial data, and most Cabinet-related documents. An editorial in the *Ottawa Citizen* said the act, "with its exemptions and with its spirit undermined, could have the reverse effect to what the public thought was intended. Instead of loosening government information, ... [it] may have merely codified the ways in which information can be suppressed" (*Ottawa Citizen* 1984, A8).

The State Prevails in "500 Ways to Say No"

Over the relatively short 30 years since the *Access to Information Act* was enacted in Canada (and every province and territory now has such acts), social, economic, technical, and political conditions have changed dramatically, while the struggle for greater openness has always been evident but stymied (Rubin 2013). Among key developments to be discussed in this chapter, of particular impact in thwarting rather than improving public access have been the effect of tightened security after 11 September 2001 and the failed effort to capitalize on making the publicity practices of government more accountable after the scandal of the 1997–2001 sponsorship program.

The number of people who use the access legislation has been very low, beginning in the 20,000 range, and now is only between 30,000 and 40,000 users a year. Many users are drawn from the corporate world, and on average, journalists account for about one-tenth of users. The number of users is further skewed because of high use by federal correction inmates, immigration requestors, and those who use access information multiple times. The most-used exemptions have been for personal information protection and commercial confidentiality. In 2000, information was disclosed in 49.8 per cent of requests. By 2006, information was disclosed in 35.6 per cent of requests, and in 2009, full disclosure fell to 22.6 per cent (Gatehouse 2010, 22). Response times to access requests have continually lengthened, so most requests rarely receive a reply in less than three months and a significant amount of requests take many more months. Although the stipulated response time is 30 days, delays can reach as long as 150 to 240 days (Pugliese 2009, B1).

Public interest users face such odds and have largely been outgunned and overwhelmed by those who have much greater resources at their command – governments, security forces, and commercial interests among them – and seek to enclose it. Successive governments have increasingly developed communications strategies and tactics and established access practices that manipulate or conceal information ranging from small and embarrassing mistakes to egregious and life-threatening information needed by Canadians to evaluate their government and participate knowledgeably in civic life. In so doing, governments have circumvented information rights and lessened usage of the *Access to Information Act* in order to promote themselves positively for public support and electoral gain.

This chapter will demonstrate how the government of Stephen Harper, as both a minority government and especially after it gained a majority, has intensified this urge to secrecy by, among other means, controlling the information environment centrally within the Prime Minister's Office (PMO) and its public service equivalent, the Privy Council Office (PCO). In 2010, *Maclean's* magazine devoted an article to increasing frustration over "literally 500 ways to say no" (Gatehouse 2010, 22). Alarmingly, several studies have shown that Canada is now consistently near the bottom on international openness ratings of the 60 countries that have freedom of information legislation.

Government Information Management and Control

The nature of information, as well as access to and manipulation of information, was and continues to be a major issue in information politics. In the initial years following passage of the *Access to Information Act*, public interest groups, the media, and parliamentarians identified many more unaddressed or emerging access issues. Yet recommendations made in the official statutory three-year review of the act in 1987–8 remain unfulfilled to this day, despite a multitude of reports and reviews that followed, many of them repeating the same areas that needed improvement (Douglas 2006, 3). Prime among the recommendations are the exclusion of Cabinet records and increasing the number of institutions that need to comply.

Changes in government made little positive impact on access issues. Prior to the 1982 act, some Conservatives in opposition led the campaign for open government. Once in power under Prime Minister Brian Mulroney, they fought battles to prevent amendments to the act that would liberalize access, for example, by reducing Cabinet secrecy exemptions and putting the details of free trade agreements under public scrutiny (Rubin 1987, A9). The Mulroney government was the first to feel the full impact of the new law and, according to critics, reacted by being "secretive and defensive, and manipulating the law and its exemptions to avoid embarrassment or controversy" (Wilson 1988, n.p.). Subsequent governments fell into a pattern: they called for more transparency while in opposition but lost their fervour for access reform after they came to power.

It was clear that the access system had problems, and governments were introducing practices to thwart transparency and prevent leaks. In the Chrétien years (1993–2003), the tradition of backbench and opposition interest in more liberal access to information continued, while the media exposed ways in which access was thwarted within and by the government. Roberts (2005, 6) has succinctly identified three common strategies in that period that characterize the federal and provincial Canadian environment: litigation is used by governments to ensure that interpretations of the access law remain restrictive, despite promises to review information laws; over time, governments have declined to include new federal organizations within the law; and governments have refined practices of administrative routines that identify and treat differently requests that are sensitive. As this chapter indicates, the urge to protect information that would have an adverse effect on one's image or reputation grows alongside the constantly developing tools to contain it.

By the mid-1990s, it became evident that government practices were slowing down and frustrating any momentum access users were achieving in getting information from the government. This was in part accomplished by a sophisticated early warning system that was institutionalized to alert ministers to access requests and to assist the government in monitoring, vetting, manipulating, and delaying the release of information to the public (Rubin 1996, 4). The pre-release practices included

- a centralized clearinghouse for reviewing potential Cabinet or ministerial confidences at the PCO through its assistant secretary and legislation and House planning counsel;
- other clearinghouses for assessing access applications bearing on matters of federal-provincial relations, international relations, national security, and financial interests of the federal government;
- a central recording place of most access requests that departments receive through a coordinated and secure computer database retrieval system, formerly called the Coordination of Access to Information Request System;
- a practice in many departmental access offices of alerting communications divisions and ministers to access requests when they are received or before their release;
- a practice in some access offices of identifying certain users, such as the media, and tailoring responses accordingly;
- an occasional practice of monitoring access requests to detect potential leaks and security threats; and
- a practice of initiating unnecessary consultation, notifications, and consent procedures with third parties.[2]

None of these administrative practices for vetting access requests were or are illegal. Most often, government insiders see them mainly as enhancing the management of access requests, including how to communicate the issues raised by the information. However, they have resulted in abuse and violation of the *Access to Information Act*. At issue is whether tipping the government off to such queries through various early warning systems is just good administration or if it has become a tool for introducing unnecessary delays in responses and a method for sidelining the public's right to information. It becomes an issue when vetting and damage control prior to the release of the information become more important than the sharing of data about government operations. That such practices are even part of the routine illustrates the penchant for secrecy that characterizes most governments. Through these practices, it has become abundantly clear that the state does not like to disclose information and looks for ways to get out of doing so.

This urge to control is more pronounced and more sophisticated over time, with, for instance, two of the above practices becoming more explicit and widespread. First, a briefing note in 2006 revealed that, under the Harper government, the segregated database and server now has the explicit purpose of keeping confidential ministerial documents out of reach of access requests and thus beyond public scrutiny (Naumetz 2006, A1). Only ministers and their political staff have access to the server.

Second, even as the *Accountability Act* became law, another internal government practice on information requests was revealed that seemed to counter the Harper government's initial position of claiming more openness and transparency. At a parliamentary inquiry, it was revealed that government departments were coordinating requests centrally and profiling frequent requesters, especially when the information was sensitive (Rubin 2006a, 7). The categories of users, and even individual names of users, have been provided regularly to those in government that put the information package together and those that vet the package politically and for communications purposes.

Internally, this practice is called an "Amber Light Process." It alerts senior management in a department that an access request might attract media attention – a practice that is both an invasion of privacy and virtually criminalizes users. Roberts's (2005, 15) research confirms that significant delays occur in processing requests if the requester is either a member of the media or the political opposition. Such an elaborate centralized monitoring system can only be built on the implicit premise that a government's policy agenda needs to be protected. More recently, cases of political interference in ministers' offices with access requests have been exposed and brought before a parliamentary committee with mixed results (Beeby 2010, A1).

From the beginning, the predominant ethos in government has been to be creatively subversive, protect the minister, and release as little information as possible. An early benchmark event is the 1994 investigation into the murder of a Somali youth in a Canadian military camp; the inquiry found that as part of the cover-up of the death, "sensitive information was written on removable post-its, which were peeled off when accessed" (Sullivan 1996, 4).[3] National Defence was the department responsible for communicating information to the media and the public. To respond to this interest and need for information, the department created a special unit to handle media and other enquiries, with the effect that much less information was actually released.

There is a parallel here with the later case of Afghan citizens who were detained by Canadian troops in their own country and became the subject of media coverage beginning in 2008. Prisoners were turned over to local handlers without concern for their safety when it was well known that such prisoners were routinely tortured. When the actions of Canadian troops became known publicly, National Defence again set up a special unit (with the code name "Tiger Team") to do damage control and deal with information demands (Rubin 2008a, 9). The government's response to the detainee issue – from Prime Minister Harper as commander in chief on down – was to bury much of the material, even from parliamentarians. These kinds of sensitive files lead to bureaucratic and political resistance that override and superimpose any normal access processing chain of command. The result, of course, is greater secrecy (ibid.).

The Somalia scandal was one of the incidents of record alterations that led a backbench MP, Colleen Beaumier, to introduce a private member's bill in 1998 that would amend the *Access to Information Act* to prevent and penalize those officials altering records. It was meant to be a psychological turning point by telling public employees to start obeying the act – 16 years after its passage (Canada 1999, 13). The detailed ways in which the *Access to Information Act* could be or had been ignored by abusing records included destroying them, switching records to a different department, using "transitory" records such as telephone messages that normally get destroyed after use, or exempting the materials from access after an access request has been received (ibid., 15–16). One such example of record abuse was revealed during the 1997 Krever inquiry into the contamination of the voluntary blood donation supply, in which 32,000 Canadians were infected either with Hepatitis C or the HIV virus between 1980 and 1990. It was discovered that Health Canada officials had destroyed relevant records, including minutes of meetings of the Canadian Blood Committee, the agency responsible for the safety of the blood supply (ibid., 15).

The Beaumier bill became the rare exception to backbenchers' bills and was passed unanimously. Although not as tough as it could have been, it imposed penalties on federal public employees for destroying, mutilating, or altering documents for the purpose of thwarting the *Access to Information Act*. The bill remains a positive example of how the legislative process can be influenced in favour of information access.

Further Legislating State Secrecy

By the time Beaumier's bill passed in 1999, dozens of federal laws with overrides on information access had eroded the 1982 act considerably. The events of 11 September 2001 had a paradigm-changing impact on access to information release. Canada's *Anti-Terrorism Act*, enacted in late 2001, provided arguably the single largest override avenue for increasing government secrecy, including broadening excluded documents issued under the *Canada Evidence Act*. Instead of moving forward, antiterrorism legislation contracted information rights. Gains made over many years in personal privacy protection and information access came under threat from the perceived needs of security and safety, and Canada, like many other nations, responded quickly with legislation that gave broad powers to the state and its security apparatus.

The *Anti-Terrorism Act* attempted to address too many issues too quickly and with the force of a recent and compelling tragedy prompting it to include sweeping powers (Daniels, Macklem, and Roach 2001). Prime among these powers were those related to changes to the *Official Secrets Act*, areas that should but did not have full public and parliamentary debate. Importantly, the *Anti-Terrorism Act* did not have a separate, permanent parliamentary joint oversight committee to review and audit security intelligence matters. Overall, the impact of the act was also psychological, as it advanced the cause of secrecy in government.

In a controversial provision, the *Anti-Terrorism Act* gave the minister of justice (Austin 2001, 256) the power to issue certificates to exclude security-related data from the public, which was in direct conflict with the minister's mandate to uphold information and privacy rights legislation. The certificates are for indefinite periods, without an opportunity of independent review and without any mechanism for revoking them, which meant little accountability for the government. Certificates could declare records to be on grounds of undefined security, international relations, and national defence, putting these records beyond the reach of public access (Canada 2001, 3–4). In terms of government accountability and access to information, the attorney general could issue a certificate that prohibits disclosure of information, thereby not allowing citizens to review their files for accuracy and impeding the public's right to know (Austin 2001, 252).

The *Anti-Terrorism Act* clearly threatened public accountability by acting outside of regular parliamentary and public debate and fair information access and protection, leaving considerable secret control in the hands of government. The act, which was nonetheless renewed in 2013, was used as an excuse to widen considerably what records could be security classified.

No case makes the connection more explicitly between the new realities of post-2001 access to information in Canada and the new antiterrorism laws than that of Maher Arar. In September 2002, Arar, a Syrian-born Canadian citizen, was returning from a vacation in Tunisia when US officials detained him during a stopover in New York. Claiming that Arar had links to the terrorist group al-Qaeda and acting on information received from the Royal Canadian Mounted Police (RCMP), US officials deported him to Syria, even though he had his Canadian passport with him. The RCMP and the Canadian Security Intelligence Service, along with the attorney general, denied any involvement or complicity with Arar's detention and deportation. Yet co-author Rubin was able to obtain records only with the consent of Arar and his wife, Monia Mazigh, that showed or hinted that these three entities were exchanging information (or misinformation) on Arar, including in meetings with Syrian intelligence (Rubin 2004d, 8). In October 2003, Arar was released and returned to Canada.

To further illustrate the extent to which authorities went to hide data on the circumstances in the Arar case, in January 2004, a 15-month-old Department of Foreign Affairs and International Trade (DFAIT) access request had one-quarter of its 240 pages blanked out completely (Aubry 2004, A1). It appeared that part of the delay was because the RCMP had vetted the file put together by DFAIT in response to the request. Arar's lawyer said such vetting was "unprecedented" and had blocked his client's access to information (ibid.). The irony is that while an investigative agency such as the RCMP could get access to the file, Arar himself could not see his entire file because of the deletions.

Even as the later public inquiry on the Arar case got underway later in 2004, a parallel process was taking place secretly in which departments and the RCMP were sifting through and judging documents that might or might not end up being viewed publicly. Some of those documents were already in the public domain. In a curious practice, some government agencies, including the RCMP, even began to reclassify data from public sources as secret. For example, the RCMP exempted parts of questions it received from reporters and hid parts of media analysis on the Arar case, even though the data was taken from open-source material (Rubin 2004b, 2). Thus, getting access to information that is already public becomes the exception, while confidentiality for purposes of national security becomes the rule (Rubin 2004c, 1). The 2006 inquiry report concluded that there was no evidence to link Arar to terrorist activity. In 2007, the Canadian government and the RCMP issued separate apologies to Arar and gave him and his family $10.5 million in compensation.

The Arar inquiry showed how the Chrétien government's desire for confidentiality in matters related to national security went beyond any existing statutory prohibitions passed by Parliament.

Attempts to Modernize Access Administration

As has been discussed previously, government officials have spent much time over the years devising back-door practices restricting access to information. They have also actively countered several private members' bills and prevented one bill produced by an information commissioner, who attempted modest reforms to access to information legislation, from getting anywhere. Instead, without initially putting forward a full-scale government-sponsored access bill, officials offered their own working papers to smother and "modernize" access legislation, as we will see with the *Accountability Act* later in this chapter.

One concerted effort to put a damper on advancing access to information legislation occurred with the Treasury Board establishing a $4 million Access Task Force composed solely of government officials. Its lengthy report in 2002 contained many regressive proposals, including even more exemptions, such as allowing personal jot notes of officials and draft audit reports to become classified as secret.

John Reid, information commissioner at the time, was highly critical of "insider" influence on the task force and felt most of its recommendations were self-interested and would actually weaken existing access and expand the government's zone of secrecy (Rubin 2002b, 7). While the Access Task Force report was buried, its input and administrative thinking was recycled in a 2005 Justice Canada discussion paper (Rubin 2005). One of the biggest disappointments during the Harper years and with the commissioners he has appointed has been that this once pivotal office has diminished in stature and has taken on some of the very administration-heavy trappings that many other Ottawa agencies possess (Rubin 2009).

Internally, government officials, who are not generally devious but very cautious, see the management of access to information, with its growing delays and backlogs that critical information commissioner reports have highlighted, as simply one of pouring more resources into their departments (and making access users respond to tighter rules). For instance, the Office of the Information Commissioner's 2008–9 report said that huge delays in fulfilling access requests were eroding the public's right to information, yet the report dismissed the bureaucracy from blame and suggested administrative arrangements that reputedly would improve the dismal practices of those departments with backlogs and delays (Canada 2009c, 1). The report and more recent annual reports in 2010 and 2011 did indicate concerns with the central agency, the PCO, for some of the longest delays, some of which emanate from PCO's role as advising on exemptions across all government departments.

Probably the most progressive of the private access bills seeking to break out of the administrative solutions mode of more resources for "modernizing" the access to information regime was that devised by Reid in 2005 and reintroduced since then several times in Parliament via private members' bills. While quite limited, the Reid bill did recommend that the act's many exemptions be subject to a public interest override, injury tests, and some time restrictions. It also asked that the government not put secrecy override clauses in other federal statutes. This meant there would be a requirement and duty to document key decisions in a climate where many decisions were increasingly taken orally and deliberately not well documented (Rubin 2005).

The Reid bill and its successors won support from the newly created House of Commons Access to Information Committee and various citizen groups. However modest a start the Reid model bill was, Harper still paid lip service to it, especially because the bill ran against his government's strategy of minimal legislative information management and control.

The Sponsorship Scandal and Its Impact on Information Access

The sponsorship scandal is the Canadian event that most defines government misbehaviour where greater access to information and oversight helped bring events to light. This high-profile case revealed the limits of transparency and information flow in government and relates specifically to the publicity practices of the Chrétien government.

During the early 2000s, information about the management of the little-known $250 million, five-year (1997 to 2001) sponsorship program began to emerge through leaks, access to information requests, and media stories. As Kozolanka has elaborated in her chapter in this volume, the program emanated from the government's attempts to stem Quebec separatism, particularly in the second referendum on sovereignty in that province in 1995. From the beginning, it was clear that the program was the product of little more than a "propaganda bureau" (Aubry 1999, A1). Access records received after a year's delay showed that the government branch that administered the contracts was acting as a private sector contract broker for various government departments, issuing subcontracts in an increasingly back-door, non-competitive manner (Rubin 2000, 7).

In 2001, the issuing branch – now part of the new department Communication Canada – was still preoccupied with national unity and still exhibiting further questionable spending practices and mandates (Kozolanka 2006; Rubin 2002a). The list of egregious qualities and actions revealed through access requests became longer: the department's actions were partisan and propagandist, too focused on fighting separation, and broke or exploited government contract spending rules, and the department hired political friends (Rubin 2002a; Aubry 1999, A1). A troubling aspect of the work of Communication Canada was its close association with the PMO of Chrétien that made it unsuitable to carry out a mandate of producing and giving out unbiased and accurate information to Canadians.

The auditor general (AG) examined the sponsorship program in two separate reports in 2002 and 2004 and confirmed the "appalling lack of documentation and extensive non-compliance with government legislation, regulations and policies that apply to financial transactions" (Cobb 2002, A4). By the time of the second AG report, little had changed in the conditions that spawned the scandal: poor controls, faculty disclosure, third-party dominance, political connections, and downright greed still existed (Rubin 2004a, 13). Documents obtained under the access act later revealed that an internal audit in 2000 had expressed deep concerns about the program. Yet it appeared that the only concrete action emanating from the audit was the preparation of media lines (MacCharles 2004, A1).

In a later 2006 public inquiry on the sponsorship program, Savoie (2010, 123), who served as research director of the Gomery Commission, points out one contributing factor that became clear through the inquiry, in terms of public employee complicity in politicized work and its repercussions: "The more one goes up the influence and power ladder, the greater the resistance to transparency requirements."

The sponsorship scandal represented a low point for accountability in government while also demonstrating the importance of a mechanism such as the *Access to Information Act* to ensure transparency, particularly when the government is using public funds to get positive publicity for political and electoral gain. Although accountability was not necessarily seen as directly related to access-to-information issues, records requested under the act played a role, along with unnamed sources and whistle-blowers, in uncovering the problems with the sponsorship program. In so doing, those records also revealed many of the already mentioned deeply embedded processes within government that supported secrecy and partisanship where neither should have existed.

Within this information-constrained, post-2001 environment, under the Jean Chrétien and Paul Martin Liberal governments and leading up to the 2006 election, access to information efforts continued to be thwarted while central control over information was exerted through the PMO. Chrétien and his government used the *Access to Information Act* as a defensive weapon to impede access, often through increased bureaucracy surrounding access requests (Rubin 2002c, 7). While Martin's efforts in his short term as prime minister were less obsessed with hiding problems such as the failings of the sponsorship program, they were hardly more transparent either.

The Harper Government, the *Accountability Act*, and Further Secrecy

The 2006 election was supposed to be a key moment. The government was about to change from Liberal to Conservative for the first time since 1993, and the latter party's call for accountability in government as a key part of its election platform struck a chord with Canadians, even if the call was not without contradictions. During the campaign, Conservative party leader Stephen Harper said, "We need to replace a culture of entitlement and corruption with a culture of accountability" (Stanbury 2010, 34). The party's electoral platform included promises to reform the *Access to Information Act* fairly substantively, including introducing some of the Reid bill reforms.

In the post–sponsorship scandal environment, the Conservative Party stressed government accountability and won the election. The new government under Harper immediately began work on public accountability legislation that became the *Federal Accountability Act.* Despite campaign rhetoric, the bill had serious substantive flaws, but more jarring was the inability or disinterest of the new government in reshaping the way Ottawa would engage in public commitment, debate, and policymaking.

Ominously, the accountability bill drafted by senior mandarins and political operatives had measures that further limited public access to certain administrative and audit records and excluded more operational records held by government agencies (Canada 2006b, 1–3 passim). One section of the bill claimed to make the contract and procurement process more fair and transparent but instead increased the level of secrecy protection for commercial and government economic interest claims – to hide, not open up, such information from the public (2).

Overall, the bill equated accountability with legislating the release of surface factual materials such as recent poll results and travel costs that can be managed as to when or if they are disclosed, but important operation and evaluation processes were given further secrecy protection (Canada 2006b, 3). Neither the PMO nor his ministers' offices were placed under public scrutiny in the bill (4). Passed in late 2006 and gradually brought into practice since then, the *Accountability Act* can hardly be viewed as curbing the existing culture of entitlement that works against a free flow of information.

The Harper government not only continued with the same anti-access practices as previous administrations but also fine-tuned ways to control information for its personal visibility and benefit, some efforts more successful than others. One such example of Harper wanting publicity both in minority and majority modes for his government was revealed in severed (edited) access records obtained. Documents showed how his government wanted to maximize positive exposure from the 2010 Winter Olympics in Vancouver for the government. In a 2007 memo, Canadian Heritage said the opening ceremony should "ensure that the event reflects the priorities of the government and helps to achieve its domestic and international branding goals" (Rubin 2008b, 16), in fact, helping to build the government's brand and profile along the way, a process Nimijean discusses in his chapter. The government spent thousands of dollars on consultants to get its brand and profile at the games right. This included producing many drafts of the games logo, as well as the way literature for the games would look. Accessed records even revealed how the extended pre-Olympic torch relay – which eventually lasted several weeks and visited most communities in Canada – was intended to build the government's profile.

The oil sands development, key to the Harper government's economic policies, is another example where the government says one thing that downplays the environmental impact but knows that such development poses a "significant environmental and financial risk to Alberta" (De Souza 2012, A4). Further, by using its majority, the government is holding more of the business of parliamentary committees as in-camera sessions (Plecash 2012, 15), denying the media and the public access to democratic discussion.

Taken together, under the Harper government, practices of hyper-control of information that might impede the government's policies and public image have fostered an access environment in which it is the norm to delay responses to requests for ever-longer periods and, when the information is finally received, to be thinner and lighter in content because of the many deletions (Rubin 2006b, 15). The combination of a government that has not responded to calls for mandatory record collection and keeping or inclusion and disclosure of decision-making records and a bureaucracy reluctant to record or release policy options or deliberations results in a lack of government transparency and less public confidence (Rubin 2010, 35).

In power, Harper's underlying credo that "less government is good government" means less record collection and recording to the point that the government has been widely criticized for its lack of respect for knowledge itself (Rubin 2011c, 11; 2012, 17). One example in 2010 was his government's rejection of collecting more in-depth, long-form census data in a more rigorous mandatory reporting manner, which would have contributed to having more solid and unbiased information. Downplaying collecting information and releasing less information make it easier for the official version of events to prevail. Finally, the public has been told repeatedly over time by the Harper government that the costs of its 65 F-35 fighter jets would be about $15 billion, but the AG's 2012 report places the costs at $25 billion (Auditor General of Canada 2012, chap. 2). This could prove to be the classic case of saying one thing and doing another.

Conclusion

Going behind the official government publicity can be difficult, but access to information, however still limited, can expose the dichotomy between what is propagated and what actually happens. Successive governments have been obsessed that certain files such as those on the oil sands development, constitutional change, climate change, and Afghanistan be hidden as much as possible by stretching access rules, creating special units, or coordinating the means to ensure all government agencies are online to resist disclosures.

Access requests obtained from Health Canada, however, still reveal the difference between the government's official communications and telling it as it really occurred. One such example is how government promoted healthy eating practices through its most widely distributed publication, "Canada's Food Guide." Access records obtained showed that development of "Canada's Food Guide" was successfully subjected to lobbying by the food industry (Rubin 2007, 15). The manipulated recommendations in the food guide reflect the interests of those industries that lobbied the government, many of them concerned about any further restrictive labelling on their less-than-healthy products.

Another example of how the government claims publicly to be acting in a responsible, balanced manner but in reality, in a deceptive fashion, is catering to special interests was uncovered through multiple access requests to various federal agencies over two and a half decades concerning its defence of the "safe use" for asbestos. Even though asbestos (now identified as a type of asbestos called chrysotile) is a recognized toxic health hazard that is heavily restricted in Canada, the governments of Canada and Quebec still pushed for its export to developing countries such as India. Documents reveal that between 1984 and 2004 alone, Canada spent almost $60 million to fund the international industry group the Asbestos Institute (now the Chrysotile Institute) to lobby for continued use of asbestos abroad, with the institute working closely with Canada's embassies abroad and Natural Resources Canada and Health Canada joining the institute's seminars overseas to conduct "awareness" workshops for its "safe use" (Rubin 2003, 19). Despite multiple public health concerns, Canada is still a worldwide leader in the marketing of this lethal commodity (Rubin 2011b, 13).

Not every government official, however, is intent on hiding or distorting data, and officials do face restrictions and gag orders and operate under limited disclosure rules. Designated access-to-information officials with limited resources are at times caught between their managers' demands to release little and the public's demands to release more. Small open-government initiatives, such as a more routine release of databases for public use, which happens in other countries such as the United States, New Zealand, and Australia, have only belatedly and modestly begun in Canada (Rubin 2011d, 13). It would seem that senior mandarins and prime ministers, who have the most to lose, along with corporate allies and law and security officials, want nothing to do with a freer flow of information. They are now seeking to also control the government message and information through their new social media sites (Galloway 2011, A4).

Political resistance and interference to open government is not new. As long ago as 1986 in Mulroney's government, the clerk of the Privy Council, the senior-ranking bureaucrat in Canada's government system, in a letter ironically released through an access request, directed that "where the records being requested relate to the prime minister or to the operations of his office, ... you should consult with ... [the] senior advisor to the prime minister" (*St. John's Evening Telegram* 1986, n.p.). This directive, a result of the release of embarrassing travel costs Mulroney racked up while abroad, not only signified the potential for interference in the information process but also sent strong signals to the bureaucracy about how to handle access requests.

During the Chrétien years, access records revealed that the former Communication Canada very often served the prime minister's interests and that of his party, although it was couched in the name of national unity. In contrast, under the Harper government, the PCO has replaced Communication Canada as the means of hypercontrolling information that might impede a positive image. A key example is how the PCO, under the direction of the PMO, was given special resources to centralize and coordinate the roll-out of the Economic Action Plan (EAP) across government, the Harper government's communications response to the economic recession of 2009. Access records helped confirm that the EAP is run centrally and is steeped in political calculations (Kozolanka 2012).

Under the right government, when supplemented by considerable spending on publicity practices that have as their bottom line the electoral interests of the party in power, this cannot be healthy for an open and transparent government. Access to information has become so institutionalized and politicized, so little used and backlogged, that it is unable to function properly under so many restrictions and exceptions

(Rubin 2011a, 30). A sea change is needed in the culture of secrecy in Ottawa, yet instead secrecy is even more actively encouraged by the Harper government, revealing the hypocrisy between the theory and practice of managing access to information in the publicity state.

Access to information needs to be seen as the bedrock condition for a democratic country and a shield against absolute power. Consider the impact that a lack of information has when governments are subject to a considerable amount of lobbying or pressure of one kind or another, as Gutstein shows in his chapter. Access to information legislation should ensure that the public and the media have counter-information that can help even the playing field in aid of open government and a strengthened democracy (Rubin 1997, 10). To appease the public, it is not enough in this Internet age to periodically release via official Web sites a few antiquated databases on travel and hospitality expenses, nor are those expensively developed Web sites always full of up-to-date information unless what is offered is the government's spin on its programs and events.

One solution to this spin cycle, where much is withheld or bits and pieces selectively released, is to move forward with passing a Public Right to Know Act.[4] Such an act would make disclosure a constitutional right where the government practices would include proactive record keeping, service, open-meeting management, and agency pro-disclosure agreements (Rubin 2008a, 9). Proactive interactive disclosure would mean health, safety, environmental, and consumer records that affect our daily lives would, by law, be immediately releasable, and the number of restrictions to instant access would dramatically drop. The sole focus of an arm's-length "Public Access Authority" would be to release as much government information as possible, with the right to appeal to an Information Commission with binding powers to order information release. We need to have a legislative plan to go beyond the morass in which Canada's access to information currently sits.

Moving beyond the frustrating conundrum of living in an information age of abundance without getting the information that we need as citizens in a democracy is difficult, but it can be done. To achieve a more transparent government, first and foremost, the political will needs to be there, and that requires public pressure for change away from being told nothing, half-truths, or outright lies. After all, what people don't know *can* hurt them, and substance instead of spin is most needed and welcome.

NOTES

1 Co-author Ken Rubin is a consumer advocate and researcher who for over
forty years has played a significant role in Canadian access legislation by
testing, using, and criticizing its shortcomings.
2 As manager of a public opinion research program in a government department in the early to mid-1990s, and thus having received access requests to
fulfil and to write media lines for, co-author Kozolanka personally can attest
to the existence of several of these practices.
3 Removable notes, as well as other transitory records such as phone message
slips (see the paragraph on records abuse related to the Somalia scandal),
are part of a "read-and-delete" (Macleod 2005, 1) and "oral" culture that
hinders access to information (Savoie 2010, 122). In 2013, PMO e-mails
related to the Senate expense scandal were found to have been deleted,
causing concern about how to preserve such documentation. The scandal
involved several Senators who had inappropriately billed and were reim-
bursed for private expenses that were not related to their official duties.
4 One proposed freedom of information model is suggested at http://www
.kenrubin.ca/reform/model-bill.html.

10 Tracing and Tracking Privacy Discourses: The Audience as Commodity

LESLIE REGAN SHADE
AND TAMARA SHEPHERD

At the nextMEDIA digital media industry conference in Toronto in November 2010, Facebook Canada's managing director, Jordan Banks, told reporters that today's consumers feel it is "their right" to receive targeted advertisements from marketers: "Isn't that the consumer's expectation these days? We're in this era of ... this two-way conversation that every consumer feels is their right. Whenever they interact with a brand these days, they want to have a say, they want to be treated personally and they want to be talked to in a timely and relevant manner." While asserting the positive impact of such targeted and branded advertising on Facebook, Banks "downplayed privacy concerns," according to the CBC (Chung 2010). This public disavowal of the threats to privacy by social network sites such as Facebook, along with the explicit promotion of targeted ads as a consumer right, demonstrates the way that commodification is immanent to social networking. More importantly, it also highlights tensions between the privacy rights of citizen-consumers and their disclosure of and access to personal information in commercial – and highly profitable – social media sites. The right of access to information is the subject of the chapter by Rubin and Kozolanka.

Mosco's (2009) analysis of commodification in the political economy of communication provides a useful and salient entry point into our discussion of how social network sites and other forms of social media have adopted techniques from the marketing sector to create two forms of commodities: the audience commodity and immanent commodification. Commodification is understood as taking objects or often noncommercial products and services and transforming them into entities valued for their marketable function and use in exchange processes. It is a phenomenon that has grown in stature and stealth as companies seek to develop and deepen new revenue streams.

The audience commodity, as elaborated by Canadian political economist Smythe (1981b), refers to the processes by which consumers are
bought and sold by the media industry. Smythe analysed how television viewers are constructed by the mass media, arguing that audiences
comprise the commodity form of mass-produced, advertiser-supported
communications under monopoly capitalism. Audiences thus engage
in unpaid labour for the media industries by viewing advertisements
in their leisure time. Embedded in the costs of ads are the costs of
the goods and services that are marketed, which are passed onto the
viewer-consumer. This notion of the audience commodity has resonated throughout the years and "has deeply influenced international
studies of audience, media and consumption in both cultural studies
and political economy. If a commodity, the audience is hardly sovereign" (Murray 2010, 84). The audience commodity is a huge industry,
comprising the media companies themselves, the advertisers that are
attracted to specific media products and the particular demographic
they can target, and the groups that track the impact of advertising on
its viewers.

Newer offshoots of marketing online – involving psychographics,
demographics, and behavioural advertising – are constitutive of what
Mosco (2009, 143) calls "immanent commodification," or the processes
wherein the audience commodity, in fact, produces new commodities.
This involves the interrelatedness of multiple practices that produce
incremental levels of exchange value, and particularly those that create

> new measurement and surveillance technologies to expand the produc-
> tion of media commodities. Internet cookies, digital television recording
> devices, "smart" cards, etc., produce new products, in the form of reports
> on viewing and shopping, containing demographic details that are linked
> to numerous databases. But these new products are more than discrete
> units. They are part of a commodification process that connects them in a
> structured hierarchy. The implications for privacy are powerful. [...] *Im-*
> *manent commodification not only produces new commodities; it creates powerful*
> *surveillance tools that threaten privacy.* (ibid.; emphasis added)

Nissenbaum's (2004) notion of "contextual integrity" and its impact
on informational privacy is also key to our discussion. Nissenbaum
argues that contextual integrity – the various informational contexts
that govern or habituate privacy norms – should be considered the
benchmark of privacy. Privacy violations are composed of variables

that are situationally dependent, including "the role of agents receiving information; their relationships to information subjects; on what terms the information is shared by the subject; and the terms of further dissemination" (137–8). Contextual integrity is used to explain our increasing unease with pervasive forms of public and covert surveillance, especially with increasingly ubiquitous computerization regimes that tend to outpace the development of policy that protects privacy rights. These issues can have a particular impact on young, new, or other vulnerable users of new media who are unaware of how their media usage affects their personal privacy. Such developments again draw attention to a shifting privacy-information rights dichotomy.

As threats to citizen rights of online privacy, immanent commodification and contextual integrity on social network sites have been central to recent policy discussions that explore whether federal privacy legislation has kept pace with technological developments. This chapter looks at several policy papers from the Office of the Privacy Commissioner of Canada (OPC) and the consumer organization the Public Interest Advocacy Centre (PIAC). These recent papers have roots in much earlier concerns around the emerging landscape of information technology in Canada, as computers were introduced into the work practices of governments and corporations amidst the creation of databanks containing citizens' personal information.

In this chapter, we situate recent Canadian policy documents from the OPC and PIAC in light of their predecessors, the *Instant World* (Canada 1970) and *Privacy & Computers* (Canada 1972) reports issued by the now defunct Department of Communications. These earlier reports also raised privacy concerns long before social network sites such as Facebook came to define what we take for granted today as mundane forms of everyday social networking. Here, we explore how the notions of immanent commodification and contextual integrity have been conceptualized and treated as policy issues – where regulation tends to lag behind technological innovation – throughout the intensification of networked communication over the last 40 years.

The Context of Canadian Privacy Legislation

Issued in the early 1970s by the Department of Communications, *Instant World: A Report on Telecommunications in Canada* and *Privacy & Computers* examined the integrity of personal information and the potential surveillance implications of nascent database technologies for sorting, tracking, and making links by governments and private industries, alongside concerns about the outsourcing of Canadian data to the detriment of national sovereignty. *Instant World* originated from the Department of Communications' Telecommission, a two-year comprehensive study of the socio-economic and political impact of telecommunications in Canadian society. The report was prescient in its predictions of the widespread use of telecommunications technologies for society and concluded that "the establishment of a Canadian right to communicate was required in order to confront the social implications of the ever-increasing centrality of technologically mediated communication to Canadian society" (Raboy and Shtern 2010, 4). *Privacy & Computers* stemmed from a joint task force of the Departments of Communications and Justice. Ten major discussion papers were commissioned by the government and from independent experts, including overviews of the privacy implications of new technologies, the increased information-gathering and processing roles of governments and corporations, security safeguards, the regulatory role of governments, law enforcement agencies, and the effect of constitutional protections. In response to these early regulatory concerns, both the OPC and PIAC were established.

The OPC was created with the passing of the Canadian *Human Rights Act* in 1977 to serve as an advocate for the privacy rights of Canadians whose personal information was stored in federal databanks. It is headed by a privacy commissioner, appointed for a seven-year term by the governor general on the recommendation of Cabinet. The privacy commissioner's powers include investigating complaints, conducting audits, and pursuing court action under the two pieces of federal privacy legislation, the *Privacy Act* (1983) and the *Personal Information Protection and Electronic Documents Act*, or *PIPEDA* (2000); reporting on public and private sector organizations that handle personal information; conducting and publishing research on privacy issues; and engendering public awareness of these issues.

The *Privacy Act* applies to the federal public sector related to data collection and places limitations on the collection, use, disclosure, and disposal of personal information held by the federal government and federal agencies (Canada 1982, 1983). *PIPEDA* applies to the federally regulated private sector with respect to the collection, use, and disclosure of personal information, but only for the transaction of commercial activities (Canada 2000). Jennifer Stoddart, commissioner from 2003 to 2013, has been a global leader for her strong stance in demanding accountability in the privacy practices of popular social media companies such as Facebook and Google and in advocating for public education on digital privacy, particularly for young people (McNish 2010).

While the privacy commissioner is an officer of Parliament and thus represents an arm of the federal government, PIAC is a non-profit organization. Founded in Ottawa in 1976, it provides legal and research services around consumer rights, especially the interests of vulnerable (i.e., low-income) consumer groups in procuring access to critical public services. In responding to the challenges of fulfilling such an ambitious mandate in the context of a small non-profit organization, PIAC (2001, 7) expressly limited its purview in the 1990s to telecommunications, the Internet, energy, privacy, and competition law. In addition, earlier courtroom activities of PIAC have since shifted to primarily research-based models of consumer advocacy, according to the principle that "public policy is best determined when all elements of the public interest are represented by informed advocates at the time decisions are made" (32).

Thus the OPC and PIAC were formed with different mandates, yet the two organizations have recently adopted similar concerns over how immanent commodification might threaten citizens' right to online privacy. Social network sites have received particular attention, for example, in the OPC's 2009 report, *Social Network Site Privacy*, and its 2010 public consultations on the practices of online tracking, profiling, and cloud computing,[1] in light of the mandated five-year review of *PIPEDA* in 2011. In compiling its final report based on these public consultations and with input from written stakeholder submissions, the OPC focused primarily on "behavioural advertising" – another term for the online tracking of user behaviour as part of a marketing strategy (Stallworth 2010). In evaluating the merits and limitations of *PIPEDA* in this context, the review also influenced the OPC's submission to the federal government's Digital Economy Consultation in July 2010, where it emphasized the need to conduct new research on areas of vexing privacy concerns. One of the main areas relevant to our discussion in this chapter reflects the immanent commodification of personal information online, particularly on social network sites.

The OPC's recommendations to the federal government on how to deal with social network site privacy take a standpoint similar to recent PIAC reports. Since 2004, PIAC has compiled policy research on the effectiveness of *PIPEDA* in protecting consumer privacy online in relation to practices such as third-party advertising, target marketing, and online behavioural tracking and how these various iterations of immanent commodification pose special risks to children and minors. While PIAC tends to use qualitative methodologies including surveys, focus groups, and interviews, many of its conclusions about the need for increased privacy protection resemble those from the OPC on the commodification of personal information online.

Moreover, both organizations tend to reproduce some of the older discourses around privacy in relation to changing technology as expressed in *Instant World* and *Privacy & Computers*. Indeed, the concerns enumerated 40 years ago are still with us today but are exacerbated with the popular increase in social media over a wide demographic – from young people to middle-aged adults – along with more complicated data-based practices such as deep packet inspection (DPI),[2] cloud computing, and behavioural tracking.[3] The next sections show clearly how early conceptions of informational privacy gave way to later discourses expressing heightened tensions about the impact of commercialization in online environments on the privacy rights of citizens' personal information.

Early Discourses: Concerns over Informational Privacy and a Right to Privacy

Informational privacy as a societal concern became a topic of prevalent public discourse in the 1960s, as computerization entered the management of government and corporate activities. Reporting on a series of public forums preceding the release of *Instant World* in 1970, the *Globe and Mail* conveyed concerns that widespread computerization would "mak[e] us the greatest data-generating, privacy-invading society ever known" (Sagi 1970, B7). Another news article summarized that "nosy people have always been a nuisance, in the society that values privacy. If they are permitted to enlist the full support of computers, such people could soon become a major threat to Canada's open, democratic life style" (Braithwaite 1970, B2). The article further reported on a proposal for a right to privacy made by A.E. Gotlieb, deputy minister of communications, who warned that if this right was not established, "power will increasingly flow to those who know how to manipulate electronic information systems," and that "with electronic memories it will be possible to collect all possible data on a given individual and this body of information will follow him [*sic*] throughout his life like a ball and chain" (ibid).

Instant World categorically called for the consideration of a "right to privacy," given the rapid uptake of information technologies to collect, store, manipulate, and distribute information. While acknowledging the "administrative economies" enabled by these new applications, the report cautioned against the discriminatory use of technologies to the detriment of citizens' privacy, especially for more vulnerable members of society (Canada 1970, 41).

Privacy & Computers similarly detailed the technical, administrative, and legal challenges of the mounting collection of personal information and its resultant privacy issues: accuracy and integrity of data; right of access to personal information; and the relationship between information, privacy, and political power. The preponderance of privacy concerns, the report noted, resided in the uncertainty about the extent of these new power structures, but the report also noted that informational privacy was "in essence, a political and not a legal issue" (Canada 1972, 19).

The report further cautioned against "presentiment[s] of a technocratic nightmare" through government and corporate misuse or abuse of information (ibid., 119, 120) and acknowledged concerns surrounding the collection of personal information, its accuracy, dissemination to third parties, and the right of individuals to access and verify the integrity of their personal information. A "right to privacy" was thus seen as a widespread social claim with respect to personal information.

Contemporary Discourses: Contextual Integrity

Earlier concerns over the context of information disclosure have proved prescient, as shown in the OPC's *Social Network Site Privacy* report, which applies Nissenbaum's (2004, 2010) notion of "contextual integrity" to describe how privacy legislation is only meaningful and effective within the context of users' expectations (see also Grimmelmann 2009). Echoing early debates around a "right to privacy" as an individual matter, Nissenbaum (2010, 236) frames contextual integrity as a concept that seeks to establish "whether socio-technical devices, systems, and practices affecting the flow of personal information in a society are morally and politically legitimate." While she cautions that contextual integrity is neither a legal right nor a legal concept of privacy, she argues that it is still useful for providing a standard for evaluating privacy legislation according to users' expectations.

It is important to note that these expectations develop not through the state's regulatory paradigms but rather through community norms in online spaces for social networking. Privacy violations are thus recognized as breaching one of two main types of norms: "the norm of what information is appropriate to collect, and the norm of how information flows and whether it is appropriate to distribute that information" (Office of the Privacy Commissioner of Canada 2009a, 5). Some of the challenges of this definition of privacy as norms based include differentiating between public and private (as noted in earlier reports from the Department of Communications) and the conundrum of determining users' attitudes towards social network sites as particular sites for communication. As the OPC report argues, users of social network sites partake in an "illusion of privacy" furnished by the controls they exert over who can see their profiles among their network of friends, without a clear understanding of how their informational privacy is breached by immanent commodification, especially through the less visible collection and use of their personal information for commercial purposes (Office of the Privacy Commissioner of Canada 2009b, 6).

The concept of contextual integrity is useful when extending definitions of privacy to newer technologically mediated spaces for communication such as social network sites, but it also bears upon older and ongoing concerns for policymakers in this area. In *Privacy in a Changing Society* (Office of the Privacy Commissioner of Canada 2010c, 3), the OPC names four central and interrelated issues that affect privacy legislation: information technology, the integrity of personal identity, genetic information, and national security. The first two concerns – information technology and the integrity of personal identity – most obviously emanate from the immanent commodification challenge of Internet technology, where the profitability of networked communication poses threats to the security of personally identifiable information.

In less apparent ways, national security is also implicated in concerns around privacy as contextual integrity. National security mandates often work in tandem with commercial data mining initiatives. For instance, the report highlights the increased challenge to privacy legislation from "ubiquitous computing," where every object and living thing (including people) can be tagged through technologies such as radio-frequency identification (RFID). In this scenario, one can imagine the integration of genetic data into personal data profiles that cannot be controlled or managed by individuals themselves, which then not only breaches the integrity of personal identity and personal information but also heightens surveillance and security mechanisms by government and corporate interests.

A series of consultations held in 2010 by the OPC also summarizes various concerns relating to privacy as contextual integrity. The three touchstone issues discussed in the consultations – tracking, profiling and targeting, and cloud computing – likewise invoke the notion of immanent commodification, especially since most of these technological advances have emerged from the marketing sector. The report based on these consultations notes that the convergence of online information has built up increasingly complete portraits of individuals, using their personal information without their explicit knowledge, consent, or control, thus creating an audience commodity. Alongside the fraught nature of tracking and profiling, protecting people's privacy presents a more complex challenge to participating in online life altogether (Office of the Privacy Commissioner of Canada 2010c, 14). In taking a more holistic approach to technologically mediated behaviours, the report invokes both the ideas of contextual integrity and immanent commodification. Because privacy is contextually dependent, where the context is always already inscribed within capitalist business practices, the OPC acknowledges the need to have privacy protections built into system defaults to meet basic regulations (Office of the Privacy Commissioner of Canada 2010d, 15).

It is apparent to us, and indeed to the OPC, that the issues of contextual integrity and immanent commodification represent a case of "new technologies, old questions" (ibid., 5). The *Instant World* and *Computers & Privacy* reports from the 1970s cautioned about power imbalances between the rights of individuals to protect and control their personal information (particularly the more vulnerable people in society) and large governments and corporations that sought citizen information for administrative tasks, record keeping, and potential consumer profiling.

Yet there are qualitative changes to the flow of data across networked spaces. As such, while the OPC boasts that Canada is a world leader in privacy protections – citing its progressive legislation, such as the *Human Rights Act* (1977), the *Charter of Rights and Freedoms* (1982), the *Privacy Act* (1983), and *PIPEDA* (2000) – federal regulation has not kept pace with technological innovation (Office of the Privacy Commissioner of Canada 2010a, 4). Especially with regard to immanent commodification, the OPC has argued that users' lack of control over their unintentional virtual profiles fundamentally reduces expectations of privacy, in effect automatically waiving privacy rights online (Office of the Privacy Commissioner of Canada 2008, 5). In addition, while Canada has no explicit recognition of privacy as a human right, there are court precedents for assuring a "reasonable expectation of privacy"; however, the spontaneous and peripatetic nature of transactions and communicative flows on social network sites renders the establishment of such "reasonable expectations" vexatious (Shade 2008).

Immanent Commodification and Privacy on Social Network Sites

Earlier policy documents primarily envisioned computers as facilitating the workflow of administrative functions through the creation and cross-referencing of private citizens' information in databases, a necessary bureaucratic function. Maintaining both the integrity of database information and allowing citizens to redress erroneous information was deemed essential. Safeguarding personal information, thus pro-⸱ tecting the informational sovereignty of Canadians, was also a major concern with the increase in transborder data flows.

As the OPC's report on online tracking notes, the introduction of the *Privacy Act* (1983) sought to protect personal information in government databanks, while *PIPEDA* (2000) addressed concerns around commercial threats to individual privacy in a changing technological landscape. Yet, despite its attempt at technological neutrality, *PIPEDA* has not even managed to keep pace with the ever more sophisticated iterations of immanent commodification online within the 14 years since it was drafted. As the 2004 PIAC review of *PIPEDA* found only three years after it was enacted, the earliest adopters of its complaint-resolution system displayed a lack of consistent complaint filing and resolution, stemming from the lack of an effective enforcement mechanism (Public Interest Advocacy Centre 2004, 13). Consent was identified as the key problem in these cases, as articulated in principle 3 of *PIPEDA*: "The knowledge and consent of the individual are required for the collection, use, or disclosure of personal information, except where inappropriate" (*PIPEDA* 2000, n.p.). PIAC's report contends that this wording is vague and unclear, leaving online commercial actors free to assume implied consent across numerous situations of information collection.

In addition to the lack of a clear consent requirement, *PIPEDA*'s effectiveness is compromised by its position as a statute tacked onto the *Privacy Act* rather than being enshrined within that act (*Privacy Act* 1983, 14). Immanent commodification of personal information thus escapes proper scrutiny as a violation of fundamental privacy rights – a violation that implicates not only corporate collection and use of personal information but that of government agencies as well. As the Federal Trade Commission emphasized in its report on consumer privacy protection in the United States, corporations should look to government models for handling personal information in determining the "privacy impact of specific practices, products, and services" (Federal Trade Commission 2010, 49). In the Canadian context, this would involve strengthening *PIPEDA* reviews to include reviews of the *Privacy Act* and the *Criminal Code* (1985) as well, since the federal government should serve as a "model user" for enforcing legislated privacy protections, thus gaining citizen trust (Office of the Privacy Commissioner of Canada 2010b, 12).

Critiques of existing privacy legislation, especially *PIPEDA*, stem not only from the shortcomings of the act but also from technological changes that outpace the development of federal regulation. As PIAC (2009, 18) notes in its report on the possibility of a Do Not Track List for Canada,[4] pre-Internet models for commodifying people's information relied on demographic segmentation, psychographics, and offline data mining – for example, in companies' computer systems about their consumers – but today, data mining has become easier and more sophisticated with e-commerce and online surveillance technologies based on tracking consumer behaviour on the Internet. This unregulated arena has a profound impact on commodification. Industry spending on behavioural tracking is estimated to be in the many billions of dollars and growing (Public Interest Advocacy Centre 2009, 19), to which the OPC (2010c, 6) has enumerated concerns that these expansionary "dataveillance" practices intrude into formerly private domestic spaces as individuals increasingly participate in commercial activities from their home computers. In this way, immanent commodification has accelerated the spread of intrusive marketing practices, such as tracking, while qualitatively changing and challenging the notion of a public-private boundary.

New and refined technologies are key to how immanent commodification poses threats to people's contextual expectations of privacy. OPC consultations on online tracking, targeting, and profiling solicited respondents' opinions on how information might be collected via cookies, log files, and DPI (Office of the Privacy Commissioner of Canada 2010c, 10). These mechanisms were associated with practices such as surveillance, dataveillance, mapping, monitoring, and geotagging – which are all able to amass personal data within only a small number of commercial and governmental organizations. This concentration of users' information incorporates relatively new sources of personal information including social network site profiles that can be arranged in data clouds (Office of the Privacy Commissioner of Canada 2010a, 7).

The OPC notes that new mechanisms, practices, and modes of data collection and storage occur not only in social network sites primarily concerned with advertising but also across many other business models: mapping technologies that integrate street-level information with data storage; location-based services for marketing and Internet search; the "Internet of things," a term that describes a host of new means of rendering objects and persons as data through advanced internetworking technologies, including sensor networks, Internet Protocol version 6, RFID tags, wireless sensors, smart technologies, and nanotechnologies; analytics such as databases and algorithms; e-health modules containing personal health records; and newly evolving business models based on Web 2.0, third-party applications, and cloud computing (Office of the Privacy Commissioner of Canada 2010a, 7–10). In all these scenarios for data collection, immanent commodification implies that the creation of virtual profiles based on people's information happens without their control or even knowledge, with audiences for such profiles including data brokers, marketers, investigators, monitors, and identity fraud scammers (Office of the Privacy Commissioner of Canada 2008, 4).

Within this broad span of data collection and usage practices online, social network sites present unique challenges to legislated privacy protections, particularly because social network sites are online spaces that invest users with the *perception* of control over their online profiles. While such intentional profiles are only the tip of the iceberg when it comes to data-based personal profiles online (Office of the Privacy Commissioner of Canada 2008, 1), users of social network sites perceive their rights to participate in these networks from the standpoint of social privacy (i.e., who can see their profile among the network) rather than informational privacy (i.e., marketers and other third-party organizations accessing users 'information).

This apparent elision of informational privacy on social network sites is crucial in allowing the sites to operate according to advertising revenue models. Advertising allows these sites to offer services for free, where user information helps marketers to target ads to users' interests and to "inject themselves into conversations and manipulate participants into being favourably disposed towards their products by using loyal consumers' word-of-mouth to communicate a firm's bottom-line to new prospects" (Public Interest Advocacy Centre 2009, 42). As Facebook Canada's Jordan Banks claims in the CBC story quoted at the beginning of this chapter, consumers welcome this "very targeted and relevant and personalized messaging" as part of developing "very meaningful and rich relationships with brands" (Chung 2010). However, online tracking on social network sites such as Facebook poses potentially serious privacy risks. These risks clash with the ideals of Facebook CEO Mark Zuckerberg's belief in "radical transparency" – the company's credo that creating more open and transparent identities creates a healthier society (Kirkpatrick 2010).

But this sense of radical transparency is also elitist. For many people, the ability to control and maintain one's personal privacy on social network sites implies a particularly high level of information literacy, especially as privacy controls and features change continually at the seeming whim of technology designers, who tend to claim that these changes are implemented for users' benefit. In this sense, privacy becomes, as Papacharissi (2010, n.p.) characterizes, a "luxury commodity," one that only those with higher socio-economic and cultural capital can regulate. There is a risk, she cautions, of a privacy divide "further enlarged by the high-income elasticity of demand that luxury goods possess" between those who can "afford greater access to privacy" and those who can't – a newer class of "have-nots." Papacharissi's comments are redolent of *Instant World*'s cautions to ensure that privacy rights do not remain elitist and to be attentive to the "less powerful" in society, "welfare recipients, the out-patient at a public clinic, or the indigent senior citizen" (Canada 1970, 42).

Considering Facebook's reliance on transparency as an ultimately fallacious way of granting users control over their personal information, the OPC report on social network privacy contends that social network sites are particularly prone to placing users' privacy in danger. As the report details, privacy policies on these sites are required by *PIPEDA* to include transparent statements about how information is collected and used.[5] Yet, even with increased transparency in privacy policies, relationships between social network sites and advertisers often remain unclear; this occurs alongside the vague process of aggregating information so that it is not "personally identifiable" (Office of the Privacy Commissioner of Canada, 2009b, 45–6).

Expanding the OPC's recommendations for clearer wording, PIAC has suggested that Canada implement a Do Not Track List, which has been proposed in the United States by the Federal Trade Commission as "a universal mechanism" through legislation or self-regulation (Federal

Trade Commission 2010, 66). Such a mechanism would allow users to bypass the numerous privacy threats posed by the collection and use of personal information on social network sites: compromised transparency; implied consent; little or no control over opting out; opt-out consent as the main model rather than opt-in; the selling of information to third parties; the packaging and aggregation of data in data mining operations; incomplete or impermanent anonymization of personal information; and more generally, the ways that online profiling can discriminate and lead to loss of consumer autonomy through predictive models of behaviour (Public Interest Advocacy Centre 2009, 49–53).

Particularly troubling about the range of privacy threats on social network sites is how to protect the rights of children and youth under the age of majority who find these sites appealing. Canadian privacy legislation includes no special laws related to the protection of minors' personal information online against commercial breaches of privacy. Children's information is an especially sensitive category of personal data, amplifying threats of misuse and abuse. Children may also disclose personal information more readily to commercial sites posing as games, termed "immersive advertising" (Public Interest Advocacy Centre 2008, 23), or on sites where ads are indistinguishable from content (Public Interest Advocacy Centre 2009, 54–5).

Moral panics about online predators have overshadowed these informational privacy threats, with federal privacy regulation containing little protection over minors' personal information. In the United States, the 1998 *Children's Online Privacy Protection Act* aims to safeguard the informational privacy of children under the age of 13, mainly through putting the onus on parents rather than on the sites themselves to make sure kids understand how to protect their information online. In practice, it is relatively easy for young Internet users to circumvent their parents' discretion and use social network sites by claiming an older birthdate (Public Interest Advocacy Centre 2008, 32). Even though Facebook requires new users to be over the age of 13, children still create profiles and use the site for social interaction – accepting the conditions of data collection and use as specified in its Terms of Service and Privacy Policies, arguably without being able to give meaningful consent (Burkell, Steeves, and Micheti 2007).

Conclusion

In the reports from the 1970s, as well as today, the primary objective of policy research in Canada has been to suggest recommendations to policymakers on how to effect legislation to protect citizens' rights more comprehensively. In regard to privacy in online social networks, recommendations from the OPC and PIAC focus on amendments to *PIPEDA*, reflecting the concern with immanent commodification in the private sector's collection and use of personal data. Yet in a more general sense, as indicated by the *Instant World* and *Privacy & Computers* reports issued long before *PIPEDA* was drafted, regulation needs to invest citizens with control over their own data online. As part of Nissenbaum's characterization of privacy as contextual integrity, control over personal information – the ability to determine what information gets collected and used in certain contexts – is critical for upholding privacy as a fundamental right of citizenship.

A first step for granting users more control over their own personal information is mandating Web sites to draft transparent privacy policies to increase public understanding of how online platforms collect and use personal information. On social network sites, for instance, the OPC (2009a, 47) would require the sites to provide a clearer and comprehensive explanation of how personal information is collected and used. PIAC (2009, 75) reiterates the importance of transparent privacy policies and suggests that companies should detail the following information for users:

> 1) what personal information about them is collected, and especially what sensitive personal information is collected (e.g., health and financial information); 2) how this information will be used for online behavioural targeted advertising; 3) how long this information will be retained by the website operator and/or the parties with which they share the information; and 4) to whom this information will be disclosed, including affiliates and third party marketers and market researchers. Definitions should be provided for "affiliates," "third party" and "partners."

The rationale behind standardizing privacy policies is to ensure that they describe exactly how personal information gets collected and used, in order to improve the reliability of informed consent (ibid., 75). The argument is that if policies offer users more transparency, the result will be increased understanding of data flows online, enabling users to grant more meaningful consent.

In addition to exercising users' capacity to give informed consent through transparency of privacy policies on social network sites and other commercial Web platforms, the OPC (2010a, 17) recommends that users apply a number of identity management tools. These rest on a similar rationale for meaningful consent, where users should know never to disclose key identifying information in online contexts (such as their Social Insurance Number, date of birth, address, or phone number). Moreover, users should be aware of how their information is used on sites, not only through reading complex privacy policies, but also through a more general understanding of how marketing works on seemingly "free" Web sites such as social network sites (Office of the Privacy Commissioner of Canada 2008, 6).

If these requirements for users seem somewhat vague and demanding, the PIAC has taken a different approach from the OPC in developing privacy management tools. Following the US Federal Trade Commission's discussion papers on a Do Not Track List, PIAC suggests that a similar mechanism might be adopted effectively in Canada. The main benefit of such a list would be to absolve consumers of responsibility for filing a complaint if they feel their rights are being breached (Public Interest Advocacy Centre 2009, 71). And while the barriers to implementing such a list include legal, operational, technological, monetary, and social constraints, PIAC's survey respondents supported the idea of a Do Not Track List, especially since it does not depend on complaint resolution as the main mechanism for federal privacy regulation (ibid., 72–7, 76).

But federal regulatory amendments such as a Do Not Track List need to be drafted in consideration of broader global privacy legislation. Recalling the issue of transborder information flows central to the much earlier *Instant World* and *Privacy & Computers* reports, PIAC's interest in the American regulatory debates indicates the importance of internationally minded revisions to existing legislation. In that regard, PIAC references American and European Union research on potential changes to *PIPEDA*'s complaint resolution framework. They argue that *PIPEDA* should be used to more reliably enforce the privacy safeguards in transnational business models based on secondary marketing (Public Interest Advocacy Centre 2004, 3).

While the OPC has not always been willing to examine *PIPEDA*'s flaws, it has also suggested potential legislative alterations in line with the international regulatory community. In an online context where state borders are more contingent – a dimension of networked technology that has only become amplified since the 1970s – federal privacy protections need to eliminate what the OPC (2008, 3) calls "jurisdictional uncertainty." The OPC has thus been following the International Standards Organization in determining how to set up more secure models for online transactions involving data, in a climate where "citizens want to know that privacy protections are in place, and businesses want to have a common set of rules to follow" (5). Likewise, the first privacy protection recommendation put forth by the OPC in the federal government's 2010 consultations on Canada's digital economy strategy emphasizes that any amendments to *PIPEDA* must underscore global flows of data by implementing privacy controls for users from the design stage of technological and business model development (Office of the Privacy Commissioner of Canada 2010a, 11).

Yet regulatory methods of granting citizens control over their personal information face several challenges related to the immanent commodification of personal information online. Internet businesses such as social network sites often depend on data transactions for generating profit (Campbell and Carlson 2002); therefore, these companies are reticent to draft more transparent privacy policies or grant users more robust privacy controls. Moreover, as discussed previously, increased transparency and privacy management tools assume a baseline level of privacy literacy on the part of citizens, making privacy a "luxury commodity" (Papacharissi 2010) in a context where publicity becomes cheap. To this end, a key element of the OPC's recommendations concerns research on and implementation of public education programs to encourage privacy literacy. Such programs face the challenge of effective implementation given that responsibility for education in Canada lies at the provincial level and there is no federal department for education (Whitehead and Quinlan 2002, 14).

Perhaps, as the OPC's report on the privacy policies of social network sites proposes, the most effective means for transmitting awareness of privacy rights to citizens is through the viral spread of information on social network sites themselves. In this regard, the development of online privacy management tools should be accompanied by "finding ways to normalize privacy choices within the SNS [social network sites] context so that not only those who are currently using SNS actively engage with them but so that as new users join, privacy becomes as viral as other behaviours" (Office of the Privacy Commissioner of Canada 2009a, 6). Yet these viral means are both difficult to manage and peripheral to the key issue of ensuring that users exercise meaningful consent, especially when it comes to younger users of social network sites and similar Web platforms. The OPC has identified children as requiring special attention in this regard, particularly on immersive advertising sites, submitting a revision to *PIPEDA* that would require a "reasonable" expectation that users understand how their information is being collected and used (Office of the Privacy Commissioner of Canada 2010c, 19). This vague stipulation on the responsibility of the sites to define the validity of consent represents but one side of the premise of individual understanding.

As part of the other side – privacy education and literacy – the OPC has attempted to inform young people about their privacy rights through its youth-oriented Web site Youthprivacy.ca. When it was launched, the site featured bright colours and the logos MyPrivacy, MyChoice, and MyLife amidst iPod-advertising-inspired action silhouettes of young people dancing, jumping, and kickboxing. Its modules include an interactive MyPrivacy Quiz, an overview of how to manage one's own privacy, an explanation of privacy legislation and the operations of the OPC, and information on what to do about privacy breaches from peers or Web sites. A blog provided updates on privacy events and issues and highlighted the annual MyPrivacy and Me National Video Competition for short youth-produced videos about personal privacy. Winning submissions, judged by a youth panel, were featured on the OPC Web site and the OPC's YouTube channel, PrivacyComm (Office of the Privacy Commissioner of Canada 2008, 6).[6]

The impact of YouthPrivacy.ca in shaping young people's knowledge of online privacy and immanent commodification online has not yet been assessed. An alternative educational approach is forwarded in PIAC's report *All in the Data Family* (2008), which proposes stringent recommendations for how social network sites themselves communicate their marketing practices to young users. In addition to the report's contention that social network sites' privacy defaults should reflect the most *closed* rather than open settings, the report also calls for the development of a specific set of guidelines for children and minors in different age groups with an increased onus on the sites to implement these, along with higher standards of privacy protection. The report recommends legislation prohibiting the collection, use, and disclosure of all personal information from children under the age of 13. It also recommends legislation requiring consent from both teens and parents for 13- to 15-year-olds and just the teen's consent for young people aged 16 to the age of majority at 18 or 19, depending on the province. Once the teen reaches the age of majority, PIAC recommends that all the teen's previously stored online data be wiped clean (4–5).

PIAC's approach to privacy protection for young users is thus instructive for privacy regulation more generally. Since it is easier to conceptualize the threat of immanent commodification when discussing children's use of social network site platforms, the recommendations around the collection and use of children's personal information tend to be more comprehensive and urgent. This urgency ought to be applied to privacy protections for all citizens, especially considering the OPC's stated contention that "the social transformation that has taken place in the span of a single generation due to the Internet is nothing short of staggering" (Office of the Privacy Commissioner of Canada 2008, 7).

The panoply of popular social media tools – Internet technologies that allow for participative communicative practices wherein users can develop, collaborate, customize, rate, and distribute Internet content – pose particular policy challenges. Our concern in this chapter is privacy, especially related to the protection of personal information, the covert pervasiveness of third-party marketing, and informational integrity. Related concerns include protection against illegal and inappropriate content, the promotion and preservation of freedom of expression, and security and safety.

Social network sites enable what Christensen (2009, n.p.) terms "complicit surveillance," in what seems to be a growing cultural acceptance that such sites are a legitimate means for corporations, employers, and the public to monitor the personal communication of citizens. Christensen comments that the often naive yet enthusiastic uptake of these technologies "is giving way to a new surveillance, where the act is consensual and guilt (of convenience and pleasure with a cost) shared" (ibid.). The sophisticated search algorithms and data mining software activated on these participatory platforms exemplify immanent commodification. Hence, an attention to the tenets and parameters of contextual integrity is key to this milieu. Privacy should not have to be a luxury to which only the more knowledgeable members of society can lay claim, nor should it be a commodity that gets shaped by the logic of supply and demand. A truly radical initiative would be to make sure that privacy rights become intrinsic to communication rights alongside access to information.

ACKNOWLEDGMENTS

This chapter has been written thanks to the generous funding from the Social Sciences and Humanities Research Council for the Young Canadians, Participatory Digital Culture and Policy Literacy research project.

NOTES

1 Cloud computing is defined by the OPC as "the provision of Web-based services, located on remote computers, that allow individuals and businesses to use software and hardware managed by third parties. Examples of these services include online file storage, social networking sites, webmail, and online business applications. The cloud computing model allows access to information and computer resources from anywhere that a network connection is available" (Office of the Privacy Commissioner of Canada 2010a).

2 DPI involves the use of network management tools to investigate the digital packets that comprise an electronic message or its transmission over a network. While typically used to ensure the security and integrity of the network, DPI can be used to infringe on users' personal privacy by facilitating third parties' ability to look into the content of messages, thus allowing for the targeting of personalized marketing messages (Office of the Privacy Commissioner of Canada 2009b).

3 Behavioural tracking is a "surreptitious tracking and targeting" of the on-line transactions of users, including their search queries, social network site content, Web pages visited, e-mail content and mobile phone location. Content is culled and analysed to create targeted and ostensibly "relevant" advertising (Center for Digital Democracy 2009).

4 Unlike a Do Not Call List for avoiding telemarketers, which relies on the federal government compiling a national registry of identifying telephone numbers, the proposed Do Not Track List would entail a browser-based system being made available to citizens. This system would run through browser cookies, indicating to behavioural marketers that they may not collect that user's information. As the Federal Trade Commission (2010, 66–7) notes, one of the many potential challenges of implementing this system would be its reliance on self-regulation by marketers.

5 Facebook was found to violate several of PIPEDA's principles, as detailed in a comprehensive complaint filed by students at the University of Ottawa's Canadian Internet Policy and Public Interest Clinic (Canadian Internet Policy and Public Interest Clinic 2008).

6 See http://www.youtube.com/privacycomm?gl=CAandhl=enandhl=en. For a video produced by the OPC about its youth initiative, see http://www .youtube.com/watch?v=eH6t20mlMVE. For the OPC's video on social networking sites, see http://www.youtube.com/watch?v=X7gWEgHeXcA.

PART THREE

Beyond the Publicity State

Introduction

In the third part of this volume, authors address strategies and practices that counter the publicity state from various sectors or perspectives. Together, they illuminate aspects of Canadian society and activity in which possibilities lie for positive change to challenge the publicity state.

Many believe that online communication has the potential to play a decisive role in fostering understanding and action that can counter state-led publicity. In their chapter, Greg Elmer, Ganaele Langlois, and Fenwick McKelvey examine the nature of campaigning in a politically interactive and networked world in which technical management for success displaces the common good, in effect privileging partisanship over governance. It also is a murkier, blurred sphere for political campaigning that demands flexibility, adaptability, and adoption from its social actors; these qualities characterize not only online campaigning but also the marketplace. As Elmer, Langlois, and McKelvey write, online "mobile partisans," in the quest for technological control over political life, join institutional actors in "constant attention to not only communication but also to the very conditions of publicity," the foremost of which is permanent campaigning. What is needed in critical analysis, the authors say, is the development of new framework concepts, including political ethics. However, they also point out that Web 2.0 provides rich political opportunities for those who challenge "centralized and hierarchical forms of political governance and campaign management."

Interest groups and social movements often can and do play a key role in political communication, but increasingly political publicity and marketing are used to control, marginalize, and delegitimize collective action that in earlier years would have been seen as freedom of association and assembly. As the individualist New Right political project deepens its hold on Canadian society, group politics and collective action are more likely to be seen as "distorting the democratic will of the people as expressed in elections," notes Miriam Smith in her chapter. In contrast, when acting as part of policy communities, other organizations – those supportive of government – can provide legitimacy to the actions of the state. The latter groups have the opportunity to influence, define, and help set the agenda for government policy. Smith concludes that economic resources are critically important for groups to get their message out through the media, as well as to be able to seek to influence government and the public. She suggests that globalization has the potential to provide new opportunities and renewed vigour for marginalized groups to network online at minimal cost and maximum visibility.

In his chapter, Herbert Pimlott points to the key role that alternative media play in countering New Right communication practices: "Alternative media ... have a fundamentally critical and unique role in any democracy, but especially where corporate interests and the publicity state threaten or distort democratic communication processes that are at the heart of democracy." Noting that the political context of any period helps determine the degree of freedom for the production of critical content, he reminds us that even publicly funded media (which we rely on for counterbalance and a broader spectrum of perspectives) have been undermined or limited by both political and economic forces in recent years. Alternative media act on behalf of marginalized voices and, in doing so, articulate counter-hegemonic narratives and reframe issues to reflect public concerns. The potential exists for alternative media to develop a broad, networked counterpublic sphere; such potential lies in the interrelationships, cross-fertilization, and networking of these media that can then provide a strong challenge to the commodification of communication.

In the current environment in which mainstream media tend to reinforce rather than challenge existing power structures, media reform is key to resist the publicity state and its "de-democratizing" tendencies. In their chapter, Kathleen Cross, Robert Hackett, and Steve Anderson explore the intersections, interventions, and opportunities that can reinvigorate a democratic public sphere through media reform. According to the authors, the media sphere is unique as the site of both economic and symbolic power to define social reality, but "no field is completely predetermined and no response ever fully certain." Like political systems, the media are not closed to change but are sites where "meanings are contested in a struggle to shape public consciousness." Cross et al. advocate positioning media reform at the centre of a multifaceted approach to the structural and political change that is necessary to achieve this vision of broader and inclusive political and citizen communication.

As the chapters in this part emphasize, Web 2.0 activism, interest groups and social movements, alternative media, and media reform all have the potential to break through the morass of the publicity state to reclaim democratic communication in political life. More importantly, their interventions are not prescriptive but are intended to be open, flexible, and grounded within the public sphere itself. They offer entry points for citizens to participate actively and positively in actions to enrich the quality of communication in our democracy, instead of fostering an imagined community based on similar consumer preferences that characterize the publicity state.

11 The Permanent Campaign Online: Platforms, Actors, and Issue-Objects

GREG ELMER, GANAELE LANGLOIS,
AND FENWICK MCKELVEY

In the past few years, there has been an undeniable shift in political communication, one marked by the rise of so-called social media – user-generated Web 2.0 platforms such as blogs, social networks (e.g., Facebook), microblogs (e.g., Twitter), video and image Web sites (e.g., YouTube and Flickr), and knowledge repositories (e.g., Wikipedia). Social media make it possible for anybody to express themselves, and this ability has directly challenged traditional modes of political communication that rely on a handful of political and media experts to control and propagate political discourses and orchestrate political events. Recent uprisings in the Middle East, dubbed the "Arab Revolutions," have also become synonymous with the democratic potential of such communication technologies. At the same time, the rise of a whole industry of political campaigning online that is aimed at helping professional political actors manage their campaign through mobilizing users, spread their messages, and fundraise across social media platforms, as became apparent with Barack Obama's 2008 presidential campaign (Harfoush 2009), also points to new strategies of political communication that seek to manage and control this distributed and networked environment. As such, professional politics, along with strategizing and managing political discourses and representations, has far from disappeared in the social media environment. Rather, media control is reinventing itself in order to meet the new possibilities and limits of the current online communication environment. In particular, as we explain in this chapter, political campaigns are faced with the complicated challenge of maintaining visibility, coherence, and durability in an environment where the risks of disappearing in a sea of information, of being the subject of infinite critiques and attacks, and of having one's message distorted are constantly present. Hence, the key critical concept of this chapter – the *permanent campaign* – seeks to address this constant effort to maintain visibility, coherence, and durability on and through online social media.

This chapter provides a theoretical framework for examining permanent campaigning online in the Canadian and US context. In particular, we examine permanent campaigning that sees alliances across different platforms and types of users, for instance, among politicians, political bloggers, the mainstream media online, and amateur video making. We argue that these new modes of permanent campaigning are increasingly defined through the technological plane as much as the rhetorical one; that is, in order to understand new modes of managing communication online, we cannot simply stop at the analysis of the content of online communication. Rather, in order to understand what is new about political communication on social media sites in the permanent campaign, we need to look at the circulation of political communication objects across platforms.

From Mediated to Networked Permanent Campaigns

In his tell-all book, Scott McClellan (2008), former White House press secretary to George W. Bush – effectively the president's chief spokesperson – denounced not only his old political boss but also the permanent campaign in Washington, the hyper-partisan, insider-driven political game that demanded a high degree of loyalty. A similar story. also played out north of the border in Canada, where Tom Flanagan, former advisor to Prime Minister Stephen Harper, similarly distanced himself from his former boss's permanent campaigning mode, one that he argued had turned the Conservatives into a "garrison party": "Just as chronic warfare produces a garrison state, permanent campaigning has caused the Conservative Party to merge with the campaign team, producing a garrison party. The party is today, for all intents and purposes, a campaign organization focused on being ready for and winning the next election, whenever it may come" (MacCharles 2010, 1). While such high-profile political operatives have invoked the permanent campaign in an effort to raise questions about the recent political past, the concept itself was first politically enacted by Patrick H. Caddell, an advisor to then president-elect Jimmy Carter. According to *Time* magazine, Caddell advised Carter, "It is my thesis governing with public approval requires a continuing political campaign" (J. Klein 2005). Caddell's remarks, of course, came at a particularly complicated and contested period in American political history, one that witnessed a renewed sense of patriotism and partisanship nearing the end of a decade defined by a loss of public confidence in post-Vietnam and Watergate political leadership. In such a politically volatile climate, where politicians came under close scrutiny from not only their political opponents but also members of the media and voters, Caddell's noteworthy report was among the very first to recommend bridging the tactics, time, and technologies of governing and electoral campaigning. Ornstein and Mann (2000, 38), however, argue that permanent campaigning is a form of "technical management" of the political sphere, an effort on the part of the political class (viz., elected representatives and their assorted operatives) to strictly control the terrain and terms of political life.

As an object of study, the permanent campaign has also served to bring together a group of American political scientists in search of empirical methods and approaches to the study of partisan governance. Murray and Howard (2002), for example, argued that politician's travel and public appearances, particularly at public events, served as a clear indicator of permanent campaigning. Likewise, Doherty's (2007, 770) study of nonelection year presidential travel indicated a pattern of visiting "large competitive states." The widespread growth of political opinion polling by government worldwide also points to an ongoing concern with electability even after elections (Murray and Howard 2002). In addition, Canadian researchers, many of them also authors of chapters in this volume, have examined shifts in political communication that foreground nonelection tactics and strategies to maintain public visibility and support.

The ensemble of strategies that constitute the permanent campaign form the underlying and necessary environment for the proliferation of publicity practices that characterize political communication in the modern publicity state. While we should be careful in distinguishing across national case studies, permanent campaigning as an emergent 24/7 cycle of partisan forms of publicity typically shares common modernist traits, which in the political sphere means resulting from (a) the bureaucratization of political parties, (b) the emergence of formalized or professionalized election apparatuses (or, in the vernacular, party "machines"), and (c) executive-dominated political cultures where backbencher legislators are rewarded for loyalty and are harshly punished for dissent from the party line and votes. Election cycles, of course, also play a significant role in mediating the ebbs and flows of partisan and political life across jurisdictions (Alesina and Roubini 1992). The splintering of electorates, through the growth of regional and linguistic, anti-immigrant, and protest parties, has also cultivated permanent campaigning, as unstable minority and coalition governments and "hung" parliaments increase the frequency or at least the possibility of shorter election cycles.

Lastly, the emergence of permanent campaigning can also be tied to the exponential rise in the publicity practices of political advertising and fundraising – much of which is raised by appealing to the more ardent and ideologically committed members of particular political parties. Similarly, governments, opposition parties, and other minor parties now routinely engage in legislative antics, set-ups, "gotcha" politics, and scheduled votes on wedge issues that attempt to draw sharp policy distinctions between parties – distinctions that, of course, touch on particularly contentious issues such as abortion, gun control, taxation, and minority and immigration rights (Hillygus and Shields 2008).

Whatever the emphasis, each of these scholars explicitly or implicitly raises the question of partisanship and permanent campaigning out of a concern for the conduct of political life, in short, for ethical reasons. This chapter is no different. Permanent campaigning suggests a waning of the central tenets of political representation, whereupon elected representatives, particularly members of the ruling party, displace their responsibility for the common good for all citizens in favour of the technical management of continued electoral success. The perils of permanent campaigning lie in the privileging of partisanship over governance. Ironically, this perilous state of affairs is, as we detail here, both constructed and destabilized by the very same set factors, namely by the rapid introduction of information and communication technologies into political life. Hess (2000) makes this important point but in the earlier content of the first railway-enabled political campaigns. Permanent campaigning then was a mediated phenomenon where mass-mediated or reported stops – "staged" or otherwise – sought greater control over political messages (see Marvin 1988).

For decades, network news has served as a key site of political debate and political campaigning, be it through the coverage of events, talk shows, or televised candidate debates. The predictability of such

244   Greg Elmer, Ganaele Langlois, and Fenwick McKelvey

coverage, in terms of its discrete broadcast timing and scheduling, however, was fundamentally altered in 1980 in the United States and later in Canada with the introduction of the Cable News Network (CNN). Similar networks around the globe, including CBC and CTV in Canada, soon joined CNN in introducing the 24-hour news cycle to political life. The subsequent need for more hours of news coverage greatly expanded political programming on television, leading to the development of an expanded class of political pundits, typically former members of the political or journalistic class, whose newfound freedom from professional conventions led to the airing of unabashed partisan sloganeering and debate. Furthermore, the multiplicity of spaces for political debate created the need for more political spokespeople – greatly valorizing communicators over legislators, orators, or parliamentarians (Cushion and Lewis 2010; Dagnes 2010).

Building upon these changes in news cycles and political communication, this chapter investigates how the introduction of the Internet and the World Wide Web has redefined and otherwise contributed to a new paradigm of permanent campaigning. This chapter, however, moves beyond discussions of expanded media time, reporting and commentary, the timing and coverage of public affairs, and even the political tone of political news coverage. In so doing, this chapter is largely concerned with understanding and seeking to develop new perspectives, methods, and theories of political communication, based upon what we see as a networked and distributed battle over political opportunities presented by the Web, one that has greatly complicated the relatively fixed roles of journalist, citizen, and politician, as discussed in Ornstein and Mann (2000). The political establishment and, to a lesser extent, the mainstream media, are faced with a destabilized set of relationships produced by distributed and interactive forms of communication and networking – techniques and technologies that afford two-way communication in real time. Contemporary forms of permanent campaigning thus continue to invoke partisan tactics and talking points (centralized message control) in a political landscape that deploys campaign-style tactics in the routine running of government. However, so-called participatory media (see Jenkins 2006) – namely Web 2.0's networked platforms (blogs, microblogs, online video, social networking) – have also challenged centralized and hierarchical forms of political governance and campaign management. Permanent campaigning today is in fact largely defined by the ongoing attempts by various political actors to harness and otherwise manage the opportunities wrought by new information and communication technologies – including media and voter management technologies (Howard 2006; Kreiss, 2012; Karpf, 2012).

Without the rigid definition afforded by traditional political roles and institutional hierarchies, contemporary permanent campaigning clearly contributes to a murkier political sphere – a blurring of temporalities, rules, conventions, and professional roles that have produced new hybrid actors such as "citizen-journalists" and venues for official government communications (e.g., Twitter). Even electoral results and ensuing claims to certain "mandates" have been remediated through this cloudy political landscape. The 2000 American presidential election marked a pivotal moment in contemporary western political history whereupon online activists, fundraisers, and pundits engaged in a protracted campaign to settle the terms of the incomplete Electoral College results. While the uncertainty of who won the 2000 presidential election (George W. Bush or Al Gore?) highlighted a crisis – a deep divide – in American political opinion, it also served to highlight the role of technology in elections through the use of, abuse of, and mistrust in voting machines, as well as the use of Internet sites to debate and spread questionable "facts" during the ensuing constitutional crisis. Similar post-electoral political dynamics have recently occurred in Canada in 2008 (this example will be discussed later in this chapter) and, more recently, the United Kingdom in 2010 when established political parties failed to secure a majority of seats in their respective Houses of Commons. Ongoing campaigns on the part of politicians, party staff, partisans, and political proxies were all evident on the Internet days and weeks after official election results were announced.

More in-depth theoretical, conceptual, and empirical studies of the socially mediated aspects of permanent campaigning must recognize not only the speed, hyper-immediacy, and the (24/7) dimensions and potential of modern political communications but also the speed at which the Web platforms, political roles, and forms of communication themselves constantly change. In other words, networked permanent campaigning is as much about flexibility, adaptability, and adoption as it is about partisan politics as such. In the remainder of this chapter, we suggest that networked permanent campaigning in particular intersects – that is, seeks to manage and is itself managed by – three constantly shifting phenomena: the spaces of communication and campaigning itself (social media platforms); partisan participation, action, and subjectivity; and lastly, the digital encoding and circulation of political communications (or "issue-objects").

Permanent campaigning then is enacted on – and across – Web-based platforms, sites such as YouTube, Facebook, and Twitter that contain their own unique set of practices, rules, and networking opportunities in three key areas. First, by understanding how such platforms interact and are themselves networked – both in terms of how one can distribute content across them and view and interact with such comments from a series of such platforms – we can begin to understand the new terrain of networked politics, the site upon which permanent campaigning is enacted.

Second, as previously noted, permanent campaigning during "off-peak" hours of the week or during particularly acute political crises where additional electoral campaign staff have not been hired or integrated into war rooms and other official partisan structures calls into question the very nature of what it means to be a political partisan in the networked age. This focus on partisan subjectivity, however, does not simply seek to understand the blurring of political roles among those interested and active within political circles (officially or otherwise); it focuses more on the role that such new subjects play in heightening and privileging continuous partisan and political activity – a central characteristic of contemporary permanent campaigning. Indeed, it logically flows from our first point above, as was the case in the development of the 24-hour news cycle, that more opportunities, spaces, and sites for political communication have also created the need for new political "staff," which means more individuals who can be called upon to contribute to debates, dialogues, and other forms of political communication that support political parties, their elected leaders, and their public policies.

Third and lastly, in the final section of the chapter, we analyse the primary mode of political campaigning in the networked landscape, the tactical and strategic deployment of issue-objects (such as videos, blog posts, digital images, graphics, and hyperlinks) for political goals. In this concluding section of the chapter, we investigate how discrete issue-objects, according to Foot and Schneider (2006), are used to unite political campaigns across platforms (as noted in the previous section) while also serving as "stand-alone" object signifiers, meaning artefacts that connote specific political meaning (i.e., political issues, positions, and ideologies) in and of themselves, that is, how they invoke and seek to influence and frame specific political issues and debates. To illustrate the networked deployment of issue-objects, we will elaborate on the role of blogging in the post-election crisis in Canada in 2008.

The Platform of Permanent Campaigning

The concept of the permanent campaign, as we argued previously – as well as the publicity practices that develop from it – is inseparable from the development of mass media systems. The transition from mass media to networked media, however, has radically changed the communicative terrain on which forms of permanent campaigning are shaped. Simply put, permanent campaigning can be defined as an ensemble of strategies to shape the parameters of political discussion (such as issues, scope, perspectives, and talking points) so as to predefine for a public the discursive and affective positions of political candidates and their opponents. The strategies of mass-mediated permanent campaigning were mostly centred on control over the airwaves and establishment of networks through which a specific agenda, stance, and image could be continually pushed to an audience. Networked media, however, fundamentally challenges long-held assumptions about media reception, participation, and political roles. The Web's distributed networked environment therefore forces us to reconceptualize and redefine the very term *political communication* – a term that must now account for the ever-expanding capacity for information storage and retrieval, multiple entry points of communication, and expanded sites and modes of self-expression. Current buzzwords used to describe online communication – Web 2.0, social media, participatory culture – all try to express the radical equalization of communication via distributed networks, where the boundaries between producers and receivers are constantly blurred and where there are seemingly no limits to the expansion and circulation of information and content. In this new context, the classical restriction of access to a handful of media and political professionals disappears only to be replaced by the rise of participatory communication models based on hosting grass-roots and independently produced content. As such, while previous forms of permanent campaigning were focused on enclosing the flows of communication, we see the main challenge for political communication today as one of managing open-ended flows of communication.

While open-ended communication is perhaps the defining characteristic of contemporary networked media, this does not imply a lack of structure or limits. The original structuring protocol of the World Wide Web, the hyperlink, served as both a protocol of communication and a device for organizing information across Web documents and spheres. As such, a central methodological approach to examining the structure and subsequent flows of information online focused on determining hyperlinking patterns across Web pages and sites (Park and Thelwall 2003). The current structure of the Web is conversely marked by the rise of the operating software platform model (Gillespie 2010; Langlois et al. 2009). Simply put, Web 2.0 platforms have emerged as largely enclosed and self-regulated operating systems that operate "on top of" existing Web protocols. As opposed to the previous Web 1.0 model that was based on the hyperlink as a universal protocol, Web 2.0 platforms manage content and users in very specific and modular ways through a proliferation of codes and protocols. The common characteristic of all participatory platforms is to accommodate (in terms of easy-to-use publishing tools and expansive databases) large amounts of user-generated content, that is, content created by a diverse range of users, from official party staff to interest groups and citizens. What distinguishes one platform from another is, in the first instance, the form taken by this content, from videos on YouTube to digital pictures on Flickr, short text on Twitter, and more multi-mediated approaches on social networking sites such as Facebook.

Each Web 2.0 platform also differs in terms of the ways in which users can relate to content – the kinds of comments they can make, the possibility of exporting content from one platform to another, and so on. However, while such interactive functions are often clearly highlighted on platform interfaces for users, the main distinguishing feature among participatory platforms concerns the ranking of information. Simply put, it is not enough for a participatory platform to be a database or repository for all kinds of information. The participatory platform must also offer specific logics by which information can be meaningfully retrieved, ranked, and circulated. Such logics differ from one platform to the next and require different arrangements and practices between software and users, thus posing significant problems for those seeking to orchestrate coherent political communications and campaigns. For instance, some platforms might push software-produced recommendations onto users. In this case, the software is in charge of extracting the meaningful information, that is, the kind of information that might be relevant to all users, specific categories of users, or individual users. For example, YouTube offers two ways of accessing videos: a general search box that will rank results in terms of popularity (most viewed) videos and personalized recommendations based on a user's personal viewing history. The first search is based on the logic that what is the most popular is most universally relevant, while the recommendations are based on personalized preferences according to users' specific patterns of viewership. Other platforms might be more focused on enabling users to establish paths of relevant content through user-generated tags and keywords, for instance, or by allowing users to create their own paths for following other user-generated content streams, as in the case of Twitter. Often, participatory platforms will multiply the different logics of retrieving and ranking content according to multiple definitions of what constitutes meaningful content.

Given the varying approaches to ranking and otherwise making visible content on Web 2.0 platforms, permanent campaigning on the Internet can thus be understood as an attempt to manage the open-endedness of communication by maximizing the potential interface time, visibility, and ranking of specific digital objects, whether they be text, video, images, or audio clips. As explained in the next section, strategic interventions in the flow of open-ended content subsequently require enlisting online partisans to participate in political debate and organizing. The Obama presidential campaign of 2008, for instance, was considered a success in large part because it mobilized users to circulate messages about the campaign onto multiple platforms, namely social networks, but also online video sites and blogs. That being said, the strategies of permanent campaigning are not simply about mobilizing users; they also seek to maximize the ways in which specific discourse, sound bites, and images can be more present, more visible, and more audible online than others. To achieve such effects requires an understanding and strategic use of the communicational logics within and across platforms that organize information according to the specific definition of meaningfulness.

It is often difficult to determine exactly how specific Web 2.0 platform logics of search, retrieval, and ranking work, because such processes are often held back from users, programmers, and others for proprietary reasons. Moreover, given the overall unique proprietary software code that governs respective Web 2.0 platforms, political networking and communicating on the Web also faces a constantly shifting set of rules among 2.0 platforms that determine what can circulate across such sites. The circulation of information across platforms is increasingly enacted by individual partisans and online party supporters "sharing" objects (via Facebook or Twitter share buttons) with other users, social networks, interfaces, and social media platforms. While these modes of sharing simplify the circulation of content from a user's perspective, they make it more difficult to actually track patterns of circulation of content across the Web because they tend also to be black-boxed, opaque software processes. The participatory platforms do not just structure information; they also manage the circulation of information within and across platforms. This takes the form of controlling the conditions under which third parties such as political parties or the mainstream media can access, retrieve, and customize the information available on participatory platforms.

Another important distinguishing characteristic of participatory platforms then, as opposed to the classic Web site model, is the means through which third parties access or data mine large sets of data on social media platforms, whether it be the user-generated content or specific information about users (such as demographic information, surfing behaviours, and content preferences). Access to such information typically occurs through so-called application programming interfaces (APIs), which are slightly more advanced components of social media or Web 2.0 platforms that allow third-party customized software programs to link to and get information from the software in charge of managing information on the participatory platform side. APIs can range from software modules launching a specific query to a platform's database and retrieving search results to more complex software modules destined to provide users with value-added content. For instance, the YouTube API makes it possible to obtain information about the most viewed videos (such as the numbers of views, the date posted, and tags). The Facebook API allows for more complex applications, such as a gaming application that require users to allow a third party to access their personal data and network of friends. The Obama campaign launched a "Yes We Can" application using Facebook's API. It served key networking and campaigning roles during the 2008 campaign: first, to promote the "Yes We Can" music video on Facebook by making it possible for users to embed the music video onto their Facebook page and, second, to gather data about potential voters by forcing users to grant access to information about themselves and their networks of friends to the creators of the API-enabled application.

As such, the open-ended field of communication that is characteristic of the participatory model offers a new terrain for permanent campaigning, one that is organized around platforms, each developing its own logic by which some content is rendered more visible or socially networked. The strategies of permanent campaigning are now centred on making use of these logics of visibility, both with regard to the mobilization and deployment of new actors and with regard to developing specific back-end software processes to intervene in and obtain information about user-created content and user profiles.

The Activation of Mobile Partisans in the New Politics

The history of political campaigning is one of expansion – of the sites, spaces, and times, in short, the opportunities to engage in political communication. Initially, political opportunities were clearly defined, in terms of formats, times, and in professional roles. Today, we see a blurring of such distinctions, with accompanying claims of a "participatory" culture on new media platforms and technologies that pave the way for political engagement (Jenkins 2006). We suggest, however, that such participation is intensely contested (cf. Scholz 2006), as much defined by relationships to existing forms of political power as to an entirely new plane of political life, which some have dubbed a Politics 2.0 (Chadwick and Howard 2008).

Such 2.0 sites, spaces, and times of political communication and activity thus present both opportunities and needs – opportunities for nontraditional actors to engage other established actors and for political parties to reach out and otherwise interact with such new political actors to, in effect, serve as "staff" for the partisan fuelling of a permanent campaign. Unlike in the past, however, these individuals are not contracted, hired, or otherwise directly employed as staff of political parties, nor are they simply volunteers or grass-roots members of political parties. With the introduction of the aforementioned 2.0 platforms, particularly those that hosted, served, and otherwise facilitated the use of so-called blogs, individuals interested in engaging with the political process, through the circulation of opinions or direct and indirect efforts to support candidates or oppose government or opposition policies, can in near real time publish their partisan opinions.

Before we turn to an analysis of the digital objects and discourses circulated across Politics 2.0, we should first begin with the core of any permanent campaign mode of governance: the intensified and expanded field of the contemporary partisan. The late conservative political theorist Schmitt (2007) offers a particularly helpful point of departure even though he has been the subject of intense criticism from radical democratic theorists such as Roberto Esposito (2005) and Chantal Mouffe (2005). Initially in *Theory of the Partisan*, Schmitt offers a rather traditional and institutionally minded definition of partisanship that invokes common military metaphors into the civil sphere: "The partisan fights at a political front, and precisely the political character of his [sic] acts restores the original meaning of the word partisan. The word derives from party, and refers to the tie to a fighting, belligerent or politically active party or group" (ibid., 15). Yet it is the more mechanically or technologically enabled forms of partisanship that Schmitt offers to our 2.0 perspective, one that not only disentangles the partisan necessarily from the party organ but also introduces a nomadic perspective to partisanship. He writes,

> His [sic] mobility is increased by his motorization to such an extent that he is in danger of becoming completely disoriented. In the situations of the Cold War, he becomes a technician of the invisible struggle, a saboteur, and a spy. Already during World War II, there were sabotage troops with partisan training. Such a motorized partisan loses his telluric character and becomes only the transportable and exchangeable tool of a powerful central agency of world politics, which deploys him in overt and covert war, and deactivates him as the situation demands. (ibid., 22)

What Schmitt's "mobile partisan" offers, then, is the figure of a political actor, motivated of course by partisan political goals, though not necessarily tied, as a matter of routine or convention, to the everyday machinations of political parties. However, while such actors exhibit nomadic traits, taking from Schmitt's definition of partisanship, they also maintain a semblance and practice of party loyalty, which he defines as one initiated or activated by political parties – the calling to arms, so to speak, of the mobile partisans for the good of the party. Bloggers, twittering politicos, YouTubers (or "vloggers"), and the like are both proactively and subtly courted by individuals, factions, or campaigns from political parties. The permanent campaign requires reliable staff; thus, online political activists are consistently monitored by the political parties, through their social media monitoring services, to determine who among the partisan bloggers can be trusted when the political stakes are raised. Of course, the nomadic, (un)tethered notion of the 2.0 actor also highlights – and some might argue acerbates – pre-existing and just-below-the-surface factions within political parties themselves. Through their ability to anonymously disseminate and otherwise promote insider political information, bloggers are consistently used by party members, leaders, and factions to disrupt and embarrass internal political agendas and personalities (Flanagan 2009, 239–40). Indeed, leadership crises and contests within political parties often exhibit the most intense and mortal coupling of online partisans and established political masters.

Through such party-based connections, partisan bloggers and other online activists establish ongoing relationships with staff and representatives of the political parties and their various appendages. The importance of reputation and the ability to consistently deliver "insider" information from political masters, on the one hand, and the ability to anonymously "leak" political information out of party offices, on the other, continues to cultivate a symbiotic relationship between individual bloggers and other online partisans and official staff from within established political parties. Such relationships therein offer a myriad of ex-distanced or otherwise virtual forms of political manoeuvring that were previously restricted to selective and sometimes surreptitiously under-the-door leaks to members of the mainstream media.

The rise of such amateur partisan actors has provided the media with compelling figures to serve as Internet-based, savvy members of the technocrati. The attempt to provide readers and viewers with commentary from technologically savvy and politically verbose newcomers is, however, but one component in this newly reconstituted sphere of political punditry and posturing. Rather, both the media and political parties and institutions call upon bloggers to enter the mainstream political discourse for strategic reasons. For the mainstream media, the growth of political consultancy, or professional talking-head punditry, has become stale, itself undermined by a near-monopolistic sphere of mediated political discourse. The tethering of such amateur political actors then mixes the vox populi – or "streeters," as the media refer to them (interviews with citizens typically walking to or from work or school) – with more politically informed punditry. Since such bloggers do not officially speak for political parties, the media can routinely turn to them in the aggregate – for example, the conservative or "republican" blogosphere – at any time of the day or night to obtain voices of the partisan political mood.

Issue-objects and Discrete and Networked Tactics

The motivations and agendas of partisans alter the terrain of political conflict. We see their presence as intensifying the ongoing shift from traditional iron triangle arrangements in the United States (those connections between Congress, interest groups, and the bureaucracy) to what Heclo (1978) described as "issue networks." Heclo noticed in the Carter administration that this "stable set of participants" that had "coalesced to control fairly narrow public programs" had given way to issue networks that "comprise a large number of participants with quite variable degrees of mutual commitment or of dependence on others in their environment" (102). The content of politics is as broad as the term *issue* – a sort of catch-all category to define all the scandals, crises, perspectives, and concerns that spark entry into the political fray. Once into the fray – through party manipulation, personal interest, or both – partisans fight to have their message heard amidst all the political noise.

Political expression in the permanent campaign entails a calculated manoeuvre to construct issues in order to gain scarce attention. Attention here refers to both the prominence of issues on the current political agenda and in the memory of the event itself (Lazzarato 2006). Actors seek not only to bring their concerns to the forefront but also to ensure their version of an event remains the preferred history. In doing so, partisans attempt to construct issues in the most favourable light possible for their agenda. Capturing attention aligns the expression of politics with the calculated, campaign style of talking points, stump speeches, and "plain speak for the little guy." Each actor carefully constructs issues in ways expedient to partisans and party goals and strategies. Partisans not only generate messages but also play a pivotal role in echoing and amplifying the message.

The permanent campaign is an attention economy, a competition over the scarce resource of political attention (Lanham 2007). Dean (2008, 107) argues that the communication of information no longer primarily includes an intended receiver: "Uncoupled from contexts of action and application, as on the Web or in print and broadcast media, the message is simply part of a circulating data stream." Often, political issues and concerns are ignored or fall on deaf ears. Bloggers, as Lovink (2008) points out, fear nothing more than zero comments – the sign that no one has read their post. Successful actors in the permanent campaign avoid the dreaded zero comments or, on the other hand, cause an opponent's message to fall on deaf ears. As Schattschneider (1960, 71) wrote, "Some issues are organized into politics while others are organized out." Political debate, in other words, hinges on capturing attention in the campaign – to win recognition or, at least, cause an opponent to be discredited.

Making an impact in the permanent campaigning, capturing and sustaining attention, is centred on discrete digital *objects*. In other words, permanent campaigning is an object-oriented form of politics (Callon, Lascoumes, and Barthe 2009; Latour 2005; Marres 2005). Among the clutter and clatter of political discourse, discrete digital objects (links, blog posts, YouTube videos, Flickr photos) not only capture and embody contemporary politics but also *orient* the field of political communication and the means of publicity towards their sustained (meaning visible) circulation. Consequently, political missteps are increasingly defined as such political objects. Consider the racial slur uttered by George Allen, the Republican incumbent in the 2006 US Senate election in Virginia. Allen uttered the slur at a campaign rally. While the actual slur might have happened before a stage full of supporters, a Democratic campaign staff recorded Allen's words on camera. The Democratic campaign recognized the potential of the video and worked to construct an object that could discredit its opponent. The campaign staff uploaded the video to YouTube and then circulated the object to the mainstream media and partisan operatives. Bloggers and news sites circulated the object by embedding it in their Web pages.

An object-oriented politics has increasingly intensified during the past few tumultuous years in Canadian politics. The 2008 coalition crisis stands out as a major crisis where parties leveraged digital media objects. Just a few months after a recent federal election, the Conservative government introduced a routine economic update that, in addition to a series of economic measures, also contained cuts to the public funding of federal political parties (see MacDermid's chapter for details). The move threatened to cripple the indebted opposition parties (as well as small parties not represented in Parliament). As a consequence, two opposition parties (the Liberals and the New Democratic Party [NDP]) joined forces to establish a coalition government, with the support of the Bloc Québécois. To pre-empt the defeat of the governing Conservatives, the prime minister abruptly ended the parliamentary session in a controversial parliamentary manoeuvre, in effect staving off defeat at the hands of the coalition government-in-waiting. With the closure of Parliament, the Internet lit up with campaigns for and against the proposed coalition government.

Through analysis of hyperlinked objects posted during the coalition crisis to the partisan blogosphere in Canada, we see in Table 11.1 that political bloggers from the respective parties deployed vastly different tactics. Overall, links of the various parties to "news and analysis" sites (i.e., mainstream media sources) dominate linking practices, with the NDP at 53 per cent, the Liberal Party at 47 per cent, and the Conservative partisan blogrolls (i.e., one's personal links to other blogs) at 50 per cent linking to this sphere. The Green Party and non-partisan bloggers, however, were far less inclined to invoke media reports during the crisis. Only 38 per cent of links from non-partisan bloggers were directed at media platforms and sites, with less than 25 per cent for Green bloggers.

Internal links within the blogosphere (i.e., bloggers linking to other blog posts) was the second most common form of hyperlinking, except for the non-partisan bloggers, who instead linked to the "issues and advocacy" sphere. After "news and analysis" and "internal" blog links, connections to other Web spheres fall off dramatically. The third-most-linked-to sphere for the Greens (15 per cent), Conservatives (10 per cent) and non-partisans (10 per cent) was the "user-generated content" sphere (typically social media platforms), while Liberal bloggers (8 per cent) more commonly linked to the sphere of "professional politics" and NDP bloggers (7 per cent) chose instead to link to the "knowledge resources" sphere.

On other social media sites, the political crisis also fractured into multiple objects as parties sought to define the event and discredit their opponents. Facebook groups – framed as either "I'm part of the 62 per cent majority" or an "undemocratic constitution" – emerged for each side. While such campaigns were obviously orchestrated, it was typically specific blog posts – or objects – that served to highlight both content and to promote activities for both sides on the issue, including protests in city streets. The coalition crisis, as it came to be known, thus demonstrated the multidimensional, multi-mediated life of an object. Objects existed in a variety of media, such as the echo of a slogan in a partisan blog post or the talking points used on a debate show. These expressions calcify to the object, fixing characteristics of an object that define its trajectory and significance. These expressions include not only content but modes of action as well, such as signing a petition or circulating a video. In sum, the research from the political

Table 11.1. Percentage of links to web sites during the 2008 coalition crisis

	News and analysis	Internal (blogs to blogs)	User-generated content	Knowledge resources	Professional politics	For-profit	Issues and advocacy	Indexing	Governmental
Conservatives	50.14%	20.33%	10.12%	4.19%	3.49%	3.88%	2.95%	2.81%	2.11%
Greens	24.19%	29.61%	14.88%	4.96%	4.81%	9.15%	7.75%	1.55%	3.10%
Liberals	46.75%	19.03%	6.60%	5.23%	8.42%	3.58%	2.48%	4.51%	3.41%
NDP	53.20%	15.39%	4.93%	6.90%	3.45%	3.76%	3.57%	3.63%	5.17%
Non-partisan	38.19%	13.19%	10.16%	3.02%	2.47%	3.02%	23.35%	4.40%	2.20%

Source: Infoscape, 2009.

crisis in 2008 demonstrates that, in current politics, studying the object involves digging into its strata to understand its formation and trajectory.

This object-oriented approach is also helpful for understanding the dynamics of the Obama "Yes We Can" campaign. First, the campaign deployed a range of multidimensional Web objects: official texts, videos, and pictures; citizen-generated video responses, critiques, and parodies; and more importantly, links that functions as deictic or pointers (Elmer 2006) to different platforms (such as the official campaign Web site, the Facebook page, YouTube videos, fundraising pages, and organizing and get-out-the-vote sites). Various "Yes We Can" Web buttons (that could be embedded in individual Facebook pages, blogs, and Web sites) facilitated political action and organizing, not simply a declaration of allegiance and voting intention. As an application, particularly the Facebook application developed by Obama campaigners, the online campaign also served as a covert polling measure to acquire information on supporters and would-be voters. As such, "Yes We Can" was a multilevel traffic tag – a digital title or tag that both enabled the wide circulation of said object and created a feedback loop from likely supporters and online organizers. From the point of view of the user, "Yes We Can" served as both political content and a deictic pointer to a broader community of like-minded individuals.

The Obama case illustrates a second important characteristic of an object: its circulation and ability to create networked ideas and technological and communicative affordances. Objects remain in motion, shifting, entangling, stabilizing, and evaporating. Some objects successfully circulate across the Web, such as viral videos, while others simply never make an impact, such as blog posts with zero comments. Circulation is a particularly significant process in a networked campaign. Circulation has intensified partly because of the need to repeat a message in order to capture attention and because the design of digital systems encourages sharing information.

Political campaigns depend on managing the circulation of content – not only attempting to promote objects (with the hopes of them going viral) but also remixing (re-editing) an object to change its initial intended purpose. Similarly, leaking a potentially damaging story to a friendly blog helps shape it as an object before potentially negative articulations emerge. Circulation also includes hijacking an object. The candidate name, for example, has become a key search term and point of entry into politics. Since interested voters conduct online searches for parties, platforms, and specific issues, campaigns routinely consider how best to position their candidate on information aggregators such as Google. Online partisans and party operatives routinely manipulate the search rankings of their opponents so that negative articles appear at the top of the list. Alternatively, politicians of all stripes also buy ads on Google to help direct voters who search specific search terms to their own campaign Web sites – or, conversely, direct voters to unflattering information on the Web sites of their political opponents. In France, the political party UMP (Union pour un Mouvement Populaire) was under assault over allegations that its candidate, Éric Woeth, had received illegal contributions from Liliane Bettencourt, heir to the L'Oréal cosmetics and beauty empire. The party bought ads for searches of "Bettencourt" to ensure its positive message entangled with hits on the controversy (Cario 2010).

While the circulation of objects occurs in the context of strategic campaign communications, at other times it evolves and devolves into an uncontrolled viral meme, an unintended consequence or accident. The management of political campaigns – and objects – is precarious with constantly shifting algorithmic rules on social media platforms and information aggregators. Therefore, an inability to master the political rules of the game – the constantly rewritten operating code used to enable social networking on the Internet –requires an ongoing rethinking of strategic political communication. In other words, it requires a constant attention to not only communication but also to the very conditions of publicity. In short, it requires a permanent campaign.

Conclusion

The chapter has focused on three interconnected components of contemporary technologically mediated and networked political life, the sum of which have cultivated an expanded political clock, an intensified form of partisanship, or a permanent campaign. New political actors (such as bloggers) have emerged as adjuncts to established institutional actors (such as political reporters, party and legislative staff, and elected representatives). Such actors or "mobile partisans" are unlike party workers or even campaign volunteers who work primarily within party structures and conventions. As self-promotional subjects, enacting an object-oriented form of politics, such online activists are proven network communicators; they know how to sustain interest for their objects (such as blog posts) through the use of network conventions such as hashtags, keywords, strategies of embedding objects, and manipulating information aggregators.

Knowledge of social media conventions provides for the necessary skills in a permanent campaign. The ability to easily publish, reedit, comment, and circulate networked political content 24/7 has started to chip away at the conventions of televised broadcast cycles in favour of a new form of temporality governed by modes of attention, and the attendant terms and forms of connectivity among partisans, as well as across and among social media platforms. Some platforms (such as Facebook) swallow political objects like a black hole, disabling their ability to circulate to other platforms, while others (particularly YouTube) actively encourage spreading their objects (such as embedded videos) across a number of sites, platforms, and formats. Political communications can, in other words, be said to be in a state of constant flux, not only because of the breakneck speed at which new platforms, such as Twitter, can emerge on the media landscape but also because of the degree to which the operating systems of such social media sites constantly change their underlying operational code, the language that governs the possibilities and limitations of the social Web. Furthermore, political parties simply do not have the expertise, time, and money to keep a firm grip on this constantly mutating, innovating, and rules-shifting sphere of networked life. As such, they have had to continuously intervene in the new 24/7, networked landscape to test out or otherwise prepare for possible elections and other political crises. Political parties and governments must be proactive in the networked environment, the consequence being a greatly expanded and partisan-filled networked landscape.

This chapter has focused on how such components of political networking both challenge and cultivate technological control over political life; how such new actors, spaces, and objects contribute to the intensification of political partisanship; and the degree to which they both contribute to and undermine the ability to conduct a top-down hierarchical form of political management over the mainstream media, political parties, organs of government, and ultimately the voting public. Moving forward, all actors in a permanent campaign will inevitably struggle to keep pace with the new sites, times, and emergent partisan voices. Given the dizzying pace at which social media platforms update their back-end operational code, the task of researching such online-enabled political campaigns will also struggle to keep pace with technological change. Yet, this is not simply a question of objectively understanding the technomanagement of contemporary politics. Instead, critical analyses of technologically mediated politics must also seek to develop a set of renewed concepts, including political ethics, to frame our understanding of how networked computers, media, institutions, and citizens invoke, enhance, or displace democratic life. While critics may decry the use of new media platforms by political war rooms and partisan operatives as merely networked forms of broadcasting speaking to, but not listening to, voters, permanent campaigning also raises serious ethical issues regarding the spheres of politics, the distinction between public and private, partisan publicity, and voter or citizen privacy. Permanent campaigning is not merely a matter of expanding times and spaces but rather of extending the opportunities and reach of partisanship across the entire political terrain.

12 The Role of Social Movements and Interest Groups

MIRIAM SMITH

Interest groups and social movements play a key role in political communication.[1] Since the 1980s, the role of groups and movements has been increasingly controversial. Right-wing parties have dubbed such groups "special interests," while street protests such as the Occupy movement and the antiglobalization protests that dogged the leaders' summits in Seattle, Quebec City, and Toronto have often conveyed an image of disorder and illegitimacy. These images suggest that collective action by groups of citizens is somehow illegitimate or undemocratic, despite an alternative perspective that freedom of association and freedom of assembly might be seen as core values of democracy. While interest groups or special interests are sometimes depicted in the media as representing a small minority, in fact, the mainstream interests in Canadian society – business, labour, agriculture, universities, the professions, and even media practitioners and companies themselves – have established associations (or interest groups) that represent the common interests of their members. These groups engage in politics in different ways. In some cases, they engage directly in partisan politics by supporting particular parties during election campaigns. In other cases, they press government for particular public policies that are of interest to their members in areas such as regulation or taxes. Still another strategy is that such groups attempt to influence public opinion on a particular policy issue. All of this is collective action by groups of citizens coming together to influence politics. In an environment in which persuasive practices of publicity are used increasingly by governments to sway the public, the ability to communicate one's own voice in policymaking is a considerable challenge.

A few recent cases of collective action in Canadian politics serve to illustrate the range and types of group and movement politics that occur and the challenges they face in fulfilling their role in political communication. When the G20 meeting of western heads of state was held in Toronto in the summer of 2010, large, peaceful demonstrations were held at Queen's Park and other locations in Toronto. Yet the media focused almost entirely on a small minority of anarchists who damaged property and burned a few police cars. The message of the peaceful demonstration, a demonstration that had been organized by the Ontario Federation of Labour, its affiliate unions, and other groups such as student organizations, was almost entirely lost as the message of disorder and urban mayhem dominated the news. Rather than focusing on or even describing social movements' critiques of the G20 meeting on issues such as the economy, the environment, and labour and women's rights, the media again focused almost entirely on actions of anarchists and the subsequent debate over police conduct. Therefore, social movements failed to communicate their message through the mainstream media.

Another example of failed collective action is provided by the case of Ontario pharmacists, a group not known for public lobbying, to call attention to its issues. In 2010, the pharmacists were upset with the McGuinty government's spring 2010 decision to eliminate professional fees paid by the provincial government to pharmacists for generic drugs. While pharmacists could speak to the provincial government regarding this issue through their professional association (Ontario Pharmacists Association 2010), once the government made its decision, pharmacists decided to engage in a publicity campaign to force the government to rethink its decision. Led by large chains such as Rexall and Shoppers Drug Mart, the pharmacists undertook a public campaign on television, radio, and the Internet and through pharmacies themselves (using notices and flyers) to convince the public to support them in their battle with the provincial government. Despite this campaign, the Ontario government stuck to its policy decision on generic drugs.

Pharmacists enjoyed the opportunity to communicate directly with the Ontario minister of health; however, once the government created a policy that was diametrically opposed to the interests of pharmacists, they resorted to a systematic media campaign in order to highlight their concerns about the policy change. Unlike the social movements involved in the G20, pharmacists undertook political communication by purchasing media access, especially to television and radio, and creating YouTube videos. In contrast, social movements protesting the G20 did not have this direct access to government. As for purchasing publicity, social movement campaigners were restricted to home-grown political communication that could be undertaken freely by activists such as online petitions, Facebook, and amateur videos. Thus, political communication varies significantly and substantially for different types of groups. The most successful groups are those who are able to turn their points of view into the common sense of everyday political discourse.

This chapter outlines the role of interest groups and social movements in the process of political communication, a process that has changed considerably in the publicity state as governments strengthen their power to influence the public. I begin by clarifying some terminology. Collective actors vary in their size, power, and level and type of organization, and this section will describe the different types of collective actors and their relationships to the state. Even for those collective actors that are media- and policy-literate, their complexity and breadth are not usually displayed in public forums. Instead, as Gutstein writes in his chapter, a narrow set of social actors enjoys unequal and quiet access to power. In the second section of the chapter, I explore the role of groups and movements in the process of political communication, considering the range of strategies that groups use to influence public policy, while also keeping in mind that access to power takes place on an uneven playing field. The third section of the chapter broadens the focus from the relationship between groups and the Canadian state to consider the role of interest groups and social movements across the system of multilevel governance. Political communication is increasingly multilayered and less focused on the state as the target of collective action. This has implications for interest groups and social movements seeking to promote their perspectives and activities beyond governments to the media and public.

Groups and Movements: A Complex Field of Action

The contrast between the tactics of the Ontario pharmacists and the G20 protesters demonstrates the different kinds of collective actors and their diverse aims. The terms used to discuss group and social movement politics reflect specific theoretical assumptions about collective action, as well as normative judgments about the validity of group politics in democratic societies. The term *collective action* often implies a rational choice approach, based on neoclassical economics, in which the calculating self-interest of the individual is seen as the basis of collective action. The once common political science term *interest group* invokes a pluralist view of society as composed of many diverse groups that contend, more or less equally, for power. The term *pressure group* also implies that groups are "pressuring" the state for their preferred policies and outcomes. Interest groups and pressure groups are sometimes defined as self-regarding, that is, out to pursue the interests of their own members and clients (Young and Everitt 2004). In contrast, public interest groups, non-profits, or non-governmental organizations (NGOs) are often defined as other-regarding, that is, as seeking to further a cause that is not directly connected to the interests of their own members, such as human rights or environmental protection. Interest groups are often distinguished from social movements in that social movements seek to transform social and political values or seek sweeping political change, whereas interest groups are more narrowly focused on obtaining selective benefits from the state. Others distinguish social movements and groups based on their extent of organization, labelling formally organized and well-resourced groups as "associations" or "interest groups" and labelling smaller scale informal networks as social movements (see Smith 2005 for a theoretical and historical overview).

There are also a number of different normative visions of the role of groups in democratic political life. Right-wing populists in Canadian politics have often defined certain forms of group activity as "special interests," a term that implies that such groups are illegitimate and undemocratic (Dobrowolsky 2000; Harrison 1995; Patten 1999). Right-wing populists have tended to label groups as "special interests" when they do not like the aims and goals of the specific groups (e.g., I. Brodie 2002). For example, the First Nations, women's organizations, and gay and lesbian groups have often been labelled "special interests," while groups such as the National Citizens Coalition are defined by Right-wing populists as legitimate and democratic representatives of the common good. Some argue that group politics undermines democracy by distorting the democratic will of the people as expressed in elections (Knopff and Morton 1992). According to critics, such groups are not necessarily democratic and do not necessarily represent the views of the people they claim to represent. In contrast, observers on the Left define class politics as the central form of collective action (Camfield 2008; Buechler 2000). Such a perspective emphasizes the importance of class-based organizations such as trade unions or business organizations that represent capitalist interests. Perhaps most importantly, a class-based perspective would emphasize the underlying power relations in which the dominant class is structurally privileged in the political system while the subordinated classes (workers) have less influence in the political system. From this perspective, business groups are often able to shape political assumptions about policy debates and, therefore, to define their views as the norm against which other views are judged. However, the dominance of class politics on the traditional Left as the lens for viewing the political world has posed challenges for understanding other progressive movements, such as the women's movement, that do not fit easily within the lens of class politics (Fraser 1995; Conway 2004).

I use the term *collective actors* to describe any group of people or organizations that comes together to influence public policy. Interest groups and social movements are types of collective actors. Political parties and think tanks may also be considered as collective actors (see the chapter by Gutstein in this volume), but they have a different purpose than interest groups and social movements. Political parties compete in elections, while think tanks produce knowledge and research, which may be used in the policy process. In contrast, interest groups and social movements do not compete in elections (although they may be allied to political parties) or principally devote themselves to producing policy-relevant knowledge (although they may produce policy-relevant research).

Groups and movements vary in their extent of organization and professionalization. Some groups are highly organized and institutionalized. They have professional staff and regular revenue that enable them to plan action strategically and carry out their activities effectively. Usually, groups that represent economic interests such as business, labour, agriculture, and professions enjoy this level of organization and resourcing. Other large-scale groups of citizens may sell individual memberships or merchandise in order to encourage people to join. On a smaller scale, informal networks of people may come together to engage in political action. Many social movements (e.g., the early women's movement; the anti-racism movement; and the lesbian, gay, bisexual, and transgender) movement had this informal quality of networking and lacked formal organization.

Some social movements are based on existing social institutions or networks and are composed of organizations, as well as individual activists. For example, Christian evangelical political organizing is based in part on networks of churches, and church leaders may play a role in urging members to political action, whether it is voting or participating in other forms of political participation. At the same time, the movement also has dedicated organizations, such as the Evangelical Christian Fellowship, which undertake a broad range of activities, including mobilizing voters behind particular candidates and parties in elections, intervening in court cases, presenting briefs to governments and parliamentary committees, and maintaining individual networks through online mobilization and direct mail (Harrison 2008; McDonald 2010). Similarly, the African American civil rights movement was based in large part on networks of churches throughout the South, which provided vital organizational infrastructure for demonstrations and direct action (McAdam 1999). Therefore, when we speak of a social movement, we most commonly refer to a network of activists and organizations that are loosely affiliated around a common purpose, such as advocating for people with disabilities or engaging in political work around a common cause such as the pro-life issue regarding abortion rights (see also the discussions in Castells 1997; Della Porta and Diani 1999; Staggenborg 2007).

Lobbying is another term that is sometimes used to denote individuals or groups of individuals who are attempting to influence government policies. However, lobbying can best be considered as a professional activity that is carried out on behalf of organized groups, associations, and firms and that, at the federal level, is subject to the regulation of the *Lobbying Act*. Lobbyists are specialists in accessing specific bureaucrats and politicians in a particular policy area, and they are hired because of their networks and connections. Generally, lobbying is a political strategy that is only open to well-heeled organizations and groups because it is expensive. Moreover, lobbying must be contrasted with participation in policy communities, in which organizations have institutionalized linkages with government departments and other stakeholders in a particular policy area. Organizations and associations with a great deal of legitimacy, who are considered to be key stakeholders because of the interests and expertise they represent, will normally not need to hire professional lobbyists to access government (Montpetit 2002).

Strategies of Influence in Political Communication

Collective actors differ in the power they bring to bear in the political process. These power relationships both shape and are shaped by political communication. Some groups work quietly in the background, while others mobilize their members in public demonstrations. Most critically, some types of groups and movements seek publicity, while others do not. In this section, I will outline the different political strategies used by groups and movements in influencing public policy within a state that has considerable communicative resources of its own to counter with. For each strategy, I will discuss the implications for political communication in the publicity state. This is a general typology; in the real world, many groups and movements will use a mix of strategies or will move through different strategies over time.

Policy Communities: Institutionalized Communication

The term *policy community* is used to refer to institutionalized relationships between organized groups and the bureaucracy, usually focusing on a particular area of public policy, such as labour, agriculture, a specific business sector, women's issues, or Aboriginal concerns. A government department or branch in the relevant policy area will develop institutionalized relationships with key groups in the sector over time. The community may also include other policy stakeholders such as think tanks or academics who are particularly knowledgeable about the sector (Howlett and Ramesh 2003).

Political communication in policy communities is characterized by an exchange of information and legitimacy that typically occurs below the media's radar. Governments seek out civil society organizations in order to obtain information regarding particular issues. For example, if the government is considering a new regulation that will affect farmers, the Canadian Federation of Agriculture (CFA) will be able to provide information regarding farmers' views. More than just a sounding board, however, the CFA will also be able to provide information and knowledge to the government about potential effects of regulatory changes. If the government is pressed to bar the use of particular pesticides or wishes to diminish pesticide use, how will this affect crop yields or the types of crops that will be grown? The CFA will have access to specialized technical information about the professional activities of its members and will spare the government the expense of having to collect that information. Organized groups may also provide information to the government about particular policies and programs and their effects on the sector. For example, if the government established a new program to open up market opportunities for particular crops or for the development of new crops, the CFA could provide information to the government on how well these new programs were working (Canadian

Federation of Agriculture 2010). Again, while government might not want to rely entirely on interest groups or social movement organizations for research and information, such groups are founts for certain types of knowledge, which can provide useful feedback and shortcuts to government. In addition to the exchange of different types of information, the government may also seek the legitimacy that can only be provided by groups representing civil society. That is, the government wants approval for its policies from those who are viewed as the stakeholders or the most knowledgeable citizens in a particular sector. If farmers do not agree with agricultural policy, this could pose a problem for government. By participating in the policy community, organized groups and social movement organizations provide legitimacy to the actions of the state.

The advantage to the institutionalization of the government-group relationship from the perspective of the group is that groups obtain information about government policy and, potentially, the opportunity to influence the bureaucracy's thinking on particular issues. The group may be able to set the agenda of government policy, define new concepts and terms in the policy process that may benefit the group in the longer run, or influence the implementation of an important new policy or regulation. At the same time, the government may plan out particular policies, select participants to "consult" whom it believes will support these policies, and then claim to have consulted society. Focus groups and surveys, discussed in Nesbitt-Larking's chapter, may also be used as more passive means of "consulting" citizens instead of working through group representatives.

Some powerful groups and networks are able to access government at the highest level, such as the Prime Minister's Office or members of the Cabinet. Political communication is based on direct relationships with government and other actors through personal networks in which information and political opinions are exchanged. In general, though, elected politicians are not the main target of group and movement influence and pressure. Except in rare cases where politicians may try to use groups to build political support for partisan ends, the legislature does not provide a route for group influence in Canadian politics. The fusion of power between the executive and the legislature combined with the rules of the "first-past-the-post" electoral system and the leader-driven nature of political parties means that most individual MPs do not have much influence in policymaking (Montpetit 2002; Smith 2005). Occasionally, groups may use MPs to capture media attention through, for example, making an appearance before a parliamentary committee; however, in general, individual MPs are not powerful enough to be extensively targeted by groups and social movements. For these reasons, the policy community is centrally important as a vehicle for state-group relations and to the process of political communication. However, because political communication in the policy community does not occur in public, it is generally not covered or noticed by the media. Yet, when the relationships in the policy community break down over a serious policy disagreement, disputes may break out in public and in the media.

Finally, as power is devolved within states, a number of public-private partnerships may also involve groups in implementing public policy on the ground. These public-private partnerships are different from traditional policy communities in that they involve the offloading of state responsibilities to arm's-length length administrative agencies or even NGOs. These types of relationships are very difficult for the public or the media to access given that they deal in specialized regulation based on professional expertise. Like policy communities, they may only burst into media attention when substantial breakdowns occur.

Citizen Engagement and Consultation

Government may also seek to engage with individuals or groups through policy-specific exercises in citizen engagement and consultation. These may range from royal commissions, which are fairly common in Canadian politics, through parliamentary committees to department-based exercises focused on specific policy issues. For groups and movement organizations, such exercises may provide an opportunity to influence policy development, and very much like institutionalized participation in the policy community, bureaucrats and politicians may enter into exchanges of information, expertise, and legitimacy with groups in order to build political support for particular policy options. Such consultations may vary in the extent to which they are open to media scrutiny. Royal commissions and parliamentary committees provide organized interests with the opportunity to voice their views in the open, and developing strategies for media dissemination or for capturing media attention may also form part of a group or movement strategy for influencing the outcome or recommendations of such an exercise (Bradford 1998; Salter 2007).

Governments may also seek to consult with individuals as a means of undermining the role of groups and movements in the policy process. The rise of professionalized polling and focus groups means that governments may seek to take the temperature of public opinion or devise deliberative or consultative exercises that invite selected individuals to give their opinion on sensitive issues. Citizens' juries or citizen forums are sometimes used to give opinions or to represent the interests of the public on delicate policy issues. These deliberative mechanisms are widely used in certain areas of policymaking. For example, in the United Kingdom, decisions on the funding of controversial drugs are made by citizens' juries and biomedical experts rather than by government acting alone. In this case, again, citizen involvement assists government by legitimating decisions or by allowing governments to pass the buck to deliberative forums (Fishkin and Luskin 2005; Gastil 2000). With this type of mechanism, collective actors such as organized groups or social movement organizations are marginalized in the policy process, and it is more difficult for groups to enter into the process of political communication through the mainstream media.

Litigation

Another key means by which organized interests and social movement organizations seek to influence public policy in Canadian politics is through the deliberate deployment of litigation as a means to an end or through intervention in a case that has already been commenced by an individual plaintiff or by the Crown against an individual. Groups ranging from the Canadian Medical Association to the Charter Committee on Poverty Issues, the Canadian Health Coalition, and the Canadian Labour Congress intervened in the Chaoulli v. Quebec case on health-care funding, in which the court ruled that private clinics were constitutionally permitted to operate in Quebec (Manfredi and Maioni 2006). The Council of Canadians with Disabilities, the DisAbled Women's Network, and other groups representing people with disabilities intervened in the 2001 case of Robert Latimer, who was convicted of killing his disabled daughter, Tracy Latimer (*R. v. Latimer* 2001; on disability litigation, see Vanhala 2009).

Intervention in or participation in a court case is an important means of political communication for organized interests and social movement organizations. While litigation is highly specialized and dominated by experts such as lawyers, it also provides an opportunity for organized groups to hire their own experts to present their views on the specific dispute. In doing so, groups may gain access to the media or draw public attention to their issue in a way that would not have been possible without a court case.

Direct Action

Direct action refers to protests, demonstrations, sit-ins, occupations, or blockades that aim to directly stop or encourage specific action by their targets (e.g., spiking a tree, blocking a roadway). Many such actions directly challenge the authority of governments or other powerful actors (e.g., corporations). Direct action must be distinguished from rioting or mob actions that are unplanned or spontaneous. In order to qualify as direct action, there must be an intention to send a political message by acting collectively. In other words, there is a meaning and an intention behind the collective action. Random looting and rioting may send a powerful political message that social conditions need to change; however, random action is quite different from collective protest and demonstrations that are planned and carried out with a common purpose. Direct action must also be distinguished from political violence and terrorism, in which collective action crosses the line into deliberately harming human beings in the service of political goals or ideals. However, direct action may include threats of violence or violence may result from the way in which the direct action is policed, whatever the intentions of protestors.

Just as participating in the institutionalized policy community entails a specific form of political communication – the exchange of information and legitimacy between groups and government – direct action is also tied closely to political communication. In fact, direct action may be considered a form of political communication. When groups and movement organizations are not consulted or when they are shut out of the corridors of power because their views are too challenging to government, then direct action is one means by which they may seek attention. Sitting-in or occupying a lunch counter or a government office, blockading a highway, or chaining oneself to a tree directly forces the authorities to confront the protest. In so doing, the protest captures media attention. This provides the opportunity for the group to convey their message. Corporate-owned media nearly always highlight the means as the message and force groups onto the defensive by suggesting that "inconveniencing the public" or "damaging private property" is criminal or immoral. In the age of the Internet, cell phone cameras, and social networking, this discourse may be challenged by the power of the individual protestors to turn the media back on itself through the relative ease of use and dissemination of video, photos, and audio of political events.

A number of social movements have engaged in well-known direct actions that have been successful in drawing public attention to political issues and, arguably, in effecting political change. Aside from examples of civil disobedience in the modern era in anticolonial movements such as Gandhi's non-violence movement in India, Canada and the United States have also seen very important cases in which direct action has shocked society. The non-violence civil disobedience of the African American civil rights movement, modelled in part on Gandhi's philosophy and strategy, was a very important case in which sit-ins, marches, and demonstrations were used to press claims for civil rights. In Canada, the environmental movement has been a pioneer of direct action. Greenpeace, which was established in Vancouver in 1971, began its political career as an organization directed at the media. One of Greenpeace's first actions was to send the ship *The Greenpeace* to the island of Amchitka, near Alaska, to stop an underground nuclear test by the United States. This was a direct action in the sense that, by sailing close to the site of the explosion, the American government would be forced to choose between conducting the test and killing Greenpeace members or stopping the test as a result of the Greenpeace action. In this case, the Greenpeace ship was turned back by the American government and the test went ahead. However, Greenpeace was successful in bringing the issue of nuclear tests to worldwide attention, joining the issues of nuclear war and the environment by targeting a nuclear test, which would result in environmental degradation to the island wildlife refuge (Greenpeace 2010; Dale 1996). Another well-known case of successful direct environmental action occurred on Clayoquot Sound on Vancouver Island in the mid-1990s, when environmental activists chained themselves to trees in order to stop the logging of the rainforest. This battle has been ongoing and still remains a live political issue (Mabee and Hoberg 2006).

Aboriginal peoples in Canada have also used direct action, especially blockades and occupations, as a form of political communication. The Oka dispute in the summer of 1990 is a good example of direct action as the Mohawks of Kahnawake stopped the expansion of a golf course into their traditional burial ground. The threat of violence and the deployment of the army at Kanehsatake attracted unprecedented media attention. A number of other blockades have occurred since the Oka dispute. Occupations and blockades are often justified by the argument that Aboriginal peoples have attempted to resolve land disputes through the process of land claims; nonetheless, there has been little progress in resolving First Nations claims. Direct action is means of forcing governments to negotiate agreements with First Nations (Ladner 2008). At the same time, occupations and blockades often attract negative attention to First Nations because some media commentators focus on the question of the legitimacy of the means of protest rather than on the substance of the issues that are being raised.

Similarly, in the antiglobalization protests that have occurred over the last 10 years from Seattle to Quebec City to Toronto and other locations, protests and demonstrations have been overshadowed by acts of violence against property. This has produced a battle over the framing of the protests as peaceful demonstrators emphasize that violence was carried out by only a small minority while much of the mainstream media focuses on the violence. Often, the images of violence against property, such as the burning of three police cars at the Toronto G20 summit in 2010, have been played over and over, while the thousands of people who demonstrated were not able to convey their views to the media. In the Toronto case, controversies also arose over policing, and the progressive coalition that had organized the demonstrations were able to reverse the framing of the event to some extent by questioning the actions of both levels of government and the actions taken by the police.

Aside from the federal government's decision to hold the summit in Toronto, the provincial government was also criticized for its confusing message over the security regulations that affected the free movement and civil rights of those passing in or near the security zone. Police were roundly criticized for having overreacted and allegedly violating the *Charter* rights of citizens. Protestors captured police actions on cell phone videos and digital cameras, and videos of specific police acts were widely circulated on the Internet. Just as the major television networks showed the few burning police cars, the cell phone videos showed only a snippet of police behaviour without context. In 2012, a report from the Office of the Independent Police Review Director, a citizen agency, criticized the police for using excessive force, arresting peaceful demonstrators illegally, and gross violations of prisoners' rights at different points in the day. The report said the police had a responsibility to balance law enforcement and the rights of citizens to demonstrate (Office of the Independent Police Review Director 2012, ix–x). The message of the G20 protests was as much about the means of protesting as it was about the substance of the actions of G20 leaders. However, unlike the Oka crisis, the media and the police were themselves under scrutiny as the ability of individuals to turn the media gaze back on the police and on the mainstream media cameras through the widespread availability of video and digital cameras and phones created a new dimension of political communication that empowered individuals. Interestingly, however, this empowerment mainly produced negative messages criticizing the police rather than an alternative social and political vision.

In summary, then, different patterns of interaction between governments, on the one hand, and organized groups and social movements, on the other hand, entail distinctive forms of political communication. In institutionalized relationships, there is an exchange of information and legitimacy, while in protest activities, the media are more directly implicated and play a major role in refracting and reframing political messages. The rise of the Internet and the advent of camera-equipped phones has empowered grass-roots groups and individuals to produce their own messages and created a new means by which these messages can be disseminated. Nonetheless, this does not mean that alternative perspectives are communicated to the broader public. Rather, at least in the case of the Toronto G20 and the worldwide Occupy movement that started in 2011, the Internet has only amplified the debate over the means and legitimacy of protest (De Lint and Hall 2009; Rosie and Gorringe 2009; Hayhtio and Rinne 2009).

Shifting Targets and Multilevel Governance

The examples given in the previous section were focused on the federal level and were based on the traditional assumption that the state is the main target of group pressure. In the Canadian case, as in other federal states, governmental targets may also vary, depending on the jurisdictions of particular policy issues. A long-standing literature in Canadian politics has explored the ways in which groups may shift from pressuring one level of government to another, depending on jurisdictional issues (Schultz 1977; see also Simeon and Robinson 1990). The complexity of Canadian federalism and the increasing importance of the urban and international levels for many political issues (e.g., the environment, trade) mean that political communication has become more complex. As governments have sought to transfer the fiscal burden from one level of government to another through downloading responsibility from the federal level to provinces and cities and as governments in general have offloaded responsibility to the private sector or to community-based organizations, the political environment has become more complex. This poses challenges for political communication when such jurisdictional complexity exists alongside the capability of governments at all levels to sell their policies and actions to the public.

For example, if interest groups want to challenge current policies on health care and argue for a greater collective commitment to the Medicare system, it is not clear if they should target the province or the federal government. Because the federal government provides crucial funding to the system, groups feel they should target the federal government. However, health-care systems are administered by a province, which suggests that groups should target provincial health-care policy. It is particularly difficult for the public to understand the system because of its complexity, and in turn, it is challenging for stakeholder groups to explain how the system works to the public and then to position their own interests in relation to this complexity. In the case of the Ontario pharmacists, for example, the Ontario Pharmacists Association took out large print ads to explain the system by which generic drugs are funded in part through professional allowances. Were these high-content print ads more effective than the simple flyers at pharmacy cash registers, which asked customers to save Ontario's local pharmacies? In either case, health-care funding is complex in a federal system, and this poses a challenge of political communication for group and movement actors.

At the same time, with the rise of globalization, the state has been displaced in favour of other sources of institutionalized power including international organizations, multinational corporations, and transnational social movements and NGOs. The ease of global communication and travel has made it qualitatively easier and cheaper for organized groups and movements to cooperate across borders, and the advent of global media and the Internet means that groups (Keck and Sikkink 1998; Smith 1997) and movements in Canada are much better informed about developments elsewhere. As power has shifted towards markets and international organizations, organized groups and social movements have responded to these shifts in a number of ways.

First, the state is no longer the sole target of collective action. While this may be a key part of a group's repertoire of collective action, it may also be quite important for the group to target actions of the United

Nations or other international organizations. Over the last 30 years, some international organizations, such as the United Nations, have officially recognized the importance of consultation with civil society stakeholders and the role that these groups play in many domestic and international conflicts. Like states, international organizations may benefit from the legitimacy that NGO support can give to their actions. Similarly, international organizations may need the information that groups can provide. Especially in regions of the world where states have failed, NGOs may provide government services and otherwise discharge some of the functions of states, a role that is increasingly criticized for its lack of democratic accountability to the peoples who live in such failed states (Jordan and van Tuijl 2006). In addition, many contemporary social movement campaigns directly target corporate behaviour, whether domestically or globally. For example, the campaign against child labour and sweatshops, sometimes combined with consumer boycotts, has shed new light on the clothing industry. Environmental campaigns have repeatedly targeted corporate conduct, whether in the oil sands of Alberta or in campaigns against pesticides. Campaigns against diamonds, ivory, and coltan and tungsten (used in cell phones and other electronics) have all used mass direct action to target the conduct of corporations (Raphael 2008).

Second, the growth of transnational social movements and NGOs has increased the opportunities for political communication. The growth of new technologies and the ease of cross-border communication make it possible for transnational organizations to exchange information and to seize media openings beyond their own national context (Shepard 2002). If the media within a particular country is closed to discussion on particular issues, these closures may themselves be targeted by transnational activists. Ongoing struggles over the openness of the Internet in China or the privacy rights of cell phone users in Saudi Arabia show how corporations such as Research In Motion, which produces the BlackBerry, and Google have become key mediators of the process of political communication in the global era. In turn, their actions are targeted by activists and by transnational NGOs. For example, Google Maps is subject to continuous action from grass-roots activists who attempt to reshape the depiction of political spaces and place names in the software application (Gravois 2010).

Third, as Keck and Sikkink (1998) and others have highlighted, transnational activists create epistemic communities, in which cross-border networks build a common framework and norms that guide the functioning of the community. They may also draw on common sources of expert knowledge such as certain forms of environmental science or business or economic expertise. This may provide new channels for political communication as transborder networks may form links with academics, think tanks, governments, and international organizations, which broaden the opportunities and methods of communicating far beyond the traditional definition of media. In addition, such networks may build their own sources of political communication, drawing on the long-standing culture of social movement organizations and networks, which traditionally deployed humble means of home-grown communication such as newsletters or phone trees to mobilize supporters. They may also found their own think tanks to influence the public agenda and to increase their media presence. In this way, they may hope to shape public debate through participation in mainstream media, using media to build public support for their cause, in addition to using media to communicate with their own supporters. Recent analyses of the rise of the Christian Right in Canada emphasize the important role of political communication in the strategies of Christian Right organizations (McDonald 2010; Warner 2010).

Social movement organizations and NGOs today may have highly developed media and publicity budgets that engage in highly professionalized messaging. A quick look at the extensive Web sites of progressive NGOs such as Doctors Without Borders or Amnesty International shows that these organizations have invested heavily in professionals to design and facilitate their online messaging. Just as some have emphasized the extent to which the Internet is increasingly corporate dominated, like other news media (Taras 2001), NGOs and interest groups need to invest in a professional Web presence in order to get their message out. Again, this process benefits those organizations with the economic resources to invest in an online presence. Finally, as Cross, Hackett, and Anderson lay out in their chapter in this volume, it is important to note that there have been a number of recent anticorporate campaigns that have focused on the media itself as a target, protesting corporate control of media in Canada and elsewhere. Some campaigns have targeted advertising itself as a medium of conveying the values of a neoliberal consumer society (Carroll and Hackett 2006; Waters 2004).

Conclusion

Interest groups and social movements continue to play a key role in political communication in the publicity state, despite the considerable challenges of access, resources, and governance. Insider groups that participate in the policy community provide a conduit of information from civil society to government regarding a vast array of highly specialized domains of economic and social life. At the same time, the government uses these insider groups to legitimate and provide political support for government action, regulations, and policies. Specialized policy communities largely do not communicate in the open and may not attract media attention, except on the rare occasions when conflict breaks out among stakeholders or between groups and government. Conflicts may then spill over into the media. Normally, however, insider participation in the policy community is a form of political communication that occurs under the public radar.

In contrast, outsider groups and movements may undertake various strategies of political communication in order to capture media attention and influence public policy. These strategies range from direct actions and protests to investments in professional publicity such as Web sites or think tanks. Governments themselves may seek to legitimate their policies through outreach to particular stakeholder groups through holding consultative exercises; alternatively, they may bypass groups by using polls, focus groups, or data mining to survey individuals. Litigation provides another venue for organized group influence (as well as a tool used by the state to chill negative publicity). By backing particular litigants, organizing or orchestrating litigation, or intervening in litigation that is already underway, organized groups and movement organizations seek to draw attention to their perspective and, beyond influencing the jurisprudence or decisions of courts, may also use court actions to draw media attention.

In the era of globalization, the traditional patterns of political communication have been both broadened and narrowed. Transnational organizing has extended the reach of political communication, while the rise of media such as the Internet enables specialized communication. The decline of state authority and the rising power of transnational advocacy networks, international organizations, and multinational corporations has created a new media landscape in which groups and social movements seek to change the conduct of companies, as well as the conduct of states. The shifting targets of political influence and activism create a more complex environment for political communication. In a federation such as Canada, the shifting targets of globalization are complemented by the complexity of policy networks across multiple jurisdictions.

In this more complex terrain, economic resources are critically important for groups that seek to get their message out through the media, as well as for groups that seek to influence governmental, nongovernmental, and corporate targets. In this sense, those with resources are more likely to have a public voice. In a political environment characterized by expensive and extensive publicity practices, this undermines the quality of democratic political life. At the same time, access to new social media provides a counterbalancing power for grass-roots groups to capture the attention of mainstream media and to organize direct action protests. The resurgence of grass-roots social movements and the outbreak of the Occupy movement, antiglobalization, and student protests may signal increasing contestations against governments and corporations as civil society groups take back the political space that has been defined by the assumptions of New Right political discourse. This may move us into a new era of political communication in which activism from below can bring considerable counterpressure to bear on the publicity state.

NOTE

1 A small portion of this text is taken from my book, *A Civil Society?: Collective Actors in Canadian Political Life* (Broadview Press, 2005).

13 Reality Check: The Counterpublicity of Alternative Media

HERBERT PIMLOTT

Alternative media play an important, if unacknowledged, role in democratic communication in Canada because they not only articulate and circulate both critiques of the status quo and free-ranging discussions of alternatives but also serve to represent views and voices that are ignored, neglected, or marginalized. Driven to represent those without access to the mass media, alternative media seek to provide balance in the public sphere of national debate. Under the New Right's communications strategy, the state has become a "formidable power" in political communication that poses a "threat to the free and diverse distribution of information" (Golding 1995 in Kozolanka 2009, 233), while its communication practices focus on mobilizing or demobilizing "exclusive target audiences" to further corporate interests (Kozolanka 2009, 224). Thus, alternative media have to act as disseminators of both "information for action" (Atton 2002, 12), since their ideal audiences are (potentially) active citizens who they seek to engage "as inclusive deliberative bodies" (Bennett and Manheim 2001, 280), and "empowering narratives of resistance" (Atton 2002, 153), which help sustain and (ideally) increase such participation. Alternative media also provide citizens with training and access to media production (for little or no cost). Since alternative media have relative independence from corporate and state control or are grounded in particular communities and movements, they are uniquely situated to counter the publicity state, if they can overcome a tendency of operating in separate silos and gain public visibility. This chapter begins with an account of competing definitions of alternative media before identifying the strengths and weaknesses of different types of alternative media and the roles that they play in organizations and movements. In the last section, the present US situation is considered as an example of how alternative media might (re)connect with diverse organizations and movements to counter the publicity state more effectively.

The term *alternative media* immediately begs the question, "Alternative to what?" (Skinner 2010, 221). It may be a field that is "notoriously hard to define" (ibid.), and some definitions appear to include just about all media, including those that self-identify as alternative. An early scholar of alternative media, John Downing (1984), argued that they are essentially politically "radical media," which he later extended to include a broader range of political perspectives, although they should be "relatively free from the agenda of the powers that be" and may be in opposition to part or parts of that agenda (Downing 2001, 8). If corporate and state media are "key bulwarks of global capitalism ... ideologically [and] economically" (Hackett 2000, 61) and if they act as a "conservatizing influence" (62), then surely alternative media could not include those that support and reinforce corporate power, racism, sexism, or other forms of domination and oppression. If alternative media are those that are outside of or opposed to traditional forms of status, power, and hierarchy, then they should only include those media that represent the progressive (i.e., Left) side of the political spectrum because they are about inclusion rather than exclusion and about greater equality rather than greater inequality (socially, politically, economically). Therefore, as part of its definition, alternative media should include all media that hold progressive, oppositional, and radical perspectives but not those with conservative, reactionary, or fascist views – what Mazepa (2012, 244) calls "regressive media."

Some argue that it is more than a political line that makes alternative media alternative. Albert (1997) argues that media are alternative when they have "special attributes" and they should be alternative to "mainstream," "dominant," "hegemonic," and "mass" (i.e., corporate and state) media. Mass media seek to maximize profits, sell an elite (niche) audience to advertisers, are "virtually always" structured hierarchically (reinforcing social, political, and economic power) and are "generally controlled by, and controlling of, other major social institutions, particularly corporations" (ibid.). Alternative media, Albert argues, not only do not exhibit any of these criteria, but they also should seek to subvert hegemonic relationships within their own structures. Therefore, alternative media must be part of a project "to establish new ways of organizing media and social activity" and remain committed to these rather than to their own preservation: prefigurative politics is integral to this definition.

Like Albert, Downing (1984) also stresses a key difference between the types of audiences promoted by mainstream and alternative media: the former encourage passive consumers, whereas the latter encourage active media users, which, in Downing's understanding, tend to be radical alternative media producers. Participatory alternative media are those that encourage consumers (viewers, readers, listeners) to become producers or "produsers" (Sandoval and Fuchs 2010). This idea of alternative media as participatory media narrowly limits the definition and overturns some earlier criticisms of the prefigurative model as a reason for the lack of success in reaching out beyond the radical ghetto: the failure to exploit marketplace mechanisms (Comedia 1984; Pimlott 2000b).

Sandoval and Fuchs (2010, 143–5) offer three criticisms of the idea that alternative media must be participatory media: the fragmentation of the public sphere, participation "as a means of profit accumulation or for advancing repressive political purposes" (144), and exclusivity. First, where the process has taken precedence over the product (or program), alternative media have put the emphasis on prefigurative politics and organization. This internal focus has undermined their ability to contribute to a counterpublic sphere or political interventions in the public sphere because they are too focused on getting their internal politics right. These alternative media fail because their success ultimately "depends on their ability to gain public visibility for their critical media content" (148).

Second, Sandoval and Fuchs (2010) argue that participatory media do not automatically mean that media are alternative because capitalist and regressive media can also be participatory.[1] In communicative capitalism, consumer participation is incorporated into accumulation and legitimation strategies, where user-generated content is incorporated as part of the potential (surplus) value of Web 2.0 (via attracting viewers to sell, in turn, to advertisers), and therefore can no longer be considered alternative as it once was (Barney 2008; Dean 2005).

Their third criticism, exclusivity, identifies the importance of "oppositional media that provide critical content, but make use of professional organization structures," but would not be considered alternative because they are not participatory (Sandoval and Fuchs 2010, 145). They argue that alternative media must be critical media in terms of their content vis-à-vis the mass media. The more radical and prefigurative models of alternative media tend to exclude other forms that are structured professionally but still produce critical content or complex forms and that may reach a broader audience via greater circulation or public visibility (148).

Sandoval and Fuchs (2010) argue that two key ingredients are necessary for defining alternative media as alternative: first, critical producers and, second, critical content and/or complex form. However, complex form is not necessarily alternative if it militates against reaching audiences or gaining public visibility, since a constant problem for alternative media is reaching publics outside their community silos or radical ghettos. If public visibility is the measure of success, then complex form cannot be part of the definition, at least not for those intent on promoting progressive social change to the broader public. While recognizing the degree of fuzziness when defining alternative media, Sandoval and Fuchs offer a broad, albeit critical, definition that includes a range of media that can counter the New Right's publicity tactics.

Counter-hegemonic Narratives and Framing

The pervasive influence of dominant frames and hegemonic narratives of the ruling elites, and the institutions and organizations through which they wield economic, political, and communicative power, make it difficult to engage in developing and disseminating a coordinated, counter-hegemonic narrative. This is true even for large organizations representing hundreds of thousands or even millions of Canadians, such as the Canadian Labour Congress (CLC), which may not always have the same influence, legitimacy, or credibility with their own members, especially when organizations with limited access to mass media, such as unions, have already been framed negatively by those media on a daily basis for decades. Organizations, such as the CLC, are therefore at a disadvantage in responding to lies and distortions peddled via the mass media because of the mass media's pervasive ability to frame issues and marginalize dissenting voices.[2]

Alternative media, therefore, have a fundamentally critical and unique role in any democracy but especially where corporate interests and the publicity state threaten or distort communication processes that are at the heart of democracy. It requires engaging in investigative journalism that exposes power to the truth, which profit-driven journalism is increasingly unlikely to do. The "phone-hacking" scandal surrounding Rupert Murdoch's *News of the World* illustrates the depths to which corporate media can corrupt public institutions. Since most alternative media remain outside of corporate control and do not seek audiences to sell to advertisers, they are able to articulate critiques and insights without worrying about any economic fallout, such as a boycott by advertisers.

The critical producers and critical content of alternative media are about creating "information for action" (Atton 2002, 12). By openly advocating on behalf of marginalized groups and by directly accessing the voices of those groups, critical producers articulate "counter-hegemonic narratives and reframe the issues to reflect public concerns" (Hackett and Carroll 2006, 58), which is a critical role, since mass media mediate the national public sphere. Therefore, alternative media need to intervene to name and (re)frame issues to (re)define reality instead of allowing corporate interests to do so. For example, "rape" was first constructed as a "sex crime" by an alternative publication one year before the *New York Times* identified it as such and four years before a major book publisher tackled the subject (Atton 2002, 12). Alternative media can have influence, but it is not guaranteed. Critical producers therefore help provide language and rhetorical strategies to counter the New Right's frames, which are circulated via the mass media. This role is of greater importance because the New Right's communication strategies have increasingly overtaken government communications and shifted it away from acting as a neutral purveyor of information (see the chapter by Kozolanka).

Alternative media do not just voice ignored and neglected concerns and issues but also articulate "empowering narratives of resistance" (Atton 2002, 153) to various publics. The process of citizens speaking to one another to debate and share critiques, ideas, and propositions, without worrying about putting off advertisers or target audiences, is at the heart of democratic communication. It is important for social movements "to attract loyal members, challenge hegemonic definitions of reality, enhance the movement's cultural capital and project its symbols into the public arena" (Hackett 2000, 79).

Alternative media need to speak truth *effectively* to power. This means that they not only need to reveal the reality behind the rhetoric of corporate and state communications and to (re)frame issues to present marginalized or neglected perspectives, but they also need to obtain greater public visibility for these views. It is through the serial, sustained, and systematic articulation of alternative viewpoints and the reframing of mass media representations of issues and events to better reflect the public interest that alternative media are best able to counter the publicity state.

Professional Journalism and New Media

Before we can consider alternative media in more detail, it is important to outline the new media developments and their impact on the two approaches to traditional or professional journalism that are often mistakenly heralded as alternative media. The rise of the interactive capabilities of Web 2.0 and the democratizing of technological skills to widen access to the less skilled have emphasized the possibilities of passive consumers morphing into active produsers. Faced with constantly disappearing readers, news media have sought to involve audiences in ways that would draw them in and retain them and thereby meet advertisers' needs (and generate revenue). Social media have provided news media with a tool to help in the production and distribution of news, which in turn raises issues that are important to alternative media.

On the one hand, news media can draw upon the contributions and (usually "free") work of audiences to attract other audiences and advertisers, lowering costs while increasing content. On the other hand, there are the problems of relying on free labour to produce and distribute news that, unlike most "commodities," may have legal implications and strict timelines and require professional filming, recording, writing, and editing skills. Of course, the implications for news production and distribution are greater than just the potential displacement of media professionals. The question of who will control and therefore frame the news remains crucial. Will ordinary citizens be the producers and consumers of news? Or will control remain with owners and professionals?

These developments have led to the rise of two different conceptions of what social media could mean for journalism: participatory journalism versus citizen journalism. While the problems associated with gatekeeping and access in traditional journalism – that is, who filters, selects, produces, interprets, and distributes the news – underlies the fundamental raison d'être for alternative media, it is with Web 2.0 that some argue readers and audiences are increasingly being encouraged and permitted to participate in the production and distribution of news by mainstream media.

So, does participation in generating content offer a way of challenging the publicity state? Following the approach of Nip (2006), I would draw a distinction between participatory and citizen journalism. It is important to note first, however, that an earlier concept of public journalism

(Rosen 1999) arose in the late 1980s and 1990s, which was an attempt to move beyond the limitations of traditional journalism and the professional standards of objectivity, such as the focus on celebrities and the horse-race coverage of politics, and engage the increasingly disaffected and disengaged citizens in selecting the issues that matter to aid reporters in developing coverage that interested the public. Some critics argued that public journalism was spurred by the looming threat to the newspaper industry of rapidly declining readerships. In other words, mainstream media interest in participatory journalism is pursued in the name of profit rather than in the interests of democratic communication and the public.

Although there are differences in what different outlets permit, online responses to news stories generally constitute the primary form of participation on Web sites of established newspapers and on the Web sites of public and private broadcasters. This participation is essentially the 21st-century version of letters to the editor, from online comments and discussion boards to blogs and photographs. Crowdsourcing is one term that appears to offer something more, though it too remains limited. For example, during the G20 summit in June 2010, the CBC had a weblog, where it "got in touch with people living in the area to write about their experience while downtown Toronto was pretty much in lockdown" (Hermida, quoted in Lynch 2011).

Participation in structures that are controlled by others has (limited) value as a counter-hegemonic strategy. Although it enables alternative views to be circulated and even challenge orthodoxy, at least to the degree that they conform to certain standards of traditional media, the range of possibilities in this form of journalism is limited by the existing structures. For example, in a study of online newspapers, participation by non-professionals is usually limited to commentary on journalists' blogs or reactions to published stories; citizen-authored stories have been primarily published in the travel section (Singer et al. 2011). Canadian interviewees "were particularly articulate about the usefulness of participatory journalism in addressing strategic marketing goals ... and viewed the various approaches to engaging audiences as indicators of good business" (ibid., 147). Thus, at least for two Canadian national Right-wing newspapers, the *Globe and Mail* and the *National Post*, forms of engaging readers become an integral strategy for marketing the news and ensuring audience numbers that can be sold to advertisers.

The Canadian Association of Journalists has hosted a series of debates on this issue, as have alternative media Web sites such as rabble.ca.

Differences in attitudes towards citizen participation in news media is partially divided by generation and media type, with younger professional journalists being more supportive than older ones, and "popular" newspapers more interested than "quality" or "elite" media (Domingo et al. 2008; Singer et al. 2011). Of course, while journalists feel the need to protect their professional self-interests, their expression of such concerns can help justify police disregard for ordinary people acting as citizen journalists under their *Charter* rights to free speech and assembly. Indeed, one could claim that since mainstream, traditional journalism is a commodity rather than a means of *democratic* communication and hence *not* free speech, especially since it is paid for and for which particular credentials or credibility are needed to access elite sources, it should not be considered as retaining a claim to *Charter* rights in the same way that citizen journalism does.

The policing of the G20 protests in Toronto included the repression of citizen journalists, some of whom were also engaged as freelance reporters or stringers by progressive mainstream media (e.g., Jesse Rosenfeld reporting for UK newspaper the *Guardian* was allegedly assaulted by police) and became a hot-button issue for some commentators who argued that not just anyone could claim to be a journalist (Blatchford 2010; Kellar 2011, 78). However, this is beginning to be challenged; one mainstream newspaper, the *Winnipeg Free Press*, is beginning an experiment to train citizen journalists. The Winnipeg Foundation and the John S. and James L. Knight Foundation, founded by owners of a US newspaper chain, have invested $400,000 in the *Winnipeg Free Press*'s News Café as part of a three-year project (2012–15) to "train and mentor citizen journalists, as well as create multimedia platforms to share their news, photos and information," which draw upon several "public library branches … as technology hubs" (Paul 2011).

Nevertheless, the potential that participatory and citizen journalisms offer as alternative media in terms of critical content and/or producers is dependent upon news professionals who act as gatekeepers, even in community newspapers (Lewis, Kaufhold, and Lasorsa 2010, 176). A 10-country study of participatory journalism indicates that there is still some distance to go before non-professional audience members are in a position to contribute to the critical work necessary in news production (Singer et al. 2011). This recognition has also extended, somewhat ironically, from the general public to the public of activists, where a study of activist reporting of the G20 in Toronto demonstrates that only a small contingent of activists were willing to act as citizen journalists (for alternative media), whereas the majority of activists, like the general public, do not appear to be interested in citizen reporting when participating in events (Poell and Borra 2011). Thus, just as mainstream media rely on a small group of journalists to produce their news, so too do alternative media. Unlike mainstream media journalists, however, citizen journalists will therefore be self-selecting and driven by their passion for public engagement.

The Continuum of Alternative Media

Canadian alternative media encompass every kind of medium imaginable: from graffiti to music to newspapers to radio to Web sites. Each type of alternative media has particular advantages and disadvantages, some of which pertain to the idiosyncratic nature of individual enterprises, or their owners or producers, or which may be an attribute of a particular technology or form or organizational structure. While recent scholarship focuses on Internet-based alternative media or cyber activism, the paucity of research on Canadian developments means that it is easy to overlook a whole range of older or more conventional forms that may be influential with internal audiences or in reaching out to the general public. The range of alternative media runs from programs located within state and corporate institutions to those of social movement organizations (SMOs), political parties, and trade unions to those that are independent or self-sustaining, as well as from individual, irregular projects to professional media with global audiences (see the chapter by Smith). Alternative media face a series of problems that impede their ability to counter the publicity state. For example, they are not monolithic and do not act in tandem with other alternative media. Their independence, or desire to remain so, can at times stop them from working together and coordinating their efforts to contest the New Right. They may spend more time trying to differentiate themselves from other media or focus only on their particular community. Alternative media remain dispersed and diffuse, and their influence, impact, and significance remain hard to measure.

Individual and Irregular Alternative Media

First of all, there are individual and irregular alternative media: small scale or low intensity, with seemingly little or no long-lasting impacts. The exceptions are those critical producers, frequently individual columnists or authors, who have national and even international visibility, such as Linda McQuaig and Naomi Klein, and who have their own Web sites. Although they can promote critical perspectives via opinion columns or guest panels in the mass media, they remain isolated voices and are always subject to the whims of owners (e.g., Rick Salutin's column was cut from the *Globe and Mail* in 2010).

While parodies, graffiti, and other forms of culture jamming that are produced at one-off or irregular intervals may have an effect on audiences that encounter them, there are limitations to what can be accomplished without a sustained, serial critique that engages people every hour, day, or week, as corporate and state media do. For example, Guerrilla Media's *Vancouver Sun* parody, which was wrapped around a real copy of the daily newspaper, provided an immediate contrast between *Vancouver Sun* stories and the parodies highlighting the biases of mainstream media, but only for one day (Murray 2009; Hackett and Carroll 2006).

Other alternative media are focused on a single event or issue and have a limited lifespan. In the 18 months leading up to the 1989 Free Trade Agreement between the United States and Canada, for example, two million copies of *What's the Big Deal?*, a pamphlet that contained cartoons and challenged the dominant pro–free trade views, were distributed across Canada by the Pro-Canada Network (PCN). The PCN (renamed Action Canada Network in 1990) was a network of trade unions, religious organizations, women's groups, and other progressive coalitions that came together to challenge the free trade agenda of the Progressive Conservative government of Brian Mulroney, corporations, and the Business Council on National Issues, renamed the Canadian Council of Chief Executives in 2005 (Conway 2006, 64–6). While the reach of this booklet is a testament to the dedication of activists, it is also a result of the combined efforts (and resources) of social movements and trade unions working together. Yet, ultimately, such one-off efforts are not enough when mass media and state communications sustain a systematic, ongoing (and one-sided) argument for free trade and undermine the balance that mass media are theoretically supposed to provide in a democracy.

Along more conventional lines, there are independent print publications, from weeklies to quarterlies, that operate in between the radical Left media and mass media. They provide for a range of interests and may rely on mainstream or alternative distribution and retail outlets. With an online presence where breaking stories can be promoted between hard-copy editions and links to organizations can be hosted, these publications represent a long-standing tradition of self-sustaining independent journalism. *This Magazine, Briarpatch,* and *Our Times* are just three examples of independent publications that cover a range of interests, from arts to labour. In British Columbia, the online publication TheTyee.ca, which is one of the most effective sources of critical communication in a province dominated by a media oligopoly, publishes regular investigative pieces and critical commentary on contemporary issues and has had some success in countering the publicity techniques of the provincial Liberal government. With a worldwide circulation of around 120,000 copies per issue, *Adbusters* operates at a global rather than a provincial or national level from its base in Vancouver. Nevertheless, while its focus may be global, its work helps foster a critical engagement with promotional communications of all kinds, which highlights the commodification of communication and its consequences.

There are a number of pirate radio operations and low-power FM stations operating in different parts of Canada, as well as online webcasting outlets, some of which only operate on a temporary, ad hoc basis (Langlois, Sakolsky, and Van Der Zon 2010). While these radio broadcasters have advantages in terms of immediacy of response and in reporting events, it is much more difficult for them to establish public visibility beyond listeners in the immediate area or involved in alternative media, despite the best intentions of their producers. It is difficult to build audiences, let alone a counter-hegemonic public sphere, through the ether.

Progressive think tanks, such as the Polaris Institute and the Canadian Centre for Policy Alternatives (CCPA), and independent researchers provide in-depth research, as do some SMOs, such as the Council of Canadians, and national and provincial unions. The CCPA, for example, publishes the *Monitor* 10 times a year to about 10,000 individuals and organizations, and while its audience may be small, its contribution to combatting the New Right's agenda and publicity is crucial. This information helps counter attempts to mislead the public, as with the government's arbitrary abolition of the long-form census, which provoked widespread public criticisms of a Conservative agenda to undermine objective tools for democratic governance, a decision that few organizations defended (e.g., the Fraser Institute and the Canadian Council of Chief Executives).

Alternative book publishers, such as Fernwood and New Star, help disseminate sustained, scholarly, and systemic critiques of power and the New Right's agenda, which contribute to a slower, long-term public sphere of ideas. For example, TheTyee.ca published a printed collection of articles analysing British Columbia's Liberal government as a public intervention before the 2005 election because of the mass media oligopoly that favoured the government (Beers 2005). It is much harder to trace the impact of individual and irregular alternative media, except over many years, in sustaining progressive ideas against the New Right's ideological hegemony.

Publicly Funded and Regulated Media as Alternative Media

Alternative media also include a range of publicly funded programs within established media, such as Challenge for Change (CFC) at the National Film Board (NFB), community cable channels, Aboriginal media, and campus radio. All of these publicly funded and regulated media cope with different restrictions and regulations that limit what can and cannot be said or done but that nonetheless permit critical producers working within these programs to produce critical content for audiences that might not normally be exposed to critical ideas.

The first example of a program within an established media organization is the CFC project, which was instituted by the NFB in Canada's centenary year (1967), and was specifically mandated to engage in animating social change, especially around poverty issues in marginalized communities (such as rural poor, Aboriginal people). Here was an example of a program within a state institution that had critical producers able to produce critical content. While many of its film projects were never intended for the general public, the involvement of subjects in making decisions about editorial content sometimes led to screenings to outside audiences, including those who were connected to the issue in some way. For example, George Stoney's 1969 documentary, *You Are on Indian Land*, about Aboriginal people protesting government inaction, was shown to police, judges, and politicians (Waugh, Baker, and Winton 2010). Unfortunately, the CFC was shut down in 1980, a reflection perhaps of the changing social and political context, just as its birth had been in response to public demands.

A second example of an institutional location was the development of community access television (CATV), which was funded by the public through subscriptions paid to corporate cable monopolies. CATV, like CFC, was a reflection of progressive social movements' demands for a voice in the 1960s and 1970s. It enabled ordinary citizens to speak to one another directly (in theory) via the "community access" cable channel. Over time, however, the community channel has been increasingly professionalized, and the independence of critical community producers (usually volunteers) has been restricted or eliminated. Now, it operates more as an arm of the corporate media oligopoly than as a means for citizens to speak to one another directly (Pimlott 2000a; Skinner et al. 2010). However, there are a few progressive programs, including those produced independently, such as Working TV, a labour program in Vancouver, which also webcasts its videos. Like CFC, CATV demonstrates that possibilities for critical content within corporate media are dependent upon the political environment for openings, and until such a time, their contribution to democratic dialogue will be limited.

Third, privately owned alternative newsweeklies represent another strand, which brought progressive perspectives and critical commentary to 1960s and 1970s urban youth. Although most evolved out of event-listing news sheets, they have contributed to a counterpublic sphere for critical news and views to reach a broad, urban, youthful audience, such as the *Georgia Straight* in Vancouver and *NOW Magazine* in Toronto (Verzuh 1989). Urban newsweeklies can be more critical than mass media despite their dependence on advertising as their primary source of income, although these are usually the exception rather than the rule (Benson 2003). Such media are usually connected to a larger corporate entity and are intended to appeal to youth in the hopes of encouraging brand or product loyalty. This tendency to embrace commercialism "as a means of survival" may encourage a more "apolitical" stance (Hackett and Carroll 2006, 59).

Fourth, there are Aboriginal media, particularly newspapers and radio stations, which can be considered alternative. Public funding cuts since the 1990s have led to the closure of many Aboriginal media, though some have survived (Skinner 2010 et al. 225), such as the *Tekawennake News*, one of the oldest, continuously published Aboriginal newspapers, which has served the Six Nations and the Mississaugas of the New Credit since 1963. These media are critical for democratic communication because they provide a neglected voice on issues that affect Aboriginal communities and portray Aboriginal peoples outside of, and in contrast to, dominant stereotypes, although their public visibility is limited.

Fifth, there are over 200 community and campus radio stations in Canada, including Aboriginal radio, most of which are funded by public revenues or located within public institutions, such as universities and colleges (Khan 2007). An important, independent, long-running example is CFRO or Vancouver Co-op Radio, which has been broadcasting since 1971. Its broad range of music, ethnic, multilingual, and news programming – including its long-running current affairs show, Red Eye, which provides in-depth, critical analyses of issues – reaches diverse audiences. By engaging diverse communities in production and decision making, CFRO provides a participatory model of engaging audiences as active participants in democratic communication.

In addition to campus radio, there are also scores of student newspapers on college and university campuses, supported by the Canadian University Press, a newsgathering cooperative for sharing news and features. Student media, with a specific focus on postsecondary issues, will likely be more critical of the status quo than corporate media, though their positions may vary and will be affected by the degree of student support for the dominant ideology or hegemonic "common sense" (Gramsci 1971) as with student media coverage of the 2012 Quebec student strike.

The province of Quebec has helped support media that preserve, protect, or promote québécois political, economic, and cultural power vis-à-vis the dominant anglophone culture of Canada. Since the provincial government supports québécois companies over community-based groups, alternative media flourish within the province for the same reasons as in the rest of Canada, because linguistic and cultural differences have not proved to be barriers to New Right publicity techniques (Langlois and Dubois 2005; Skinner et al. 2010).

Overall, these media can be considered alternative to the extent to which they provide critical content because critical producers operate with a degree of editorial independence from institutional control and economic forces. However, these forms of alternative media have become increasingly subject to political and economic forces, which undermine or limit their critical content and the independence of critical producers. The political context of a period helps determine the degree of freedom for the production of critical content, and at this particular conjuncture, there are few opportunities for marginalized communities to speak because of the development of the publicity state.

Oppositional and Radical Political Alternative Media

Since the 1990s, the focus of scholars has been on alternative media of the socialist-anarchist tradition (Downing 2001). Yet there are a range of radical Left media that are clearly counter-hegemonic and operate in a more sustained way than many prefigurative alternative media, in part because of an allegiance to a particular philosophy or ideology, such as Leninism, which stipulates the need for a vanguard party to direct working-class struggles (Pimlott 2006).

Since print media remained a primary form of entertainment for the working class during the 19th and early 20th centuries, many newspapers catered to the radical politics of their audiences, which contributed to the rise of Left parties, from social democratic to communist. These parties also published their own pamphlets and books to provide the public with counter-hegemonic views. During the 1930s, for example, shortly after the founding of the Cooperative Commonwealth Federation (CCF), the precursor to the New Democratic Party (NDP), the CCF had six newspapers in six provinces supported by a central news cooperative providing alternative perspectives to the dominant Liberal and Conservative press (Black and Silver 2001, 173). However, mainstream-oriented, progressive political parties, such as the social-democratic NDP, now rely on the mass media, despite the latter's anti-NDP bias, to reach the public, while using internal communications to engage members in support of electoral strategy and fundraising.

However, it is the smaller, more ideologically consistent, radical Left political organizations that continue to publish and distribute newspapers, magazines, and pamphlets, in part because of the constitutive role print media play for such organizations (Pimlott 2006). Such publications include *People's Voice*, the paper of the Communist Party of Canada (CPC), founded in 1922 and affiliated with the old pro-Soviet Communist parties, and *Socialist Worker*, the paper of the (Trotskyist) International Socialists, which is explicitly opposed to the CPC's Communism. While this focus on print might seem counterintuitive when moving online can substantially reduce the costs of print media, there are still some important advantages to print media. For example, face-to-face interactions with (potential) readers when distributing leaflets and papers on the streets or at rallies and demonstrations can be crucial to recruit new members and "push" potential readers, who would otherwise be unaware of them, to Web sites (Pimlott 2011).

Other (non-Leninist) Left political organizations such as the New Socialist Group, which publishes the *New Socialist* webzine, and the collective that publishes *Canadian Dimension*, represent a broader orientation to radical Left politics. The *Canadian Dimension*'s editorial collective, for example, is more open to dialogue with other Left groups, and its members hold a range of opinions on various issues. These political groups use digital media to try to reach beyond their base, although their use of new media forms (such as podcasts and videos) is more orientated towards an internal or self-selecting audience.

One group, however, that is engaged in a more innovative use of print and digital media is the Socialist Project. It publishes a range of materials, available electronically for free via the Web site or in print for a fee via bookstores or post (with discounts for bulk orders). These include the electronic bulletin (*The Bullet*), sent out by e-mail and available via the Web site, along with *Relay*, a political-cultural magazine; an online video service called LeftStreamed, which provides videos of public talks and discussions; and additional materials, such as a pamphlet series called *Interventions*. Nevertheless, the Socialist Project's public visibility remains limited at present.

The advantage of print media is the ability to provide a serial, sustained, systematic argument, which is necessary to be able to persuade people of the counter-hegemonic solutions to social, political, and economic problems. However, print communication can be undermined when radical Left groups use jargon or draw upon assumptions that operate against or outside of hegemonic "common sense" (Pimlott 2006).

Social Movement and Trade Union Media

Print media have provided an important and constitutive function for trade unions and SMOs. For example, from the late 1960s, there were well over 300 feminist publications, including journals, magazines, and newsletters of various degrees of longevity with an average of 40 to 50 "between the late 1980s and the mid-1990s" (Freeman 2012, 86). Feminist periodicals, such as *Kinesis*, *Pandora*, and *Broadside*, provided key platforms for analysis and commentary that was largely excluded from mainstream media, while other publications such as *La vie en rose* were more successful in reaching out to different audiences; they illustrate the diversity of feminist print media that was important in constituting and sustaining the movement for several decades (Godard 2002; Freeman 2012; Marshall 1995).

Although the circulation estimates remained low, rarely exceeding 2,000 to 3,000 per issue, these publications nonetheless influenced the broader public sphere through the circulation of their ideas via various networks. These networks were enhanced by a variety of organizations, groups, and individuals, such as bookstores, community centres, and the National Action Committee on the Status of Women, with differing degrees of permanency and financial support, which were important in establishing "infrastructures of dissent," that is, "the means of analysis, communication, organization and sustenance that nurture the capacity for collective action" (Sears 2005, 32). Clearly, while some publications received government or other forms of public funding, others did not. All, however, played an integral part in developing a vital feminist movement that has had considerable influence on policies and publics, although many of these achievements are under threat from the New Right.

While Smith's chapter in this volume discusses the contribution of social movements and interest groups to democratic life in Canada, it is important to recognize here their contribution to democratic communication, much of it online and focused on reaching beyond national boundaries. For example, the rise of the anticorporate globalization movement has been helped by the spread of e-mail lists, Web sites, and social media: many of these media maintain a commitment to a nonhierarchical, consensus-based process of decision making and organization. Scholars have focused primarily upon electronic alternative media, such as the network of Independent Media Centres (IMCs), or Indymedia (Skinner et al. 2010; see also chapter by Cross, Hackett, and Anderson). IMCs first gained prominence during the "Battle of Seattle" in 1999 and coalesce around meetings of the G8 or G20 countries. While representing the work of thousands of activists around the globe, IMCs are also local and have both advantages and disadvantages. Media that seek to adopt a policy of open publishing and yet seek to avoid discrimination or behaviours that reinforce "axes of domination" (Hackett and Carroll 2006, 58), such as sexism and racism, will find a need to engage in debates over editorial policies and practices (Skinner et al. 2010). Dependent upon volunteers, IMCs go through periods of low levels of activity even as they maintain something of a global reach (ibid.). More broadly, electronic media such as e-mail listservs and Web sites have become standard for many SMOs because of low costs and ease and speed of use, although potential publics have to be "pushed" towards SMO Web sites among the millions in cyberspace.

Other independent alternative media that are closely aligned with social movements, such as rabble.ca and *The Dominion* (a reader-supported media co-op with Web site and print editions, locals in four cities, and working groups in several smaller locales), provide an important nexus for activists to link up through these Web sites. For example, rabble.ca runs an online discussion forum, called Babble, for readers to engage in discussions over all sorts of different issues. It has also begun an "activist toolkit" to support activists in everything from running a meeting to designing media releases. Although these Web sites and their supporting activities and "produsers" offer great promise, their public visibility also remains limited.

Most media affiliated with or run by unions and SMOs have been neglected or ignored. For unions and social movements, while internal communications link the leadership with the rank and file, the opportunities for communicating with external audiences is uneven. Over the last 30 years, as corporate wealth and power have increased substantially at the expense of the great majority of Canadians, workers and consumers find themselves being squeezed to pay for the 2008–9 financial meltdown and bank bailouts. Thus, unions and SMOs are seeking to mobilize both members and allies to reach the general public, on which the decentralized Occupy movement has had an impact.[3]

SMOs and unions expend considerable amounts of resources (money and staff) on both "free" media, news coverage via public relations practices, and "paid for" media (advertising). Since advertising is quite expensive, it is only used by those organizations with substantial resources (such as Greenpeace). Primarily, SMOs and unions attempt to get free media, via public relations practices, to reach the public, which emphasize the newsworthiness of one-off events and photo opportunities.

Unions provide funding for alternative media such as *Our Times* and rabble.ca by purchasing advertising or donating funds, which also help reach non-union, external audiences. Unfortunately, while unions have to rely upon corporate and state media to reach the general public (and sometimes even their own members), including spending money on advertising, these mass media remain indifferent, if not explicitly hostile, which makes it difficult for unions to get their messages out unaltered (e.g., Kumar 2007; Martin 2004). Corporations fund mass media through advertising, and the media in turn maintain business sections, which employ specialist reporters providing a business angle on industries, law, and policies, whereas labour beat reporters, who drew upon union contacts, have all but disappeared.

SMOs and unions are also suppliers of newsworthy (and critical) reports on industries, public services, health and safety hazards, and other issues. Besides research and analysis, unions also take on issues that affect the workforce generally, including non-unionized workers and the public. Examples include the campaign to expand the Canada Pension Plan launched in 2010 and the Canadian Union of Public Employees' research on the high cost to taxpayers of public-private partnerships.[4] Corporate media, however, may ignore union-sponsored newsworthy reports, especially when they contradict New Right frames.

Union communicators' use of publicity techniques is generally less successful with the mass media because of the inherent establishment bias in professional news practices. Not only do union and social movement communicators have to counter negative, anti-union, anti-protester, and pro-business biases of corporate and state media, but they have to also counter the mass media's negative framing and stereotyping of union leaders and community activists (as "bosses" and "rent-a-mobs").

SMOs and union media can sometimes counteract the influence of the publicity state, especially where the interests of the workers may be directly counterposed to the objectives articulated through government communications. National unions produce their own communications and media, frequently to professional standards, but these are usually produced just for members and therefore have limited public visibility. Yet, even as these alternative media are working at a disadvantage in terms of resources and public visibility, as union members may have other identities or interests that militate against accepting counter-hegemonic framing and perspectives, SMOs and union media are able to overcome these obstacles at times because of the immediate material interests of their members-cum-audiences.

While there are various forms of control and top-down communication that one finds in most organizations, union locals do vary in the degree of freedom that they have in internal and external communications. For example, horizontal internal communication will be more likely at local or branch level than at provincial or national level. To communicate with members, most unions use a range of media, from printed leaflets and newsletters to phone trees, e-mail lists, and Web sites to audio and video webcasting. Unions have also begun to make use of new and social media for organizing and solidarity activities, including LabourStart, which provides frequent updates on labour issues throughout the world and local and global links for labour activists (Cain 2010; Wolfson 2008).

To sum up, the single recurring problem facing alternative media is public visibility. Alternative media need to start connecting their efforts at a national level; otherwise, the efforts of critical producers and audiences will be unable to strengthen democratic communication to counter New Right publicity tactics. It is a process that US alternative media have already started.

Reconnecting the Counterpublic Sphere

The New Right's success in the US national public sphere was established through a long-term "war of position" (Gramsci 1971) of more than 30 years, by which public opinion was shifted inexorably to the Right. The emphasis was on first building an infrastructure of think tanks and small journals in which conservative, free-market fundamentalist ideas were circulated among small groups of intellectuals. As the chapter by Gutstein in this volume demonstrates, as the number of institutions and public intellectuals involved in disseminating free-market ideas grew, they were able to sustain continuous political interventions in national debates. The New Right was able to achieve hegemony by reaching beyond political and corporate elites to the public and its success in the mass media has been predicated upon dual inputs: a commercial journalistic establishment that accepts unquestioningly, or is cowed into following, conservative messaging and an "echo chamber" of conservative media that drowns out critical ideas (Brock 2004; Rampton and Stauber 2004).

The New Right's coordination of messaging and framing of issues via its echo chamber sets an example of what progressives need to do. In the United States, alternative media have begun a process of cooperating to push back against the "swiftboating"[5] of progressive candidates and conservative messaging on numerous issues, from health care to bailouts, and to establish a mutually supportive network to counteract the "Fox effect"[6] (Clark and Van Slyke 2010). They found that alternative media audiences do not overlap as much as had been assumed, and through the efforts of the Media Consortium (a grouping of alternative media), for example, they have begun to build a much larger, progressive counterpublic sphere that is successfully challenging the New Right agenda (78). Brave New Films, Robert Greenwald's media company, has sought to react swiftly against the New Right's publicity tactics since 2002, and as of December 2010, its videos were reaching 50 million viewers. While progressives may still have a long way to go to achieve a more democratic balance to counter New Right publicity, their efforts at working together are beginning to have an impact in enhancing open, democratic communication in the public interest.

The potential of alternative media to construct and distribute a counter-hegemonic narrative that is both persuasive and pervasive requires coordinated action and messaging. The first stage is to build a counterpublic sphere through alternative media, even though their audiences may be limited for any number of reasons (e.g., technological, geographic, financial). The cross-fertilization of alternative media audiences would help overcome the fragmentation of the counterpublic sphere, and this base in turn would provide the foundation upon which alternative media could link with trade unions, social movements, and community organizations to develop a broader public network for a counterpublic, which would bridge separate issue and community silos.

Trade unions and certain SMOs, such as the Council of Canadians, which have greater resources and staff to help fund and support such a progressive media network, could be at the heart of a network of alternative media, connected to different audiences across labour, environmental, social, and political movements, which would begin to coordinate the reframing of issues and could provide the critical mass to create an echo chamber of voices of marginalized communities, consumers, and workers to combat the New Right's publicity tactics. This network could engage in a reciprocal dialogue to facilitate the exchange of ideas, critiques, and propositions, even possibly sharing ideas, personnel, and stories, as well as providing material, moral, and intellectual support for each other. It could share the most persuasive slogans, messages, rhetorical strategies, and frames that, if reiterated through every alternative media outlet, would create an echo chamber effect compelling mass media coverage. Drawing upon alternative media, citizens would have information for action to respond to New Right publicity tactics through such forums as talk radio and letters to the editor, thereby creating a buzz around an issue or perspective that might otherwise be ignored.

This interrelationship and networking among different alternative media production and distribution sites could develop into a broad, networked counterpublic sphere, which would enable greater public visibility for a range of neglected views. For example, the cross-fertilization of members of the Council of Canadians with anti-poverty activists and environmental groups – of which there are hundreds, even thousands – across the country, would go some way in establishing a dialogue that could bring many of these groups together to see how their issues intersect and overlap. Ideally, such a network would enable progressive forces of sufficient capacity to intervene in the national public sphere and thus challenge the commodification of communication to reclaim an active, participatory citizenship for all Canadians. It is the only way to ensure that communication is open, democratic, and in the public interest.

Conclusion

As this chapter demonstrates, alternative media include a range of programs and outlets, from the irregular to the daily, and a variety of organizational structures, from the participatory and nonhierarchical to the hierarchical and professional, but all of which have critical producers producing critical content. Since alternative media provide a voice for those news and views excluded from access to the mass media, and because they are also frequently situated within marginalized communities and because they avoid the commodification of ideas by addressing their audiences as citizens rather than as consumers, their role is crucial to enhancing democratic communication to reverse the current trajectory of political communication and the development of the publicity state.

Yet the weakness of alternative media lies within their fragmentation into separate silos or ghettos and a lack of public visibility, the consequence of which is the colonization of the national public sphere via New Right publicity practices. Alternative media have to move towards reaching out and connecting with each other and their diverse audiences if they are to counter the publicity state and enhance democratic communication. While the range of alternative media is great, the relationship of system-orientated, counter-hegemonic alternative media with social, labour, and environmental movements is key to building a counterpublic sphere that has the potential to harness the cumulative impact of serial, sustained critiques to counter the publicity state and the present trajectory of political communication in Canada.

NOTES

1 Also using a critical perspective, Kozolanka, Mazepa, and Skinner (2012) take a different but complementary approach, characterizing such media as alternative by virtue of the existence of one or more, but not necessarily all, of structure, participatory nature, or activism.
2 The case of Ken Georgetti, president of the CLC, whose position on the North American Free Trade Agreement was "misrepresented" by mainstream media in September 2004, is one such example.

3 The unexpected response of the public to Republican attacks on public
   sector workers in Wisconsin in February 2011, which spread to other states,
   foreshadowed the rapid spread of support for Occupy Wall Street.
4 In P3s, public taxes pay part of the costs of public facilities, like hospitals,
   while the private sector manages them and keeps the profits.
5 Swiftboating is a term that refers to aggressive negative advertising based
   upon falsifications and distortions aimed at destroying a candidate's credibility. It is named after the Swift Boat Veterans for Truth, who attacked
   Democratic Party candidate John Kerry during the 2004 US presidential
   election because his military service on the swift boats in the Viet Nam war
   was considered a threat to then-President George W. Bush's credibility.
6 The Fox effect is named for Rupert Murdoch's Fox News Corporation and
   refers to partisan commentary that is passed off as news or legitimate commentary and the ways in which mass media adopt similar approaches to
   news and opinion.

14 Publicity State or Democratic Media? Strategies for Change

KATHLEEN A. CROSS, ROBERT A. HACKETT, AND STEVE ANDERSON

The past 20 years have witnessed numerous developments that have had negative effects on the democratic public sphere. One of the most worrisome of these developments has been the emergence of a publicity state in which the media's role as intermediary between state and public has been eroded by persuasive political communication. For example, Gutstein (2009 and in this volume) notes how the success of expensive political persuasion campaigns on the part of specialized interests has manipulated both the news media and public discourse. Raboy and Shtern (2008) lament the erosion of public interest elements in Canadian communication regulations and policies. And Kozolanka (2006) has mapped the politicization of government communications activities. Public relations tactics and long-term publicity strategies, once the domain of business, have been adopted by political parties and governments, thereby increasing the need for independent review and democratic protection from abuses of power. However, rather than sound the alarm on these and other developments that undermine democratic communications, the dominant news media appear to have acquiesced to, if not collaborated with, these changes. For some, journalism no longer represents the fourth estate whose role is to "speak truth to power," and instead has taken part in what many have come to call a "democratic deficit" of public discourse (Hackett and Carroll 2006). Although by international standards the Canadian media system is better off than many in the world (Raboy and Shtern 2008), there is growing concern for the failure of institutions of public communication to promote the needs of a functioning democracy. Indeed, as Hackett and Carroll (2006, 2; emphasis in original) remark, "Media are not only *failing to furnish citizens with ready access to relevant civic information* ... but also, and more broadly, they are *failing to help constitute a democratic public sphere*."

It almost need not be said that the news media are central actors in political communication and, by extension, the publicity state. As Fletcher notes in his chapter in this volume, media represent significant symbolic power as the source of political information for most Canadians. They take part in the social construction of reality by making some perspectives or messages part of the public discourse and by neglecting or omitting others. They also have significant economic power as components of large corporate conglomerates and therefore can influence public policy, as well as the diversity and openness of their own public content. Indeed, it is because of the central role of the media in contemporary society that the reform, reinvigoration, and restructuring of the media system is a pivotal strategy for rescuing the public sphere from the emergence of market-based politics. How do we recreate a media system that champions the broad public interest rather than merely repeating the dominant discourse and echoing the interests of the elite?

A burgeoning academic literature on media reform is helpful in this project (e.g., Dichter 2005; Klineberg 2005, 2007; McChesney 2004). Such literature has recognized media reform as both a site of conflicting power and as a nascent social movement in the United States and internationally. In Canada, we have a strong tradition of critical communication scholarship, including notable attention to communication and cultural policy (Moll and Shade 2008; Raboy 1990, 1995), and discussions of media content and structures, partly due to our unique, mixed public-private media system (Skinner and Gasher 2005). Unfortunately, while the urgent need for a reinvigorated democratic public sphere through media reform is a common refrain, little has been published to date in the way of Canadian examples. This is a unique situation, since, as will be elaborated in this chapter, Canada's media landscape differs from that of the United States in terms of structures and institutions, as well as the political and cultural appetite for a strong public interest media, which actively invites public participation.

This chapter explores some of the most promising possibilities for challenging the dominant media systems by considering what can be done to reform the media so that they are more representative of what Hackett (2000) has called "communicative democracy" rather than play a narrow and instrumental role as message carriers within the publicity state. What are the intersections, interventions, and opportunities that make such democracy possible? What are the most effective, efficient, and promising activities and developments in attempts to resist the publicity state and its accompanying de-democratizing tendencies?

More importantly, the intention here is not to posit a nostalgic return to a non-existent pre–public relations world of participatory citizenship but rather to help envision broader and inclusive political and citizen communication within the present and for the future and to position the media at the centre of this vision for democratic communication and enhanced political discourse.

Theories of Structure and Change

This approach to the potential for social and political change *in* and *through* the media has been informed and influenced by numerous scholars of both communication and social change. However, two theorists in particular are key to understanding institutional power and how to effect political and social change: Antonio Gramsci and his development of the concept of *hegemony* and *counter-hegemony* and Pierre Bourdieu's useful and influential *field theory*.

The concept of hegemony was developed by Gramsci to help explain the way capitalist societies within liberal democratic political systems maintain political stability, even though they are characterized by substantial inequalities and conflicting interests (Gramsci 1971). Gramsci noted that no ruling group can establish stable long-term dominance through physical coercion alone; it must seek the *consent* to rule. This is done, he theorized, by translating dominant interests into universal ones, which entails the permeation through society of an entire system of values, attitudes, and beliefs that in one way or another support the established order. Such permeation is never total and is not achieved merely through propaganda or falsehood; rather, it works by defining the ways we already live and view the world in a context that supports the dominant order and marginalizes alternative views. More importantly in this perspective, neither the media nor political systems are closed to change – both are sites where meanings are contested in a struggle to shape public consciousness. Through this struggle, power is translated into authority, an authority that appears to be exercised in the general interest by seemingly "neutral" agencies such as the state, the courts, and the media. Thus, we can recognize the media as *hegemonic institutions*, one of the ways that the dominant interests become naturalized and regarded as inevitable or beyond history and politics.

Hegemonic ideology is a helpful concept for analysing the news media and their relationship to political communication. First, this approach recognizes the power of symbolic content and the pivotal role of media in political life without subscribing to a propaganda model that sees the audience as completely passive. The audience, in fact, may withhold consent by refusing to accept the preferred perspective being offered by the dominant media discourse. Thus, the concept of hegemony takes into account both *consent* and *dissent*. It recognizes media discourse as neither neutral nor passive, but as a site of struggle for symbolic power – a struggle that is not taking place between equals but between a dominant "power bloc" (or set of dominant interests) and the rest of the population. More importantly, the elite not only have more power than the dominated classes or groups in a society but also are themselves a differentiated diverse group. Hegemony implies not only ideological domination but also the creation of alliances between elite groups to maintain a particular social order. It also indicates that maintaining hegemonic power entails the need to adapt to changing economic, social, and political conditions.

From this perspective, then, the media in general and political communication in particular are seen as primary sites of the struggle over political and ideological leadership, places where the symbolic content of media is part of invisible – and usually successful – attempts to gain consent for domination. While media actors (owners, managers, and editors) and political actors (politicians and political interest groups) may not have absolute control, they are all part of the negotiation for control of media and symbolic authority and, in this process, are supported by and, in turn, support the political and economic systems that sustain them. Thus we can see the affinities and alliances created between public relations companies, corporate media, and major political parties. Yet, while the media system may be structured in dominance, it can be resisted and changed. However, Gramscian approaches are somewhat limited in their articulation of the options for resistance and political change. The route to challenging hegemonic ideology appears to reside solely in massive oppositional politics and the building of a counter-hegemonic movement across all groups and classes in a united front to challenge political power. This may indeed be what is necessary, but it gives little possibility for transitional interventions – actions for resisting political and economic dominance in the short term and as part of building that movement.

More recently, French philosopher Bourdieu's concept of social fields has provided fertile ground for a number of scholars seeking to engage with shifting structures and pressures on cultural production and meaning (Allan 2004; Atton 2008; Benson and Neveu 2005; Couldry 2003). In Bourdieu's work, media power can be understood as acting within a set of institutional *fields*, each of which has its own internal hierarchies and logics allowing relatively autonomous actions that are nevertheless still potentially influenced by other fields. Within each field, there is a tension between logics that are intrinsic to the field (therefore *autonomous*) and those *heteronomous* logics that are embedded in the field by virtue of the demands of external institutions. For example, the extensive use of audience ratings to make programming decisions in commercial television demonstrates the influences of the economic field on the overall media field. Similarly within the *journalistic* media field there are dominant modes of discourse, conventions of selecting and constructing media content, and other routinized practices and principles that form the "habitus" of the work of reporting news. Yet none of these formal and informal practices and assumptions is unalterable. Much of this media work appears autonomous; all of it is situated within larger fields of power, such as the state and economic system (for more discussion of fields of power, see Bourdieu 1990, 1993, 2005). Thus, the field of journalism and the cultural forms of production it entails can be influenced, albeit unevenly, by pressures from the economic and political fields (Benson 2006; Benson and Neveu 2005). This theory recognizes that the autonomy of each field of power is itself *relational to* and *contingent upon* its proximity and association to other fields. For example, the media field's autonomy of cultural production can be seen to be constrained by economic and political pressures, such as the increased concentration of ownership and the increased use of content produced by public relations firms (see, e.g., McChesney 1999; Gutstein 2009; and chapter 4 of this volume).

Using Bourdieu's approach, Hackett and Carroll (2006, 200) analysed the media as a field with distinct characteristics – notably, porous boundaries, a high capacity to intrude upon other fields, and vulnerability to influence from political and economic fields. Journalism can be recognized as having "the distinct feature of combining economic power (the production of profit) and symbolic power, which is ultimately the capacity to define social reality" (32). This indicates the significant influence media can have on other fields of power while remaining itself structured in dominance. By looking at the potential impact of media activism on forms of public communication, the authors were able to recognize how media reformers found opportunities to effect change by responding to opportunities in shifting political discourse and emerging policy debates. Indeed, the capacity of other potential allied groups to recognize the impact of the media field on their own area of activism has created a necessary awareness of the role of the dominant media in any resistance or oppositional movement.

Given the possibilities inherent within field theory, how do we imagine the options of intervening in the hegemony of market and neoliberal domination in the political field of power? Because of its unique, porous, and relatively autonomous nature, the media field can be challenged by both external and internal forces. Externally, pressures such as calls for change to government policy, critiques, organized reactions from civil society organizations, and overall opposition to commercial constraints, can, if successful, have significant impact on the media field. Fields can also be challenged from inside, for example, through shifts in demographics (who makes up the class of actors in the field) and resultant challenges to the taken-for-granted assumptions about the meaning of the cultural works. Since no field is completely predetermined and no response ever fully certain, field theory offers the possibility of intermediate actions and interventions that can, if persistent and sustained by multiple pressures, reshape aspects of the media field and move us towards resistance to dominant political discourse. While hegemony posits that change is possible, field theory suggests that a multifaceted approach to structural and political change is not only advantageous to resistance but also necessary. Such a strategy could include, for example, policy changes, political pressure, demographic and situational changes, internal and external creative strategies, and counter-hegemonic media. It is within this context that we can evaluate and develop alternatives to the neoliberal publicity state and intervene in the symbolic and economic power of the media.

A Three-part Strategy for Resistance and Change

The recognition of the media as a site of struggle for democratic participation is in part a response to the deterioration of the media landscape in terms of public interest communication. As has been argued by McChesney (2004) and others (Baker 2007; Bennett 2009), the ability of corporate journalism to examine and challenge the publicity-dominated power centres is itself so weak as to have reached a crisis point. In response, a nascent movement to change and transform the media has emerged. In the United States, hundreds of local and national groups working in independent media, media education, and policy advocacy have been joined by Free Press,[1] a national flagship for media reform, with hundreds of thousands of supporters. Perhaps a key factor in the renewed interest in media democracy is the new opportunities afforded by the emergence of the Internet, combined with a crisis in traditional journalism that has left many previously disengaged citizens with a willingness to invest time and effort in the media democracy movement. The perceived unique openings in both media production and the structure of media make up essential ingredients for media activism.

In this regard, Canadians have not been idle. The veteran non-profit organization Friends of Canadian Broadcasting, founded in 1985 and with over 60,000 supporters, is probably the largest and oldest current media reform group in anglo-Canada.[2] Several smaller organizations lobby on telecommunications issues and copyright from a consumer rights perspective, and some unions have developed detailed policy proposals and collaborated on policy-oriented campaigns (e.g., the Communications, Energy and Paperworkers Union 2004). Further, international movements and organizations have come to recognize the central place of democratic communications and communication rights in democracy. UNESCO's World Summit on Information Society in 2005,[3] like the McBride Commission 20 years earlier, put democratic communication at the centre of global needs for public information, education, and development. This time, the neoliberal model of global media power was challenged by the inclusion of the notion of civil society in the formal discussions (see Calabrese 2004; Raboy 2004). The World Association for Christian Communication,[4] an ecumenical non-governmental organization (NGO), recently moved its global headquarters to Toronto and is seeking to build alliances in North America and create a Web portal in support of communication rights for all.

As an example of the development of the media reform movement in Canada, Media Democracy Days has been an active voice in championing the public interest in media structures and communication policy. The first Media Democracy Day was held in 2001, organized by local Toronto and Vancouver members of the Campaign for Press and Broadcasting Freedom (CPBF), an organization modelled after the British group of the same name. CPBF Canada was a coalition of concerned citizens, researchers, academics, and activists that emerged in 1996 in response to the takeover by Conrad Black's Hollinger Inc. of much of the Canadian press and the perceived threat to diversity of content posed by such an unprecedented concentration of ownership. Since then, the mediascape has changed. Concentration of ownership trends have continued including the convergences of media and tele-communications companies, and the current issues related to media policy have become even more crucial to the potential for democratic communication, as we will note later. The CPBF has been reorganized and renamed as OpenMedia.ca (see the discussion later in this chapter) and has been advancing media reform issues such as net neutrality, or the principle of non-discrimination in Internet access. The 10th Media Democracy Day, held on 6 November 2010 at the Vancouver Public Library, saw record-breaking attendance, over three-quarters of whom had never attended the event before. Close to 1,000 people participated in workshops on areas such as communication and copyright policy, representation of the environment and gender in media, and documentary film production. Since 2010 the annual event has been expanded to two days (thus the name change to Media Democracy Days) and has led to an expanded organization called the Media Democracy Project, which holds events throughout the year.

The founders of the CPBF and Media Democracy Day envisaged the need for action in three distinct but mutually necessary fields in order to make media change and to challenge the corporate media structures: a three-pronged strategic framework for media activism encapsulated in the slogan: "Know the media. Be the media. Change the media."

1. Know the Media

To know the media demands citizen engagement, critical discussion, and analytical dissection of how meaning and information are produced today. This means interrogating the political economy of communication, opening up the back rooms of the production and distribution chain, and highlighting the biases of representation embedded therein.

– *Media Democracy Day Web site*, 2010

The Canadian context for understanding the shifting role of the mass media in the publicity state is linked to its historical and policy origins, which are significantly different from those in the United States. Citizen activism of the 1930s, notably the Canadian Radio League guided by Graham Spry, was influential in creating Canada's public broadcaster (the CBC), as well as a number of key public interest elements embedded in Canadian policy instruments such as the

Broadcasting Act 1991. For example, Canadian ownership of Canadian media; Canadian content requirements; specific supports for community, ethnic, and Aboriginal programming; and some limits to the concentration of ownership of media companies are all unique Canadian regulatory requirements (Raboy and Shtern 2008).

The goal of *knowing the media* is to promote critical audiences and citizens by analysing the state of the Canadian in three distinct but interrelated areas: the political economy of *ownership structures*, the formal and informal regulation of *media production and practices*, and the *discursive content of media products*. Each of these areas of research and analysis offers necessary empirical evidence for effective critique of the existing system and help in discovering critical junctures for intervention and change.

OWNERSHIP STRUCTURES

Since 1996 and the "Black Sunday" purchase of a large sector of Canada's media sector by Hollinger Inc., mergers and acquisitions have dominated Canada's media landscape. In 2001, Canada's mass media industries were described as being one of the most concentrated in the western world (Nesbitt-Larking 2001). By 2008, a media "triopoly" dominated the industry, receiving over half of all Canadian media revenue (Winseck 2008, 31). Further, the Canadian government has been steadily allowing increased levels of minority ownership by foreign companies, primarily American (Moll and Shade 2008). Most recently, the mediascape was further shaken up by a substantial restructuring and converging of mass media giants with two of the largest telecommunications companies in Canada. On 3 May 2010, Shaw Cable bought all the broadcast holdings previously owned by the struggling Canwest Corporation, including the entire Global Television Network of stations, as well as 30 other TV stations in eight provinces, and a number of specialty channels. A few months later, on 10 September 2010, Bell Canada's parent company, BCE, announced it was buying the entire CTV broadcast network. While these purchases represented a significant convergence of media and telecommunications companies, the Canadian Radio-television and Telecommunications Commission (CRTC) approved the deals.

In contrast to the growing corporate ownership structures of the commercial media systems, the public and community broadcast sector has, conversely, suffered over the last two decades. Regulatory and funding support for Canada's public broadcaster, the CBC, has been shrinking, and community broadcasting has been struggling with minimal resources, suggesting that the commitment to the policy of public ownership of broadcast airways may be losing its fundamental place in Canada. Attempts by non-government groups to stem the neoliberal tide of mergers and acquisitions through submissions and presentations to the CRTC have fallen on deaf ears.

Corporate concentration of ownership as we find in Canada today has been demonstrated to be contradictory to a vibrant and diverse public sphere of political discourse. It creates less diversity of opinions and views in public discourse and diminishes local content in favour of less expensive national coverage (Hackett and Zhao 1998; Bagdikian 2004). Such market-based concentration of ownership has other structural implications as well. Advertisers gravitate to larger markets, drawing more revenue to corporations and marginalizing smaller independent media. Merger-induced debts lead large corporations to maximize profit in any way possible, most often at the expense of informational content and investigative journalism (Hackett and Zhao 1998; McChesney 1999). The corporatization of media ownership results in increased political power and gives companies substantial persuasive weight with regulatory bodies and government departments alike.

The dominance of the commercial media structure highlights the paradox of the overall media system: the dual and fundamentally competing roles of mass media as the profit-seeking businesses that most are, and the responsibility of providing citizens with information they need in a democratic society. This tension between the commercial and the public interests inherent in the media field is often at the centre of the ownership debates and has historically been mediated to some extent by the regulatory aspects to protect and enhance the public interest. However, these regulatory structures have been steadily eroded over the last 20 years. Handing responsibility for the major symbolic content to one source of power in our society (commercial-based media) is akin to shutting down debate about interests outside of those held by the corporate entities.

MEDIA PRODUCTION AND PRACTICES

While ownership types and structures of the industry in Canada shape the overall mediascape, we must also understand the complexity of the journalistic field of practice. Journalists use routinized practices that help define how they undertake their work. Unwritten conventions such as specific and historically situated approaches to "journalistic objectivity" (Hackett and Zhao 1998) and the habitual use of certain types of sources to help define news content (Ericson, Baranek, and Chan 1987) have become so entrenched in media work as to constitute regimes of practice. These occupational constraints are based on both professional codes and the organizational needs of a commercial media system constrained by deadlines and limited resources, allowing reporters a degree of autonomy in their work while ensuring a conformity and standard of content.

For example, current research notes that the experts featured on television newscasts are presented as objective and non-partisan and yet have largely conservative views representing a narrow selection of elite pro-market groups (Bennett 2009; Hackett and Gruneau 2000). Further, external organizations that can afford to hire public relations professionals as convenient and articulate spokespeople will generally have an advantage in media access and thus gain preferred access to public discourse (Gutstein 2009; Manning 2001). The question of who is quoted can also be the result of the need for "symbolic representations" of the already decided news narrative (Cross 2010). Thus, the diversity of opinion is constrained by both external sourcing practices and internalized preferred narratives, both of which are influenced by the emergence of political marketing.

In addition, significant changes have occurred in the way journalists in Canada do their work, leading scholars Compton and Benedetti (2010, 488) to note that journalism is undergoing significant restructuring. While the increase in blogging and so-called citizen journalism has created potential openings for audience production, it does not necessarily result in improved democratic communication. Countervailing constraints on democratic deliberation, such as the fragmentation of the audience into self-reinforcing "opinion tribes," and the rise of excess partisanship may only serve to reinforce polarized perspectives rather than provide meaningful debate. Further, traditional news organizations may encourage user-generated content to keep costs of creating content down while undermining journalistic standards. Indeed, the drive for corporate profits has resulted in "intensified rationalization" and the reduction of the labour cost of reporters, especially investigative journalists (Compton and Benedetti 2010, 490). The Canadian Media Guild estimates that some 3,000 media workers were laid off between January and April of 2009 alone. Declining staff means heavier workloads along with content and deadline pressures that can lead to press release dependent news, welcomed as free content subsidies for overworked newsrooms (McChesney 2004, 71–2).

DISCURSIVE CONTENT OF MEDIA PRACTICES

Promoting critical audiences also necessitates analysing media content to discover the meaning-making texts that inhabit our cultural norms and values. Invisible or stereotypical representations of race, poverty, or politics, for example, shape our cultural conceptions of what is an acceptable topic for political discourse and what is not. The news media define and construct what is good and important, what is bad and dangerous, and what is altogether insignificant, both through the treatment and very presence or absence of a subject within the news discourse (Allan 2004; Johnson-Cartee 2005). Further, news media content has an effect on how we understand and interpret the political world (the *cognitive* dimension) and on our emotional response to it (the *affective* dimension) (van Dijk 1988, 1998; Johnson-Cartee 2005).

The symbolic power of media content has inspired a rich resource of quantitative and qualitative research seeking to *know the media*. As one example, a 2010 study from the Global Media Monitoring Project (GMMP) found that women remain dramatically under-represented in Canadian news (Global Media Monitoring Project 2010).[5] Only 30 per cent of the news subjects – people who are interviewed or whom the news is about – are female, and less than 18 per cent of the quoted "experts" in the news are women. Men were two and a half times more likely to be news subjects and three times more likely to be found in stories about politics and government. The overall finding that women are marginalized as subjects in the news is a persistent pattern of gender portrayal that, as Tuchman (1978, 3) argued over 30 years ago, leads to the "symbolic annihilation" of women as diverse social actors. Indeed, a number of Canadian scholars have continued to demonstrate how the news is situated within a gendered, masculinist discourse (Robinson 2005; Trimble and Everitt 2010; Jiwani 2006).

Another example of research into media content has found a tendency to focus on horse-race politics, scandals, and conflict in much of the news about parliamentary politics and at the expense of stories about policy issues (Hallin 1997; Taras 2001; Nesbitt-Larking 2001; McNair 2007; Soroka and Andrew 2010). The news media's focus on political strategy at the expense of policy considerations – known as "strategic frames" – have been shown to affect voter turnout, cynicism, and the political and communication strategies of parties (Capella and Jamieson 1997; Gingras, Sampert, and Gagnon-Pelletier 2010). The weakening of political knowledge and the long-term decline in voter participation rates (especially among 18- to 25-year-olds; see Blais, Gidengil, and Nevitte 2004) are indications of de-democratizing tendencies that are at least in part a response to political communications. Indeed, the emergence of the "marriage of public relations and politics" (Lees-Marshment 2001, 692) as a strategy of political communication transforms political discourse, public policy, party behaviour, and *politicians themselves* into commodities – products to be sold to political consumers by public relations and professional practitioners. Within this view, voters are reconceptualized as merely markets to be harnessed. The news media's active participation in the reframing of politics reduces citizens to the role of passive observers, mere consumers of political news and marketed political products, rather than active political participants in democratic deliberations

Thus, research has demonstrated how news content not only reflects but also, importantly, reinforces and constructs our social and political reality and contributes to the democratic deficit in Canada. Representations in news media must be seen as sites of ideological struggles between what is legitimized and what is marginalized, what is dominant and what is invisible, and what is natural and what is deviant. Identifying the constraints and narrowness of political discourse can help put both internal and external pressure on the journalistic field by appealing to its own commitment to democratic communication.

2. Be the Media

To be the media means taking charge of the myriad opportunities available for citizens to participate actively in the creation of meaning within the culture. Media Democracy Day promotes this engagement by providing attendees with free workshops focused on how to transform and denaturalize the hierarchical audience-producer binary established by decades of corporate control of the media.

– *Media Democracy Day Web site*, 2010

If the key values of communicative democracy include participation, diversity, and equality (as noted by Hackett and Carroll 2006, chap. 4), then the opportunities to "be the media" by taking part in the creation of counter-hegemonic cultural content are strategies that encourage and promote agency on the part of citizen-audiences. Indeed, frustration with gaps and omissions in the mainstream media has encouraged a diversity of "alternative" or "citizen" media products and organizations that generally seek to provide a voice for groups and opinions not commonly present in the dominant media (Skinner 2010). While by no means a new phenomenon (note the emergence of underground newspapers in the 1960s and 1970s), independent, non-profit media potentially offer a counterweight to the narrow views and underrepresentation or misrepresentation found in the much of the dominant news and entertainment media. Such media are recognized as a fundamental and complementary route to both communicative democracy and social change (e.g., Couldry and Curran 2003; Downing 2001; Hanke 2005; Rodriguez 2001). The alternative mediascape in Canada has been outlined elsewhere (Skinner 2010; Kozolanka, Mazepa, and Skinner 2012) and in Pimlott's chapter in this volume, but a few comments on the importance of such media are appropriate here.

We are actually talking about two dynamics at play. One dynamic concerns content. "Radical" alternative media challenge dominant ideologies or interpretive frames. An example would be *Canadian Dimension*, which defines itself as a magazine "for people who want to change the world," or the online news site rabble.ca, which offers "news for the rest of us" – in other words, the majority of people who are not part of privileged elites. A second dynamic concerns audience participation in the production process. Recent years have witnessed the emergence of "citizen journalism," which Rosen (2008, cited in Deuze 2009, 256) defines as what happens "when the people formerly known as the audience employ the press tools they have in their possession to inform one another." The concept of "citizenship" alluded to is not a formal legal status (such as membership in a national state) but rather active engagement by people in the daily life of their society. So, citizen journalism is produced by ordinary people (rather than professional journalists), acting as individuals or in groups, and its forms can range from eyewitness accounts of unfolding disasters or mundane community events to opinionated political blogs and critiques of mainstream media reportage.

Alternative media achieve their most democratizing potential when they combine counter-hegemonic content with participatory processes that encourage citizen engagement, as can be seen in both *Canadian*

Dimension and rabble.ca. Downing (2001, 3), for example, notes that the "radical alternative media" critically activate audiences and "expresses oppositional strands, overt and covert, within popular cultures." Many of these organizations engage in 'crowdsourcing' and non-hierarchical organizational models and are non-profit. As such, they are typically financially unstable and often relying on volunteer or marginally paid labour with minimal training. The emergence of new media has reduced the production costs of creating alternative content to some degree, allowing a proliferation of Web site and networks for cultural politics and engagement (Hackett and Anderson 2010). However, the somewhat transient nature of not-for-profit media means that the communicative landscape can change from year to year and community to community. Still, the capacity building and skill development for those engaged in these practices cannot be underestimated.

These new and parallel media fields, as Bourdieu would call them, offer a vision for communicative democracy, capacity building for active participation in political discourse, and challenges to the material conditions and symbolic power of corporate media (Hackett and Carroll 2006, 52). As counter-hegemonic movements, they denaturalize the dominant structures and content of mass media. They can also promote change by providing benchmarks of comparison with profit-based corporate media. Indeed, as Project Censored in the United States has found, some of the most valuable and significant investigative journalism reports are found in the non-corporate, non-profit alternative media.[6]

While alternative media movements may offer a challenge to dominant media, the two fields are not completely separate. Dominant media have tried to domesticate citizen journalism, turning it into "user-generated content" as "a way to generate news and marketing opportunities at little or no cost, using the free labor of citizen-volunteers" (Deuze 2009, 255). For example, including the ability for readers to post comments on stories in online versions of newspapers might be promoted as a way to enhance readers' engagement and interactivity with the news organization (an example is the *Winnipeg Free Press*'s Café; see Pimlott's chapter) but has resulted in mixed results at best. Indeed, the model appears more market-driven than a tool for enhancing democratic speech, characterized by personal attacks and unrelated opinions that drive up attention and entertainment but provide no actual value to the news coverage (Paskin 2010).

Online citizen journalism has arguably been most effective when it has both maintained its independence and broken through the filters of the dominant media to influence the mainstream news agenda. This process can be understood as one of *amplification*, where the original story from citizen journalism is taken up and repeated by the mainstream media, resulting in significant outcomes. One early example was cyber-journalist Matt Drudge's 1998 release of the allegations of President Bill Clinton's affair with a White House intern, a story that engulfed the administration in scandal once it was amplified by the dominant media (Allan 2009, 21–2). Another prominent political example was the downfall of Right-wing US Senator Trent Lott, after a citizen journalist amplified Lott's endorsement of racist politician Strom Thurmond, a story that the Washington press corps had missed.

More recently, the youthful movements that triggered the overthrow of governments in Tunisia and Egypt engaged in a form of citizen journalism, using social media sites such as Facebook to organize protests and share information and support. While primarily an organizing tool, their "Arab Spring" multiplied and spread to other countries when conventional media, notably the Al Jazeera international television network, amplified their story. A similar pattern characterized the Occupy Wall Street movement, which was inspired by the Arab Spring rebellions. Initially ignored by dominant media, Occupy Wall Street's message nonetheless resonated with middle-class anxieties and changed the conversation of American politics, thus succeeding in expanding the dominant media agenda to include serious discussion of economic inequality. Indeed, *Time* magazine selected "The Protester" as its Person of the Year for 2011. Thus, alternative media may be swimming upstream against a media system still dominated by corporate and commercial imperatives, but its potential includes the ability to broaden the dominant political discourse and media agendas when working with large-scale social movements.

3. Change the Media

To change the media requires that we harness both political-economic inquiries and media production to the task of transformation. By gathering independent and activist media outlets in one place around common themes, Media Democracy Day hopes to transform a loose association of like-minded groups into a coherent movement capable of mounting a legitimate challenge to the dominance of the corporate, mainstream media.

– *Media Democracy Day Web site*, 2010

Given what we know about the media system, what possibilities exist to change the media field? While the New Right's policies have heavily restructured Canada's mediascape over the last 20 years, civil society has also generated a growing movement seeking to change the media. To explore the overall present state of media reform activities in Canada, a research project by Hackett and Anderson (2010) sought to identify the building blocks for a coalition movement that would work towards communicative democracy.[7] The authors conducted a triangulated research approach that included an online survey of 57 NGOs in different stakeholder sectors (political, professional or service, independent media, arts and culture, gender, religion, human rights, labour, First Nations, environment, etc.), supplemented by 18 in-depth interviews. The results of this research provide us with a sketch of the possibilities and constraints associated with the various interventions undertaken by a number of media activist groups.

First, it was widely acknowledged by the respondents (84.7 per cent agreed) that the quality and diversity of Canadian journalism affected their work, yet 62 per cent expressed dissatisfaction with the mainstream media coverage of their organization and issues (although CBC fared better than commercial news sources). Independent media were seen as far more helpful to their interests. Many NGOs have tried to reduce their dependency on mainstream media partially by putting more effort into their own Web sites, blogs, or published reports than into news releases or other ways to attract traditional media. Not surprisingly then, respondents were nearly unanimous (88 per cent) that Internet access for Canadians and for their own work is moderately or very important. They valued the Internet for very tangible and instrumental reasons: research, public access, mobilization, outreach, education, advocacy, collaboration, building community, and networking. Many of the respondents were emphatic. "It is our oxygen," said one respondent (Hackett and Anderson 2010, 18).

More generally, on the abstract question of Canadian media's performance of their role in a democratic society, over half of respondents (55 per cent) rated it as poor or very poor, though 45.1 per cent rated media as average or better. Most of the 24 respondents who offered additional comments were critical, in ways resonating with the potential agenda for media reform. First, 13 respondents pointed to aspects of corporate control, media concentration, or state policy. Ten mentioned biased or inadequate coverage. Some respondents linked bias to corporate control, but others emphasized resource constraints (the third most common theme of critics), cultural power differentials, or journalists' own inadequacies. The themes suggest somewhat divergent emphases for media reform: reduce market concentration, replace corporate ownership with public or community ownership, subsidize journalism, or change the cultural background and assumptions of journalists and their publics. These approaches are not necessarily mutually exclusive, however. Possibly by contrast with their American counterparts, Canadian NGOs do not appear to put much faith in market forces and greater competition as an antidote to concentrated corporate control. Conversely, there was widespread support for using the instrumentality of the state to achieve democratic reform of media. While there were differences of opinion in relation to relative support for mainstream journalism, public service media, and community media, there was no such ambiguity around the issue of fair access to the Internet, however. A full 98 per cent agreed that bandwidth throttling, the practice of prioritizing Internet traffic according to ability to pay, would negatively affect their work.

Overall, the extent of familiarity with media reform issues was encouraging. At least half of respondents were familiar with key Canadian media democracy entities – more so than with their US counterparts. The Friends of Canadian Broadcasting and rabble.ca appear to have gained particular recognition. Such awareness of these issues suggests that respondent organizations could be mobilized to support regulatory protections of public interest elements of the media, such as those found in the *Broadcasting Act 1991*. The research study made a number of conclusions as suggestions for moving towards more effective media reform. First, given the abstract and secondary nature of democratic communication as a political concept for most people, the diversity of specific issues it entails, and the diversity of potential constituencies for it, it was recognized that activists might need to frame their campaigns carefully and adopt different frames for different issues and constituencies.[8] Second, NGOs were most likely to invest resources in issues that affected their organizational mandates and sustainability. Third, "positive" frames, such as support for community media or for reinvigorating Canadian journalism, may find broader (albeit likely less intense) support than would adversarial frames, such as opposition to corporate concentration. Fourth, the issue of Internet access and net neutrality was likely to find wide support and to provide an entrée to ongoing collaboration for future campaigns. Finally, the frame of "open media" could appeal to younger activists and complements a focus on equitable access to digital media. At the very least, it should take its place alongside other current frames reflecting different emphases, such as media justice, free press, media democratization, and communication rights (Hackett and Carroll 2006).

Media Activism in Canada: One Example

As a particular example of the media reform movement in Canada, with a focus on digital media, OpenMedia.ca provides an important case study for understanding both the opportunities for effecting change and the kinds of pressures that can be placed on the media field. OpenMedia.ca emerged from a loose association of like-minded groups and individuals into the very kind of coherent movement that is able to organize effective campaigns on major communication policy issues in Canada and therefore is one model of resistance and reform.

OpenMedia.ca was initiated in May 2007 when the University of Windsor convened a communications conference called "20 Years of Propaganda." Participants, including prominent academics, media activists, and NGO representatives, agreed that Canada needed a media policy reform network – an organization that would work to bring public participation into media policy development. Several participants called for creating an organization focused on media reform generally and on public engagement campaigns and movement building specifically, similar to Free Press in the United States. Simultaneously, the annual Media That Matters[9] gathering was taking place on the West Coast and reaching similar conclusions. Shortly after these two workshops, participants from both originating groups, as well as representatives from unions and other NGOs, organized a campaign around the CRTC's Diversity of Voices Hearing, launching the Stop the Big Media Takeover campaign. The network for democratic media reform grew out of this campaign and involved a diverse coalition of labour groups, consumer groups, small businesses, independent and community media outlets, grass-roots organizations, media watchdog organizations, academics, bloggers, and others. A national not-for-profit organization was formally established in 2007, initially called the Campaign for Democratic Media (CDM). The campaign saw nearly 2,000 Canadians submitting comments to the CRTC calling for media reform to prevent further loosening of media concentration rules. It drew national media attention and led the CRTC to hold a hearing on community broadcasting.

In 2008, the CDM began to organize around an emerging media issue – net neutrality, which is when every user is treated equally. CDM launched the SaveOurNet.ca coalition, bringing together citizens, businesses, and public interest groups to protect equal access to the Internet. Recognizing the connection between Canada's digital divide and net neutrality, CDM worked through the SaveOurNet.ca coalition in 2009 to organize several Open Internet Town Hall Meetings in Toronto, Vancouver, and Ottawa. Coalition members and network experts appeared before the CRTC at the "traffic management" hearings set up to discuss proposals by Internet providers to introduce "Internet traffic management practices to address possible congestion in their networks" (Canadian Radio-television and Telecommunications Commission 2009). The CDM's public campaigns garnered extensive national media attention, resulting in thousands of Canadians sending comments to the CRTC. This effort helped propel net neutrality from an obscure issue into a national movement to secure open and equal access to the Internet. In October 2009, the CRTC ruled to adopt new traffic management guidelines resembling some of the rules put forth by SaveOurNet.ca. and the Canadian Internet Policy and Public Interest Clinic.

In 2010, CDM was "rebranded" to reflect its shift to online communications and Web-based tools, and the growing strength of the "open" movement aimed at advancing the causes of innovation and democracy in governance both in the public and private sector. OpenMedia.ca, the new name, reflects the organization's stated commitment to pursuing and creating an open, accessible media system in Canada. Most recently, OpenMedia.ca launched the Stop The Meter campaign in 2010 to intervene in a decision by the CRTC to allow wholesale Internet providers the power to impose "usage-based billing" (pay per byte) on independent Internet service providers and thus most Canadian Internet users. At the time of writing, the campaign had received national attention and over 400,000 signatures on its Stop The Meter petition – an unprecedented level of public engagement around telecommunications policy in Canada.

Conclusion

The fundamental importance of journalism to a functioning democracy is uncontested. The value of a democratic media system remains as essential today as a hundred years ago and is central to contemporary emerging democracies. However, as noted in this chapter, many of the developments of the last 20 years have diminished democratic communications in the media systems on which we rely. Journalism has become a corporate version of public relations for the elite at a time when governments and political parties have adopted public relations strategies that undermine the public interest. Commercial media have successfully lobbied regulatory structures to allow a level of concentration of ownership that not only undermines the diversity of content but also undermines the investigative journalism that could expose public relations politics. Corporate bottom lines and reliance on public relations content reduce the informational capacity of the media and, consequently, the normative goal of a vibrant and diverse public sphere of political discourse. Media content has tended to reinforce, rather than challenge, existing power structures at the same time as representations of politics and policies have become more like product marketing than the deliberation of ideas.

If we are to resist the developments and implications of the publicity state, it is clear that we need an informational media system that enhances the democratic public sphere; decentralizes political, civic, and symbolic power; encourages diversity and equality of voice; and provides a strong support for media regulation in the public interest. As a whole, this list of laudable goals is intimidating. Yet, drawing on theories of hegemony and social fields, we can see the possibilities for resistance and change. Hegemonic ideology can be contested by counter-hegemonic pressures from other social fields, such as those brought to bear on the CRTC by Openmedia.ca. Indeed, the media field, as we noted previously, is not unalterable. It is vulnerable to influence from within, as well as from other fields of power, including political pressure and citizen engagement. The growing evidence, both from academic and activist examples, supports the emergence of media reform as a nascent social movement concerned with communicative democracy and thus recognizes the vital importance of a media system that enhances democratic goals such as equality, participation, and diversity of opinion.

The goal for effective resistance to a publicity state, then, is to act on the range of opportunities and strategies for change in the media system. The three-part strategy outlined in this chapter gives some structure to the options for change by breaking these goals down into manageable projects and sites of struggle. To *know the media, be the media, and change the media* represents a multifaceted approach that works from a number of positions and on a number of social fields at once. Such an approach holds the greatest possibility for enhancing political discourse and the public sphere in Canada.

NOTES

1 Free Press is a US-based media reform group founded by media scholars Robert W. McChesney and Josh Silver in 2002. At the time of writing, the organization claimed over half a million members. See http://www .freepress.net.

2 Friends of Canadian Broadcasting was founded in 1987 to protest the first major cuts to the budget of the CBC. It has over 100,000 members. See http://www.friends.ca for more information.

3 The World Summit on Information Society was held in two phases: in Geneva in 2003, attended by over 11,000 participants from over 175 countries, and in Tunis in 2005 with 19,000 participants. The objective of the summit was to come to international agreements about Internet governance and communication rights in the digitalized world.

4 The World Association for Christian Communication is a group that works with both faith-based and secular member groups to promote "communication for social change." It identifies its key concerns as media diversity, communication rights, and media and gender justice. See http://www .waccglobal.org for more information.

5 Begun in 1995, the GMMP monitors the presence of women in the news across the globe very five years, the longest and most extensive research on gender in the news media ever conducted. The fourth GMMP report was published in 2010 and involved 107 countries. See http://www.whomakes thenews.org.

6 Every year the researchers at US-based Project Censored (founded in 1976) publish a list of the top 25 under-reported stories in the mainstream news. See http://www.projectcensored.org.

7 Some of the material for this chapter, particularly the discussion of media reform, draws from "Revitalizing the Media Reform Movement in Canada," a research paper by Robert Hackett and Steve Anderson, with collaborative assistance and support from OpenMedia.ca and WACC. Funding assistance for the research came from the Necessary Knowledge for a Democratic Public Sphere Program of the Social Science and Humanities Research Council. Different versions of this report were published in the *CCPA Monitor*

(July–August 2010) and in the *Canadian Journal of Communication* in 2011 in a special issue on democratizing communication policy in Canada.

8 Gitlin's (1980) classic discussion of news framing is helpful here, as is Lakoff's (2004) more recent work on the need for effective framing of social justice campaigns as a fundamental political strategy and as a formative influence on public policy.

9 The Media That Matters conference is held annually at Hollyhock Educational Retreat on Cortes Island in British Columbia.

References

Advertising Standards Canada. 2011. "The Canadian code of advertising standards." http://www.adstandards.com/en/Standards/canCodeOfAdStandards.aspx.

Ajzen, I., and M. Fishbein. 1980. *Understanding attitudes and predicting social behavior*. Englewood Cliffs, NJ: Prentice Hall.

Albert, M. 1997. "What makes alternative media alternative?" *Z Magazine Online*, October. Accessed 11 June 2001. http://subsol.c3.hu/subsol_2/contributors3/alberttext.html.

Alesina, A., and N. Roubini. 1992. "Political cycles in OECD economies." *Review of Economic Studies* 59 (4): 663–88. http://dx.doi.org/10.2307/2297992.

Allan, S. 2004. *News culture*. 2nd ed. New York: Open University Press.

Allan, S. 2009. "Histories of citizen journalism." In *Citizen journalism: Global perspectives*, edited by S. Allan and E. Thorsen, 17–32. New York: Peter Lang.

Althusser, L. 1971. *Lenin and philosophy and other essays*. New York: Monthly Review Press.

An, J., M. Cha, K. Gummadi, and J. Crowcroft. 2011. "Media landscapes in Twitter: A world of new conventions and political diversity." Proceedings of the 5th International Conference on Weblogs and Social Media, Barcelona, Spain, July.

Anderson, P. 2000. "Renewals." *New Left Review* 1: 1–20.

Anholt, S. 2004. "Branding places and nations." In *Brands and branding*, edited by R. Clifton, J. Simmons, and S. Ahmad, 213–26. Princeton, NJ: Bloomberg.

Anholt, S. 2009. "Nation 'branding': Propaganda or statecraft?" *Public Diplomacy Magazine*, Summer, 88–90.

Anker, L. 2005. "Peacekeeping and public opinion." *Canadian Military Journal* 6 (2): 23–32.

Anonymous. 2001. "What role should branding play in politics?" *Brand Channel*. Accessed 24 May 2004. http://brandchannel.com/forum.asp?bd_id=5.

Armstrong, P. 1996. "From caring and sharing to greedy and mean?" In *Language, culture and values in Canada at the dawn of the 21st century*, edited by P. Smart, A. Lapierre, and P. Savard, 251–68. Ottawa: Carleton University Press.

Aronczyk, M., and D. Powers, eds. 2010. Introduction to *Blowing up the brand: Critical perspectives on promotional culture*. New York: Peter Lang.

Assange, J. 2006. "Conspiracy as governance." Accessed 4 January 2011. http://cryptome.org/0002/ja-conspiracies.pdf.

Atlantic Institute for Market Studies. 2011. "Charles Cirtwill." Accessed 21 March 2011. http://www.aims.ca/en/home/aboutus/staff/charlescirtwill.aspx.

Atton, C. 2002. *Alternative media*. Thousand Oaks, CA: Sage.

Atton, C. 2008. "Alternative media theory and journalism practice." In *Digital media and democracy: Tactics in hard times*, edited by M. Boler, 213–27. Cambridge, MA: MIT Press.

Aubry, J. 1999. "Unity contracts handed out without tender." *Ottawa Citizen*, January 27, A1.

Aubry, J. 2004. "Arar denied full access to own file." *Ottawa Citizen*, January 27, A1.

Aubry, J. 2006. "Don't sound so American, advisers told Tories." *Ottawa Citizen*, September 21, A2.

Aucoin, P. 2012. "New political governance in Westminster systems: Impartial public administration and management performance at risk." *Governance: An International Journal of Policy, Administration and Institutions* 25 (2): 177–99. http://dx.doi.org/10.1111/j.1468-0491.2012.01569.x.

Auditor General of Canada. 2012. *2012 Spring Report of the Auditor General*. Accessed 25 June 2012. http://www.oag-bvg.gc.ca/internet/English/parl_oag_201204_e_36455.html.

Austin, L. 2001. "Is privacy a casualty of the war on terrorism?" In *The security of freedom: Essays on Canada's anti-terrorism bill*, edited by R.J. Daniels, P. Macklem, and K. Roach, 251–68. Toronto: University of Toronto Press.

Bachrach, P., and M.S. Baratz. 1963. "Decisions and nondecisions: An analytical framework." *American Political Science Review* 3 (57): 632–42. http://dx.doi.org/10.2307/1952568.

Bagdikian, B.H. 2004. *The new media monopoly*. Boston: Beacon Press.

Baker, C.E. 2007. *Media concentration and democracy: Why ownership matters*. New York: Cambridge University Press.

Bakvis, H., and M.D. Jarvis. 2012. *From new public management to new political governance: Essays in honour of Peter Aucoin*. Montreal: McGill-Queen's University Press.

Barney, D. 2008. "Politics and emerging media: The revenge of publicity." *Global Media Journal – Canadian Edition* 1 (1): 89–106.

Barry, A. 2001. *Political machines: Governing a technological society*. London: Athlone Press.

Bastedo, H., W. Chu, and J. Hilderman. 2012. "Occupiers and legislators: A snapshot of political media coverage." Samara Foundation. http://www.sama racanada.com/what-we-do/current-research/occupiers-and-legislators.

Baudrillard, J. 1996. "The masses: The implosion of the social in the media." In *Media studies: A reader*, edited by P. Marris and S. Thornham, 60–8. Edinburgh: Edinburgh University Press.

Beauchesne, E. 1994. "Welcome to the third world, think tank says you owe $61,188." *Edmonton Journal*, May 12, A3.

Beck, U. 1999. *The reinvention of politics: Rethinking modernity in the global social order*. Cambridge, UK: Polity Press.

Beeby, D. 2010. "Tories blocked full release of sensitive public works report." *Globe and Mail*, February 7, A1.

Beers, D., ed. 2005. *Liberalized*. Vancouver: New Star Books.

Bennett, W.L. 1983. *News: The politics of illusion*. New York: Longman.

Bennett, W.L. 2009. *News: The politics of illusion*. 8th ed. New York: Pearson/ Longman.

Bennett, W.L., R.G. Lawrence, and S. Livingston. 2007. *When the press fails: Political power and the news media from Iraq to Katrina*. Chicago: University of Chicago Press.

Bennett, W.L., and J.B. Manheim. 2001. "The big spin: Strategic communication and the transformation of pluralist democracy." In *Mediated politics: Communication in the future of democracy*, edited by W.L. Bennett and R.M. Entman, 279–98. Cambridge, UK: Cambridge University Press.

Benson, R. 2003. "Commercialism and critique: California's alternative weeklies." In *Contesting media power: Alternative media in a networked world*, edited by N. Couldry and J. Curran, 111–27. Lanham, MD: Rowman & Littlefield.

Benson, R. 2006. "News media as a 'journalistic field': What Bourdieu adds to new institutionalism, and vice versa." *Political Communication* 23 (2): 187–202. http://dx.doi.org/10.1080/10584600600629802.

Benson, R., and E. Neveu. 2005. *Bourdieu and the journalistic field*. London: Polity Press.

Bernays, E. (1928) 2005. *Propaganda*. Brooklyn: Ig.

Best, P. 2009. "Flaherty a big fan of a new think tank." *Globe and Mail*, June 18, B2.

Billig, M. 1995. *Banal nationalism*. London: Sage.

Billig, M. 2001. "Humour and hatred: The racist jokes of the Ku Klux Klan." *Discourse & Society* 12 (3): 267–89. http://dx.doi.org/10.1177/095792650101 2003001.

Black, E., and J. Silver. 2001. *Building a better world: An introduction to trade unionism in Canada*. Halifax: Fernwood.

Blais, A., E. Gidengil, R. Nadeau, and N. Nevitte. 2002. *Anatomy of a Liberal victory: Making sense of the vote in the 2000 Canadian election*. Peterborough, ON: Broadview.

Blais, A., E. Gidengil, and N. Nevitte. 2004. "Where does turnout decline come from?" *European Journal of Political Research* 43 (2): 221–36. http://dx.doi .org/10.1111/j.1475-6765.2004.00152.x.

Blake, S. 2011. "Managing the media mosaic: Diversity of voices and deliberative policy making in English Canadian media." MA thesis, Ryerson University and York University, Toronto.

Blanchfield, M., and J. Bronskill. 2010. "Documents expose Harper's obsession with control." *Toronto Star*, June 6, A1.

Blatchford, C. 2010. "Self anointed G20 'journalists' should get real." *The Globe and Mail*, June 26. http://www.theglobeandmail.com/news/national/self-anointed-g20-journalists-should-get-real/article1386500.

Blumler, J.G. 1990. "Elections, the media and the modern publicity process." In *Public communication: The new imperatives: Future directions for media research*, edited by M. Ferguson, 101–14. London: Sage.

Blumler, J.G., and M. Gurevitch. 1995. *The crisis of public communication*. London: Routledge.

Boatright, R.G. 2009. "Interest group adaptations to campaign finance reform in Canada and the United States." *Canadian Journal of Political Science* 42 (1): 17–43. http://dx.doi.org/10.1017/S0008423909090027.

Boeder, P. 2005. "Habermas' heritage: The future of the public sphere in the network society." *First Monday* 10 (9). http://dx.doi.org/10.5210/fm.v10i9.1280.

Boesveld, S. 2011. "Canada's royal rebrand: Conservative majority makes swift symbolic moves." *National Post*, September 10, A4.

Boily, C. 2006a. "Canadian young adults and information." Paper presented at the Canadian Media Research Consortium Conference on Youth and the News, Vancouver, April 3–4.

Boily, C. 2006b. *The 18–24 age group and the news*. Quebec: Centre d'études sur les medias.

Boswell, R. 2007. "We're no mouse; we're a wolverine: Harper." *Montreal Gazette*, February 20, A15.

Boswell, R. 2012. "War of 1812 commemoration takes shape; $28 million to mark 200th anniversary." *Ottawa Citizen*, March 20, A5.

Bourdieu, P. 1990. *The logic of practice.* Stanford, CA: Stanford University Press.

Bourdieu, P. 1993. *The field of cultural production: Essays on art and literature.* Edited by R. Johnson. Cambridge, UK: Polity.

Bourdieu, P. 2005. "The political field, the social science field, and the journalistic field." In *Bourdieu and the journalistic field,* edited by R. Benson and E. Neveu, 29–47. London: Polity.

Bowman, K. 2000. "Polling to campaign and to govern." In *The permanent campaign and its future,* edited by N.J. Ornstein and T.E. Mann, 54–74. Washington, DC: American Enterprise Institute & Brookings Institution.

Brader, T. 2006. *Campaigning for the hearts and minds: How emotional appeals in political ads work.* Chicago: University of Chicago Press.

Bradford, N. 1998. *Commissioning ideas: Canadian national policy innovation in comparative perspective.* Toronto: Oxford University Press.

Braithwaite, C. 1970. "Invasion of privacy is feared from computer manipulation." *Globe and Mail,* May 23, B2.

Brock, D. 2004. *The Republican noise machine: Right-wing media and how it corrupts democracy.* New York: Crown Publishers.

Brodie, I. 2002. *Friends of the court: The privileging of interest group litigants in Canada.* Albany: State University of New York Press.

Brodie, J. 2002. "Citizenship and solidarity: Reflections on the Canadian way." *Citizenship Studies* 6 (4): 377–94. http://dx.doi.org/10.1080/13621020220000 41231.

Brown, C. 2010. "White noise: The blogosphere and Canadian politics." In *Mediating Canadian politics,* edited by S. Sampert and L. Trimble, 173–83. Toronto: Pearson.

Bruner, M.L. 2002. *Strategies of remembrance: The rhetorical dimensions of national identity construction.* Columbia: University of South Carolina Press.

Bruno, J. 2012a. "Privy Council Office to cut $17.6 million in budget, 139 employees." *Hill Times,* May 7, 1.

Bruno, J. 2012b. "PBO gets constitutional lawyer to help fight for details on feds $5.2 billion spending cuts." *Hill Times,* June 18, 1.

Buechler, S.M. 2000. *Social movements in advanced capitalism.* Oxford: Oxford University Press.

Bumsted, J.M. 1994. *The Winnipeg General Strike of 1919: An illustrated guide.* Toronto: Watson Dwyer.

Burkell, J., V. Steeves, and A. Micheti. 2007. *Broken doors: Strategies for drafting privacy policies kids can understand.* Ottawa: Privacy Commissioner of Canada. http://www.idtrail.org/files/broken_doors_final_report.pdf.

Butler, D. 2011. "Accounting for accountability." *Ottawa Citizen.* March 24, A1.

Butler, D. 2012. "Government analyzing its surveys." *Ottawa Citizen,* June 24, A3.

Butler, P.M. 2007. *Polling and public opinion: A Canadian perspective.* Toronto: University of Toronto Press.

Cabinet Office. 2008. *Cabinet Manual.* Wellington, New Zealand: Cabinet Office. http://cabinetmanual.cabinetoffice.govt.nz.

Cain, S. 2010. "Grassroots global solidarity: LabourStart's different kind of conference." *Our Times* 29 (4): 11–13.

Calabrese, A. 2004. "The promise of civil society: A global movement for communication rights." *Continuum (Perth)* 18 (3): 317–29. http://dx.doi.org/10.1080/1030431042000256081.

Calgary Herald. 1994. "Sky is not falling yet." May 18, A4.

Callon, M., P. Lascoumes, and Y. Barthe. 2009. *Acting in an uncertain world: An essay on technical democracy.* Cambridge, MA: MIT Press.

Camfield, D. 2008. "The working-class movement in Canada: An overview." In *Group politics and social movements in Canada*, edited by M. Smith, 61–83. Peterborough, ON: Broadview and University of Toronto Press.

Campbell, J.E., and M. Carlson. 2002. "Panopticon.com: Online surveillance and the commodification of privacy." *Journal of Broadcasting & Electronic Media* 46 (4): 586–606. http://dx.doi.org/10.1207/s15506878jobem4604_6.

Canada. 1958. Privy council office, *Organization of the Government of Canada.* June. Ottawa: Queen's Printer.

Canada. 1962–3. Royal Commission on Government Operations. [Glassco Commission]. Ottawa: Queen's Printer.

Canada. 1970. *Instant world: A report on telecommunications in Canada.* Department of Communications Ottawa: Government of Canada.

Canada. 1972. *Privacy & computers. Department of Communications/Department of Justice.* Ottawa: Information Canada.

Canada. 1980. *Organization of the government of Canada.* Ottawa: Queen's Printer.

Canada. 1981a. *Government communications guide.* Ottawa: Privy Council Office.

Canada. 1981b. *Government communications: Principles and mandates.* Ottawa: Privy Council Office.

Canada. 1982. *Charter of Rights and Freedoms.* Ottawa: Government of Canada.

Canada. 1983. *Privacy Act*, R.S.C., 1985, c. P-21. Accessed 2 April 2011. http://laws-lois.justice.gc.ca/eng/acts/p-21/index.html.

Canada. 1991. *Reforming electoral democracy: Final report*, vols. 1–2. Royal Commission on Electoral Reform and Party Financing. Ottawa: Ministry of Supply and Services Canada.

Canada. 1999. Proceedings of the Standing Senate Committee on Social Affairs, Science and Technology. The Senate. March 9.

Canada. 2000. Personal Information Protection and Electronic Documents Act, S.C. 2000, c.5. Accessed 2 April 2011. http://laws-lois.justice.gc.ca/eng/acts/P-8.6/index.html.

Canada. 2001. *Evidence. Standing Committee on Justice and Human Rights.* House of Commons. October 30. Accessed 4 May 2010. http://www.parl.gc.ca/HousePublications/Publication.aspx?DocId=1041077&Language=E&Mode=1&Parl=37&Ses=1.

Canada. 2002. *Communications policy of the government of Canada.* Ottawa: Treasury Board.

Canada. 2003a. *A year of review: Annual report of the government of Canada's advertising, 2002–03.* Ottawa: Communication Canada.

Canada. 2003b. *Report of the Auditor General of Canada: Government-wide audit of sponsorship, advertising, and public opinion.* Ottawa: Public Works and Government Services Canada.

Canada. 2005. *Who is responsible?: Phase 1 report.* [Gomery Report] Ottawa: Commission of Inquiry into the Sponsorship Program and Advertising Activities.

Canada. 2006a. *Communications policy of the government of Canada.* Ottawa: Treasury Board Secretariat. Accessed 7 June 2011. http://www.tbs-sct.gc.ca/pol/doc-eng.aspx?id=12316.

Canada. 2006b. *The grids. Office of the Information Commissioner of Canada.* November 14. www.infocom.gc.ca. Accessed 20 December 2010. [Canada Federal Court. (Rubin v. Canada (CMHC) 1989 (Appeal-108–97) 1 FC p. 265 C. A.; 52 D.L.R. (4th) 671; 21 C.P.R. (3d). 1989.]

Canada. 2006c. *Restoring accountability: Recommendations. Commission of Inquiry into the Sponsorship Program and Advertising Activities.* [Gomery Report] Public Works and Government Services. Accessed 23 June 2010. http://epe.lac-bac.gc.ca/100/206/301/pco-bcp/commissions/sponsorship-ef/06-02-10/www.gomery.ca/en/phase2report/recommendations/cispaa_report_full.pdf.

Canada. 2007a. *House of Commons Debates. Official report (Hansard).* No. 157, May 18. Accessed 18 May; updated 1 November 2013. http://www.parl.gc.ca/HousePublications/Publication.aspx?DocId=2965260&Language=E&Mode=1.

Canada. 2007b. *About the PBO.* Library of Parliament. Accessed 23 March 2011; updated 30 November 2013. http://www.pbo-dpb.gc.ca/en/ABOUT.

Canada. 2008. *Economic and fiscal statement.* Ministry of Finance, 1–11. November 27. Accessed 9 July 2011. www.fin.gc.ca/ec2008/speech/speech-eng.html.

Canada. 2009a. *Government electronic directory.* Prime Minister's Office. February 18. Accessed 4 January 2011. http://sage-geds.tpsgc-pwgsc.gc.ca/cgi-bin/direct500/eng/XEou%3dPMO-CPM%2co%3dGC%2cc%3dCA.

Canada. 2009b. *Connecting Canadians with their government - Annual report on government of Canada advertising activities 2008–2009.* Accessed 7 June 2011. http://www.tpsgc-pwgsc.gc.ca/pub-adv/rapports-reports/2008-2009/tdm-toc-eng.html.

Canada. 2009c. *Out of time: 2008–2009 report cards: Systemic issues affecting access to information in Canada.* Office of the Information Commissioner of Canada. Accessed 12 July 2010. http://www.infocom.gc.ca/eng/rp-pr_spe-rep_rap-spe_rep-car_fic-ren_2008-2009_2.aspx.

Canada. 2010a. *The cheques report: The use of partisan or personal identifiers on ceremonial cheques or other props for federal funding announcements.* Office of the Conflict of Interest and Ethics Commissioner. Ottawa: Parliament of Canada.

Canada. 2010b. "Auditor general tables report on former public sector integrity commissioner." News release, December 10. Office of the Auditor General.

Canada. 2010c. *Discontinuance report.* Ottawa: Office of the Conflict of Interest and Ethics Commissioner. http://ciec-ccie.gc.ca/resources/Files/English/Public%20Reports/Examination%20Reports/The%20Discontinuance%20Report.pdf.

Canada. 2010d. Address by Minister Van Loan to Fraser Institute. September 23, Ottawa. Foreign Affairs and International Trade. Accessed 21 March 2011. http://news.gc.ca/web/article-eng.do?m=/index&nid=561539.

Canada. 2010e. *Report on plans and priorities 2010–11.* Privy Council Office. Accessed 23 June 2010. http://www.tbs-sct.gc.ca/rpp/2010-2011/inst/pco/pco-eng.pdf.

Canada. 2011a. Testimony. A.M. Smart, Assistant Secretary to the Cabinet, Communications and Consultations, Privy Council Office. Standing Committee on Government Operations and Estimates, 40th parliament, 3rd session. March 10, 11:25 a.m.

Canada. 2011b. *2009–2010 Annual report on Government of Canada advertising activities.* Public Works and Government Services. Accessed 23 June 2010. http://www.tpsgc-pwgsc.gc.ca/pub-adv/rapports-reports/2009-2010/chapitre-chapter-2-eng.html.

Canada Revenue Agency. 2009. Registered charity information return for Aurea Foundation. Accessed 21 March 2011. http://www.cra-arc.gc.ca/chrts-gvng/lstngs/menu-eng.html.

Canadian Association of Journalists. 2010. "Ottawa's information lockdown and what journalists should do about it." Annual conference keynote panel

featuring H. Buzzetti, Pierre Duchesne, Kady O'Malley, Rob Russo, and
Mary Agnes Welch, Montreal, May 29.

Canadian Federation of Agriculture. 2010. "CFA News." http://www.cfa-fca.ca/.

Canadian Internet Policy and Public Interest Clinic (CIPPIC). 2008. "PIPEDA
complaint: Facebook." May 30. Accessed 2 April 2011. http://citeseerx.ist
.psu.edu/viewdoc/download?doi=10.1.1.121.4912&rep=rep1&type=pdf.

Canadian Newspaper Association. 2010. "Daily newspapers: 2010 circulation
by ownership group." Accessed 12 August 2011. http://www.newspaper
scanada.ca/sites/default/files/2010%20Circ%20byOwnership%20
Groups.pdf.

Canadian Press. 2010a. "Prorogation controversy takes hit on Tory lead, Harper's popularity: Poll." January 15.

Canadian Press. 2010b. "A list of groups opposed to scrapping of long-form
census." July 20.

Canadian Press. 2011. SNC Lavalin confirms it is building jail in Libya. *CBC
News*. February 24. Accessed 26 September 2013. http://www.cbc.ca.

Canadian Radio-television and Telecommunications Commission. 2009. "Traffic management." http://www.crtc.gc.ca/eng/pol/pdr-epr3.htm.

Capella, J.N., and K.H. Jamieson. 1997. *The spiral of cynicism: The press and the
public good*. New York: Oxford University Press.

Capstick, I. 2010. "From Facebook to filling the streets." *Globe and Mail*,
January 23. http://www.theglobeandmail.com/news/politics/
from-facebook-to-filling-the-streets/article4302566/.

Cario, E. 2010. "Pour se défendre, l'UMP achète « Bettencourt »." écrans,
July 8. http://www.ecrans.fr/Pour-se-defendre-l-UMP-achete,10347.html.

Carroll, W., and R.A. Hackett. 2006. "Democratic media activism through
the lens of social movement theory." *Media Culture & Society* 28 (1): 83–104.
http://dx.doi.org/10.1177/0163443706059289.

Carstairs, C. 2006. "Roots nationalism: Branding Canada cool in the 1980s and
1990s. *Histoire sociale / Social History* 39 (77): 235–55.

Castells, M. 1997. *The power of identity*. Oxford: Blackwell.

CBC News. 2006a. "Harper touts Canada's emerging role in NYC address."
September 21. http://www.cbc.ca/news/world/harper-touts-canada-s-
emerging-role-in-nyc-address-1.583875/.

CBC News. 2006b. "Soldiers' deaths in Afghanistan the price of leadership:
Harper." October 6. http://www.cbc.ca/news/canada/soldiers-deaths-
in-afghanistan-the-price-of-leadership-harper-1.592410/.

CBC News. 2006c. "Canada committed to Afghan mission, Harper tells
troops." March 13. http://www.cbc.ca/news/world/canada-
committed-to-afghan-missionharper-tells-troops-1.573722/.

C.D. Howe Institute. 1995. *1994 annual report*. Toronto: G.D. Howe Institute.

C.D. Howe Institute. 2008. *Annual report*. http://www.cdhowe.org/pdf/
AR_English_2008.pdf.

Center for Digital Democracy. 2009. "Online behavioral tracking and
targeting: Legislative primer." http://www.democraticmedia.org/
privacy-legislative-primer.

Centre for Research and Information on Canada. 2004. *Portraits of Canada 2003*.
Ottawa: Centre for Research and Information on Canada.

Cerulo, K.A. 1995. *Identity designs: The sights and sounds of a nation*. New Brunswick, NJ: Rutgers University Press.

Chadwick, A., and P. Howard, eds. 2008. *Routledge handbook of Internet politics*.
New York: Routledge.

Chase, S., and T. Grant. 2010. "Statscan chief falls on sword over census."
Globe and Mail, July 22, A1.

Chase, S., G. Galloway, and L. Perreaux. 2011. "Harper says he'll scrap per-
vote subsidy if elected." *Globe and Mail*, April 2, A8.

Cheadle, B. 2009a. "Economy media blitz trumps swine flu fight." *Toronto Star*,
September 21, A1.

Cheadle, B. 2009b. "Taxpayers on hook for $1.7-million as PMO rolls out
video." *Globe and Mail*, December 8. http://www.theglobeandmail.com/
news/politics/taxpayers-on-hook-for-17-million-as-pmo-rolls-out-video/
article4294919/.

Cheadle, B. 2009c. "Tories mum over vanishing Harper photos." *Toronto
Star*, September 22. http://news.ca.msn.com/canada/cp-article.aspx?
cp-documentid=21848281.

Cheadle, B. 2011a. "Harper government's ad buy costs taxpayers $26m."
Canadian Press, March 13. Accessed 21 March 2011. http://www.ctvnews.ca/
harper-government-s-ad-buy-costs-taxpayers-26m-1.618202.

Cheadle, B. 2011b. "Tories re-brand government in Stephen Harper's name."
Globe and Mail. March 3, A4.

Cheadle, B. 2011c. "Harper government spends $26 million on winter ad blitz."
Globe and Mail, March 12. http://www.theglobeandmail.com/news/politics/
harper-government-spends-26-million-on-winter-ad-blitz/article571061/.

Cheadle, B. 2011d. "No 'formal directive' on use of 'Harper Government,' just
direction, says PCO." *Winnipeg Free Press*, March 7.

Cheadle, B. 2011e. "How PMO orchestrated a taxpayer-funded online
marketing coup." *Globe and Mail*, February 24. http://m.theglobeandmail
.com/news/politics/how-pmo-orchestrated-a-taxpayer-funded-online-
marketing-coup/article567843/?service=mobile.

Cheadle, B. 2011f. "Documents show economic action plan marketing blitz a PMO production from the get-go." *Canadian Press*, February 24.

Chief Electoral Officer of Canada. 2008. *Report of the Chief Electoral Officer of Canada on the 40th general election of October 14, 2008*. Ottawa: Elections Canada.

Chrétien, J. 2000. "The Canadian way in the 21st century." Speech at the Progressive Governance for the 21st Century Conference, Berlin, June 2–3.

Chrétien, J. 2007. *My years as prime minister*. Toronto: Random House.

Christensen, M. 2009. "Watching me watching you: Complicit surveillance and social networking." *Le Monde Diplomatique*, October. http://mondediplo .com/2009/10/02networking.

Christie, J. 1990. "Participaction's propaganda." *Globe and Mail*, May 7, A1.

Chung, E. 2010. "Consumers want targeted marketing: Facebook." *CBC News*, November 30. http://www.cbc.ca/news/technology/consumers-want-targeted-marketing-facebook-1.975290.

Clark, C. 2011. "Canada protests 'one-sided' resolutions with pro-Israel stand at UN." *Globe and Mail*, November 10. http://www.theglobeandmail .com/news/politics/canada-protests-one-sided-resolutions-with-pro-israel-stand-at-un/article4181837/.

Clark, C., and S. Chase. 2010. "Canada's $9 billion jet fighter deal raises questions." *Globe and Mail*, July 17. http://www.theglobeandmail.com/news/politics/canadas-9-billion-jet-fighter-deal-raises-questions/article1212443/.

Clark, I. 1985. "Recent changes in the cabinet decision-making system in Ottawa." *Canadian Public Administration* 28 (2): 185–201. http://dx.doi .org/10.1111/j.1754-7121.1985.tb00510.x.

Clark, J., and T. Van Slyke. 2010. *Beyond the echo chamber: Reshaping politics through networked progressive media*. New York: New Press.

Clifton, R., J. Simmons, and S. Ahmad, eds. 2004. *Brands and branding*. Princeton, NJ: Bloomberg.

Cobb, C. 2002. "Ads: Government paid third party to deal with crown corporation." *Ottawa Citizen*, June 6, A4.

Cohen, B. 1963. *The press and foreign policy*. Princeton, NJ: Princeton University Press.

Coleman, R., and M. McCombs. 2007. "The young and agenda-less? Exploring age-related differences in agenda setting on the youngest generation, baby boomers and the civic generation." *Journalism & Mass Communication Quarterly* 84 (3): 495–508. http://dx.doi.org/10.1177/107769900708400306.

Coleman, S., and J.G. Blumler. 2009. *The Internet and democratic citizenship*. Cambridge, UK: Cambridge University Press. http://dx.doi.org/10.1017/CBO9780511818271.

Coletto, D., and M. Eagles. 2011. "The impact of election finance reforms on local party organization." In *Money, politics and democracy: Canada's party finance reforms*, edited by L. Young and H.J. Jansen, 104–29. Vancouver: University of British Columbia Press.

Coletto, D., H. Jansen, and L. Young. 2011. "Stratarchical party organization and party finance in Canada." *Canadian Journal of Political Science* 44 (01): 111–36. http://dx.doi.org/10.1017/S0008423910001034.

Comedia. 1984. The alternative press: The development of underdevelopment. *Media, Culture & Society* 6 (2): 95–102.

Communications, Energy and Paperworkers Union. 2004. *Canadian media: How to make it diverse, democratic and responsive.* http://www.cep.ca/docs/en/mediapolicy_e.pdf.

Comor, E. 2008. *Consumption and the globalization project: International hegemony and the annihilation of time.* New York: Palgrave Macmillan. http://dx.doi.org/10.1057/9780230582996.

Compton, J.R., and P. Benedetti. 2010. "Labour, new media and the institutional restructuring of journalism." *Journalism Studies* 11 (4): 487–99. http://dx.doi.org/10.1080/14616701003638350.

Conacher, D. 2011. "Making the government more accountable." Letter to the editor, *Ottawa Citizen*, June 27, A8.

Conservative Party of Canada. 2011. *Here for Canada.* Accessed 25 November 2013. http://www.conservative.ca/media/2012/06/Conservative Platform2011_ENs.pdf.

Conway, J.M. 2004. *Identity, place, knowledge: Social movements contesting globalization.* Halifax: Fernwood.

Conway, J.M. 2006. *Praxis and politics: Knowledge production in social movements.* New York: Routledge.

Cook, P. 1994. "The bad news on the budget never sleeps." *Globe and Mail,* October 12, B2.

Copeland, D. 2005. "New rabbits, old hats." *International Journal (Toronto, Ont.)* 60 (3): 743–62. http://dx.doi.org/10.2307/40204061.

Corcoran, T. 1994. "Spending crisis closing in on Ottawa." *Globe and Mail,* October 12, B2.

Cormack, P. 2008. "'True stories' of Canada." *Cultural Sociology* 2 (3): 369–84. http://dx.doi.org/10.1177/1749975508095617.

Corner, J. 2007. "Mediated politics, promotional culture and the idea of 'propaganda.'" *Media Culture & Society* 29 (4): 669–77. http://dx.doi.org/10.1177/0163443707078428.

Cosgrove, G. 1999. "Laurier Club membership has its privileges." *National Post*, December 11, B11.

Couldry, N. 2003. "Media meta-capital: Extending the range of Bourdieu's field theory." *Theory and Society* 32 (5–6): 653–77. http://dx.doi.org/10.1023/B:RYSO.0000004915.37826.5d.

Couldry, N., and J. Curran. 2003. *Contesting media power: Alternative media in a networked world*. Lanham, MD: Rowman and Littlefield.

Cowley, P. 2007. "Bringing education into the market place: Part I – The report card on schools." *Fraser Forum*, September: 6–9.

Cross, K.A. 2010. "Experts in the news: The differential use of sources in election television news." *Canadian Journal of Communication* 35 (3): 413–29.

Crozier, M., S. Huntington, and J. Watunaki. 1975. *The crisis of democracy: Report on the governability of democracies to the Trilateral Commission*. New York: New York University Press.

Curry, B. 2011. "Selling policy or party? Tories to spend $4 million on budget ad blitz." *Globe and Mail*, March 10, A1.

Cushion, S., and J. Lewis. 2010. *The rise of 24-hour news television: Global perspectives.* New York: Peter Lang.

Dagnes, A. 2010. *Politics on demand: The effects of 24-hour news on American politics*. Santa Barbara, CA: Praeger.

Dale, S. 1996. *McLuhan's children: The Greenpeace message and the media*. Toronto: Between the Lines.

Daniels, R.J., P. Macklem, and K. Roach, eds. 2001. *The security of freedom: Essays on Canada's anti-terrorism bill*. Toronto: University of Toronto Press.

Davis, A. 2007. *The mediation of power: A critical introduction*. London: Routledge.

Davis, J. 2009a. "Liberal-era diplomatic language killed off." *Embassy*, July 1. http://www.embassynews.ca/news/2009/07/01/liberal-era-diplomatic-language-killed-off/37788?absolute=1.

Davis, J. 2009b. "Leaked DFAIT memo documents struggle between Conservative political staff and foreign service." *Embassy*, July 29. http://www.embassynews.ca/news/2009/07/29/leaked-dfait-memo-documents-struggle-between-conservative-political-staff-and-foreign/37888?absolute=1.

Davis, J. 2010. Opposition parties attack feds' $89-million advertising strategy. *The Hill Times*, April 5.

Davis, S. 2010. "Facebook and democracy." *National Post*, January 22, A12.

Deacon, D., and P. Golding. 1994. *Taxation and representation: The media, political communication and the poll tax*. London: John Libbey.

Dean, J. 2002. *Publicity's secret: How technoculture capitalizes on democracy*. Ithaca, NY: Cornell University Press.

Dean, J. 2005. "Communicative capitalism: Circulation and the foreclosure of politics." *Cultural Politics* 1 (1): 51–74. http://dx.doi.org/10.2752/174321905778054845.

Dean, J. 2006. *Žižek's politics*. New York: Routledge.

Dean, J. 2008. "Communicative capitalism: Circulation and the foreclosure of politics." In *Digital media and democracy: Tactics in hard times*, edited by M. Boler, 101–22. Cambridge, MA: MIT Press.

Dean, J. 2009. *Democracy and other neoliberal fantasies: Communicative capitalism and left politics*. Durham, NC: Duke University Press.

Decima Research. 2011. "National TV networks, local dailies will reach the largest number of Canadian voters." Press release. With School of Journalism and Communication, Carleton University.

Delacourt, S. 2009. "It's all about who?" *Toronto Star*, June 16. http://thestar.blogs.com/politics/2009/06/its-all-about-who-.html.

Delacourt, S. 2012. "Canada's Conservative government: In picture-story book form." *Toronto Star*, June 1. http://www.thestar.com/news/canada/2012/06/01/canadas_conservative_government_in_picturestorybook_form.html.

De Lint, W., and A. Hall. 2009. *Intelligent control: Developments in public order and policing in Canada*. Toronto: University of Toronto Press.

Della Porta, D., and M. Diani. 1999. *Social movements: An introduction*. Oxford: Blackwell.

De Souza, M. 2010. "Spending good for 'visibility,' bureaucrats told Baird." *Ottawa Citizen*, February 18, A3.

De Souza, M. 2012. "Oilsands 'significant' risk to Alberta, memo says." *Ottawa Citizen*, February, A4.

Deuze, M. 2009. "The future of citizen journalism." In *Citizen journalism: Global perspectives*, edited by S. Allan and E. Thorsen, 255–64. New York: Peter Lang.

Dichter, A. 2005. "Together we know more: Networks and coalitions to advance media democracy, communication rights and the public sphere 1990–2005." Paper presented at the Social Science Research Council Necessary Knowledge Workshop, New York.

Dickens, C. 1848. *Dombey and son*. Philadelphia: Lea and Blanchard.

Ditchburn, J. 2007. "PMO failed to reveal its own research." *Globe and Mail*, May 7, A7.

Dobbin, M. 1998. *The myth of the good corporate citizen: Democracy under the rule of big business*. Toronto: Stoddart.

Dobbin, M. 2003. *Paul Martin: CEO for Canada?* Toronto: James Lorimer.

Dobbin, M. 2010. "Harper's hitlist: Thirteen months, two prorogations of parliament." rabble.ca, March 4.

Dobrowolsky, A. 2000. *The politics of pragmatism: Women, representation, and constitutionalism in Canada*. Don Mills, ON: Oxford University Press.

Doern, G.B. 1977. "The policy-making philosophy of prime minister Trudeau and his advisors." In *Apex of power: The prime minister and political leadership in Canada*, 2nd ed., edited by T.A. Hockin, 189–96. Scarborough, ON: Prentice-Hall.

Doherty, B. 2007. "Elections: The politics of the permanent campaign: Presidential travel and the Electoral College, 1977–2004." *Presidential Studies Quarterly* 37 (4): 749–73. http://dx.doi.org/10.1111/j.1741-5705.2007.02623.x.

Domingo, D., T. Quandt, A. Heinonen, S. Paulussen, J.B. Singer, and M. Vujnovic. 2008. "Participatory journalism practices in the media and beyond: An international comparative study of initiatives in online newspapers." *Journalism Practice* 2 (3): 326–42. http://dx.doi.org/10.1080/17512780802281065.

Dominion Institute. 2008. "In wake of constitutional crisis, new survey demonstrates that Canadians lack basic understanding of our country's parliamentary system." News release, December 15. Accessed 12 August 2011. http://www.dominion.ca/DominionInstituteDecember15Factum.pdf.

Douglas, K. 2006. "The *Access to Information Act* and recent proposals for reform." Publication No. 2005-55-E, Library of Parliament, Ottawa. Accessed 30 November 2013. http://www.parl.gc.ca/Content/LOP/ResearchPublications/2005-55-e.pdf.

Downing, J. 1984. *Radical media*. Boston: South End.

Downing, J. 2001. *Radical media: Rebellious communication and social movements*. With T. Villarreal Ford, G. Gil, and L. Stein. Thousand Oaks, CA: Sage.

Easton, B. 1994. "How did the health reforms blitzkrieg fail?" *Political Science* 46 (2): 215–33. http://dx.doi.org/10.1177/003231879404600205.

Easton, D. 1965. *A framework for political analysis*. Englewood Cliffs, NJ: Prentice Hall.

Economist. 2003a. "Campaign finance in Canada: Closing the private purse." July 10, 1–2.

Economist. 2003b. "Northern tiger loses growl." February 20, 34.

Ekos Research. 2010. "Canadians support decriminalization of minor pot possession and lean to not reintroducing death penalty." March 19. http://www.ekos.com/admin/articles/cbc-2010-03-19.pdf.

Elections Canada. 2008. Return Summary. Financial reports. Registered Parties Financial Returns. Conservative Party of Canada. Accessed 25 November 2013. http://www.elections.ca/WPAPPS/WPF/PP/SelectParties?act=C2&returntype=1&period=0.

Elections Canada. 2009. Financial Reports of Political Parties. Statements of Assets and Liabilities and Statements of Revenues and Expenses – 2009 Fiscal

Period. http://www.elections.ca/content.aspx?section=fin&document=index&dir=pol/asset/2009&lang=e.

Elections Canada. 2012. "Remarks of the Chief Electoral Officer in response to concerns arising from allegations of wrongdoing during the 41st general election before the Standing Committee on Procedure and House Affairs." March 2. Accessed 4 April 2012. http://www.elections.ca/content.aspx?section=med&document=mar2912&dir=spe&lang=e.

Elections Canada. 2013. Financial Reports of Political Parties. Statements of Assets and Liabilities and Statements of Revenues and Expenses. http://www.elections.ca/content.aspx?section=fin&document=index&dir=pol/asset&lang=e.

Elmer, G. 2006. "Re-tooling the network: Parsing the links and codes of the Web world." *Convergence* 12 (1): 9–19.

Eltahawy, M. 2011. "Tunisia: The first Arab revolution." *Guardian*, January 16. http://www.theguardian.com/commentisfree/2011/jan/16/tunisia-first-arab-revolution-ben-ali.

Ericson, R., P. Baranek, and B. Chan. 1987. *Visualizing deviance: A study of news organization*. Toronto: University of Toronto Press.

Esposito, R. 2005. *Catégories de'impolitique*. Paris: Seuil.

Ewen, S. 1992. *Channels of desire: Mass images and the shaping of American consciousness*. Minneapolis: University of Minnesota Press.

Fan, Y. 2010. "Branding the nation: Towards a better understanding." *Place Branding and Public Diplomacy* 6 (2): 97–103. http://dx.doi.org/10.1057/pb.2010.16.

Federal Trade Commission. 2010. *Protecting consumer privacy in an era of rapid change: A proposed framework for businesses and policymakers*. Washington, DC: Federal Trade Commission.

Fekete, J. 2012. "Critics see omnibus bill as abusive, unethical." *Ottawa Citizen*, May 4, A3.

Ferguson, J. 1994a. "Deficit-bashing rhetoric seen as corporate agenda." *Toronto Star*, September 17, D1.

Ferguson, J. 1994b. "'Historical' stand on deficit praised." *Toronto Star*, October 18, C2.

Ferguson, P., and C. de Clercy. 2005. "Regulatory compliance in opinion poll reporting during the 2004 Canadian election." *Canadian Public Policy* 31 (3): 243–57. http://dx.doi.org/10.2307/3552440.

Fishkin, J.S. 2006. "Beyond polling alone: The quest for an informed public." *Critical Review* 18 (1–3): 157–65. http://dx.doi.org/10.1080/08913810608443654.

Fishkin, J.S., and R.C. Luskin. 2005. "Experimenting with a democratic ideal: Deliberative polling and public opinion." *Acta Politica* 40 (3): 284–98. http://dx.doi.org/10.1057/palgrave.ap.5500121.

Fitzpatrick, M. 2011. "F-35 jets cost to soar to $29B: watchdog." CBC News, March 10; updated November 30, 2013. http://www.cbc.ca/news/politics/f-35-jets-cost-to-soar-to-29b-watchdog-1.983367.

Flanagan, T. 2009. *Harper's team: Behind the scenes in the conservative rise to power*. 2nd ed. Montreal: McGill-Queen's University Press.

Flanagan, T. 2010. "Campaign strategy: Triage and concentration of resources." In *Election*, edited by H. McIvor, 155–72. Toronto: Emond Montgomery.

Flanagan, T., and S. Harper. 1998. "Conservative politics in Canada: Past, present and future." In *After liberalism: Essays in search of freedom, virtue and order*, edited by W.D. Gairdner, 168–92. Toronto: Stoddart.

Fletcher, F. 1977. "The prime minister as public persuader." In *Apex of power: The prime minister and political leadership in Canada*, 2nd ed., edited by T.A. Hockin, 130–40. Scarborough, ON: Prentice-Hall.

Fletcher, F. 2004. "Media and democracy: Does the news meet citizen needs?" Presentation at the School of Journalism, University of British Columbia, Vancouver, January.

Fletcher, F. 2005. "Public perceptions of ownership concentration in the Canadian news media." Paper presented with K. Wozniak at the Annual Conference of the Canadian Communication Association, London, Ontario, June.

Fletcher, F. 2007. "The future of news in the digital era." *Australian Policy Online*, July 9. Accessed 12 August 2011. http://www.apo.org.au/apo_search/results/Fred%20Fletcher.

Fletcher, F. 2010. "Quality journalism: Engaging audiences." PowerPoint presentation to the Reinventing Media Conference, Public Policy Forum, Ottawa, May 19.

Fletcher, F. 2011. "The Harper government's communication strategy: The message, the message, the message." *Canada Watch*, Spring, 37–8, 43.

Fletcher, F., and R. Everett. 2004. "The media and Canadian politics in an era of globalization." In *Canadian politics in the 21st century*, edited by M. Whittington and G. Williams, 427–48. Toronto: Thomson Nelson.

Fletcher, F., D. Logan, A. Hermida, and D. Korell. 2011. *Even in the digital era, Canadians have confidence in the mainstream news media*. Vancouver: Canadian Media Research Consortium.

Foot, K.A., and S.M. Schneider. 2006. *Web campaigning*. Cambridge, MA: MIT Press.

Foot, R. 2007. "Harper casts Canada as firmly distinct from the U.S." *Ottawa Citizen*, July 17.

Francoli, M., J. Greenberg, and C. Waddell. 2011. "The Campaign in the digital media." In *The Canadian federal election of 2011*, edited by J. Pammett and C. Dornan, 219–46. Toronto: Dundurn.

Franklin, B. 2004. *Packaging politics: Political communications in Britain's media democracy*. London: E. Arnold.

Franks, C.E.S. 2004. "Putting accountability and responsibility back into the system of government." *Policy Options* (October): 64–6.

Franks, C.E.S. 2009. "Parliament and public policy: What's to be done?" Presentation at the Public Policy Forum, "Inside Ottawa: Back to School," Ottawa, Canada, September 9.

Fraser Forum. 2007. "Fraser Institute Foundation receives generous gift." December 2007–January 2008, 6.

Fraser Institute. 1997. "Toward the new millennium: A five year plan for the Fraser Institute." Draft, Vancouver, January.

Fraser Institute. 1999. *Challenging perceptions: Twenty-five years of influential ideas: A retrospective 1974–1999*. Vancouver: Fraser Institute.

Fraser Institute. 2002. *The Fraser Institute 2002 annual report*. Vancouver: Fraser Institute.

Fraser Institute. 2007. *2007 Annual report: Changing the world*. Vancouver: Fraser Institute. Accessed 29 June 2011. http://www.fraserinstitute.org/uploadedFiles/fraser-ca/Content/About_Us/Who_We_Are/2007_Annual_Report.pdf.

Fraser Institute. 2009. *Fraser Institute annual report*. Vancouver: Fraser Institute. http://www.fraserinstitute.org/uploadedFiles/fraser-ca/Content/About_Us/Who_We_Are/2009-annual-report.pdf.

Fraser Institute. 2010. Fraser Institute Founder's Award gala dinner, June 3. Accessed 19 May 2010. http://www.gifttool.com/registrar/ShowEventDetails?ID=180&EID=6152.

Fraser, N. 1995. "From redistribution to recognition? Dilemmas of justice in a 'postsocialist' age." *New Left Review* 212 (July–August): 68–93.

Freedman, P., M. Franz, and K. Goldstein. 2004. "Campaign advertising and democratic citizenship." *American Journal of Political Science* 48 (4): 723–41. http://dx.doi.org/10.1111/j.0092-5853.2004.00098.x.

Freeman, A. 2007. "Change tune on war, PM told." *Globe and Mail*, July 13.

Freeman, B.M. 2012. "'One part creativity and nine parts hard work': The legacy of Canada's feminist periodicals." In *Alternative media in Canada*, edited by K. Kozolanka, P. Mazepa, and D. Skinner, 85–103. Vancouver: University of British Columbia Press.

Friedman, M. 1951. "Neo-liberalism and its prospects." *Farmand* 17 (February): 89–93.

Friedman, M. 1995. "Public schools: Make them private." *Washington Post*, February 19, C7.

Frontier Centre for Public Policy. 2010. 2009 Annual Report. http://www.fcpp.org/annual-reports/pdfs/annual-report-2009.pdf.

Frost, G. 2002. *Antony Fisher: Champion of liberty*. London: Profile Books.

Fuchs, C. 2010. "Grounding critical communication studies: An inquiry into the communication theory of Karl Marx." *Journal of Communication Inquiry* 34 (1): 15–41. http://dx.doi.org/10.1177/0196859909338409.

Galloway, G. 2010. "Tories skeptical of their own 10-point lead." *Globe and Mail*, July 8. http://www.theglobeandmail.com/news/politics/ ottawa-notebook/tories-skeptical-of-their-own-10-point-lead/article 4353462/.

Galloway, G. 2011. "Ottawa cautiously dipping its toe in social-media pool." *Globe and Mail*, December 29, A4.

Garbacz Rawson, E.A. 2007. "Perceptions of the United States of America: Exploring the political brand of a nation." *Place Branding and Public Diplomacy* 3 (3): 213–21. http://dx.doi.org/10.1057/palgrave.pb.6000067.

Gastil, J. 2000. "Is face-to-face citizen deliberation a luxury or a necessity?" *Political Communication* 17 (4): 357–61. http://dx.doi.org/10.1080/ 10584600050178960.

Gatehouse, J. 2010. "500 ways to say no." *Maclean's*, May 17, 22.

Geer, J. 2006. *In defense of negativity: Attack ads in presidential campaigns*. Chicago: University of Chicago Press. http://dx.doi.org/10.7208/ chicago/9780226285009.001.0001.

Geertz, C. 1973. "Thick description: Toward an interpretive theory of culture." In *The interpretation of cultures: Selected essays*, 3–30. New York: Basic Books.

Geisler, M.E. 2005. "What are national symbols – And what do they do to us?" In *National symbols, fractured identities: Contesting the national narrative*, edited by M.E. Geisler, xiii–xlii. Lebanon, NH: University Press of New England.

George, S. 1997. "How to win the war of ideas: Lessons from the Gramscian right." *Dissent*, Summer, 47–53.

Giddens, A. 1983. "Four theses on ideology." *Canadian Journal of Political and Social Theory* 7: 18–21.

Gillespie, T. 2010. "The politics of 'platforms.'" *New Media & Society* 12 (3): 347–64. http://dx.doi.org/10.1177/1461444809342738.

Gingras, A.-M., S. Sampert, and D. Gagnon-Pelletier. 2010. "Framing Gomery in English and French newspapers: The use of strategic and ethical frames." In *Mediating Canadian politics*, edited by S. Sampert and L. Trimble, 277–93. Toronto: Pearson.

Gitlin, T. 1980. *The whole world is watching: Mass media in the making and unmaking of the new left*. Berkeley: University of California Press.

Global Media Monitoring Project. 2010. *Canada national report*. Toronto: WACC.

Globe and Mail. 1994. "Putting off pain likely to magnify it." October 12, A7.

Godard, B. 2002. "Feminist periodicals and the production of cultural value: The Canadian context." *Women's Studies International Forum* 25 (2): 209–23. http://dx.doi.org/10.1016/S0277-5395(02)00231-5.

Golding, P. 1992. "Communicating capitalism: Resisting and restructuring state ideology." *Media Culture & Society* 14 (4): 503–22. http://dx.doi .org/10.1177/016344392014004002.

Golding, P. 1995. "The mass media and the public sphere: The crisis of information in the 'information society." In *Debating the future of the public sphere: Transforming the public and private domains in free market societies*, edited by S. Edgell, S. Walklate, and G. Williams, 25–40. Aldershot: Avebury.

Gordon, S. 2003. "Separatism dead." *Montreal Gazette*, September 10, A12.

Government Advertising Act. 2004. S.O., ch. 20.

Grabe, M.E., and E.P. Bucy. 2009. *Image bite politics: News and the visual framing of elections*. New York: Oxford University Press. http://dx.doi.org/10.1093/ acprof:oso/9780195372076.001.0001.

Gramsci, A. 1971. *Selections from the prison notebooks*. Edited and translated by Q. Hoare and G.N. Smith. New York: International.

Grant, R. 2004. "Federal government advertising." *Research Note*, June 21. Canberra: Parliamentary Library.

Gratton, M. 1987. *"So, what are the boys saying?": An inside look at Brian Mulroney in power*. Toronto: McGraw-Hill Ryerson.

Gravois, J. 2010. "The agnostic cartographer: How Google's open-ended maps are embroiling the company in some of the world's touchiest geopolitical disputes." *Washington Monthly*, July–August. Accessed 9 August 2010. http://www.washingtonmonthly.com/features/2010/1007.gravois .html.

Gray, J. 2009. "Will the real Stephen Harper please stand up?" *Canadian Business*, March 2, 44–7.

Greenpeace. 2010. "About us: History." http://www.greenpeace.org/canada/ en/About-us/History/.

Greenspon, E., and A. Wilson-Smith. 1996. *Double vision: The inside story of the Liberals in power*. Toronto: Doubleday.

Grimmelmann, J. 2009. "Saving Facebook." *Iowa Law Review* 94: 1137–206.

Groves, R.M. 2006. "Nonresponse rates and nonresponse bias in household surveys." *Public Opinion Quarterly* 70 (5): 646–75. http://dx.doi.org/ 10.1093/poq/nfl033.

Guibernau, M. 2004. "Anthony D. Smith on nations and national identity: A critical assessment." *Nations and Nationalism* 10 (1–2): 125–41. http://dx.doi .org/10.1111/j.1354-5078.2004.00159.x.

Gutstein, D. 2009. *Not a conspiracy theory: How business propaganda hijacks democracy*. Toronto: Key Porter.

Gutstein, D. 2010a. Reframing public education: Countering school rankings and debunking the neoliberal agenda. Donald Gutstein (blog), July 31. http://donaldgutstein.com/press/reframing-public-education-countering-school-rankings-and-debunking-the-neoliberal-agenda/.

Gutstein, D. 2010b. "Regime change: New citizenship handbook twists 'the Canadian story.'" TheTyee.ca, March 3.

Gwartney, J., and R. Lawson. 1997. *Economic freedom of the world 1997 annual report.* Vancouver: Fraser Institute.

Gwartney, J., J. Hall, and R. Lawson. 2010. *Economic freedom of the world 2010 annual report.* Vancouver: Fraser Institute. http://www.fraserinstitute.org/uploadedFiles/fraser-ca/Content/research-news/research/publications/economic-freedom-of-the-world-2010.pdf.

Ha, T.T. 1995. "National unity 'perpetual crisis' Chrétien believes." *Globe and Mail*, December 19, A1.

Habermas, J. 1975. *The legitimation crisis.* Trans. T. McCarthy. Boston: Beacon Press.

Habermas, J. 1984. *The theory of communicative action.* Cambridge, UK: Polity Press.

Habermas, J. 1989. *The new conservatism: Cultural criticism and the historians' debate.* Cambridge, MA: MIT Press.

Habermas, J. 1991. *The structural transformation of the public sphere: An inquiry into a category of bourgeois society.* Trans. T. Burger. Cambridge, MA: MIT Press.

Hackett, R.A. 2000. "Taking back the media: Notes on the potential for a communicative democracy movement." *Studies in Political Economy* 63: 61–86.

Hackett, R.A., and S. Anderson. 2010. *Revitalizing a media reform movement in Canada.* Vancouver: Creative Commons. http://aegir.openmedia.ca/revitalizing-media-reform-movement-canada.

Hackett, R.A., and W.K. Carroll. 2006. *Remaking media: The struggle to democratize public communication.* London: Routledge.

Hackett, R.A., and R. Gruneau. 2000. *The missing news: Filters and blind spots in Canada's press.* With D. Gutstein, T.A. Gibson, and Newswatch Canada. Toronto: Garamond Press; Ottawa: Candadian Centre for Policy Alternatives.

Hackett, R.A., and Y. Zhao. 1998. *Sustaining democracy? Journalism and the politics of objectivity.* Toronto: Garamond.

Hall, C. 2009. "Inside the PMO ... where communications is key." *Inside Politics Blog*, November 2. http://www.cbc.ca/newsblogs/politics/inside-politics-blog/2009/11/pmo-communications.html.

Hallin, D.C. 1997. "Sound bite news: Television coverage of elections." In *Do the media govern? Politicians, voters, and reporters in America*, edited by S. Iyengar and R. Reeves, 57–65. London: Sage.

Hanke, B. 2005. "For a political economy of Indymedia practice." *Canadian Journal of Communication* 30 (1): 41–64.

Harfoush, R. 2009. *Yes we did: An inside look at how social media built the Obama brand*. Berkeley, CA: New Riders.

Harper, S. 2003. "Rediscovering the right agenda." *Citizens Centre Report*, June 1. Accessed 21 March 2011. http://www.highbeam.com/doc/1G1-105677553.html.

Harper, S. 2011a. "The red Friday ladies." http://www.pm.gc.ca/eng/news/2011/02/15/redfriday-ladies.

Harper, S. 2011b. Statement by the Prime Minister of Canada while in Trapani, Italy, September 1. http://pm.gc.ca/eng/news/2011/09/01/statementprime-minister-canada-while-trapani-italy.

Harper, S. 2011c. PM Harper speaks at Calgary Southwest constituency association barbecue, July 9. Accessed 2 May 2012. http://www.conservative.ca/?p=160.

Harper, S., and T. Flanagan.1996. "Our benign dictatorship." *Next City*, Winter, 34–40, 54–6.

Harrison, T. 1995. *Of passionate intensity: Right-wing populism and the Reform Party of Canada*. Toronto: University of Toronto Press.

Harrison, T. 2008. "Populist and conservative Christian evangelical movements: A comparison of Canada and the United States." In *Group politics and social movements in Canada*, edited by M. Smith, 203–24. Peterborough, ON: Broadview and University of Toronto Press.

Harvey, D. 2005. *A brief history of neoliberalism*. New York: Oxford University Press.

Hayek, F. 1944. *The road to serfdom*. Chicago: University of Chicago Press.

Hayek, F. 1949. "The intellectuals and socialism." *University of Chicago Law Review* 16 (3): 417–33. http://dx.doi.org/10.2307/1597903.

Hayhtio, T., and J. Rinne. 2009. "Little brothers and sisters are watching: Reflexive civic watch through computer-mediated communication." *Information* 12 (6): 840–59.

Heclo, H. 1978. "Issue networks and the executive establishment." In *The new American political system*, edited by A.S. King, 87–124. Washington, DC: American Enterprise Institute for Public Policy Research.

Held, D., ed. 1983. *States and societies*. Oxford: Martin Robertson.

Henton, D. 2012. Redford under fire for $1.3m ad campaigns. *The Calgary Herald*, March 7. http://pialberta.org/content/redford-under-fire-13m-ad-campaigns.

Herman, E., and R. McChesney. 1997. *The global media: The new missionaries of global capitalism*. London: Cassell.

Hermida, A. 2010a. "Twittering the news: The emergence of ambient journalism." *Journalism Practice* 4 (3): 297–308. http://dx.doi.org/10.1080/17512781003640703.

Hermida, A. 2010b. "From TV to Twitter: How ambient news became ambient journalism." *M/C Journal* 13 (2): 1–7.

Hermida, A., D. Logan, F. Fletcher, and D. Korell. 2011. *Social networks transforming how Canadians get the news.* Vancouver: Canadian Media Research Consortium. Accessed 12 August 2011.

Hillygus, D.S., and T.G. Shields. 2008. *The persuadable voter: Wedge issues in presidential campaigns.* Princeton, NJ: Princeton University Press.

Hockin, T.A., ed. 1977. *Apex of power: The prime minister and political leadership in Canada.* 2nd ed. Scarborough, ON: Prentice-Hall.

Holt, D.B. 2004. *How brands become icons: The principles of cultural branding.* Boston: Harvard Business School Press.

Hood, C., and M. Lodge. 2006. *The politics of public service bargains: Reward, competency, loyalty, and blame.* Oxford: Oxford University Press. http://dx.doi.org/10.1093/019926967X.001.0001.

Horkheimer, M., and T. Adorno. (1947) 2002. *Dialectic of enlightenment.* Trans. E. Jephcott. Stanford, CA: Stanford University Press.

Howard, P. 2006. *New media campaigns and the managed citizen.* New York: Cambridge University Press.

Howell, A. 2005. "Peaceful, tolerant and orderly? A feminist analysis of discourses of 'Canadian values' in Canadian foreign policy." *Canadian Foreign Policy* 12 (1): 49–69. http://dx.doi.org/10.1080/11926422.2005.9673388.

Howlett, M., and M. Ramesh. 2003. *Studying public policy: Policy cycles and policy subsystems.* 2nd ed. Toronto: Oxford University Press.

Ivison, J. 2009. "The Tory guide to a blue Canada." *National Post*, November 13.

Iyengar, S. 1991. *Is anyone responsible? How television frames political issues.* Chicago: University of Chicago Press. http://dx.doi.org/10.7208/chicago/9780226388533.001.0001.

Jansen, H., and L. Young. 2010. "How much state money goes to Canada's political parties?" Paper presented to the Annual Meeting of the Prairie Political Science Association, Winnipeg, Manitoba, October 2.

Jeffrey, B. 1999. *Hard right turn.* Toronto: HarperCollins.

Jenkins, H. 2006. *Fans, bloggers, and gamers: Exploring participatory culture.* New York: New York University Press.

Jenson, J. 1991. "Innovation and equity: The impact of public funding." In *Comparative issues in party and election finance. Royal Commission on Electoral*

Reform and Party Financing, vol. 17, edited by F.L. Seidle, 111–77. Toronto: Dundern.

Jessop, B. 2003. *The future of the capitalist state*. Malden, MA: Polity.

Jessop, B. 2008. *State power: A strategic-relations approach*. Malden, MA: Polity.

Jiwani, Y. 2006. *Discourses of denial: Mediation of race, gender, and violence*. Vancouver: University of British Columbia Press.

Johnson, B. 2010. "Individual contributions: A fundraising advantage for the ideologically extreme?" *American Politics Research* 38 (5): 890–908. http://dx.doi.org/10.1177/1532673X09357500.

Johnson, W. 2009. "The outsider." *Walrus*, March, 22–9.

Johnson-Cartee, K.S. 2005. *News narratives and news framing: Constructing political reality*. Lanham, MD: Rowman and Littlefield.

Jordan, L., and P. van Tuijl, eds. 2006. *NGO accountability: Politics, principles and innovations*. London: Earthscan.

Karabegovic, A., and N. Veldhuis. 2009. "At Conference Board, poverty is forever." *National Post*, September 25, FP11.

Karstens-Smith, G. 2012. "Federal watchdog agencies are planning to reduce staff." *Ottawa Citizen*, May 12, A4.

Katz, R.S. 2011. "Finance reform and the cartel party model in Canada." In *Money, politics, and democracy: Canada's party finance reforms*, edited by L. Young and H.J. Jansen, 60–81. Vancouver: University of British Columbia Press.

Keane, J. 1991. *The media and democracy*. Cambridge, UK: Polity.

Keck, M., and K. Sikkink. 1998. *Activists beyond borders: Advocacy networks in international politics*. Ithaca: Cornell University Press.

Kellar, D. 2011. "Presenting the movement's narratives: Organizing alternative media." In *Whose streets? The Toronto G20 and the challenges of summit protest*, edited by T. Malleson and D. Wachsmuth, 71–80. Toronto: Between the Lines.

Kelly, F.J., and B. Silverstein. 2005. *The breakaway brand: How great brands stand out*. New York: McGraw-Hill.

Kemming, J.D., and C. Humborg. 2010. "Democracy and nation brand(ing): Friends or foes?" *Place Branding and Public Diplomacy* 6 (3): 183–97. http://dx.doi.org/10.1057/pb.2010.19.

Kennedy, M. 2010. "PMO breaking bank for 'propaganda.'" *Ottawa Citizen*, October 30, A4.

Khan, S. 2007. "Community radio and the frequency of struggle." *Briarpatch* 36 (4): 4–6.

Killeen, P. 2010. "Facebook and prorogation." Rideau Institute, Ottawa, January 21. http://www.rideauinstitute.ca/?s=Killeen&x=-1263&y=-36.

Kinsella, W. 2001. *Kicking ass in Canadian politics*. Toronto: Random House.

Kirkpatrick, D. 2010. *The Facebook effect: The inside story of the company that is connecting the world.* New York: Simon & Schuster.

Klein, J. 2005. "The perils of the permanent campaign." *Time*, October 3. http://content.time.com/time/magazine/article/0,9171,1124332,00.html.

Klein, N. 2000. *No logo: Taking aim at the brand bullies.* Toronto: Knopf.

Klein, S. 1996. "Good sense versus common sense: Canada's debt debate and competing hegemonic projects." MA thesis, Simon Fraser University, Burnaby.

Klineberg, E. 2005. "Channelling into the journalistic field: Youth activism and the media justice movement." In *Bourdieu and the journalistic field*, edited by R. Benson and E. Neveu, 174–92. London: Polity.

Klineberg, E. 2007. *Fighting for air: The battle to control America's Media.* New York: Metropolitan/Henry Holt.

Knight, G. 1998. "Hegemony, the press and business discourse: Coverage of strike-breaker reform in Quebec and Ontario." *Studies in Political Economy* 55: 93–125.

Knopff, R., and F.L. Morton. 1992. *Charter politics.* Scarborough, ON: Nelson Canada.

Knuttia, M., and W. Kubik. 2000. *State theories.* 3rd ed. Halifax: Fernwood.

Koring, P. 2007. "What Ottawa doesn't want you to know." *Globe and Mail*, April 25. http://v1.theglobeandmail.com/servlet/story/RTGAM.20070424 .wdetaineereport0425/front/Front/Front/.

Kozolanka, K. 2006. "The sponsorship scandal as communication: The rise of politicized and strategic communications in the federal government." *Canadian Journal of Communication* 31 (2): 343–66.

Kozolanka, K. 2007. *The power of persuasion: The politics of the new right in Ontario.* Montreal: Black Rose Press.

Kozolanka, K. 2009. "Communication by stealth: The new common sense in government communication." In *How Ottawa spends, 2009–2010: Economic upheaval and political dysfunction*, edited by A.M. Maslove, 222–40. Montreal: McGill-Queen's University Press.

Kozolanka, K. 2012. "'Buyer' beware: Pushing the boundaries of marketing communication in government." In *Political marketing in Canada*, edited by A. Marland, T. Giasson, and J. Lees-Marshment, 107–22. Vancouver: University of British Columbia Press.

Kozolanka, K., P. Mazepa, and D. Skinner, eds. 2012. *Alternative media in Canada.* Vancouver: University of British Columbia Press.

Kreiss, D. 2012. *Taking our country back: the crafting of networked politics from Howard Dean to Barack Obama.* New York: Oxford University Press.

Kumar, D. 2007. *Outside the box: Corporate media, globalization, and the UPS strike.* Urbana: University of Illinois Press.

Ladner, K. 2008. "*Aysaka'paykinit*: Contesting the rope around the nation's neck." In *Group politics and social movements in Canada*, edited by M. Smith, 227–49. Peterborough, ON: Broadview and University of Toronto Press.

Lakoff, G. 2004. *Don't think of an elephant: Know your values and frame your debate*. White River Junction, VT: Chelsea Green.

Lalonde, M. 1971a. "The changing role of the prime minister's office." Paper presented to the 23rd annual meeting of the Institute of Public Administration of Canada, Ottawa. http://dx.doi.org/10.1111/j.1754-7121.1971.tb00296.x.

Lalonde, M. 1971b. "The changing role of the prime minister's office." *Canadian Public Administration* 14 (4): 509–37. http://dx.doi.org/10.1111/j.1754-7121.1971.tb00296.x.

Langille, D. 1987. "The Business Council on National Issues and the Canadian state." *Studies in Political Economy* 24 (Autumn): 41–85.

Langlois, A., and F. Dubois, eds. 2005. *Autonomous media: Activating resistance and dissent*. Montreal: Cumulus.

Langlois, A., R. Sakolsky, and M. Van Der Zon, eds. 2010. *Islands of resistance: Pirate radio in Canada*. Vancouver: New Star Books.

Langlois, G., G. Elmer, F. McKelvey, and Z. Devereaux. 2009. "Networked publics: The double articulation of code and politics on Facebook." *Canadian Journal of Communication* 34 (3): 415–33.

Lanham, R.A. 2007. *The economics of attention: Style and substance in the age of information*. Chicago: University of Chicago Press.

LaPiere, R. 1934. "Attitudes vs. actions." *Social Forces* 13 (2): 230–7. http://dx.doi.org/10.2307/2570339.

Lasswell, H.D. 1953. "The structure and function of communication in society." In *Reader in public opinion and communication*, 2nd ed., edited by B. Berelson and M. Janowitz, 178–90. New York: Free Press.

Lasswell, H.D. 1971. "The structure and function of communication in society." In *The process and effects of mass communication*, rev. ed., edited by W. Schramm and D. Roberts, 84–99. Urbana: University of Illinois Press.

Latour, B. 2005. "From realpolitik to dingpolitik or how to make things public." In *Making things public: Atmospheres of democracy*, edited by B. Latour and P. Weibel, 14–41. Cambridge, MA: MIT Press.

Laycock, D. 2001. *The new right and democracy in Canada*. Don Mills, ON: Oxford University Press.

Lazarsfeld, P.F., and R.K. Merton. 1971. "Mass communication, popular taste and organized social action." In *The process and effects of mass communication*, rev. ed., edited by W. Schramm and D. Roberts, 554–78. Urbana: University of Illinois Press.

Lazzarato, M. 2006. "The concepts of life and the living in the societies of control." In *Deleuze and the social*, edited by M. Fuglsang and B.M. Sørensen, 171–90. Edinburgh: Edinburgh University Press. http://dx.doi.org/10.3366/edinburgh/9780748620920.003.0009.

Lees-Marshment, J. 2001. "The marriage of politics and marketing." *Political Studies* 49 (4): 692–713. http://dx.doi.org/10.1111/1467-9248.00337.

Lees-Marshment, J. 2004. *The political marketing revolution: Transforming the government of the UK.* New York: Manchester University Press.

Lessig, L. 2011. *Republic lost: How money corrupts congress – and a plan to stop it.* New York: Hachette.

Lewis, J. 2001. *Constructing public opinion: How political elites do what they like and why we seem to go along with it.* New York: Columbia University Press.

Lewis, S.C., K. Kaufhold, and D.L. Lasorsa. 2010. "Thinking about citizen journalism: The philosophical and practical challenges of user-generated content for community newspapers." *Journalism Practice* 4 (2): 163–79. http://dx.doi.org/10.1080/14616700903156919.

Lilleker, D.G. 2006. *Key concepts in political communication.* London: Sage.

Lilleker, D.G. 2008. "Stifling cognitive gears: Exploring the boundary between citizen and consumer." In *Voters or consumers: Imagining the contemporary electorate*, edited by D.G. Lilleker and R. Scullion, 186–208. Newcastle, UK: Cambridge Scholars.

Lilleker, D.G., and R. Scullion, eds. 2008. *Voters or consumers: Imagining the contemporary electorate.* Newcastle, UK: Cambridge Scholars.

Little, B. 1994. "Slash deficit, Martin urged: Group says time is ripe for fiscal, social reforms." *Globe and Mail*, October 12, A1.

Logan, D., F. Fletcher, C. Brin and A. Reid. 2004. *Report on the Canadian news media.* Vancouver: Canadian Media Research Consortium.

Logan, D., F. Fletcher, A. Hermida, and D. Korell. 2010. "Audiences and the future of news." Unpublished data file, Canadian Media Research Consortium.

Logan, D., F. Fletcher, A. Hermida, and D. Korell. 2011. *Canadian consumers unwilling to pay for news online.* Vancouver: Canadian Media Research Consortium.

Lovink, G. 2008. *Zero comments: Blogging and critical Internet culture.* New York: Routledge.

Lower Canada. 1830. *First report of the Special Committee on Internal Communications.* Quebec: Legislature. House of Commons. Special Committee on Internal Communications.

Lynch, L. 2011. "Participatory journalism: An interview with Alfred Hermida." J-source.ca, November 10. http://j-source.ca/article/participatory-journalism-interview-alfred-hermida.

Mabee, H., and G. Hoberg. 2006. "Equal partners? Assessing comanagement of forest resources in Clayoquot." *Society & Natural Resources* 19 (10): 875–88. http://dx.doi.org/10.1080/08941920600901668.

MacCharles, T. 2004. "Audit sounded early warning." *Toronto Star*, February 26, A1.

MacCharles, T. 2010. "Stephen Harper's former campaign director paints unflattering picture of PM's leadership." *Toronto Star*, June 1, 1–2.

MacDermid, R. 1999. *Funding the common-sense revolutionaries: Contributions to the Progressive Conservative Party of Ontario, 1995–97.* Toronto: Centre for Social Justice.

MacDermid, R. 2000. "Tories tipped the odds in Ontario election." *Straight Goods.* http://www.straightgoods.com/item378.shtml.

MacDermid, R. 2006. "Television ad strategies in the 2004 Canadian election." Paper presented at the Canadian Political Science Annual General Meetings, June.

MacIntyre, A. 1972. "Is a science of comparative politics possible?" In *Philosophy, politics and society*, edited by P. Laslett, W.C. Runciman, and Q. Skinner, 8–26. Oxford: Basil Blackwell.

MacLeod, H. 2009. "$34-million ad campaign for economic action plan priming voters for election." *Hill Times*, August 17, 1.

Macleod, I. 2005. "'Culture of secrecy' undermines good government." *Ottawa Citizen*, May 28, 2.

Magnusson, W., ed. 1984. *The new reality: The politics of restraint in British Columbia.* Vancouver: New Star Books.

Manfredi, C.P., and A. Maioni. 2006. "The last line of defence for citizens: Litigating private health insurance in *Chaoulli v. Quebec.*" *Osgoode Hall Law Journal* 44: 249–71.

Manning, P. 2001. *News and news sources: A critical introduction.* London: Sage.

Marcuse, H. 1964. *One-dimensional man.* Boston: Beacon.

Marland, A., and M. Kerby. 2010. "The audience is listening: Talk radio and public policy in Newfoundland and Labrador." *Media Culture & Society* 32 (6): 997–1016. http://dx.doi.org/10.1177/0163443710379669.

Marres, N. 2005. "Issues spark a public into being: A key but often forgotten point of the Lippmann-Dewey debate." In *Making things public: Atmospheres of democracy*, edited by B. Latour and P. Weibel, 208–17. Cambridge, MA: MIT Press.

Marshall, B.L. 1995. "Communication as politics: Feminist print media in English Canada." *Women's Studies International Forum* 18 (4): 463–74.

Martin, C. 2004. *Framed: Labor and the corporate media*. Ithaca, NY: ILR.

Martin, L. 2010. *Harperland: The politics of control*. Toronto: Viking.

Marvin, C. 1988. *When old technologies were new: Thinking about electric communication in the late nineteenth century*. New York: Oxford University Press.

Marzolini, M. 2002. "Polling alone: Canadian values and liberalism." In *Searching for the new liberalism: Perspectives, policies, prospects*, edited by H. Aster and T. Axworthy, 85–102. Oakville: Mosaic.

May, K. 2012. "Expert backs page in fight for cuts data." *Ottawa Citizen*, June 19, A3.

Mayeda, A. 2007. "Harper celebrates one year of Tory power." *Ottawa Citizen*, January 24, A4.

Mayhew, L.H. 1997. *The new public: Professional communication and the means of social influence*. New York: Cambridge University Press. http://dx.doi .org/10.1017/CBO9780511520785.

Mazepa, P. 2012. "Regressive social relations, activism and media." In *Alternative media in Canada*, edited by K. Kozolanka, P. Mazepa, and D. Skinner, 244–63. Vancouver: University of British Columbia Press.

McAdam, D. 1999. *Political process and the development of black insurgency, 1930–1970*. Chicago: University of Chicago Press. http://dx.doi.org/10.7208/ chicago/9780226555553.001.0001.

McBride, S., and J. Shields. 1997. *Dismantling a nation: The transition to corporate rule in Canada*. 2nd ed. Halifax: Fernwood.

McChesney, R.W. 1999. *Rich media, poor democracy: Communication politics in dubious times*. Urbana: University of Illinois Press.

McChesney, R.W. 2004. *The problem of the media: U.S. communication politics in the 21st century*. New York: Monthly Review Press.

McClellan, S. 2008. *What happened: Inside the Bush White House and Washington's culture of deception*. New York: PublicAffairs.

McCombs, M. 2004. *Setting the agenda*. Cambridge, UK: Polity.

McDonald, M. 2004. "The man behind Stephen Harper." *Walrus*, October, 34–49.

McDonald, M. 2010. *The Armageddon factor: The rise of Christian nationalism in Canada*. Toronto: Random House.

McGregor, G. 2009. "Tory ridings the winners from stimulus; analysis reveals more than half of big-money projects went to blue districts." *Ottawa Citizen*, October 20, A1.

McGregor, G. 2013. "Economic Action Plan ads are 'junk': Poll." *Ottawa Citizen*, March 9, A3.

McKay, I., and J. Swift. 2012. *Warrior nation: Rebranding Canada in a fearful age*. Toronto: Between the Lines.

McKenna, B. 1994. "Canada a third world debtor, think tank says." *Globe and Mail*, May 12, B8.

McKenna, B. 2011. "Economic Action Plan ad blitz a snow job on taxpayer's dime." *Globe and Mail*, March 6, 1–3.

McNair, B. 2007. *An introduction to political communication*. 4th ed. New York: Routledge.

McNish, J. 2010. "Jennifer Stoddart: Making your privacy her business." *Globe and Mail*, December 10. http://www.theglobeandmail.com/report-on-business/careers/careers-leadership/jennifer-stoddart-making-your-privacy-her-business/article1319261/.

McQuaig, L. 1995. *Shooting the hippo*. Toronto: Viking.

McQuaig, L. 2009. "Tories keep the faith, such as it is." *Toronto Star*, June 30, A17.

MediaStats. 2010. http://www.mediastats.com.

Metropolitan Police. 2008. "2008 counter-terrorism advertising campaign launched." http://content.met.police.uk/Campaign/nationwide counterterrorism.

Meyer, C. 2011. "DND: Military's 'values' shape 'Canada's identity.'" *Embassy*, November 23, 1. http://www.embassynews.ca/news/2011/11/23/dnd-militarys-values-shape-canadas-identity/40997?absolute=1.

Millard, G., S. Riegel, and J. Wright. 2002. "Here's where we get Canadian: English-Canadian nationalism and popular culture." *American Review of Canadian Studies* 32 (1): 11–34. http://dx.doi.org/10.1080/02722010209481654.

Miller, M.C. 2005. Introduction to *Propaganda*, by Edward Bernays, 9–33. Brooklyn: Ig.

Minsky, A., and E. Thompson. 2011. "Bureaucrats linked to G8 funds." *Ottawa Citizen*, August 16, A4.

Mirowski, P. 2009. "Postface: Defining neoliberalism." In *The road from Mont Pèlerin: The making of the neoliberal thought collective*, edited by P. Mirowski and D. Plehwe, 417–55. Cambridge, MA: Harvard University Press.

Mitchell, T. 2009. "How neoliberalism makes its world." In *The road from Mont Pèlerin: The making of the neoliberal thought collective*, edited by P. Mirowski and D. Plehwe, 386–415. Cambridge, MA: Harvard University Press.

Mohammed, A. 2011. "Between the hammer and the anvil: Blogs, bloggers and the public sphere in Egypt." PhD diss., McGill University, Montreal.

Moll, M., and L.R. Shade, eds. 2008. *For sale to the highest bidder: Telecom policy in Canada*. Ottawa: Canadian Centre for Policy Alternatives.

Montpetit, É. 2002. "Pour en finir avec le lobbying: comment les institutions canadiennes influencent l'action des groupes d'intérêts." *Politique et Sociétés* 21 (3): 91–112. http://dx.doi.org/10.7202/000498ar.

Morozov, E. 2011. *The net delusion: The dark side of Internet freedom*. New York: PublicAffairs. http://dx.doi.org/10.1017/S1537592711004026.

Mosco, V. 1996. *The political economy of communication*. London: Sage.

Mosco, V. 2004. *The digital sublime: Myth, power and cyberspace.* Boston: MIT Press.

Mosco, V. 2009. *The political economy of communication.* 2nd ed. Thousand Oaks, CA: Sage.

Mouffe, C. 2005. *The return of the political.* New York: Verso.

Munk Debates. 2009a. "Be it resolved that climate change is mankind's defining crisis and demands a commensurate response." December 1. http://munkdebates.com/The-Debates/Climate-Change.

Munk Debates. 2009b. "Foreign aid does more harm than good." June 1. http://munkdebates.com/The-Debates/Foreign-Aid.

Munk Debates. 2010. "I would rather get sick in the United States than Canada." June 7. http://munkdebates.com/debates/Healthcare.

Murray, C. 2010. "Audience-making: Issues in Canadian audience studies." In *Mediascapes: New patterns in Canadian communication,* 3rd ed., edited by L.R. Shade, 83–103. Toronto: Nelson Canada.

Murray, G. 2009. "CanWest sues satirists for their Vancouver Sun parodies." *CCPA Monitor,* March 5.

Murray, S.K., and P. Howard. 2002. "Variation in White House polling operations: Carter to Clinton." *Public Opinion Quarterly* 66 (4): 527–58. http://dx.doi.org/10.1086/343754.

Nadeau, R., and T. Giasson. 2003. *Canada's democratic malaise: Are the media to blame?* Montreal: Institute for Research on Public Policy.

National Citizens Coalition. 2013. "NCC Success Stories." https://nationalcitizens.ca/index.php/about-us/ncc-heritage.

Naumetz, T. 2006. "Access denied." *Ottawa Citizen,* October 14, A1.

Nesbitt-Larking, P. 2001. *Politics and the media: Canadian perspectives.* Peterborough, ON: Broadview.

Nesbitt-Larking, P. 2007. *Politics, society and the media.* 2nd ed. Peterborough, ON: Broadview.

Nevitte, N., and C. Cochrane. 2007. "Value change and the dynamics of the Canadian partisan landscape." In *Canadian parties in transition,* edited by A.-G. Gagnon and A.B. Tanguay, 255–75. Peterborough, ON: Broadview.

Nimijean, R. 2005a. "The paradoxical nature of the Canadian identity." *Teaching Canada* 23: 25–31.

Nimijean, R. 2005b. "Articulating the 'Canadian way': Canada™ and the political manipulation of the Canadian identity." *British Journal of Canadian Studies* 18 (1): 26–52. http://dx.doi.org/10.3828/bjcs.18.1.2.

Nimijean, R. 2006a. "Brand Canada: The brand state and the decline of the Liberal Party." *Inroads* 19: 84–93.

Nimijean, R. 2006b. "The politics of branding Canada: The international-domestic nexus and the rethinking of Canada's place in the world." *Revista Mexicana de Estudios Canadienses* 11: 67–85.

Nimijean, R. 2007. "It's all in the brand." *Ottawa Citizen*, August 1.

Nip, J.Y.M. 2006. "Exploring the second phase of public journalism." *Journalism Studies* 7 (2): 212–36. http://dx.doi.org/10.1080/14616700500533528.

Nissenbaum, H. 2004. "Privacy as contextual integrity." *Washington Law Review* 79 (1): 101–39.

Nissenbaum, H. 2010. *Privacy in context: Technology, policy, and the integrity of social life*. Stanford, CA: Stanford University Press.

Noelle-Neumann, E. 1995. "Public opinion and rationality." In *Public opinion and the communication of consent*, edited by T. Glasser and C. Salmon, 33–54. New York: Guilford.

Norris, P. 2000. *A virtuous circle: Political communication in postindustrial societies*. Cambridge, UK: Cambridge University Press. http://dx.doi.org/10.1017/CBO9780511609343.

Office of the Auditor General of Ontario. 2010. *Annual report*. Toronto: Queen's Printer.

Office of the First Minister and Deputy Minister. 2006. *A review of government advertising in Northern Ireland, final report*. Belfast: Office of the First Minister and Deputy First Minister.

Office of the Independent Police Review Director. 2012. *Policing the right to protest: G20 systemic review report*. Toronto: Office of the Independent Police Review Direction. https://www.oiprd.on.ca/CMS/getattachment/Publications/Reports/G20_Report_Eng.pdf.aspx.

Office of the Privacy Commissioner of Canada (OPC). 2008. *Meeting of two worlds: The legal and information technology (IT) universes – online identity: Between privacy and virtual profiles. February*. Ottawa: Office of the Privacy Commissioner.

Office of the Privacy Commissioner of Canada (OPC). 2009a. *Social network site privacy: A comparative analysis of six sites. February*. Ottawa: Office of the Privacy Commissioner.

Office of the Privacy Commissioner of Canada (OPC). 2009b. *Deep packet inspection: A collection of essays from industry experts*. Ottawa: Office of the Privacy Commissioner. http://www.priv.gc.ca/information/research-recherche/dpi_index_e.asp.

Office of the Privacy Commissioner of Canada (OPC). 2010a. "Notice of consultation and call for submissions privacy implications of cloud computing." http://www.priv.gc.ca/resource/consultations/notice-avis_02_e.asp.

Office of the Privacy Commissioner of Canada (OPC). 2010b. "Privacy, trust and innovation – Building Canada's digital advantage." Submission from the Office of the Privacy Commissioner of Canada to the Digital Economy Consultation, July 9. Ottawa: Office of the Privacy Commissioner.

Office of the Privacy Commissioner of Canada (OPC). 2010c. *Privacy in a changing society*. Ottawa: Office of the Privacy Commissioner.

Office of the Privacy Commissioner of Canada (OPC). 2010d. *Draft report on the 2010 Office of the Privacy Commissioner of Canada's consultations on online tracking, profiling and targeting and cloud computing*. Ottawa: Office of the Privacy Commissioner.

Olasky, M. 1985. "Bringing order out of chaos: Edward Bernays and the salvation of society through public relations." *Journalism History* 12 (1): 17–21.

Olsen, T. 2004. "Take up health battle, Harris tells Klein." *Calgary Herald*, October 14, A6.

Ontario Pharmacists Association. 2010. *Drug pricing*. http://www.opatoday.com/. Accessed 15 October 2010.

Ornstein, N., and T. Mann. 2000. *The permanent campaign and its future*. Washington, DC: American Enterprise Institute Press.

O'Shaughnessy, N.J. 2004. *Politics and propaganda: Weapons of mass seduction*. Ann Arbor: University of Michigan Press.

Ottawa Citizen. 1984. "A code of secrecy." June 7, A8.

Ottawa Citizen. 2010. "The high cost of spin." November 2, A14.

Oxford English Dictionary. 2010. 3rd ed. Oxford: Oxford University Press.

Page, C. 2006. *The roles of public opinion research in Canadian government*. Toronto: University of Toronto Press.

Paillé, D. 2007. *Public Opinion Research Practices of the Government of Canada*. Independent Advisor's Report to the Minister of Public Works and Government Services.

Paltiel, K.Z. 1970. *Political party financing in Canada*. Toronto: McGraw-Hill.

Panitch, L., ed. 1977. *The Canadian state: Political economy and political power*. Toronto: University of Toronto Press.

Papacharissi, Z. 2010. "Privacy as a luxury commodity." *First Monday* 15 (8). http://dx.doi.org/10.5210/fm.v15i8.3075.

Paré, D., and F. Berger. 2008. "Political marketing Canadian style? The Conservative Party and the 2006 federal election." *Canadian Journal of Communication* 33: 39–63.

Park, H.W., and M. Thelwall. 2003. "Hyperlink analyses of the World Wide Web: A review." *Journal of Computer-Mediated Communication* 8 (4): 1–36.

Paskin, D. 2010. "Say what? An analysis of reader comments in bestselling American newspapers." *Journal of International Communication* 16 (2): 67–83. http://dx.doi.org/10.1080/13216597.2010.9674769.

Pateman, C. 1980. "The civic culture: A philosophical critique." In *The civic culture revisited*, edited by G. Almond and S. Verba, 57–102. Boston: Little Brown.

Patten, S. 1996. "Preston Manning's populism: Constructing the common sense of the common people." *Studies in Political Economy* 50: 95–132.

Patten, S. 1999. "The Reform Party's re-imagining of the Canadian nation." *Journal of Canadian Studies* 34 (1): 1–23.

Paul, A. 2011. "Grants to help News Café train citizen journalists." *Winnipeg Free Press*, September 28. http://www.winnipegfreepress.com/breaking-news/Grants-to-help-News-Cafe-train-citizen-journalists-130682843.html.

Paulsen, M. 2010. "Prorogation provokes online uprising." TheTyee.ca, January 11. http://thetyee.ca/Mediacheck/2010/01/11/PaulsenProrogue/.

Payton, L. 2011. "Conservative party fined for breaking election laws." CBC News, November 10. http://www.cbc.ca/news/politics/conservative-party-fined-forbreaking-electionlaws-1.1076877/.

Perlman, M. 2011. Testimony to Standing Committee on Government Operations and Estimates. House of Commons. March 10, 12:10 p.m.

Personal Information Protection and Electronic Documents Act. 2000. S.C., c. 5. http://www.priv.gc.ca/leg_c/leg_c_p_e.asp.

Phillips-Fein, K. 2009. "Business conservatives and the Mont Pèlerin Society." In *The road from Mont Pèlerin: The making of the neoliberal thought collective*, edited by P. Mirowski and D. Plehwe, 280–301. Cambridge, MA: Harvard University Press.

Pilkington, E. 2012. "Bradley Manning's treatment was cruel and inhuman, UN torture chief rules." *Guardian*, March 12. http://www.theguardian.com/world/2012/mar/12/bradley-manning-cruel-inhuman-treatment-un.

Pimlott, H. 2000a. "Limited horizons (inc.): Access, democracy and technology in community television in Canada." In *Technology and Inequality*, edited by S. Wyatt, P. Senker, F. Henwood, and N. Miller, 86–108. London: Routledge.

Pimlott, H. 2000b. "Mainstreaming the margins: A case study of *Marxism Today*." In *Media Organisations in Society*, edited by J. Curran, 193–211. London: Arnold.

Pimlott, H. 2006. "Marxism's 'communicative crisis'? Mapping debates over Leninist print-media practices in the 20th century." *Social Studies* 2 (2): 57–77.

Pimlott, H. 2011. "'Eternal ephemera' or the durability of 'disposable literature': The power and persistence of print in an electronic world." *Media Culture & Society* 33 (4): 515–30. http://dx.doi.org/10.1177/0163443711398690.

Pitts, L. 2001. "No such thing as objective media." *Charleston Gazette*, December 17, A4.

Plecash, C. 2012. "PBO page challenges Finance Department to deliver promise to release long-term fiscal report." *Hill Times*, February 20, 1.

Poell, T., and E. Borra. 2011. "Twitter, YouTube, and Flickr as platforms of alternative journalism: The social media account of the 2010 Toronto G20 protests." *Journalism* 13 (8): 1–19.

Pritchard, D., P.R. Brewer, and F. Sauvageau. 2005. "Changes in journalists' views about the social and political roles of the news media: A panel study, 1996–2003." *Canadian Journal of Political Science* 28 (2): 287–306.

Privy Council Office. 2004. Table A-1 – Resources by strategic outcomes and business lines. DPR 2003–4 [Departmental plans and priorities], 1. http://www.collectionscanada.gc.ca/webarchives/search/results/index-e.html?q=Privy+Council+Office.+2004.+Table+A-1+–+Resources+by+strategic+outcomes+and+business+lines.+DPR+2003–4++. Accessed 30 November 2013.

Project for Excellence in Journalism. 2007. *The state of the news media 2007*. Accessed 10 April 2008. http://stateofthemedia.org.

Public Interest Advocacy Centre (PIAC). 2001. *PIAC: 25 years representing the public interest*. Ottawa: Public Interest Advocacy Centre. http://www.piac.ca/files/25years.pdf.

Public Interest Advocacy Centre (PIAC). 2004. *Consumer privacy under PIPEDA: How are we doing?* Ottawa: Public Interest Advocacy Centre.

Public Interest Advocacy Centre (PIAC). 2008. *All in the data family: Children's privacy online*. Ottawa: Public Interest Advocacy Centre.

Public Interest Advocacy Centre (PIAC). 2009. *A "do not track list" for Canada?* Ottawa: Public Interest Advocacy Centre.

Public Safety Act, 2002. 2004. S.C., c. 15.

Pugliese, D. 2009. "Access to information." *Ottawa Citizen*, May 10, B1.

Pugliese, D. 2010. "Selling Canada on the need for fighter jets." *Vancouver Sun*, December 11. http://www.vancouversun.com/technology/Selling+Canada+need+fighter+jets/3964547/story.html.

Pugliese, D. 2012. "Ceremony to celebrate Libyan war victory cost double original budget: documents." *The Ottawa Citizen*. Accessed 24 April 2012. http://www.ottawacitizen.com/news/Ceremony+celebrate+Libyan+victory+cost+double+original+budget+documents/6290176/story.html.

Qualter, T. 1985. *Opinion control in the democracies*. New York: St. Martin's Press.

R. v. Latimer. 2001. 1 S.C.R. 3, SCC 1.

Raboy, M. 1990. *Missed opportunities: The story of Canada's broadcasting policy.* Montreal: McGill-Queen's University Press.

Raboy, M. 1995. "The role of public consultation in shaping the Canadian broadcasting system." *Canadian Journal of Political Science* 28 (3): 455–77. http://dx.doi.org/10.1017/S0008423900006697.

Raboy, M. 2004. "The World Summit on the Information Society and its legacy for global governance." *Gazette: The International Journal for Communication Studies* 66 (3–4): 225–32. http://dx.doi.org/10.1177/0016549204043608.

Raboy, M., and J. Shtern. 2008. "The horizontal view." In *Media divides: Communication rights and the right to communicate in Canada*, edited by M. Raboy and J. Shtern with W.J. McIver, L.J. Murray, S.Ó Siochrú, and L.R. Shade, 63–90. Vancouver: University of British Columbia Press.

Raboy, M., and J. Shtern. 2010. *Media divides: Communication rights and the right to communicate in Canada.* Vancouver: University of British Columbia Press.

Raj, A. 2011. "CC-150 Polaris: Stephen Harper gets his way on repainting of VIP airbus." *Huffington Post*, November 17. http://www.huffingtonpost.ca/2011/11/17/cc-150-harper-plane_n_1100162.html.

Rampton, S., and J. Stauber. 2004. *Banana republicans: How the right wing is turning America into a one-party state.* New York: Jeremy P. Tarcher/Penguin.

Rancière, J. 1995. *On the shores of politics.* London: Verso.

Rancière, J. 1999. *Disagreement: Politics and philosophy.* Translated by J. Rose. Minneapolis: University of Minnesota Press.

Raphael, A. 2008. "Cell phone boycott protests war in Congo." *Common Dreams*, October 23. http://www.commondreams.org/headline/2008/10/23-10.

Rau, K. 1996. "A million for your thoughts." *Canadian Forum*, July–August, 11–17.

Reicher, S.D. 2004. "The context of social identity: Domination, resistance, and change." *Political Psychology* 25 (6): 921–45. http://dx.doi.org/10.1111/j.1467-9221.2004.00403.x.

Reicher, S.D., and N. Hopkins. 2001. *Self and nation.* London: Sage.

Roberts, A.S. 2005. "Spin control and freedom of information: Lessons for the United Kingdom from Canada." *Public Administration* 83 (1): 1–23. http://dx.doi.org/10.1111/j.0033-3298.2005.00435.x.

Roberts, A., and J. Rose. 1995. "Selling the goods and services tax: Government advertising and public discourse in Canada." *Canadian Journal of Political Science* 28 (2): 173–248. http://dx.doi.org/10.1017/S0008423900018862.

Robertson, G. 1971. "The changing role of the Privy Council Office." *Canadian Public Administration* 14 (4): 487–508. http://dx.doi.org/10.1111/j.1754-7121.1971.tb00295.x.

Robinson, D.J. 1999. *The measure of democracy: Polling, market research, and public life, 1930–1945*. Toronto: University of Toronto Press.

Robinson, G. 2005. *Gender, journalism and equity: Cánadian, US, and European Perspectives*. Cresskill, NJ: Hampton.

Robson, W. 1994. *Digging holes and hitting walls: Canada's fiscal prospects in the mid-1990s*. Toronto: C.D. Howe Institute.

Rodriguez, C. 2001. *Fissures in the mediascape: An international study of citizens' media*. Cresskill, NJ: Hampton.

Rose, J. 1993. "Government advertising in a crisis: The Quebec referendum precedent." *Canadian Journal of Communication* 18 (2): 154–75.

Rose, J. 2000. *Making "pictures in our heads": Government advertising in Canada*. Westport, CT: Praeger.

Rose, J. 2003. "The marketing of nations: Old wine in new bottles?" Paper presented to the Political Marketing Conference, London, September.

Rose, J. 2010. "The branding of states: The uneasy marriage of marketing to politics." *Journal of Political Marketing* 9 (4): 254–75. http://dx.doi.org/10.1080/15377857.2010.520238.

Rosen, J. 1999. *What are journalists for?* New Haven, CT: Yale University Press.

Rosen, J. 2008. "A most useful definition of citizen journalism." *PressThink*, July 14. http://archive.pressthink.org/2008/07/14/a_most_useful_d.html.

Rosie, M., and H. Gorringe. 2009. "What a difference a death makes: Protest, policing and the press at the G20." *Sociological Research Online* 14 (5). http://dx.doi.org/10.5153/sro.2047.

Rubin, K. 1975. "Brief to the Standing Joint Committee on Regulations and Other Statutory Instruments." October, 1–3.

Rubin, K. 1977. *The public's right to information act in the federal government as viewed by cabinet ministers, members of parliament and senators*. Ottawa: ACCESS.

Rubin, K. 1983. "Rules will hinder open access to federal records." *Ottawa Citizen*, June 22, 9.

Rubin, K. 1987. "Penchant for secrecy is gutting access law." *Ottawa Citizen*, November 18, A9.

Rubin, K. 1996. "Early warning system undermines access requests." *Hill Times*, November 4, 4.

Rubin, K. 1997. "Canada's access act on the ropes." *ACCESS Reports Canada*, June 19, 3–5.

Rubin, K. 2000. "Behind the back-door bidding at government service's CAC." *Hill Times*, January 17, 7.

Rubin, K. 2002a. "A high price for hot air." *Globe and Mail*, April 8, A13.

Rubin, K. 2002b. "Federal government plans to keep more public records secret, including documents on advertising, sponsorship." *Hill Times*, June 24, 7.

Rubin, K. 2002c. "Here's the deal: The little guy hates access to information." *Hill Times*, June 17, 7.

Rubin, K. 2003. "Canada should stop soft-pedalling asbestos." *Hill Times*, September 22, 19.

Rubin, K. 2004a. "Conditions for future sponsorship, advertising scandals still exist." *Hill Times*, February 22, 13.

Rubin, K. 2004b. "Further public submission on the disclosure motion of government of Canada documents filed on behalf of Maher Arar." Presentation to the Commission of Inquiry into the Actions of Canadian Officials in Relation to Maher Arar, June 14, 1–2. http://epe.lac-bac .gc.ca/100/206/301/pco-bcp/commissions/maher_arar/07-09-13/www .ararcommission.ca/eng/26.htm. Accessed 30 November 2013.

Rubin, K. 2004c. "Public submission on the disclosure motion of government of Canada documents filed on behalf of Maher Arar." Presentation to the Commission of Inquiry into the Actions of Canadian Officials in Relation to Maher Arar, June 11, 1. http://epe.lac-bac.gc.ca/100/206/301/pco-bcp/ commissions/maher_arar/07-09-13/www.ararcommission.ca/eng/26.htm. Accessed 30 November 2013.

Rubin, K. 2004d. "Struggle to get at the facts in Maher Arar case." *Hill Times*, August 8, 8.

Rubin, K. 2005. "Access commissioner John Reid produces his own bill." *Hill Times*, October 10, 19.

Rubin, K. 2006a. "Amber alert: Access to information users targeted as the bad kids on the block." *Hill Times*, October 2, 7.

Rubin, K. 2006b. "Conservatives striking out on crucial access to information reform, but they don't care about transparency." *Hill Times*, October 23, 15.

Rubin, K. 2007. "Behind Canada's new food guide." *Hill Times*, February 12, 15.

Rubin, K. 2008a. "Oh, what to make of military's codenamed 'Tiger Team'?" *Hill Times*, January 7, 9.

Rubin, K. 2008b. "On Olympic branding, it's much better to stick to the image of Canada in winter, and hockey players." *Hill Times*, September 1, 16.

Rubin, K. 2009. "Our right to know hits rock-bottom." *Hill Times*, November 16, 9.

Rubin, K. 2010. "Long and short end: Restoring faith and ending interference and documentation let-downs." *Hill Times*, September 27, 35.

Rubin, K. 2011a. "The myth of access to information." *Hill Times*, January 31, 30.

Rubin, K. 2011b. "Research data on asbestos exposure hidden." *Toronto Star*, May 18, 13.

Rubin, K. 2011c. "Occupy Ottawa: Against record destruction." *Hill Times*, November 7, 11.

Rubin, K. 2011d. "It's time for more open government and an 'opendata .gc.ca'." *The Hill Times*. October 1, 13.

Rubin, K. 2012. "Is a massive destruction of records on the way?" *Hill Times*, May 21, 17.

Rubin, K. 2013. "Three decades of secrecy under the Access to Information Act." *Toronto Star*. June 19. http://www.thestar.com/opinion/commen tary/2013/06/19/three_decades_of_secrecy_under_the_access_to_ information_act.html.

Russell, P.H., and L. Sossin, eds. 2009. *Parliamentary democracy in crisis*. Toronto: University of Toronto Press.

Ryan, P. 1995. "Miniature Mila and flying geese: Government advertising and Canadian democracy." In *How Ottawa spends 1995–96: Midlife crises*, edited by S. Phillips, 263–87. Ottawa: Carleton University Press.

Ryckewaert, L. 2012. "Lead 'robocalls' investigator experienced in 'politically charged' investigation." *Hill Times*, May 31, 1.

Sadinsky, I.R., and T.K. Gussman. 2006. "Federal government advertising and sponsorships: New directions in management and oversight." In *Restoring accountability: The public service and transparency*. Research Studies, vol. 2. Ottawa: Public Works and Government Services.

Sagi, D. 1970. "Government may regulate computer information because systems pose threat to privacy." *Globe and Mail*, June 2, B7.

Salter, M. 2007. "Canadian post-9/11 border policy and spillover securitization: Smart, safe, sovereign?" In *Critical Policy Studies*, edited by M. Orsini and M. Smith, 299–319. Vancouver: University of British Columbia Press.

Samara Foundation. 2011. "The best moment in our democracy, according to you." http://www2.samaracanada.com/blog/post/Samarae28099s-2010-Best-Moment-in-Canadian-Democracy.aspx.

Sampert, S. 2012. "Verbal smackdown: Charles Adler and Canadian political talk radio." In *How Canadians communicate politically: The next generation*, edited by D. Taras and C. Waddell, 295–315. Edmonton: Athabasca University Press.

Sandoval, M., and C. Fuchs. 2010. "Towards a critical theory of alternative media." *Telematics and Informatics* 27 (2): 141–50. http://dx.doi.org/10.1016/j.tele.2009.06.011.

Sanina, M. 2011. "WikiLeaks cables help uncover what made Tunisians revolt." *PBS NewsHour*, January 25.

Saunders, D. 2011. "The business of doing business in Gadhafi's oil kingdom." *Globe and Mail*, February 26. http://www.theglobeandmail.com/commentary/the-business-of-doing-business-in-gadhafis-oil-kingdom/article622569/.

Saurette, P. 2010. "The Harper government's decision to make the long-form census voluntary is terrible policy, but there's method in this madness." *The Mark News*, July 23.

Saurette, P., and S. Gunster. 2011. "Ears wide shut: Epistemological populism, argutainment and Canadian conservative talk radio." *Canadian Journal of Political Science* 44 (1): 195–218. http://dx.doi.org/10.1017/S0008423910001095.

Savoie, D. 1999. *Governing from the centre: The concentration of power in Canadian politics*. Toronto: University of Toronto Press.

Savoie, D. 2003. *Breaking the bargain: Public servants, ministers, and Parliament*. Toronto: University of Toronto Press.

Savoie, D. 2008. *Court government and the collapse of accountability in Canada and the United Kingdom*. Toronto: University of Toronto Press.

Savoie, D. 2010. *Power: Where is it?* Montreal: McGill-Queen's University Press.

Scammell, M. 2007. "Political brands and consumer citizens: The rebranding of Tony Blair." *Annals of the American Academy of Political and Social Science* 611 (1): 176–92. http://dx.doi.org/10.1177/0002716206299149.

Schacter, M. 1999. "Cabinet decision-making in Canada: Lessons and practices." With P. Haid. A paper prepared for the Ottawa Institute on Governance. http://mercury.ethz.ch/serviceengine/Files/ISN/121951/ipublicationdocument_singledocument/4b76d2a9-7d6d-4e45-b2ac-b9af5ae7ffea/en/cabinet2.pdf. Accessed 30 November 2013.

Schattschneider, E.E. 1960. *The semisovereign people: A realist's view of democracy in America*. New York: Holt, Rinehart and Winston.

Schiller, H. 1973. *The mind managers*. Boston: Beacon.

Schmitt, C. 2007. *Theory of the partisan: Intermediate commentary on the concept of the political*. New York: Telos.

Schneiderman, D. 2011. "Constitutional reform by stealth: The creeping transformation of executive authority." *Canada Watch*, Spring, 20–2.

Scholz, T. 2006. "The participatory challenge." In *Curating immateriality: The work of the curator in the age of network systems*, edited by J. Krysa, 189–207. Brooklyn: Autonomedia.

Schultz, R. 1977. "Interest groups and intergovernmental negotiation: Caught in the vise of federalism." In *Canadian federalism: Myth or reality*, 3rd ed., edited by J.P. Meekison, 375–96. Toronto: Methuen.

Schuman, H., and S. Presser. 1980. "Public opinion and public ignorance: The fine line between attitudes and nonattitudes." *American Journal of Sociology* 85 (5): 1214–25. http://dx.doi.org/10.1086/227131.

Scott, W.A. 1957. "Attitude change through reward of verbal behavior." *Journal of Abnormal and Social Psychology* 55 (1): 72–5. http://dx.doi.org/10.1037/h0040249.

Sears, A. 2005. "Creating and sustaining communities of struggle: The infrastructure of dissent." *New Socialist*, July–August, 32–3.

Seiler, R.M. 2002. "Selling patriotism/selling beer: The case of the 'I am Canadian!' commercial." *American Review of Canadian Studies* 32 (1): 45–66. http://dx.doi.org/10.1080/02722010209481657.

Shade, L.R. 2008. "Reconsidering the right to privacy in Canada." *Bulletin of Science, Technology & Society* 28 (1): 80–91. http://dx.doi.org/10.1177/0270467607310591.

Shakespeare, W. 2003. The comedy of errors. In *The complete works of William Shakespeare*, 1–10. http://www.shakespeare-literature.com/The_Comedy_of_Errors/4.html.

Shepard, B. 2002. "Introductory notes on the trail From ACT UP to the WTO." In *From ACT UP to the WTO: Urban protest and community-building in the era of globalization*, edited by B. Shepard and R. Hayduk, 11–20. London: Verso.

Shirky, C. 2009. "Newspapers and thinking the unthinkable." *Clay Shirky Blog*, March, 4–5.

Simeon, R., and I. Robinson. 1990. *State, society and the development of Canadian federalism*. Toronto: University of Toronto Press.

Simon, R. 1982. *Gramsci's political thought: An introduction*. London: Lawrence and Wishart.

Simpson, J. 2002. "Canada's widening rhetoric/reality gap." *Globe and Mail*, September 24, A17.

Sinclair, J., and S. Younane. 2007. "Government advertising as public communication: Cases, issues and effects." In *Government communication in Australia*, edited by S. Young, 204–26. Cambridge, UK: Cambridge University Press.

Singer, J.B., A. Hermida, D. Domingo, A. Heinonen, S. Paulussen, T. Quandt, Z. Reich, and M. Vujnovic, eds. 2011. *Participatory journalism: Guarding open gates at online newspapers*. Oxford, UK: Wiley-Blackwell. http://dx.doi.org/10.1002/9781444340747.

Skinner, D. 2010. "Minding the growing gaps: Alternative media in Canada." In *Mediascapes: New patterns in Canadian communication*, 3rd ed., edited by L.R. Shade, 227–36. Toronto: Nelson Education.

Skinner, D., J.R. Compton, and M. Gasher, eds. 2005. *Converging media, diverging politics: A political economy of news media in the United States and Canada*. Lanham, MD: Lexington Books.

Skinner, D., and M. Gasher. 2005. "So much by so few: Media policy and ownership in Canada." In *Converging media, diverging politics: A political economy of news media in the United States and Canada*, edited by D. Skinner, J.R. Compton, and M. Gasher, 51–76. Lanham, MD: Lexington Books.

Skinner, D., S. Uzelman, A. Langlois, and F. Dubois. 2010. "Indymedia in Canada: Experiments in developing glocal media commons." In *Making our media: Global initiatives toward a democratic public sphere: Volume 1: Creating new communication spaces*, edited by C. Rodriguez, D. Kidd, and L. Stein, 183–201. Cresskill, NJ: Hampton.

Slater, J., and J. Ibbitson. 2010. "PM hails Canada as model global citizen in UN bid." *Globe and Mail*, September 24, A4.

Small, T.A. 2008. "The Facebook effect? Online campaigning in the 2008 Canadian and US elections." *Policy Options* 29 (10): 85–7.

Smith, J. 1997. "Characteristics of the modern transnational social movement sector." In *Transnational social movements and global politics: Solidarity beyond the state*, edited by J. Smith, C. Chatfield, and R. Pagnucco, 42–58. Syracuse, NY: Syracuse University Press.

Smith, M. 2005. *A civil society?: Collective actors in Canadian political life*. Peterborough, ON: Broadview.

Smythe, D. 1981a. *Dependency road: Communications, capital, consciousness and Canada*. Norwood, NJ: Ablex.

Smythe, D. 1981b [2006]. On the audience commodity and its work." In *Media and cultural studies: Keyworks*, edited by M.G. Durham and D.M. Kellner, 230–56. Malden, MA: Blackwell.

Soderlund, W.C., and K. Hildebrandt, eds. 2005. *Canadian newspaper ownership in the era of convergence: Rediscovering social responsibility*. Edmonton: University of Alberta Press.

Soley, L. 1998. "Heritage clones in the heartland." Fairness and Accuracy in Reporting, September 1. http://fair.org/extra-online-articles/heritage-clones-in-the-heartland/.

Soroka, S. 2010. "Census call part of trend on data collecting." *Globe and Mail*, July 28, A15.

Soroka, S., and B. Andrew. 2010. "Media coverage of Canadian elections: Horse-race coverage and negativity in election campaigns." In *Mediating Canadian politics*, edited by S. Sampert and L. Trimble, 113–28. Toronto: Pearson.

Sparks, C. 2007. "Extending and refining the propaganda model." *Westminster Papers in Communication and Culture* 4 (2): 68–84.

St. John's Evening Telegram. 1986. "Information and the PMO." December 4.

Staggenborg, S. 2007. *Social movements*. Oxford: Oxford University Press.

Stallworth, B. 2010. "Future imperfect: Googling for principles in online behavioural advertising." *Federal Communications Law Journal* 62 (2): 465–91.

Stanbury, W.T. 1991. *Money in politics: Financing federal parties and candidates in Canada*. Toronto: Dundurn.

Stanbury, W.T. 2010. "The chasm between what Harper promises on access to information and what we got." *Hill Times*, November 29, 34.

Stengel, R. 2010. "TIME's Julian Assange interview: Full transcript." *Time*, December 1.

Streeck, W. 2012. "Citizens as consumers: Considerations on the new politics of consumption." *New Left Review* 76 (July–August): 27–47.

Stuckey, M.E. 2004. *Defining Americans: The presidency and national identity.* Lawrence: University Press of Kansas.

Sullivan, A. 1996. "Access act slammed by experts, reporters." *Hill Times*, October 14, 4.

Sussman, G. 2010. *Branding democracy: U.S. regime change in post-soviet Eastern Europe.* New York: Peter Lang.

Swift, R. 1999. "One-trick pony." *New Internationalist* 314, 16–17.

Taras, D. 2001. *Power and betrayal in the Canadian media.* Peterborough, ON: Broadview.

Tatevossian, A.R. 2008. "Domestic society's (often-neglected) role in nation-branding." *Place Branding and Public Diplomacy* 4 (2): 182–90. http://dx.doi.org/10.1057/pb.2008.8.

Therborn, G. 1982. *The ideology of power and the power of ideology.* London: Verso.

Thomas, P.G. 2010. "Who is getting the message? Communications at the centre of government." In *Public policy issues and the Oliphant Commission: Independent research studies*, edited by C. Forces, 77–136. Ottawa: Minister of Public Works and Government Services Canada.

Thurlow, W.S. 2008. "Financing Canadian elections." *Canadian Parliamentary Review* 31 (4): 28–32.

Tiffen, R. 2011. "Unprincipled ads just subtract from government messages." *Sydney Morning Herald*, April 8, 1–2. http://www.smh.com.au/federal-politics/political-opinion/unprincipled-ads-just-subtract-from-government-messages-20110407-1d63o.html.

Trimble, L., and J. Everitt. 2010. "Belinda Stronach and the gender politics of celebrity." In *Mediating Canadian politics*, edited by S. Sampert and L. Trimble, 51–74. Toronto: Pearson.

Tuchman, G. 1978. *Making news: A study in the construction of reality.* New York: Free Press.

Tupper, A. 2003. "New public management and Canadian politics." In *Reinventing Canada: Politics of the 21st century*, edited by J. Brodie and L. Trimble, 231–42. Toronto: Prentice Hall.

Turk, J.L. 1997. "Days of action: Challenging the Harris corporate agenda." In *Mike Harris's Ontario: Open for business, closed to people*, edited by D. Ralph, A. Regimbald, and N. St-Amand, 165–76. Halifax: Fernwood.

United Kingdom. 2007. "Preparing for emergencies: What you need to know." http://www.direct.gov.uk/prod_consum_dg/groups/dg_digitalassets/@dg/@en/documents/digitalasset/dg_176618.pdf.

Valpy, M. 2008. "What the Tories know about you." *Globe and Mail*, September 12. http://www.theglobeandmail.com/news/politics/what-the-tories-know-about-you/article709606/.

Vancouver Sun. 1994. "Canada teetering on Quebec's portion of debt." December 2, D18.

van Dijk, T.A. 1988. *News as discourse*. Hillsdale, NJ: Lawrence Erlbaum.

van Dijk, T.A. 1998. *Ideology: A multidisciplinary approach*. London: Sage.

Vanhala, L. 2009. "Disability rights activists in the Supreme Court of Canada: Legal mobilization theory and accommodating social movements." *Canadian Journal of Political Science* 42 (4): 981–1002. http://dx.doi.org/10.1017/S0008423909990709.

van Ham, P. 2001a. "Interview with the author." *Foreign Affairs*, September 1. http://www.foreignaffairs.com/articles/64201/peter-van-ham/interview-with-the-author.

van Ham, P. 2001b. "The rise of the brand state: The postmodern politics of image and reputation." *Foreign Affairs* 80 (5): 2–6. http://dx.doi.org/10.2307/20050245.

van Ham, P. 2002. "Branding territory: Inside the wonderful worlds of PR and IR theory." *Millennium* 31 (2): 249–69. http://dx.doi.org/10.1177/03058298020310020101.

van Ham, P. 2008. "Place branding: The state of the art." *Annals of the American Academy of Political and Social Science* 616 (1): 126–49. http://dx.doi.org/10.1177/0002716207312274.

Van Horn, R., and P. Mirowski. 2009. "The rise of the Chicago school of economics and the birth of neoliberalism." In *The road from Mont Pèlerin: The making of the neoliberal thought collective*, edited by P. Mirowski and D. Plehwe, 139–78. Cambridge, MA: Harvard University Press.

Verma, S. 2010. "WikiLeaks suspect thought actions might 'actually change something.'" *Globe and Mail*, December 7. http://www.theglobeandmail.com/news/world/wikileaks-suspect-thought-actions-might-actually-change-something/article1318637/.

Verzuh, R. 1989. *Underground times: Canada's flower-child revolutionaries*. Toronto: Deneau.

Vongdouangchanh, B. 2010. "Clement most lobbied minister in cabinet. *Hill Times*, October 18, A1.

Waddell, C. 2009. "The campaign in the media 2008." In *The Canadian federal election of 2008*, edited by J.H. Pammett and C. Dornan, 217–56. Toronto: Dundurn.

Waldie, P. 2011. "SNC-Lavalin defends Libyan prison project." *Globe and Mail*, February 24. http://www.theglobeandmail.com/globe-investor/snc-lavalin-defends-libyan-prison-project/article568518/.

Warner, T. 2010. *Losing control: Canada's social conservatives in the age of rights.* Toronto: Between the Lines.

Washington Post. 2001. "Text: President Bush addresses the nation." September 20. http://www.washingtonpost.com/wp-srv/nation/specials/attacked/transcripts/bushaddress_092001.html. Accessed 6 September 2011.

Waters, S. 2004. "Mobilising against globalisation: Attac and the French intellectuals." *West European Politics* 27 (5): 854–74. http://dx.doi.org/10.1080/0140238042000283292.

Waugh, T., M.B. Baker, and E. Winton, eds. 2010. *Challenge for change: Activist documentary at the National Film Board of Canada.* Montreal: McGill-Queen's University Press.

Weber, M. 1969. *From Max Weber: Essays in sociology.* Edited and translated by H.H. Gerth and C. Wright Mills. New York: Oxford University Press.

Wells, P. 2006. *Right side up: The fall of Paul Martin and the rise of Stephen Harper's new conservatism.* Toronto: McClelland & Stewart.

Wells, P. 2010. "Jason Kenney: Harper's secret weapon." *Maclean's,* November 29. http://www2.macleans.ca/2010/11/29/harper%E2%80%99s-secret-weapon/.

Wherrey, A. 2012. "What the world must become in the future ... is what Canada is today." *Maclean's,* July 8. http://www2.macleans.ca/2012/07/08/what-the-world-must-become-in-the-future-is-what-canada-is-today/.

Whitaker, R. 1977. *The government party: Organizing and financing the Liberal Party of Canada, 1930–58.* Toronto: University of Toronto Press.

Whitaker, R. 2001. "Virtual political parties and the decline of democracy." *Policy Options* 22 (5): 16–22.

White, C. 2010. "Facebook: Not just a distraction for students, but a tool for organizing change." rabble.ca, January 18. http://rabble.ca/blogs/bloggers/campus-notes/2010/01/facebook-not-just-distraction-students-tool-organizing-change.

Whitehead, M.J., and C.A. Quinlan. 2002. "Canada: An information literacy case study." White paper prepared for UNESCO, the U.S. National Commission on Libraries and Information Science, and the National Forum on Information Literacy, for use at the Information Literacy Meeting of Experts, Prague, Czech Republic, July.

Whitson, D. 2004. "Bringing the world to Canada: 'The periphery of the centre.'" *Third World Quarterly* 25 (7): 1215–32. http://dx.doi.org/10.1080/014365904200281230.

Whitson, D. 2005. "Olympic hosting in Canada: Promotional ambitions, political challenges." *Olympika: The International Journal of Olympic Studies* 14: 29–46.

Whitson, D., and J. Horne. 2006. "Underestimated costs and overestimated benefits? Comparing the outcomes of sports mega-events in Canada and Japan." *Sociological Review* 54 (2): 71–89. http://dx.doi.org/10.1111/j.1467-954X.2006.00654.x.

Wiener, N. 1948. *Cybernetics: Or control and communication in the animal and the machine*. New York: Wiley.

Wilson, J. 1988. "Government secrecy veil is still spread too far." *Kitchener-Waterloo Record*, June 18.

Winseck, D. 2008. "Media merger mania." *Canadian Dimension* 42 (1): 3–32.

Winseck, D. 2011a. *Media ownership and concentration in Canada. The International Media Concentration Research Project*. New York: Columbia University.

Winseck, D. 2011b. "Politics, the press and bad news for democracy: Newspaper endorsements update on last day before election." *Mediamorphis*, May 1. http://dwmw.wordpress.com/2011/05/01.

Winter, J. 1997. *Democracy's oxygen: How corporations control the news*. Montreal: Black Rose Books.

Wolfson, C. 2008. "Union organizing 2.0: Labour enters the Facebook matrix." *Briarpatch* 37 (7): 16–18.

Woods, A. 2006. "Tory poll on 5 priorities 'unnecessary.'" *Ottawa Citizen*, September 5, A3.

Woods, A. 2007a. "Support for Afghan mission can grow: Polls." *Toronto Star*, August 1. http://www.thestar.com/news/canada/2007/08/01/support_for_afghan_mission_can_grow_polls.html.

Woods, A. 2007b. "To sell Canada on war, try 'hope' but not 'liberty.'" *Toronto Star*, February 17. http://www.thestar.com/news/2007/02/17/to_sell_canada_on_war_try_hope_but_not_liberty.html.

Woods, A. 2011. "Canada looking at building military bases in Arctic." *Toronto Star*, July 14. http://www.thestar.com/news/canada/2011/07/14/star_exclusive_canada_looking_at_building_military_bases_in_arctic.html.

Yalnizyan, A. 2005. *Canada's commitment to equality: A gender analysis of the last ten federal budgets (1995–2004)*. Ottawa: Canadian Feminist Alliance for International Action.

Young, L., and J. Everitt. 2004. *Advocacy groups*. Vancouver: University of British Columbia Press.

Young, L., and H.J. Jansen, eds. 2011. *Money, politics, and democracy: Canada's party finance reforms*. Vancouver: University of British Columbia Press.

Young, S. 2007. "A history of government advertising in Australia." In *Government communication in Australia*, edited by S. Young, 181–203. Cambridge, UK: Cambridge University Press.

Young, S., and J.-C. Tham. 2006. "Political finance in Australia: A skewed and secret system?" *Democratic Audit of Australia*. http://democraticaudit.org.au/?page_id=15.

Zaller, J.R. 1992. *The nature and origins of mass opinion*. Cambridge, UK: Cambridge University Press. http://dx.doi.org/10.1017/CBO9780511818691.

Zamaria, C., and F. Fletcher. 2012. *Banner tables, Canadian Internet project survey 2011*. Toronto: Canadian Internet Project Research Group.

Žižek, S. 2011. "Egypt: Tariq Ramadan and Slavoj Žižek." Interview by Riz Khan. Al Jazeera, February 3. http://www.aljazeera.com/programmes/rizkhan/2011/02/2011238843342531.html.

Contributors

Steve Anderson is the founder and executive director of OpenMedia .ca. An open Internet advocate and commentator, his writings have appeared in various publications. He is a contributing author to *The Internet Tree* (CCPA).

Darin Barney is Canada Research Chair in Technology and Citizenship and an associate professor in the Department of Art History and Communication Studies at McGill University.

Kathleen Cross is an assistant professor in the School of Communication at Simon Fraser University, national coordinator for the Global Media Monitoring Project, and chair of Media Democracy Days in Vancouver.

Greg Elmer is Bell Globemedia Research Chair and director of the Infoscape Centre for the Study of Social Media at Ryerson University. He is a co-author of *The Permanent Campaign: New Media, New Politics* (Peter Lang, 2012).

Fred Fletcher is a university professor emeritus in communication studies and political science at York University. He has published extensively on the role of news media in Canadian politics.

Donald Gutstein is an adjunct professor in the School of Communication at Simon Fraser University. Author of *Not a Conspiracy Theory* (Key Porter, 2009), he is writing his next book about Stephen Harper, think tanks, and neoliberalism.

Robert A. Hackett, communication professor at Simon Fraser University, co-founded Media Democracy Days and other media reform groups. His collaborative publications include *Expanding Peace Journalism* (2011) and *Remaking Media* (2006).

Kirsten Kozolanka is an associate professor in the School of Journalism and Communication at Carleton University. The author of *The Power of Persuasion* (2007), her research is on political and government communication.

Ganaele Langlois is an assistant professor in the Communication Program at the University of Ontario Institute of Technology and associate director of the Infoscape Centre for the Study of Social Media.

Robert MacDermid is a professor of politics at York University. He teaches, researches, and writes about political parties, election campaigns, and money in politics.

Fenwick McKelvey is an assistant professor in communication studies at Concordia University. He researches how software enacts new forms of control in digital media.

Paul Nesbitt-Larking is a professor of political science at Huron University College. His publications include *Politics, Society, and the Media* (University of Toronto Press, 2007) and the *Political Psychology of Globalization* (Oxford University Press, 2011).

Richard Nimijean teaches in the School of Canadian Studies at Carleton University. His research examines the branding of Canada internationally and links to domestic politics and national identity.

Herbert Pimlott's research interests include alternative media, public communication, and cultural politics. His first book is *"Wars of Position": Marxism Today, Cultural Politics and the Remaking of the Left Press, 1979–90* (2014).

Jonathan Rose teaches political communications at Queen's University. He has written extensively about government and political advertising and provides ongoing advice to the Ontario Auditor General on the Government Advertising Act.

Ken Rubin, an investigative researcher, citizens' advocate, and *Hill Times* columnist, is a frequent commentator and consultant on freedom of information. His work has resulted in hundreds of media stories and includes benchmark court cases.

Leslie Regan Shade is an associate professor at the Faculty of Information, University of Toronto. Her research focusses on the social and policy aspects of information and communication technologies (ICTs).

Tamara Shepherd is a postdoctoral fellow in the Ted Rogers School of Information Technology Management at Ryerson University.

Miriam Smith is a professor in the Department of Social Science at York University. Her areas of interest are Canadian and comparative politics, social movements, and lesbian and gay politics.